AF845613

CONSTITUTIONAL FOUNDINGS IN NORTHEAST ASIA

This new book in the Constitutionalism in Asia series considers the idea of origins, and of change and continuity in terms of 'constitution-making', which is an on-going process in the Northeast Asian states.

The book examines the drafting, nature, core values and roles of the first modern constitutions during the founding of the eight modern states/territories in Northeast Asia: China (1949), Taiwan (1947), Hong Kong SAR (1997), Macau SAR (1999), Japan (1889), North Korea (1948 and 1972), South Korea (1948) and Mongolia (1924).

The collection provides:

- an exploratory description of the process and substantive inputs in the making of the first constitutions of these nations/territories;
- analysis of the internal and external (including intra-regional) forces surrounding the making of these constitutions; and
- theoretical construction of models to conceptualise the nature and role of the first constitutions (including constituent documents) in the founding of the modern nation-states/territories and their subsequent impact on state-building in the region.

Constitutionalism in Asia series

NUS National University of Singapore | Centre for Asian Legal Studies Faculty of Law

Constitutional Foundings in Northeast Asia

Edited by
Kevin YL Tan
and
Michael Ng

•HART•
OXFORD • LONDON • NEW YORK • NEW DELHI • SYDNEY

HART PUBLISHING
Bloomsbury Publishing Plc
Kemp House, Chawley Park, Cumnor Hill, Oxford, OX2 9PH, UK
1385 Broadway, New York, NY 10018, USA
29 Earlsfort Terrace, Dublin 2, Ireland

HART PUBLISHING, the Hart/Stag logo, BLOOMSBURY and the Diana logo are trademarks of Bloomsbury Publishing Plc

First published in Great Britain 2022

Copyright © The editors and contributors severally 2022

The editors and contributors have asserted their right under the Copyright, Designs and Patents Act 1988 to be identified as Authors of this work.

All rights reserved. No part of this publication may be reproduced or transmitted in any form or by any means, electronic or mechanical, including photocopying, recording, or any information storage or retrieval system, without prior permission in writing from the publishers.

While every care has been taken to ensure the accuracy of this work, no responsibility for loss or damage occasioned to any person acting or refraining from action as a result of any statement in it can be accepted by the authors, editors or publishers.

All UK Government legislation and other public sector information used in the work is Crown Copyright ©. All House of Lords and House of Commons information used in the work is Parliamentary Copyright ©. This information is reused under the terms of the Open Government Licence v3.0 (http://www.nationalarchives.gov.uk/doc/open-government-licence/version/3) except where otherwise stated.

All Eur-lex material used in the work is © European Union, http://eur-lex.europa.eu/, 1998–2022.

A catalogue record for this book is available from the British Library.

Library of Congress Cataloging-in-Publication data

Names: Tan, Kevin, editor. | Ng, Michael (Writer on law), editor.

Title: Constitutional foundings in Northeast Asia / edited by Kevin YL Tan and Michael Ng.

Description: Oxford ; New York : Hart, 2022. | Series: Constitutionalism in Asia series | Includes bibliographical references and index.

Identifiers: LCCN 2021044680 (print) | LCCN 2021044681 (ebook) | ISBN 9781509940189 (hardback) | ISBN 9781509956746 (paperback) | ISBN 9781509940202 (pdf) | ISBN 9781509940196 (Epub)

Subjects: LCSH: Constitutional history—East Asia.

Classification: LCC KNC527 .C658 2022 (print) | LCC KNC527 (ebook) | DDC 342.502/9—dc23/eng/20211013

LC record available at https://lccn.loc.gov/2021044680

LC ebook record available at https://lccn.loc.gov/2021044681

ISBN: HB: 978-1-50994-018-9
ePDF: 978-1-50994-020-2
ePub: 978-1-50994-019-6

Typeset by Compuscript Ltd, Shannon

To find out more about our authors and books visit www.hartpublishing.co.uk. Here you will find extracts, author information, details of forthcoming events and the option to sign up for our newsletters.

Contents

List of Contributors

EDITORS

Kevin YL TAN is one of Singapore's leading constitutional law scholars and its foremost legal historian. He graduated from the Faculty of Law of the National University of Singapore with an LLB (Hons) and obtained an LLM and JSD from Yale Law School. He specialises in constitutional and administrative law, the Singapore legal system, law and society, legal history and human rights. He is the author and editor of over 50 books on the law, history and politics of Singapore and the region, including *Constitutionalism in Asia* (Hart Publishing, 2014) and *The Singapore Constitution: A Contextual Analysis* (Hart Publishing, 2015). He is currently Adjunct Professor at the Faculty of Law, National University of Singapore and at the S Rajaratnam School of International Studies, Nanyang Technological University. He is also Executive Editor of the *Asian Journal of Comparative Law*, Consulting Editor of the *Asian Yearbook of International Law*, and Editorial Board member of the *Korean Journal of International and Comparative Law*. He is, with Li-ann Thio, also General Editor of the Hart series, *Constitutionalism in Asia*.

Michael NG LLB (HKU), MSocSc (Criminology, HKU), PCLL, (HKU); MA (History, CUHK), PhD (History, CUHK); Solicitor (HK, non-practising), Certified Public Accountant (HK and US, non-practising) is a legal historian focusing on the legal history of China and Hong Kong in the nineteenth and twentieth centuries. He specialises in researching the history of legal transplantations in China, the history of law and colonialism in Hong Kong, and the history of the role of law in Chinese businesses. Dr Ng authored *Political Censorship in British Hong Kong – Freedom of Expression and the Law (1842–1997)* (Cambridge University Press, 2022) and *Legal Transplantation in Early 20th Century China – Practicing Law in Republican Beijing (1910s–1930s)* (Routledge, 2014), and co-edited *Chinese Legal Reform and the Global Legal Order – Adoption and Adaptation* (Cambridge University Press, 2018) and *Civil Unrest and Governance in Hong Kong – Law and Order from Historical and Cultural Perspectives* (Routledge, 2017). His works have appeared in leading international refereed journals such as *Law and History Review*, *China Quarterly*, *Law and Literature*, *International Journal of Asian Studies*, *Business History* and *Journal of Comparative Law*, amongst others. He has been appointed as visiting fellow of the University of Cambridge, visiting scholar of the University of Melbourne and the National University of Singapore, and visiting Associate Professor of National Taiwan University. Prior to joining HKU Faculty of Law, Dr Ng served in the legal, business and finance sectors for more than 15 years.

CONTRIBUTORS

Amarsanaa BATBOLD is Associate Professor and Chair in the Department of Private Law, National University of Mongolia. He also Vice Director of the National Legal Institute of Mongolia and a member of the Judicial Qualifications Committee of Mongolia, and of the Administrative Law Tribunal/Supervisory Board. His areas of research include company law, comparative law, private international law and insurance law. He is Subject Editor with the *Asian Journal of Comparative Law*.

Albert HY CHEN is Cheng Chan Lan Yue Professor of Constitutional Law at the University of Hong Kong. He previously served as Head of the Department of Law (1993–96) and Dean of the Faculty of Law (1996–2002) of HKU. He is one of Hong Kong's pre-eminent scholars in the fields of constitutional law and the legal systems of the Hong Kong SAR and the PRC. He has written over 200 articles and book chapters, and has written or edited over 30 books in English or Chinese on the subjects of his expertise. Chen has served on the Law Reform Commission of Hong Kong (2002–08), the Commission for Strategic Development of the Hong Kong Government (2005–12), and is currently a member of the Committee for the Basic Law of the Hong Kong SAR under the Standing Committee of the National People's Congress of the PRC (1997–).

Chaihark HAHM is Professor of Law at Yonsei University School of Law. His research has revolved around the nexus of constitutional interpretation, democratic political theory, Confucian philosophy, comparative law and legal history. His works in English have appeared in *Journal of Democracy*, *American Journal of Comparative Law*, and *I•CON: International Journal of Constitutional Law*, amongst others. He is the co-author of *Making We the People: Democratic Constitutional Founding in Postwar Japan and Korea* (Cambridge University Press, 2015), which was a historically informed theoretical meditation on the relationship between popular sovereignty and constitutional founding. Previously, he has held fellowships at the National Endowment for Democracy, the Netherlands Institute for Advanced Study/the Hague Institute for the Internationalization of Law, and the Center for Advanced Study in the Behavioral Sciences. He holds law degrees from Seoul National University, Yale, Columbia and Harvard, and a degree in theology from Yale.

Humphrey KO is Adjunct Associate Professor at the University of Hong Kong Faculty of Law, Associate of the China Centre at the University of Oxford, and Visiting Research Fellow in East Asian Studies at the School of Languages, Culture and Society of the University of Leeds. He received his legal education at the University of Hong Kong and holds a DPhil in Modern Chinese History from the University of Oxford. Originally trained in system research at Imperial College London, he began studying the systemic effects of legal reforms on late Imperial and early Republican China during his doctoral studies. He is interested in the historical understanding of the interconnected relationships between state building, constitutional failure and modern corporate entities. He is also interested in the historical processes and systemic consequences of the sequential imposition of modern liberal and Soviet constitutions on China after the Revolution of 1911. He taught modern Chinese history in the Institute for Chinese Studies at the University of Oxford and teaches legal history at the University of Hong Kong. He is the author of *The Making of the Modern Chinese State: Cement, Legal Personality and Industry* (Palgrave Macmillan, 2016).

Chien-Chih LIN is currently an Associate Research Professor at Institutum Iurisprudentiae, Academia Sinica (Taiwan). He received BA and MA degrees from National Taiwan University and LLM and JSD degrees from the University of Chicago. Before studying abroad, he was an attorney at law in Taipei for two years, working mainly on cases regarding administrative law and state compensation. His academic interests focus on comparative constitutional law in Asia, judicial politics and judicial behaviour. Lin has published several articles and essays in the United States, Taiwan and China. His articles can be found in both peer-reviewed and student-edited law journals, as well as in edited volumes, including *Oxford Handbook of Constitutional Law in Asia*, *American Journal of Comparative Law*, *International Journal of Constitutional Law*, *Georgetown Journal of International Law*, *National Taiwan University Law Review* and *Asian Journal of Law & Society*. He has served as Executive Editor of *Academia Sinica Law Journal* (2019–20) and is currently Book Review Editor of the *International Journal of Constitutional Law*.

Kentaro MATSUBARA is Professor of Legal History at the Graduate Schools for Law and Politics at the University of Tokyo. A graduate of the University of Tokyo and of Oxford University (where he obtained his DPhil), he works in the intersecting area of legal history and comparative law, focusing on property regimes and state structures in East Asia. His most recent works include 'East, East and West: Comparative Law and the Historical Processes of Legal Interaction in China and Japan' (2019) 66(4) *American Journal of Comparative Law* 769. He is currently working on a manuscript on *Law of the Ancestors: Lineage Property-Holding and Social Structures in 19th Century South China*. He has held visiting appointments at Columbia Law School, the University of Hong Kong, the National University of Singapore and Yale University.

Erik MOBRAND is Associate Professor of Korean Studies in the Graduate School of International Studies at Seoul National University. With broad interests in the field of politics, he is especially keen to better understand the interplay of informal power relationships and formal political arrangements. Most of his research focuses on Korean and Chinese societies. Through research on these jurisdictions, he engages in wider discussions about politics in Asia and the developing world. One stream of his work examines the resistance of poor people in Korean and Chinese cities to central state projects. Another offers a reinterpretation of South Korea's democratisation through a focus on elite management of political institutions. He is the author of *Top-Down Democracy in South Korea* (University of Washington Press, 2019). His ongoing project, anchored in South Korea, traces the variety of political uses of anti-corruption rhetoric and action.

Chadraabal UNURBAYAR is Associate Professor at the Department of Public Law, National University of Mongolia, where he teaches and researches on the History of Constitutionalism, Jurisprudence and the History of State Laws. He was educated at the School of Law, National University of Mongolia, and at Edinburgh University. From 2014 to 2017, he served as Human Rights and Legal Policy Adviser to the President of Mongolia. In this capacity, he provided legal and policy advice on over 40 legislative enactments.

Xiaobo ZHAI is Associate Professor at the Faculty of Law of the University of Macau. His areas of research interest are legal theory, Bentham studies and constitutional theory. His articles have appeared in *Law and Philosophy*, *The Journal of Legal History*, *International Journal of Constitutional Law*, *Chinese Journal of Law*, etc. He has also published co-edited volumes, *Bentham's Theory of Law and Public Opinion* with Cambridge University Press, *Bentham Around the World* with Wildy, Simmonds and Hill Publishing, and two monographs on Chinese constitutional law with presses in Beijing.

1

Northeast Asian Constitutional Foundings: The Weight of History

KEVIN YL TAN

INTRODUCTION

THIS IS THE third volume in a series I first devised back in 2017 with Bui Ngoc Son.[1] Initially, I had not thought of extending the survey of first or founding constitutions beyond Southeast Asia, but the chance to collaborate with a couple of old friends has led to two further studies: a survey of first constitutions of South Asia[2] with Ridwanul Hoque; and this volume, with Michael Ng.[3] This volume builds on the two previous ones and takes seriously the idea of origins – how things are formed, how they relate to their present and future in terms of 'constitution-making'. Of the three regions covered in the series, Northeast Asia is probably the most intensely studied. This should come as little surprise, especially since comparative legal scholars have always included China and Japan (as well as India) as 'representative' Asian states. The same cannot be said for Macau, Mongolia or North Korea. This volume examines the drafting, nature, core values and roles of the first modern constitutions of the eight states/territories in Northeast Asia, specifically those of China (1949: Taiwan (1947); Hong Kong SAR (1997); Macau (1993); Japan (1889); North Korea (1948/1972); South Korea (1948); and Mongolia (1924).

Contributors to this volume attempt to explain the process and substance of constitution-making through the wide context of state formation, history and politics. The wider objective of this interdisciplinarity is to enable us to better appreciate the process of constitution-making and the relationship between (i) founding constitutions and state building; and (ii) the impact of the foundings

[1] Kevin YL Tan and Bui Ngoc Son (eds), *Constitutional Foundings in Southeast Asia* (Hart Publishing, 2019).

[2] Kevin YL Tan and Ridwanul Hoque (eds), *Constitutional Foundings in South Asia* (Hart Publishing, 2021).

[3] As this volume goes to press, discussions are afoot to extend this series to Central Asia, the Caucasus and Western Asia.

on subsequent constitutional developments. This book is also contextual in its overall approach and has a strong comparative underpinning. We do not use the term 'comparative' in any normative or methodological sense,[4] but rather to identify commonalities and differences in constitutional responses to the challenge of the founding new nation-states as well as to the start of new constitutional epochs. Indeed, we take seriously Benedict Anderson's exhortation that 'comparison is not a method or even an academic techinque' but rather 'a discursive strategy'.[5]

For each study, we asked contributors to offer three things. First, to provide an *exploratory description of the process and substance* in making the first modern constitution in their respective countries of study. In particular, we asked each country expert to answer these questions:

(a) How was the constitution-making body constituted and who were its members?
(b) How was the Constitution drafted?
(c) What were the fundamental constitutional questions that the drafters considered?
(d) How were these questions debated in the constitution-making body and, if at all, among members of the public?
(e) And how was the Constitution approved?

Second, we asked our contributors to provide an *explanatory analysis of the internal and external factors* involved in the making of their respective founding constitutions. Internal factors would include a polity's political-legal tradition, colonial past, revolution, socio-economic condition, political/civil/ethnic conflicts, social division, ideology and local intellectual environment/movements. External factors, on the other hand, would include the influence of foreign constitutional experiences and ideas or/and international bodies or experts, and how these externalities interacted with the internal factors at the time of constitutional founding.

Third, we asked the contributors to offer *some reflections on the role of the first constitutions* in the founding of their respective modern nation-states and the subsequent state-building processes. They were also asked to specifically address the following questions:

(a) How did the constitution impact the founding of state institutions – the legislature, the executive government, courts and others?
(b) Did the founding Constitution influence the subsequent constitutional developments and practices?
(c) Does the founding Constitution still influence contemporary constitutional design and structural reform plans and, if so, how?

[4] On the theory and practice of constitution-making in a comparative setting, see David Landau and Hanna Lerner (eds), *Comparative Constitution-Making* (Edward Elgar, 2019).

[5] Benedict Anderson, 'Frameworks of Comparison' (2016) 38(2) *London Review of Books* 15, 20.

In developing the above framework of analysis, we relied on this volume's successful predecessors – *Constitutional Foundings in Southeast Asia* and *Constitutional Foundings in South Asia*, both published by Hart Publishing.[6] This introductory chapter addresses some common themes in Northeast Asian constitutional foundings rather than summarising each of these studies. References to summaries and conclusions of various chapters serve mainly to locate the respective state's/territory's experience in founding its constitution within the general study of constitutional history.

I. WHY THIS BOOK?

This volume focuses on the making, nature, fundamental values and roles of first modern constitutions during the founding period of the modern nation-states in Northeast Asia. As I intimated earlier, the scholarship on the constitutional history of this region is better served than that of other parts of Asia. However, even in jurisdictions that have benefitted from a strong scholarly tradition or have been the subject of major comparative studies – such as China, Japan and, to a lesser extent, Taiwan – much of that work has either been locally or thematically focused.[7] Since China and Japan were arguably never colonised, their founding constitutions will be contextualised with reference to their respective evolving constitutional histories and political settings.

Like its companion volumes, this book makes three significant contributions to constitutional knowledge, practice and theory. *First*, it helps plug the knowledge gap in comparative constitutional history in Northeast Asia with specific reference to constitution-making, constitutional breakdown and constitutional endurance in the region. Second, it furthers our understanding of contemporary constitutional practices and anticipates possible developmental trajectories in light of the foundational values embedded in and manifested through these constitutions. Third, we hope that with a comparative historical study of these founding constitutions, plausible theoretical models may be devised to substantiate and enhance our understanding of Northeast Asia's constitutional history, which, despite commonalities, continues to remain locally diverse and unique.

There is currently no book examining all the first constitutions in all the countries of Northeast Asia. While there has been heightened growth in Asian constitutional scholarship and the renewed burgeoning of Northeast Asian

[6] Tan and Son (eds) (n 1); and Tan and Hoque (eds) (n 2).

[7] Thematically-focused studies include: Rosalind Dixon and Tom Ginsburg (eds), *Comparative Constitutional Law in Asia* (Edward Elgar, 2014); Albert HY Chen, 'Pathways of Western Liberal Constitutional Development in Asia: A Comparative Study of Five Major Nations" (2010) 8(4) *International Journal of Constitutional Law* 849; Albert HY Chen and Andrew Harding (eds), *Constitutional Courts in Asia: A Comparative Perspective* (Cambridge University Press, 2018); Tom Ginsburg, *Judicial Review in New Democracies: Constitutional Courts in Asian Cases* (Cambridge University Press, 2003).

comparative constitutional scholarship in recent years, most scholars tend to focus generally on contemporary constitutional issues. On the subject of continuity and change, the region's contemporary constitutional law and practice is inevitably shaped by its constitutional past. And constitution-making and design in the region has seen more cross-learning than ever before. That said, Asian constitutional history is generally largely understudied, hence this series.

In terms of Northeast Asian constitutional history, there are some monographic and detailed studies of the region's founding constitutions but the focus has not been on the significance of their historical founding. While there are numerous research monographs and textbooks on legal interpretations of constitutions of the People's Republic of China enacted at various times (1954, 1975, 1978, 1982), only a handful of them are in English, and deal with their historical founding and the social political contexts from which they emerged.[8] Others deal tangentially with issues related to these foundings.[9] Hong Kong and Macau SAR were both given a new constitution (Basic Law) when China resumed sovereignty over them (Hong Kong in 1997, Macau in 1999). Most academic publications on their Basic Laws to date focus only on doctrinal interpretation and legal implications, and only scant mention is made of the historical contexts in which they were so negotiated and designed.[10] With the recent release of archival files in relation to the drafting and negotiation process of Basic Laws, a huge scholarly gap waits to be filled.

In Taiwan, the history, process and implication of constitution-making have received scant critical analysis, with some notable exceptions, such as Jiunn-rong Yeh and Wen-Chen Chang's article 'The Emergence of East Asian

[8] Notable works in constitutional history of PRC include: Hon Dayuan, *Drafting Process of 1954 Constitution* (Law Press, 2014); Pan Wei-Tung, *The Chinese Constitution: A Study of Forty Years of Constitution-Making in China,* 2nd edn (Institute of Chinese Culture, 1946); Zhang Jinfan, *Constitutional History of China* (Zhongguo fazhi chubanshe, 2016); and Hui Zhao, *Rethinking Constitutionalism in Late 19th and 20th Century China*, PhD thesis (Harvard University, 2012).

[9] See, eg, Changchang Wu, 'Debates on Constitutionalism and the Legacies of the Cultural Revolution' (2016) 227 *China Quarterly* 674; Neil Diamant and Xiaocai Feng, 'The PRC's First National Critique: The 1954 Campaign to "Discuss the Draft Constitution" (2015) 73 *The China Journal* 1; Rogier Creemers, 'China's Constitutonalism Debate: Content, Context and Implications' (2015) 74 *The China Journal* 91; Jiang Shigong, 'Written and Unwritten Constitutions: A New Approach to the Study of Constitutional Government in China' (2009) 35(1) *Modern China* 12; Li Buyun, 'Constitutionalism and China' in Ye Keping, *Democracy and the Rule of Law in China* (Brill, 2010) 197; and Byron Wang, 'Some Key Aspects of the 1982 Draft Constitution of the People's Republic of China' (1982) 91 *The China Quarterly* 492.

[10] Historical foundings form only a part of the short introduction of doctrinal study into the Basic Laws, eg, Chen Wenmin and CL Lim, *Law of the Hong Kong Constitution* (Sweet & Maxwell, 2015); and Yash Ghai, *Hong Kong's New Constitutional Order: The Resumption of Chinese Sovereignty and the Basic Law* (Hong Kong University Press, 1997). There is also a Master's degree thesis on the drafting process: Lawrence KK Ho, 'Implementation of China's Hong Kong Policy: A Study of the Drafting of Hong Kong Basic Law, 1985–90', MPhil Thesis (The University of Hong Kong, 2000). A very recent exception to this is Richard Cullen, *Hong Kong Constitutionalism: The British Legacy and the Chinese Future* (Routledge, 2020). An interesting pre-Basic Law work is GB Endacott, *Government and People of Hong Kong, 1841–1962: A Constitutional History* (Hong Kong University Press, 1964).

Constitutionalism',[11] Chien-Chih Lin's article 'Courts and Constitutions in Authoritarian Chinese Regimes'[12] and Wen-chen Chang's 'Comparative Discourse in Constitution-Making: An Analysis on Constitutional Framers as Dialectic Agent'.[13] Of these works, only Chang's single-authored piece looks specifically at Taiwan, whilst the others discuss constitutional founding in Taiwan through a comparative prism. The sub-title of Suisheng Zhao's 1996 study[14] – *Constitution-Making in Nationalist China* – is deceptive in that it is much less a study of the historical forces that shaped the Republic of China Constitution, than a public choice theory analysis of how Chiang Kai-shek favoured a presidential system to maximise his power. One possible exception is a book by Peter Yu, which looks at the role the 1949 Constitution has played in the relationship between mainland China and Taiwan since its inception.[15] This work is more of a political history – with the 1949 Constitution as a backdrop – than a focused study of the making of that Constitution. Several reasons may account for the Taiwanese people's remoteness from their constitutional identity. To begin with, many constitutional clauses that had been implemented in Taiwan were extremely awkward because the Constitution was enacted for a geographically immense country, not for a tiny island-state. Moreover, the participation of Taiwanese representatives in the constituent assembly was symbolic at best. After the catastrophic Chinese civil war, the authoritarian and iron-fisted rule imposed by the ruling party that promulgated the Constitution made many Taiwanese believe it to be an imposed constitution. Interestingly, the Republic of China Constitution is one of the most enduring in Asia, and Taiwan has consistently received high marks in the domain of political rights and civil liberties. Even more paradoxically, given the achievements of human rights protection, the Constitution still demands unification with China. How does an imposed and ill-suited constitution gradually build legitimacy and ensure compliance? What normative implications can we distil from the survival and success of the Constitution? Lin's chapter, 'The Birth of the Constitution of the Republic of China' (chapter 5) answers these questions by weaving together several threads of history, law and politics.

Japan's current Constitution, promulgated in 1946, was enacted as an amendment to the 1889 Meiji Constitution, in accordance with the earlier

[11] Jiunn-rong Yeh and Wen-Chen Chang, 'The Emergence of East Asian Constitutionalism' (2011) 59(3) American Journal of Comparative Law 805–839.

[12] Chien-Chih Lin, 'Constitutions and Courts in Chinese Authoritarian Regimes: China and Pre-Democratic Taiwan in Comparison' (2016) 14(2) *International Journal of Constitutional Law* 351.

[13] Wen-chen Chang, 'Comparative Discourse in Constitution-Making: An Analysis on Constitutional Framers as Dialectic Agent' in Chang-fa Lo, Nigel NT Li and Tsai-yu Lin (eds), *Legal Thoughts between the East and the West in the Multilevel Legal Order. Economics, Law, and Institutions in Asia Pacific* (Springer, 2016).

[14] Suisheng Zhao, *Power by Design: Constitution-Making in Nationalist China* (University of Hawaii Press, 1996).

[15] Peter Kien-Hong Yu, *The Second Long March: Struggling Against the Chinese Communists Under the Republic of China (Taiwan) Constitution* (Continuum, 2011).

Constitution's amendment clause.[16] While the regime change was abrupt and has been described by Miyazawa Toshiyoshin – the most influential constitutional scholar of the early post-War era – as an August Revolution,[17] procedural continuity was secured by submitting the draft of the new Constitution in the name of the Emperor to the Imperial Diet for deliberation.[18] Thus the foundations of the current Constitution can be directly traced to the 1889 Meiji Constitution, which was the first Westernised constitution in East Asia. English language studies of the drafting process of the Meiji Constitution have focused either on the Meiji oligarchs' initiatives in the reception of Western ideas,[19] and how they may be reconciled with Japanese society, or on the creation of a regime that integrated certain constitutional values but was ultimately authoritarian. The adoption of Prussian/German models, the power of the Emperor and limitations on civil liberties, are the mainstay of such arguments.[20] What has been less explored is how the process also involved the reinterpretation and/or creative recycling of certain elements in Japanese history, and the invention of particular Japanese traditions that were conceptualised within a framework of Western constitutional ideas.

South Korea has been better served in terms of scholarship relating to its constitutional foundings, especially in *Making We the People: Democratic Constitutional Founding Postwar Japan and South Korea*,[21] a fairly recent book by Chaihark Hahm (who also authored chapter 7 on South Korea in this volume) and Sung Ho Kim. A much briefer attempt at articulating the issue of 'peoplehood' in both North and South Korea is Justine Guichard's 'In the Name of the People: Disagreeing over Peoplehood in the North and South Korean Constitutions',[22] but, like most others, it is not concerned specifically with the founding moments of the Korean Constitution. Hardly any work on

[16] Art 73, Dai-Nippon Teikoku Kenpô.

[17] Miyazawa Toshiyoshi, *Kenpô no Genri* [Principles of Constitutional Law] (Iwanami Shoten, 1967).

[18] Yoichi Higuchi (ed), *Five Decades of Constitutionalism in Japanese Society* (University of Tokyo Press, 2001) 1–2.

[19] See, eg, Takii Kazuhiro, *Ito Hirobumi: Japan's First Prime Minister and Father of the Meiji Constitution* (Routledge, 2014); and Joseph Pittau, *Political Thought in Early Meiji Japan, 1868–1889* (Harvard University Press, 1967).

[20] George Beckmann, *The Making of the Meiji Constitution: The Oligarchs and the Constitutional Development of Japan, 1868–1891* (University of Kansas Press, 1957); George Akita, *Foundations of Constitutional Government in Japan, 1868–1900* (Harvard University Press, 1967); Takii Kazuhiro, *The Meiji Constitution: The Japanese Experience of the West and the Shaping of the Modern State* (International House of Japan, 2007); and T Iyenaga, *The Constitutional Development of Japan, 1953–1881* (John Reprint, 1973).

[21] Chaihark Hahm and Sun Ho Kim, *Making We the People: Democratic Constitutional Founding Postwar Japan and South Korea* (Cambridge University Press, 2015). This is a vastly expanded version of their work and ideas first expressed in Chaihark Hahm and Sung Ho Kim, 'To Make "We the People": Constitutional Founding in postwar Japan and South Korea' (2010) 8(4) *International Journal of Constitutional Law* 800.

[22] (2017) 4(2) *Asian Journal of Law and Society* 405.

the foundation of the Constitution of the Democratic Republic of Korea (North Korea) is available in the English language.[23]

Although Mongolia's current Constitution dates from 1992, it has had three previous Constitutions (1924, 1940 and 1960) all of which were drafted during the socialist era (1924–92). The 1924 Constitution, which is the subject of study in chapter 9 of this volume, is considered foundational because of how it established a separate, independent Mongolian state after many years of Chinese domination. Academic work on these earlier Constitutions is scant, especially in the English language.[24] One exception is a very recent book chapter by Ivan Sablin, Bargal Badagarov and Irina Sonomova, entitled 'Khural Democracy: Imperial Transaformations and the Making of the First Mongolian Constituiton, 1911–1924'.[25] Beyond these works, there is hardly anything available to anyone hoping to learn more about the establishment and impact of the 1924 Mongolian Constitution.

It can thus be seen that a thorough examination of the first Northeast Asian constitutions is still much needed. Given the problematic characterisation of the first constitution in many of these states/territories, contributors have been invited to theorise on the idea of what a founding constitution is and means in the context of regional specificities.

II. THE WEIGHT OF HISTORY

Having adopted a broad contextual approach that is both historical and comparative, we encouraged our contributors to take an interdisciplinary approach to the study of founding constitutions to enable readers to have a better understanding of the process and substance of constitution-making. Our starting hypothesis is that the framing or drafting of first modern constitutions is foundational to the creation of the modern nation-state in Northeast Asia. The 'founding' thus relates to the establishment of the nation-state, or to a major and fundamental political transition within a state, such as when an *ancien regime* or empire is displaced by a republican government. It is not an exercise in simply having contributors provide a historical narrative of the constitution-making process.

[23] There is a brief paper by Sung Yoon Cho prepared for the Library of Congress, entitled 'The Constitution of the Democratic People's Republic of Korea' (Washington DC: Law Library, Library of Congress 1986).

[24] See, eg, George Ginburgs, 'Mongolia's "Socialist" Constitution' (1961) 34(2) *Pacific Affairs* 141; William B Ballis, 'The Political Evolution of a Soviet Satellite: The Mongolian People's Republic' (1956) 9(2) *Western Political Quarterly* 93.

[25] Ivan Sablin, Jargal Badagarov and Irina Sonomova, 'Khural Democracy: Imperial Transformations and the Making of the First Mongolian Constitution, 1911–1924' in Simon Wickhamsmith and Philip P Marzluf (eds), *Socialist and Post-Socialist Mongolia: Nation, Idenity and Culture* (Routledge, 2021) 14.

Consequently, despite some related terminology and ideas, our hypothesis differs from those dealing with constitutional foundationalism[26] or theories of constitutional constructivism.[27] Our enterprise may be distinguished in two ways. First, while recognising the critical role of new and foundational constitutions in the creation of a new political order, we do not see such constitutions necessarily as a clean break with the past. Instead, we accept that legal and political change ebbs and flows in and through a series of changes and continuities in the constitutional trajectories of all states. A constitutional founding is thus informed and impacted by the pre-existing political and legal culture and practice, and thus impacts subsequent constitutional trajectories. Second, acknowledging the idea of constitutional continuity, we accept that these first constitutions did not necessarily create liberal democratic states. Indeed, we argue that in many cases, the constitution's primary role is to lay down the foundational framework for Northeast Asia's modern nation-states, and does not serve purely to limit state power and protect individual liberties. To be sure, the creation of a new political order as a component of this founding may incorporate modern constitutional ideas and institutions. However, this order is not necessarily that of a liberal constitutional democracy.

Several geo-political realities help explain the pattern of constitutional development in Northeast Asia. Of the states studied in this volume, China and Japan have the longest civilisational histories, and have never been conquered or colonised even if they both experienced varying degrees of foreign domination between the nineteenth and twentieth centuries. Indeed, Japan was to become the only Asian colonial power in the twentieth century, when it conquered and occupied a number of Asian territories, including Taiwan and Korea. Mongolia was, up until 1924, an autonomous region within China, while Hong Kong and Macau – territories previously occupied by the British and Portuguese – were returned to China in 1997 and 1999 respectively. The circumstances that led to each of these individual constitutional foundings were thus quite different, even if the reasons were generally similar.

In the majority of cases, new constitutions were crafted to mark a polity's clear break from the past. In the case of China (and Taiwan), the modern constitution-making enterprise came about following its break from its imperial past and its transformation into a modern republican state in 1911, and then its revolutionary transformation into a communist state in 1949. In 1911, following the Xinhai Revolution, the Qing Dynasty, which had ruled China for almost 300 years, collapsed and thus put an end to some 2,000 years of imperial rule. On 1 January, the Republic of China was proclaimed, with Sun Yat-sen as its

[26] Bruce Ackerman, *The Future of Liberal Revolution* (Yale University Press, 1992); see also, Mark Tushnet, 'Comparative Constitutional Law' in Mathias Reimann and Reinhart Zimmermann (eds), *The Oxford Handbook of Comparative Law*, 2nd edn (Oxford University Press, 2019) 1193, 1200–02.

[27] Ruti Teitel, *Transitional Justice* (Oxford University Press, 2000).

first President. However, the proclamation of the new Republic was met by years of turmoil and uncertainty as China descended into lawlessness and warlordism. The establishment of the Chinese Communist Party (CCP) in 1921 led to greater internecine conflict between the communists and the nationalist Kuomintang (KMT). Japan's invasion of Manchuria in 1931 and the establishment of a puppet state of Manchukuo in February 1932 led to even greater internal strife in China. Things only got worse after the Marco-Polo Bridge incident in 1937, which led to the outbreak of the Second Sino-Japanese War that lasted till the end of the Pacific War in 1945. Japan's surrender in September of that year did not bring peace to China, for almost immediately, civil war broke out between the CCP and KMT forces. The Chinese Civil War, which lasted till 1949, resulted in the CCP's victory and the expulsion of Chiang Kai-shek and his KMT forces to Taiwan, where they proceeded to establish a government in exile under the 1946 Constitution that had been enacted in Nanjing. The CCP proclaimed China the People's Republic of China (PRC) and adopted a 'Common Programme' of the Chinese People's Political Consultative Conference, which gave the CCP complete control over the state apparatus, a situation that continued till 1954 when the first PRC Constitution was promulgated. The 1954 Constitution represented yet another major break from the past – this time, an ideological one – in establishing a socialist state in China.

As mentioned earlier, the framing of constitutional orders for Hong Kong SAR in 1997 and Macau in 1999 signified breaks of a different nature. In 1997, Hong Kong, which had originally been part of China's Guangdong Province but which had been ceded to Britain at the end of the First Opium War in 1841, was returned to China under terms agreed upon in the Sino-British Joint Declaration of 1984. China guaranteed Britain that Hong Kong would be allowed to retain its political and economic system for 50 years after 1997. Macau was originally leased to Portugal as a trading post in 1557 but was ultimately ceded to Portugal in 1887 under the Sino-Portuguese Treaty. In 1986, China and Portugal began negotiations over the future of Macau, and in 1987 a Joint Declaration on the Question of Macau was signed. Under the Joint Declaration, Portugal agreed to transfer the colony back to China in 1999 and, as in Hong Kong's case, China guaranteed that Macau could retain its political and economic system for 50 years after the transfer. These arrangements resulted in both Hong Kong and Macau being administered as Special Administrative Regions (SARs). The Basic Laws of Hong Kong and Macau are thus the de facto constitutions of these two territories.

After the eclipse of the Mongol Yuan dynasty in China in the fourteenth century, the Mongols retreated to the Mongolian Plateau and established the Northern Yuan Dynasty, which lasted till 1635. Eventually, and as a result of internal power struggles and infighting, Mongolia became increasingly weak and was conquered by Qing forces. The Mongolian homeland thus became incorporated as part of China as Outer Mongolia. However, during the Xinhai Revolution of 1911 that toppled the Qing Dynasty, Mongolia declared itself independent from China. Nevertheless, it was not till 1921 that Mongolia, with the help of Russian forces, established itself as an independent state. It adopted a modern constitution in 1924 to signify its independence from China and to mark its new-found statehood.

Japan, which has the distinction of being the first Asian state to promulgate its own constitution, drafted the 1889 Meiji Constitution as part of its modernisation programme, and to signify a clear break from its feudal past. Japan's revolutionary modernisation effort began in 1868 with the restoration of imperial rule and the displacement of the powerful Tokugawa Shogunate in what has become known as the Meiji Restoration. In the process, Japan threw open its doors to western influences and technology in a bid to reform its institutions and military to catch up with the western powers. Japan looked eagerly to the West in a bid to modernise everything, including its constitutional order. And while it studied the British Navy in its effort to modernise its own navy, it fashioned its 1889 Constitution along the lines of a Prussian constitutional monarchy.

The Meiji reforms were exceedingly successful, and by the turn of the twentieth century Japan had become the leading industrial and military power in all of Asia. It began asserting its influence on neighbouring territories, most notably the Korean peninsula, then under Chinese protection. Japan's increasingly aggressive imperialism led to the First Sino-Japanese War, fought over some nine months between 1894 and 1895. China lost the war, and under the Treaty of Shimonoseki ceded control over Taiwan Province to Japan. Japan was to occupy Taiwan till 1945. Japan began forcing Korea to open itself up to trade – much in the same way it was forced to open up to trade by Commodore Perry – through the Japan-Korea Treaty of 1876. In 1897, the Korean Empire became a protectorate of Japan, which then proceeded to formally annex Korea under the Japan-Korea Treaty of 1910.

Japan's defeat in the Pacific War led to the liberation of both Taiwan and Korea. Taiwan, which eventually became the seat of the defeated KMT forces, did not draft a new constitution but instead continued to function under the 1946 Republic of China Constitution. During the Second World War, the Allied leaders fighting Japan agreed that when liberated, Korea would be placed under an international trusteeship till the Koreans were ready for self-rule. However, the Soviet Union – who only declared war on Japan on 8 August 1945, two days after the Americans had dropped the atomic bomb on Hiroshima – was anxious to exert its influence in the Korean peninsula as well. The Americans thus proposed dividing Korea into two occupation zones, with the 38th parallel as the dividing line. The territory south of the line would be placed under American control, while the territory north of the line would fall within Soviet control. This division was intended to be temporary and was to have been dissolved when the trusteeship came into being. However, after two years of negotiations, the trusteeship plan collapsed and Korea has remained divided ever since. The Korean question was referred to the United Nations, which failed to find a solution agreeable to both the Soviets and the Americans. In 1948, the United Nations supervised elections in the American-occupied south, and the American-backed Syngman Rhee won the election under the 1948 Constitution of the Republic of Korea (ROK), which had been drafted in six weeks primarily by Professor Yu Chin-o. In the meantime, a communist regime had been established in the North with the support of Soviet Union, and a Soviet-style socialist constitution was adopted, also in 1948. Thus, the drafting of constitutions in North and South Korea signified both their liberation from Japan as well as the ideological and political break between these territories as a result of the Cold War.

III. THE LEGACIES OF CONSTITUTIONAL FOUNDINGS

In no other part of Asia has ideology featured so strongly in constitution-making as in Northeast Asia. The rise of communism, starting in Russia and then spreading steadily eastwards and westwards, saw the establishment of communist parties in Mongolia, China and, later, North Korea. Of the world's five remaining communist states, two of them – China and North Korea – are in Northeast Asia. In addition, Mongolia was a communist state for almost 70 years, from 1924 till 1992, when it abandoned communism and replaced its socialist-style constitution with a liberal democratic one. Russia (initially and then, from 1922, the Soviet Union) played a key role not only in exporting revolution to these states, but also in ensuring that its 'assistance' – through the deployment of Soviet experts – manifested in constitutions that mirrored those of the Soviet Union, whether drafted in 1924 or 1936.

Constitutional borrowings occurred in the cases of the Japanese and South Korean constitutions. In the case of the Meiji Constitution of 1889, its drafters studied various models, including that of America, and concluded that the Prussian model of a constitutional monarchy suited Japan's conditions and purposes best, especially since one of the main purposes of the Meiji Restoration was to return the Emperor to his place of prominence as head of state. South Korea, occupied by America after the War, drafted its constitution under the watchful eyes of the entire international community, especially when the United Nations undertook to supervise the first general election to take place after the founding of the South Korean state. As Hahm states in chapter 7:

> Although there was no direct foreign involvement in the drafting process, the presence of outside forces was unmistakable. It was the United Nations that decided to hold the general election which created the National Assembly, in a territory occupied by foreign troops and in a context defined by the emerging Cold War. The members of the National Assembly were keenly aware that their actions and decisions were being closely watched by the international community.

Perhaps the most interesting constitution under consideration is that of the Republic of China. This 1946 Constitution may be considered the most autochthonous of all the constitutions discussed in this volume. Its home-grown character is seen in how the constitution-drafting committee took seriously

Sun Yat-sen's constitutional and political theory and crafted a unique five-power constitution. In that sense, it is unlike any other constitution in all of Asia.

Finally, something needs to be said about the unique Basic Laws that were enacted to facilitate the return of Hong Kong and Macau to China and yet provide for the continuation of their existing political and economic systems. This One-Country-Two-Systems model is unique not only because it is not modelled on any other existing system, but also because of its finite nature. It is set to expire in 2047 for Hong Kong and 2049 for Macau, after which both territories will have to administer Chinese law under the Constitution of the People's Republic of China 1982. In legacy terms, it will be interesting to see how the people of Hong Kong and Macau cope when this happens. Will these territories continue to see a lingering of the old legal and constitutional orders, or will that be swept away in revolutionary fashion like obsolete relics of a humiliating past.

IV. A NOTE OF ACKNOWLEDGEMENT

I would like end with a word of acknowledgement. Thanks to the Centre for Asian Legal Studies (CALS) at the Faculty of Law, National University of Singapore, for supporting this project and to the contributors and commentators who generously contributed to the workshop and to this volume. This book is a victim of the COVID-19 pandemic that broke out in late 2019 and reached Singapore's shores in January 2020. Originally, these chapters were to have been presented at a in-person workshop at the Law Faculty of National University of Singapore between 27 and 28 March 2020. The COVID-19 outbreak led to a postponement of the event to July 2020. However, as air travel had by this time become highly problematic worldwide, we decided to workshop each paper online via Zoom over two days, from 24 to 25 September 2020. Joining us for these workshops and serving as wonderful commentators and discussants were Chang Wen-chen, Fu Hualing, Marie Seong-Hak Kim, Patricia Goedde, Lam Peng Er and Bui Ngoc Son. Following the workshop, the country experts were invited to revise their papers in light of the comments received. Again, delays were occasioned by major adjustments that everyone had to make in view of the COVID-19 situation, which required many of us to teach online and which also limited physical access to library facilities and materials. It is thanks to the perseverance of the authors that this volume has finally come to fruition. Lastly, my gratitude to Hart Publishing, for its unwavering support of the constitutional foundings series of books.

2

The 1954 Constitution of China: Empire State Building

HUMPHREY KO

INTRODUCTION

On 20 September 1954, Liu Shaoqi, the newly-elected Chairman of the Standing Committee of the National People's Congress (NPCSC), stood on the rostrum during the First Session of the National People's Congress (NPC) in Beijing and delivered a report on the Draft Constitution of the People's Republic of China (PRC). Six years earlier, on 1 October 1949, standing atop Tiananmen, the imposing entrance gate tower of the old imperial palace, Mao Zedong had proclaimed the People's Republic of China. A new political order had been established in the new unitary state lying within the boundaries of the former Qing Empire.[1] From 1954, this new unitary state was governed under the Draft Constitution that had been passed by the NPC – the 1954 Constitution of the PRC.[2] Thus was established the secondary and permanent constitutional order for the country.

In 1956, Liu Shaoqi became the First Vice Chairman of the Chinese Communist Party (CCP), and then President in 1959.[3] But Liu's political fortunes waned after the 1966 Cultural Revolution. In 1967 he was arrested, subjected to repeated public humiliation and beatings, and, in November 1969, found dead while under confinement in a room in a distant, disused provincial house. After that he was denounced as a traitor and his family was imprisoned.[4] Years later, in 1980, Liu was posthumously rehabilitated, and in December 2018, President Xi Jinping 'saluted' Liu's 'high spirit' at the Great Hall of the People in Beijing to commemorate the 120th anniversary of Liu's birth.[5]

[1] Kuang Chen and Pan Liang, *Women de 1950 Niandai* [Our Times in the 1950s] (Zhongguo youyi chuban gongsi, 2005) 64–67.

[2] Liu Shao-Chi, *Report on the Draft Constitution of The People's Republic of China: Constitution of the People's Republic of China* (Foreign Language Press, 1962).

[3] Lowell Dittmer, *Liu Shaoqi and the Chinese Cultural Revolution* (ME Sharpe, 1998).

[4] ibid.

[5] An Baijie, 'Xi Salutes Late Leader Liu Shaoqi's High Spirit,' *China Daily* (24 November 2018) at www.chinadaily.com.cn/a/201811/24/WS5bf88740a310eff30328ac72.html.

In 1966, while Liu was the President of the PRC, law and order broke down entirely across the former Empire. Instigated by Mao under the banner of the Great Proletariat Cultural Revolution in 1965,[6] the constitutional order totally collapsed. State institutions were suspended and the country descended into violent chaos in the name of 'continuing revolution'.[7] Student 'Red Guards' roamed the streets, vandalised homes, and terrorised and even murdered ordinary people from all walks of life.[8] While China maintained its territorial integrity, the settlement achieved by the 1954 Constitution was no more. What happened? How could this happen after a tried and tested modern (albeit Leninist) constitutional order was implemented? In normal circumstances, China should have become a heavily regulated, stable, rigid and controlled party-state. What went wrong? This chapter examines the constitutional foundation of China and shows that a glitch in the drafting of the Leninist Constitution destabilised Chinese politics, leading to the large-scale political and socio-economic calamity in the PRC.

I. NATIONAL REVIVAL

It is an often overlooked fact that the PRC is the one of two modern successor states – the other being the Republic of China in Taiwan – of a millennia-old imperial tradition and state.[9] Modern Chinese history shows that modern Chinese constitutionalists regarded the key aim of a Chinese Constitution to be to 'reboot' the decrepit and declining Empire and transform it into a successful, modern, multi-ethnic nation-state. This concept of revival is encapsulated in the Chinese term *fuxing*. During the chaotic years between the first Opium War (1839–42) and the founding of the PRC in 1949, several generations of constitutionalists sought a constitutional arrangement that would either reform the Chinese Empire and save it from collapse, or unify it afterwards. From 1842, when the Treaty of Nanking (the first of the unequal treaties) was signed, the revival of China's political fortune became of paramount concern and the ultimate objective.[10]

China's history from 1842 to 1949 was marked by internal rebellion, civil war and external threats.[11] Western powers and Japan were also carving up China

[6] ibid.

[7] Dittmer (n 3) 366.

[8] Roderick MacFarquhar, *The Origins of the Cultural Revolution*, vol 3: *The Coming of the Cataclysm 1961–1966* (Oxford University Press and Columbia University Press, 1997).

[9] John K Fairbank and Denis C Twitchett (eds), *The Cambridge History of China*, 15 vols (Cambridge University Press, 1978–2019).

[10] John K Fairbank and Kwang-Ching Liu (eds), *The Cambridge History of China*, vol 11: *Late Ch'ing 1800–1911, Part 2* (Cambridge University Press, 1980).

[11] Albert Feuerwerker, *Rebellion in Nineteenth-Century China.* (Center for Chinese Studies, University of Michigan, 1975); Frederic Wakeman, *Strangers at the Gate: Social Disorder in South China, 1839–1861* (University of California Press, 1966).

through military action and unequal treaties.[12] Until the arrival of the Soviet model – indigenously developed by Russian Communists – none of the pre-1949 draft constitutions succeeded in reunifying China and stabilising its territory.[13] Lenin and his comrades had developed a constitutional model to govern a diverse and multinational Russian Empire and prevent it from unravelling in an age of self-determination.[14] Using the Russian model as a guide, framers of the 1954 PRC Constitution made yet one more attempt to establish a constitutional order.[15] Alas, it failed to instil stability in domestic politics[16] because of an unwise, casual tweak to the Soviet constitutional model by the awkward grafting of the office of President onto it. This upset the power balance and led to a decade-long political turmoil beginning in 1965. It was only remedied in 1982, when political stability was finally achieved, albeit precariously.

II. THE CONSTITUTION AS SAVIOUR OF THE CHINESE EMPIRE

History is the crux to understanding modern China, and the PRC can be seen as an incarnation of the former Empire.[17] Table 2.1 sets out the most relevant events in Chinese history in this regard.

Table 2.1 Relevant Events in Chinese History

Year	Event	Impact
1842	First Opium War	Hong Kong is ceded to the United Kingdom
1850	Taiping Rebellion	Half of China is lost to rebels
1856	Second Opium War	Old Summer Palace is razed
1894	First Sino-Japanese War	Taiwan ceded to Japan
1900	Boxer Rebellion	Eight-Nation Alliance sacked Beijing
1908	Emperor Guangxu dies	Three year-old Emperor Puyi enthroned

(continued)

[12] Rana Mitter, *China's War with Japan 1937–1945: The Struggle for Survival* (Allen Lane, 2013); Fairbank and Twitchett (eds) (n 9) vols 10–15.

[13] William L Tung, *The Political Institutions of Modern China* (M Nijhoff, 1964); Pan Wei-tung, *The Chinese Constitution: A Study of Forty Years of Constitution-Making in China* (Catholic University of America Press, 1946); Zhang Qianfan, *The Constitution of China: A Contextual Analysis* (Hart Publishing, 2012).

[14] 1918 Constitution (Fundamental Law) of the Russian Socialist Federated Soviet Republic; Richard Pipes, *The Formation of the Soviet Union: Communism and Nationalism, 1917–1923*, rev edn (Harvard University Press, 1997).

[15] Tung (n 13).

[16] Roderick MacFarquhar, *The Politics of China: Sixty Years of the People's Republic of China*, 3rd edn (Cambridge University Press, 2011).

[17] Fairbank and Twitchett (eds) (n 9); Zheng Yangwen, *Ten Lessons in Modern Chinese History* (Manchester University Press, 2018).

Table 2.1 *(Continued)*

Year	Event	Impact
1912	Republic of China	Sun Yat-sen is Provisional President and Capital is Nanjing
1912	Beiyang Government	Yuan Shikai is President. Capital moves to Beijing
1914	World War I	
1922	Guangzhou Military Government	Borodin sent by Soviet Union. Capital is Guangzhou.
1928	National Government	Chiang Kai-shek heads the Government. Capital moves back to Nanjing.
1937	Second Sino-Japanese War	Nanjing is sacked.
1939	World War II	European theatre
1946	Civil War	Nationalists vs Communists
1949	People's Republic of China	Mao Zedong heads the Government. Capital is Beijing.
1958	Great Leap Forward	Collectivisation
1966	Cultural Revolution	Red Guards' anarchy
1971	Lin Biao Incident	Failed *coup d'état*
1972	Nixon visits China	
1976	Mao Zedong dies	
1978	Deng Xiaoping in power	Reform era begins
1980	Shenzhen established as Special Economic Zone	

For our account of constitution-making, the year the Second World War ended, in 1945, provides a good entry point.[18] From 1946 to 1949, China was embroiled in a civil war between the Kuomintang (KMT) and the CCP. Constitutional initiatives aimed at incorporating both parties ended in failure.[19] An abortive constitutional conference in 1946 – the Political Consultative Conference (PCC) – that brought together the KMT, CCP and minority parties failed to forge a coalition government.[20] In 1949, the victorious CCP established a new constitutional order – the PRC – and the capital was moved back to Beijing, the old imperial capital.[21] The KMT and its army, led by Chiang Kai-shek, retreated to the small

[18] Mitter (n 12) ch 19.

[19] Jing Zhiren, *Zhongguo Lixian Shi* [Constitutional History of China] (Linking Publishing Company, 1984) 401–61; Tung (n 13) chs VII–IX; Suzanne Pepper, *Civil War in China: The Political Struggle, 1945–1949* (Rowman & Littlefield Publishers, 1999); Odd Arne Westad, *Decisive Encounters: The Chinese Civil War, 1946–1950* (Stanford University Press, 2003).

[20] Jing (n 19) 437–45.

[21] Craig Dietrich, *People's China: A Brief History*, 3rd edn (Oxford University Press, 1986) 50–65.

but defensible province of Taiwan.[22] The KMT saw this as a matter of political and strategic expedience and a temporary solution, but the Republic of China has remained in Taiwan ever since.[23]

III. CHINESE CONSTITUTIONAL ATTEMPTS SINCE THE QING DYNASTY

From the beginning, the establishment of a constitution for China was an imperial restoration project. It started out as an effort in the late nineteenth century to stabilise the declining empire before it collapsed in 1911,[24] and continued as a national constitutional project to rebuild the vast empire into a unified republic amidst ongoing internal wars and Japanese invasion.[25] From 1908 to 1954, the Chinese state, whether the Republic of China (ROC) or PRC, experimented with various constitutional models. From 1908 to 1911, a British-Japanese constitutional monarchy was debated,[26] and this was followed by an American-Weimar model from 1914.[27] When the Communists came to power in 1949, the mission fell on them. They needed to find a constitution that could stabilise the politics and achieve economic development for a unified state, and it was the Soviet model that was adopted in 1954.[28] Table 2.2 summarises the key constitutional experiments and amendments undertaken between 1908 and 1982.

Table 2.2 Constitutions and Constitutional Documents of China, 1908–82

22 Aug 1908	*Principles of the Constitution* 23 articles
13 Oct 1911	*The Organic Law of the Provisional Government* 4 chapters and 21 articles: presidential government
Nov 1911	*The Nineteen Articles* 19 articles
11 Mar 1912	*Provisional Constitution of the Republic of China* 7 chapters and 56 articles
1 May 1914	*Constitutional Compact* 10 chapters and 68 articles: presidential government

(continued)

[22] John K Fairbank and Roderick MacFarquhar (eds), *The Cambridge History of China*, vol 14: *The People's Republic. Part 1: The Emergence of Revolutionary China, 1949–1965* (Cambridge University Press, 1987).

[23] Zhang Yufa, *Zhongguo Jindai Shi* [A modern history of China] (Donghua shuju, 2001).

[24] Albert HY Chen, *An Introduction to the Legal System of the People's Republic of China*, 3rd edn (LexisNexis, 2018) chs 1–4.

[25] John King Fairbank, *The Great Chinese Revolution* (Harper & Row, 1986) 157 and 172.

[26] Jing (n 19) 69–168.

[27] Shen Yu-chung, 'Semi-presidentialism in Taiwan A Shadow of the Constitution of the Weimar Republic' (2001) 7(1) *Taiwan Journal of Democracy* 135; Tung (n 13).

[28] Chen (n 24) ch 4; Flemming Christiansen and Shirin M Rai, *Chinese Politics and Society: An Introduction* (Prentice Hall/Harvester Wheatseaf 1996),ch 5; Dietrich (n 21).

Table 2.2 *(Continued)*

10 Oct 1923	*Constitution of the Republic of China* 13 chapters and 141 articles: presidential government Bicameral legislature with provinces, counties and cities defined
1 Jun 1931	*Provisional Constitution of the Republic of China for the Period of Political Tutelage* 8 chapters and 89 articles: direct Leninist party rule
7 Nov 1931	[*Draft Basic Law of the Chinese Soviet Republic* 8 chapters and 78 articles]*
Jan 1934	[*Basic Constitutional Programme of the Chinese Soviet Republic* 17 articles]*
25 Dec 1946	*Constitution of the Republic of China* 13 chapters and 151 articles: presidential government 'The Five-Power Constitution'
21 Sep 1949	*Common Programme of the Chinese People's Political Consultative Conference* 2 chapters and 16 articles: direct Leninist party rule (in a coalition)
20 Sep 1954	*Constitution of the People's Republic of China* 4 chapters and 106 articles
17 Jan 1975	*Constitution of the People's Republic of China* 4 chapters and 30 articles
5 Mar 1978	*Constitution of the People's Republic of China* 4 chapters and 60 articles
4 Dec 1982	*Constitution of the People's Republic of China* 4 chapters and 138 articles

* The Chinese Soviet Republic was a small communist revolutionary mountain enclave in a remote and exceedingly impoverished area in Jiangxi Province headed by Mao Zedong. The Constitutions are included here for completeness.[29]

IV. THE DEATH OF THE LIBERAL DEMOCRATIC MODEL IN CHINA

The ROC, which was established on 1 January 1912 by the Organic Law of the Provisional Government of the Republic of China (dated 13 October 1911),[30] was as tenuous as the document that established it. During the Republican period (1912–49), there were several Western-inspired constitutions, but none could hold the former imperial state together. Dr Sun Yat-sen, widely-regarded as the Father of Modern China, was an outspoken revolutionary who trained as a medical doctor in Hong Kong. He became Provisional President of the

[29] WE Butler (ed), *The Legal System of the Chinese Soviet Republic, 1931–1934* (Transnational Publishers Inc, 1983) 1–52.
[30] Tung (n 13).

ROC from 1 January 1912. However, by March 1912, lacking both economic and military clout, he handed power over to Yuan Shih-kai, the last Prime Minister of the Qing Government. Yuan, who had no regard for any constitutional order or norms, died in 1916 following his farcical attempt to restore imperial rule. After his death, and as central political authority fragmented and devolved into the hands of Yuan's military protégés and subordinates, 'warlordism' emerged and China descended into chaos. These warlord factions, supported by different foreign powers, were unable to defeat one another. A nominal Central Government in Beijing administered the custom duties collected by the British, but it had no control over the separate and devolved militarised regions of the original Qing Empire.[31]

Two Constitutions were promulgated in this period: (i) the Provisional Constitution of the Republic of China (11 March 1912); and (ii) the Constitutional Compact (1 May 1914).[32] However, the ROC's constitutional plans were aborted following the assassination of Song Jiaoren, leader of the majority KMT, on 22 March 1913 at Shanghai railway station while he was on his way to parliament. This murder, widely suspected to have been ordered by Yuan himself, effectively dashed any hope of unifying China under a liberal democratic constitution.[33] Yuan's disregard for any sort of constitutional order was evident from the time he installed himself as Emperor in 1915. His reign lasted for a laughable 102 days. Following this, Zhang Xun, a former Qing bureaucrat, attempted to restore Puyi, the last Qing Emperor, to the throne.[34]

By 1917, even Sun had no choice but to turn to militarism to counter the warlords.[35] Styling himself as Grand Marshal, he moved to the southern Guangdong provincial capital Guangzhou, bringing about half of the legislators from the capital. Sun established a separate southern Guangzhou Military Government and claimed to be the legitimate Central Government.[36] This became known as the Constitutional Protection Movement that protested the discarding of the 1912 Provisional Constitution of the Republic of China. A new Constitution of the Republic of China (10 October 1923) was promulgated by the northern Government in Beijing, but it neither controlled the south nor administered the notional ROC.[37] Although Sun still kept faith in liberal

[31] Marie-Claire Bergère, *Sun Yat-Sen*, tr Janet Lloyd (Stanford University Press, 1998); Jerome Ch'en, *Yuan Shih-K'ai*, 2nd edn (Stanford University Press, 1972); Andrew J Nathan, *Peking Politics, 1918–1923: Factionalism and the Failure of Constitutionalism* (University of California Press, 1976); Arthur Waldron, *From War to Nationalism: China's Turning Point*, 1924–1925 (Cambridge University Press, 2003).

[32] Tung (n 13).

[33] Zhang (n 23); Wu, Xiangxiang, *Song Jiaoren Zhuan: Minzhu Xianzheng de Xianqu* [The Biography of Song Jiaoren: The Pioneer of Constitutional Democracy] (Zhuanji Wenxue chubanshe, 1985).

[34] Zhang (n 23); Ch'en (n 31); Fairbank (n 25) 169–74.

[35] Fairbank (n 25) 211.

[36] C Martin Wilbur, *The Nationalist Revolution in China, 1923–1928* (Cambridge University Press, 1984).

[37] ibid; Tung (n 13).

democratic constitutions,[38] he had to concede that they had achieved nothing for the ROC.[39] Pragmatically, Sun turned to Lenin.[40]

V. THE BIRTH OF LENINIST CONSTITUTIONALISM IN CHINA

In 1922, the Soviet Communists helped Sun Yat-sen to reform the Nationalist Party he founded. Lenin dispatched Mikhail Borodin to advise Sun on how to reorganise the Chinese Nationalists Party along Leninist lines. Crucially, this included adding a party army, to be trained on the island of Whampoa in the main tributary of the Pearl River, with arms supplied by the Soviets. Later, through the Communist International (Comintern), the Soviet Union also aided and assisted the Chinese Communist Party separately. This laid the ground for the eventual and fateful civil war between two Leninist party armies between 1947 and 1949.[41] This resulted in China's splitting into two separate republics, each with its own national constitution and each claiming legal and political jurisdiction over the entire country.[42]

In 1923, after failing both to make workable a liberal democratic constitutional order in China and firmly rejecting federalism, Sun planned a Northern Expedition to militarily reconquer China.[43] Unfortunately, Sun died two years later in March 1925, and it was left to his protégé, Chiang Kai-shek, to lead the Northern Expedition (1926–27) and defeat all the northern 'warlords' while they were in disarray.[44] After successfully reconquering China with the help of the Communists, Chiang brutally murdered his Communist partners and established a 'Central' Nationalist National Government (*Guomindang Guominzhengfu*) in Nanjing in 1928. This Nationalist Government also managed to nominally unify the different hostile armed factions of the KMT.[45] In the new capital, a Provisional Constitution of the Republic of China for the Period of Tutelage (1 June 1931) was promulgated.[46] This Provisional Constitution gave the KMT direct party rule. Doctrinally, this move flowed from Sun's belief that a period of 'Tutelage' under KMT leadership was necessary before China could move on to liberal democratic constitutional rule.[47] This Constitution enabled the KMT to rule under a party constitution rather

[38] Peng-yuan Chang, *From Democracy to Authoritarianism: The Theory and Practice of Tutelage in Sun Yat-sen and His Followers* (Academia Sinica, 2015) ch 2.
[39] ibid ch 3.
[40] Fairbank (n 25) 210–12.
[41] ibid.
[42] Art 3, 1946 Constitution of the ROC; Art 3 and Art 20, 1954 Constitution of the PRC.
[43] Wilbur (n 36).
[44] Waldron (n 31).
[45] Wilbur (n 36).
[46] Tung (n 13).
[47] Peng-yuan Chang (n 38).

than a fully functioning state constitution.[48] It was only in 1946, under the pressure from United States, and pending the outbreak of the civil war, that Chiang agreed to convene a constitutional convention – the Political Consultative Conference (PCC) – involving the other political parties, including the Communists.[49] He had hoped to form a post-War coalition government that incorporated the Nationalists, Communists and other smaller non-militarised political parties. The PCC was to draft and promulgate another liberal democratic constitution, the 1946 Constitution of the Republic of China. Unfortunately, negotiations failed after almost two years. Thus, in the absence of the Communists, the PCC proceeded to vote on on the draft that became the 1946 Constitution on 25 December 1946.[50]

Ironically, just four months after implementing this liberal democratic Constitution, and in the midst of a Communist boycott and military clashes, the National Assembly appended to this Constitution the 'Temporary Provisions against the Communist Rebellion' in April 1948.[51] This nullified many of the liberal provisions by granting broad emergency powers to the President. This empowered Chiang to continue almost dictatorially and spelt the end of liberal democratic ideology in mainland China. Moreover, this was appended to the Constitution two days before Chiang's election as the new President of the ROC, making a mockery of the PCC's work since 1945.[52] The Communists denounced this Constitution as illegitimate and commenced military action against the KMT, defeating them in 1949. Chiang's National Government and the KMT fled to the island of Taiwan with the remnants of their army and China's gold reserve.[53]

The Communist victory on the mainland wedded China to Russia's constitutional tradition, on which the Soviet Union's own constitution was also based. The 1954 PRC Constitution[54] was based on the 1918 Russian Socialist Federated Soviet Republic Constitution,[55] as well as the 1924[56] and the 1936 Constitutions of the Union of Socialist Soviet Republics.[57] The last one is commonly referred to as the 'Stalin Constitution'.[58] This was an important turning point. For the

[48] Yang *Hongnian, Zhongguo Zhengzhi Shi* [History of the Chinese Political System] (Anhui jiaoyu chubanshe, 1989) 433–39.

[49] Tung (n 13) 198.

[50] Jing (n 19) 447–48.

[51] Tung (n 13) 213.

[52] ibid 214.

[53] Fairbank (n 25) 263–69; Diana Lary, *China's Civil War: A Social History, 1945–1949* (Cambridge University Press, 2015); Hans van de Ven, *China at War: Triumph and Tragedy in the Emergence of the New China* (Harvard University Press, 2018) 256.

[54] Constitution of the People's Republic of China promulgated 20 September 1954.

[55] Constitution (Fundamental Law) of the Russian Socialist Federated Soviet Republic promulgated 10 July 1918.

[56] Constitution (Fundamental Law) of the Union of Soviet Socialist Republics of promulgated 31 January 1924.

[57] Constitution (Fundamental Law) of the Union of Soviet Socialist Republics of promulgated 5 December 1936.

[58] WP Coates and Zelda K Coates, *From Tsardom to the Stalin Constitution* (George Allen and Unwin, 1942).

first time in over a century, peace reigned in China, and the old Qing Empire had been prevented from fragmenting. Now, the Communists would begin remoulding the reunified empire into a republic, albeit a Leninist one.

VI. THE 1954 CONSTITUTION: THE GREAT CONSOLIDATION OF POWER

In September 1949, a few months before the CCP's victory in the civil war, it convened, with other sympathetic non-communist parties, a constitutional convention to replace the PCC. This was the Chinese People's Political Consultative Conference (CPPCC). A 'Common Programme' of the CPPCC was proposed and China was renamed the PRC. In the interim, a Common Programme acted as the provisional constitution and the CPPCC acted as the PRC's legislative body.[59] It is important to note that although power was shared under the Common Programme, it gave the CCP *effective control* of the state. This arrangement lasted until 20 September 1954, when the First Session of the NPC was set up. This First Session immediately passed the 1954 Constitution of the PRC into law.[60] Unfortunately, what this new Constitution did was to create a new structure that unintentionally turned the party against the state.[61] As will be seen, this is because the new PRC Constitution departed slightly from the Soviet constitutional model. The result was catastrophic.

A. The Soviet Model: What was Adopted?

Exactly what did China adopt in 1954? The 1954 PRC Constitution was based on the 1936 Constitution of the Soviet Union, but also retained arrangements and features of the 1918 Russian and 1924 Soviet Union Constitutions. The transplantation of a Russian Constitution into China had profound implications. In a single stroke, the basis for rebuilding the Chinese state shifted from that of an Anglo-American/German model premised on a homogeneous society, to a Russian and Austro-Hungarian model that had been developed to accommodate and harmonise multi-ethnic territories.[62] This was a fundamental and profound shift, since it was completely alien to the prevalent intellectual

[59] Christiansen and Rai (n 28), 84; also see Franz Schurmann, *Ideology and Organization in Communist China* (University of California Press, 1968) 178–80.

[60] Kuang Chen and Pan Liang (n 1) 64–67.

[61] Zheng Shiping, *Party vs State in Post-1949 China: The Institutional Dilemma* (Cambridge University Press, 1997).

[62] Tom Bottomore and Patrick Goode, *Austro-Marxism* (Clarendon Press, 1978); Mark E Blum and William Smaldone, *Austro-Marxism: The Ideology of Unity*, vol 1: *Austro-Marxist Theory and Strategy* (Haymarket Books, 2016); Joseph Stalin, *Marxism and the National and Colonial Question: A Collection of Articles and Speeches* (Lawrence & Wishart, 1936).

discourse on constitutions in China.[63] The Soviet model[64] was developed to deal with the many problems left over by the old Russian Empire, and with Continental European issues arising from the collapse of the Austro-Hungarian Empire.[65] These included the issue of self-determination that American President Woodrow Wilson had fervently promoted at the Versailles Peace Conference of 1919.[66] This idea facilitated the break-up of old empires and the formation of many new smaller nation-states in the aftermath of the First World War.[67]

The top-down Soviet model was designed to ensure the continuity of the old imperial bureaucracy under the new Council of People's Commissars.[68] The 1918 Constitution replaced the 1908 Russian Constitution, which had the Tsar at the apex as the Autocrat and Emperor with unchecked power.[69] After Tsar Nicholas II's abdication in March 1917 and the revolutionary seizure of power in October 1917, the Russian autocratic constitutional arrangement was transformed into a Lenin-led Bolshevik party-state dictatorship of the 'workers and toilers'.[70] This new Government had to grapple with how to rule the most massive land empire in history from above. This required the new Bolshevik Government to maintain political dominance over a vast territory, with a diverse multi-ethnic and multi-religion population, straddling two continents. At the same time, the new constitutional arrangement had to reflect the revolutionary theoretical ideals and Lenin's pledge of 'all power to the Soviets', and to share state power with worker councils throughout the old empire.[71]

Built up by conquests over a millennium, the Russian Empire had many similarities with the Chinese Empire, including the fact that they both had

[63] Xia Xinhua, *Jindai Zhongguo Xianzheng Licheng: Shiliao Huicui* (Zhongguo zhengfa dahue chubanshe, 2014); Gugong bowuyuan Ming Qing dang'an bu ed, *Qingmo choubei lixian dang'an shiliao* [Historical materials for the Late Qing preparation for the establishment of a Constitution] (Chunghua shuju, 1979); Guo Wei and Lin Jidong, *Zhonghua Minguo xianfa shiliao* [Historical materials for the Republic of China Constitution] (Xian Yonghe Zhen: Wenhai chubanshe youxiangongsi, 1981).

[64] William Benton Whisenhunt, *In Search of Legality: Mikhail M Speranskii and the Codification of Russian Law* (Columbia University Press, 2001); Andrey N Medushevsky, *Russian Constitutionalism: Historical and Contemporary Development* (Routledge, 2006); William E Pomeranz, *Law and the Russian State: Russia's Legal Evolution from Peter the Great to Vladimir Putin* (Bloomsbury Academic, 2019).

[65] A.J.P Taylor, *The Habsburg Monarchy, 1809–1918: A History of the Austrian Empire and Austria-Hungary* (H Hamilton, 1948).

[66] EJ Hobsbawm, *Nations and Nationalism Since 1780: Programme, Myth, Reality* (Cambridge University Press, 1990).

[67] Alan Sharp, *The Versailles Settlement: Peacemaking after the First World War, 1919–1923*, 3rd edn (Palgrave, 2018); see also Norman A Graebner, and Edward M Bennett, *The Versailles Treaty and its Legacy: The Failure of the Wilsoniam Vision* (Cambridge University Press, 2011).

[68] TH Rigby, *Lenin's Government: Sovnarkom 1917–1922* (Cambridge University Press, 1979).

[69] Geoffrey A Hosking, *The Russian Constitutional Experiment: Government and Duma, 1907–1914* (Cambridge University Press, 1973).

[70] 1918 Constitution.

[71] First published in *Pravda* No 99, 18 July 1917; 'All Powers to the Soviets,' marxist.org, last accessed 23 July 2020 at www.marxists.org/archive/lenin/works/1917/jul/18.htm; Richard Sakwa, *Soviet Politics in Perspective*, 2nd edn (Routledge, 1998) 115.

multinational inhabitants living across the vast expanse of their territories.[72] As noted, the liberal democratic Chinese Constitutions promulgated between 1912 and 1949 failed to work. On the other hand, the Soviet model, developed to deal with another fallen continental empire, seemed eminently suitable for a post-imperial Chinese environment. This fact has often been overlooked, because the Russian Communists had systematically subsumed these ideas in modern-looking constitutions and toned down the radical Communist ideas against laws by adopting 'socialist legality'.[73] This was approximately what China adopted in 1954. The most important difference is the addition of a state President (or 'Chairman' in old translations) in the Chinese case. This apparently superficial addition caused the collapse of the system. To understand how this happened, we need to examine the Constitution and its model more carefully.

VII. STRUCTURE OF THE 1954 CONSTITUTION

The PRC's 1954 Constitution contains a Preamble, four chapters and 106 articles. It follows the general layout of the Constitution (Fundamental Law) of the Russian Socialist Federated Soviet Republic (RSFSR) of 1918, the Constitution (Fundamental Law) of the Union of Soviet Socialist Republics of 1924 and the Constitution (Fundamental Law) of the Union of Soviet Socialist Republics of 1936 (the 'Stalin Constitution').[74] Table 2.3 shows the major milestones in the development of the Russian and Chinese constitutions.

Table 2.3 List of Constitutions of Russian Lineage, 1918–54

1	10 Jul 1918	*Constitution (Fundamental Law) of the Russian Socialist Federated Soviet Republic (RSFSR)* 6 sections and 90 articles
2	31 Jan 1924	*Constitution (Fundamental Law) of the Union of Soviet Socialist Republics (USSR)* 11 chapters and 72 articles
3	5 Dec 1936	*Constitution (Fundamental Law) of the Union of Soviet Socialist Republics (USSR)* 13 chapters and 146 articles
4	20 Sep 1954	*Constitution of the People's Republic of China* 4 chapters and 106 articles

[72] Geoffrey A Hosking, *Russia and the Russians: A History*, 2nd edn (Belknap Press, 2011).

[73] Anna Louise Strong, *The New Soviet Constitution. A Study in Socialist Democracy* (H Holt & Co, 1937); Sidney Webb and Beatrice Webb, *Soviet Communism: A New Civilisation*, vols I and II (Longmans, Green, 1944); Samantha Lomb, *Stalin's Constitution: Soviet Participatory Politics and the Discussion of the 1936 Draft Constitution* (Routledge, 2018); Olga Velikanova, *Mass Political Culture Under Stalinism: Popular Discussion of the Soviet Constitution of 1936* (Palgave Macmillan, 2018); Chen (n 24), 27; Andrey Yanuaryevich Vyshinsky, *The Law of the Soviet State*, tr Hugh W Babb (Macmillan, 1948).

[74] Aryeh L Unger, *Constitutional Development in the USSR: A Guide to the Soviet Constitutions* (Methuen & Co, 1981).

At this point it must be noted that while the pre-1911 Chinese state lacked a set of fundamental laws or a constitution to regulate the state and its government, the pre-1917 Russian state had a written, albeit autocratic, constitutional arrangement that lasted till September 1917.[75] Any post-1917 Russian constitution would have to continue regulating the same geographical and demographical space.[76] Thus, the 1832 edition of the Fundamental Laws in the Code of Laws of the Russian Empire preceded the 1906 edition of the Fundamental Laws. This in turn preceded the 1918 Constitution (Fundamental Laws) of RSFSR.[77]

A. The Model and Chinese State Building

We cannot understand the theoretical underpinnings of the 1954 PRC Constitution through the lens of classical separation of powers analysis. Instead, this Constitution needs to be understood in light of its Russian lineage. We must therefore consider the document from two perspectives: (i) the imperial (ancient and concerns rule); and (ii) the revolutionary (modern, socialism and democracy).

From 1917 to 1924, when the Soviet Union was established, Russia was in a state of civil war. To stabilise the country, it was necessary to unite, placate and incorporate the divergent political forces in the former empire.[78] Political power was thus shared and distributed by the constitutions. These included the Congress of the Soviets, Executive Committees of the Congress of the Soviets, the geographical regions, the multi-ethnic nations, the old bureaucracy seized and controlled by Lenin, and (lastly) the judiciary.[79] Each of these controlled a segment of political power, and they were thus fiefdoms in their own right. Save for the courts, each accrued to itself different levels of executive and legislative powers.[80] Thus, there could be no 'separation of powers' in the Anglo-American or Montesquieu sense. Such was the political reality.

It is significant that each of these institutional pillars is theoretically an executive 'branch' but with legislative powers.[81] Thus, under the 1906 Russian Constitution, the State Council, State Duma and Emperor all had legislative powers at the same time. Whether one body had more functional executive or legislative power depended on how it evolved within the Soviet state.[82] By the time these were adopted in China, their procedures and hence their relative powers were settled. Furthermore, it must also be noted when the Bolsheviks seized power, they took over the old state structures, including the imperial

[75] Medushevsky (n 64); Hosking (n 69).

[76] Richard Pipes, *The Russian Revolution, 1899–1919* (Collins Harvill, 1990).

[77] Medushevsky (n 64) ch 3.

[78] Rigby (n 68) Part Three.

[79] cf Jerome Alan Cohen, 'China's Changing Constitution' (1978) 76(4) *The China Quarterly* 810.

[80] Chen (n 24) ch 6.

[81] ibid.

[82] Rigby (n 68) ch 12.

Russian military.[83] Unlike the Russian military, the Chinese military was built up from a guerrilla force by Mao Zedong as a party army that was loyal to him as party Chairman and commander-in-chief. Mao and his party army gained ultimate state power by successful military conquest and not by political *coup d'état*. Moreover, they had fought the Japanese invaders and then the Nationalist party army in turn, their campaigns lasting over a decade from 1937 to 1949.[84] It was on account of Mao's prestige and personal power that the 1954 PRC Constitution included something not found in the Soviet Constitutions – the office of President, which Mao duly occupied in 1954.[85] In the Soviet Union, the Chairman of the Supreme Soviet assumed the role of head of state.[86]

i. Section I: The National People's Congress

The Soviet 'All-Russian Congress of Soviets of Workers, Peasants, Cossacks and Red Army Deputies', when transposed into China, became the NPC.[87] The NPC had all the powers and limitations of its Soviet counterpart under the 1936 Soviet Constitution. Apart from legislative powers, the NPC has executive prerogatives. These prerogatives are derived from the manner in which the 1917 Russian Revolution established the RSFSR and, after the civil war, the USSR.[88] Like its Russian and Soviet counterparts, the NPC cannot exercise much of the executive power it theoretically possesses. The reason, as we shall see, is historical.

Japan defeated Russia in the Russo-Japanese War of 1905. This led to widespread social unrest, and the Russian Revolution of the same year forced Tsar Nicholas II to reluctantly concede a constitution in 1906.[89] The Constitution or Fundamental State Laws of 23 April 1906 established an elected multiparty State Duma as the lower house, but procedurally mirrored by an appointed State Council as the upper house. This arrangement was a concession extracted from Nicolas II. Otherwise, the Russian Empire remained an autocracy, with the Emperor wielding unfettered executive, legislative and judicial powers, including

[83] Leon Trotsky, *History of the Russian Revolution* (Penguin Books, 2017); Rex A Wade, *The Russian Revolution, 1917*, 3rd edn (Cambridge University Press, 2017); Pipes (n 76); Sheila Fitzpatrick, *The Russian Revolution* (Oxford University Press, 1994); John LH Keep, *The Russian Revolution: A Study in Mass Mobilization* (Norton, 1976); Graeme J Gill, *Peasants and Government in the Russian Revolution* (Macmillan, 1979); Martin McCauley, *The Russian Revolution and the Soviet State, 1917–1921: Documents* (Macmillan, 1980); Robert Service, *The Russian Revolution, 1900–1927* (Palgrave Macmillan, 2009); Harold Shukman, *Lenin and the Russian Revolution* (BT Batsford Ltd, 1966); Leonard Schapiro, *1917: The Russian Revolutions and the Origins of Present-Day Communism* (Maurice Temple Smith, 1984); Orlando Figes, *A People's Tragedy: The Russian Revolution 1891–1924* (The Bodley Head, 2014).

[84] Mitter (n 12); Westad (n 19); Pepper (n 19).

[85] 1954 Constitution of the PRC, Ch Two, Sec II.

[86] Donald Gasper, 'The Chinese National People's Congress' in Daniel Nelson and Stephen White (eds), *Communist Legislatures in Comparative Perspective* (Macmillan, 1982) 160, 174.

[87] Pt III, 1918 Constitution.

[88] Unger (n 74) ch 1.

[89] Hugh Seton-Watson, *The Russian Empire, 1801–1917* (Clarendon Press, 1967) 579–627.

the power to declare war (Article 13). There was no separation of powers, since the executive and legislative powers of both the State Duma and the State Council existed in conjunction with each other, as well as with the Tsar's executive and legislative powers (Article 7). All laws passed by the State Duma and the State Council must be approved by the Tsar (Article 8). Furthermore, the 1906 Constitution in practice empowered the Tsar to pass any law, even when the State Duma and the State Council were not in session (Article 45).[90]

Soviets or workers' councils began to form throughout the Russian Empire in 1906. These began life as workers' strike committees and were initially organised informally. However, they eventually evolved into the constitutional foundation of the state when their executive committees exerted power in the plenums. The Bolshevik Party itself played little role in 1905, but the 1906 Constitution failed to create a genuine constitutional monarchy. Instead Nicolas II and his advisers took this opportunity to draft a constitution that strengthened the autocracy,[91] and the 1906 Constitution failed to provide a broad suffrage. The State Duma failed as a parliament that could hold the Government accountable for its actions. Nicolas II finally alienated all support by declaring war on the Austro-Hungarian Empire in 1914, and participated in the First World War. He was eventually forced to abdicate in March 1917 amid food shortages and widespread unrest. A 'Provisional Committee' of the Duma gained power and became the Provisional Government, while sharing power with a soviet, the Provisional Executive of the Petrograd Soviet.[92]

The period from March to October 1917 was a period of 'dual power'. Soviets were mushrooming across the country and the new Government had to share power with them. Socialist politicians and intellectuals in the executive committees of these loosely organised soviets came to dominate the rank-and-file delegates in the plenums.[93] After the 1917 October Revolution, the new 1918 Constitution removed the 'All-Russian Emperor' (Article 4, 1906 Constitution)[94] and replaced it with the 'All-Russian Congress of Soviets of Workers', Peasants', Cossacks', and Red Army Deputies' (abbreviated as the 'All-Russian Congress') (Article 12).[95] When the 1936 Constitution model reached China, the equivalent incarnation was the NPC (the direct Chinese translation is 'All-China Congress of People's Representatives'). The NPC thus represents the wide powers that were once possessed by the Russia Emperor, introduced through the adoption of the Russian model. This was an executive body with legislative and judicial powers mirroring the inherent power of the Russian Emperor. The NPCSC possesses the theoretical power to pass laws like the Russian Emperor when

[90] ibid; Marc Szeftel, *The Russian Constitution of April 23, 1906: Political Institutions of the Duma, Monarchy* (Éd de la librairie encyclopédique, 1976).
[91] Sakwa (n 71), 13.
[92] Seton-Watson (n 89) 598–727.
[93] Sakwa (n 71) 17.
[94] Art 4, 1906 Constitution.
[95] Art 12, 1918 Constitution.

the State Dumas and State Council were not in session. Once we understand the autocratic origins of the NPCSC, it is not hard to understand why, unlike constitutional systems following the classical 'separation of powers' model, the NPCSC also has the power to interpret laws (Article 31(3)).[96]

ii. Section VI: The People's Courts and the People's Procuratorates

Once we understand the imperial Russian sovereign origin of the NPC and NPCSC models, the apparently contradictory Articles 78 and Article 80 of the 1954 Constitution concerning judicial independence can be analogously appreciated as a concession from the Russian Emperor, who had unlimited autocratic constitutional power. Article 78 states that the People's Courts 'are independent, subject only to the law', while Article 80 states that the Supreme People's Court is 'responsible' to the NPC and 'reports to it'.

The idea of judicial independence in the PRC's 1954 Constitution follows the Russian tradition that began with the Judicial Reforms of 1864.[97] These include enforcing a more unified civil code across Russia and imposing a 'rule through law' system. This also led to the establishment of legal procedures and institutions that served as a modest curb on imperial state power. Judges were given life tenure and were conferred the right to interpret laws. Trial by jury was also introduced. With the passing of time, however, the increasingly independent judges began challenging the Emperor's unlimited constitutional power. Gradually, the loss of the imperial prerogative was reversed by the increasing micromanagement of the judges, who were required to explain their judgments to the sovereign's agents. The judges and their decisions were subjected to new rules that subjugated the courts to bureaucratic scrutiny. The 1917 Revolution, however, brought the liberal reforms to a complete end. In the first decade after the Revolution, Soviet Russia diverged from the procedures established by the 1864 Reforms. The independence of the judiciary that had developed since the reforms was reversed.[98] Under the new revolutionary regime, courts were subjugated to the Congress of Soviets and the Central Executive Committee.[99] These bodies are analogous to the NPC and NPCSC under China's 1954 Constitution.

The 1894 Judicial Reforms also transformed the Procuracy, the Soviet model of China's Procuratorate. In imperial times, this body had power to supervise the Russian state on behalf of the Emperor.[100] After the Reform, the Procuracy was reduced to providing state prosecutors. Under the Soviet model, the Procuracy

[96] Art 31, 1954 Constitution of the PRC.
[97] Pomeranz (n 64) 38.
[98] ibid chs 3, 4 and 5.
[99] Art 43, Ch Nine, 1918 Constitution.
[100] The prosecutor's office (*prokuratura*) was founded by Peter the Great in 1722; Pomeranz (n 64) 18.

was restored to that of imperial times,[101] and this was followed closely by China in 1954. Article 81 states that the Supreme People's Procuratorate of the People's Republic of China exercises procuratorial authority over all departments of the State Council, all local organs of state, person working in organs of state and citizens, to ensure observance of the law. Like the courts, the Procuratorate 'is responsible' to the NPC (Article 84).

In summary, the People's Courts and the People's Procuratorates in Section VI of Chapter Two of the 1954 Constitution also derived their theoretical power from its origins in the Russian Empire. They have the least or no executive powers. The People's Courts under the 1954 Constitution are also endowed with an insignificant amount of legislative power, though it is enough to further demonstrate that there is no 'separation of powers' in this adopted system.[102]

iii. Section III: The State Council

China's State Council is equivalent to the Soviet Council of Ministers (or Council of People's Commissars before 1948), which was created under the 1918 Constitution.[103] The Council of Ministers acquired the entire functioning bureaucratic machine of the Russian Empire and combines executive and legislative powers.[104] Lenin took personal charge of this Council, exerting executive central power until his death in 1924.[105] The Council could issue decrees with the force of law.[106] Alternatively, decrees would go either through the Supreme Soviet or to its Presidium for ratification.[107] This procedure was another legacy of the old Russian Empire. Ratifying decrees that had been passed (*ukases* or orders; an imposition, meaning a decree with the force of law) was usual and commonplace.[108] Between 1938 to 1956, fewer than 25 direct laws were passed, but many thousands of decrees were ratified.[109]

Again, the structure and functions of China's State Council were based on the Russian model. The power to issue decrees with the force of law was provided for in the 1954 Constitution,[110] with a slight difference. Since the Chinese State

[101] ibid 87; power of legislative initiative granted in 1933 and Art 113 of the 1936 Constitution assigned the procuracy '[s]upreme supervision over the strict execution of the laws by all People's Commissariats and their subordinate institutions, as well as by individual officials and by citizens of the USSR'.

[102] George Gainsburgs and Arthur Stahnke, 'The Genesis of the People's Procuratorate in Communist China 1949–1951' (1962) 20 *The China Quarterly* 1.

[103] Ch Eight of the 1918 Constitution.

[104] Rigby (n 68), Pt One.

[105] ibid, Pt Two.

[106] Art 9, 1918 Constitution.

[107] Pomeranz (n 64), 82; Peter Vanneman, 'The Hierarchy of Laws in the Communist Party-State System in the Soviet Union' (1974) 8 *International Lawyer* 285.

[108] Pomeranz (n 64), 13, 82 and 86; D Richard Little, 'Legislative Authority in the Soviet Political System' (1971) 30 *Slavic Review* 57.

[109] SE Finer, *Comparative Government* (Allen Lane, 1970) 407.

[110] Art 49, 1954 Constitution.

Council did not inherit a powerful bureaucracy like the Russian Council of Ministers, it was left to the 1954 Constitution to create China's ministerial bureaucracy – the State Council – which, among other things, was charged with developing the economy.

iv. Section V: Self-government of National Autonomous Areas

Section V of the 1954 Constitution attempted to neutralise nationalism within the boundaries of the old Empire. The Constitution closely followed the principles but not the structure of the 1936 Soviet Constitution. As was noted earlier, the socialist organisation of the Soviet state needed to confront the rising tide of ethnic nationality challenges.[111] In 1912, Lenin dispatched Joseph Stalin to Vienna, capital of the Austro-Hungarian Empire, on an investigative mission. Stalin later published a theoretical pamphlet entitled *Marxism and the National and Colonial Question*,[112] which he wrote in January 1913 while in Vienna. This established him as the leading thinker on the topic and formalised the Bolshevik nationality policy that was incorporated into the Russian and Soviet Constitutions of 1924 and 1936.[113]

In this pamphlet, Stalin argued against Otto Bauer's 'personal principle' that organises nations 'not in territorial bodies but in simple association of persons', and instead advanced the concept of 'national delimitation'. By the time of the 1936 Constitution, Stalin's ideas were concretised. Well-defined national territorial units were created as Soviet Socialist Republics (SSRs), Autonomous Soviet Socialist Republics (ASSRs), and other regional organisations as oblasts, rations and okrugs.[114] This structure was generally adopted by the PRC and superimposed (with modifications) on the original provincial structure of the ROC.[115] After 1936, the Supreme Soviet became a bicameral chamber and the nationalities were represented by one of the two chambers, the Soviet of the Nationalities.[116] This bicameral constitutional formulation with a chamber for nationalities was not adopted, however, in the 1954 PRC Constitution.

The Bolshevik Government also promulgated the *Declaration of Rights of the Toiling and Exploited Peoples of Russia* in January 1918.[117] This freed and conferred notional independence on the different nationalities, and successfully increased support for the Bolsheviks in the Revolution. The Declaration

[111] Jeremy Smith, *The Bolsheviks and the National Question, 1917–23* (Palgrave Macmillan, 1999); Pipes (n 14).
[112] Stalin (n 62).
[113] ibid.
[114] Unger (n 74), 91.
[115] Yang (n 48) 479–98; Tung (n 13) 44, 57–58; Xu Congde, *Zhonghua Renmin Gongheguo Xianfashi shi, shangjuan* [Constitutional History of the People's Republic of China, vol 1] (Fujian renmin chubanshe, 2005) 218–30.
[116] 1936 Constitution, Ch VII; AI Denisov and MG Kirichenko, *Soviet State Law* (Foreign Languages Publishing House, 1960).
[117] Pipes (n 14) 242–43.

proclaimed self-determination and secession for the national minorities and ethnic groups. Effectively, they gained full independence, but were supposed to hold together as proletariats under socialism and not as nationalists.[118] In both the 1924 USSR and the 1954 PRC Constitutions, a measure of cultural and administrative autonomy was granted to the national minorities within the state. This is because the Red Army and the CCP's People's Liberation Army (PLA) both triumphed in these areas in their respective civil wars.[119] In the RSFSR, there was a notional federal solution under the Constitution for nationalities in the form of 'autonomous' regions or districts,[120] while in the PRC, the solution was outright unitary and non-federal. Thus, in China the regions were defined as 'autonomous' but 'inalienable'.[121]

In the areas where the Red Army was unsuccessful, a form of federalism was introduced.[122] On the western and southern fringes of the Russian Empire, Finland, Poland, Estonia, Latvia and Lithuania gained independence after 1917.[123] In other territories of the Ukraine, the Caucasus, Belorussia and Central Asia, the Red Army won after formal independence had been declared and recognised.[124] Furthermore, the RSFSR had already agreed treaties of peace and alliance in the military and economic realms with some of these newly formed republics.[125] Some of these republics, such as Ukraine, had entered into diplomatic and military relations with foreign powers.[126] The old Russian Empire was thus pieced back together as a federal state by 1924.[127] This process culminated in the 1936 federal Constitution of the Soviet Union.[128] As time went on, more republics were created in Central Asia, and breakaway imperial Russian territories like Estonia, Latvia, Lithuania, Moldavia and Karelia-Finland all returned to the Soviet fold under the federal arrangements after the outbreak of the Second World War.[129] Eventually, the Soviet Union would break up along these federal fault lines in 1991, even if the RSFSR remained intact.[130] China, on the other hand, had never implemented any kind of federal system. With the CCP's victory over the KMT in 1949,[131] the old nineteenth-century Chinese

[118] ibid 44.
[119] Finer (n 109) 396–98.
[120] Art 11, 1924 Constitution (USSR); Unger (n 74) 19 and 45; Art 53, 1954 Constitution (China); Pipes (n 14) 248.
[121] Art 3, 1954 Constitution.
[122] Ronald Grigor Suny, *The Revenge of the Past: Nationalism, Revolution, and the Collapse of the Soviet Union* (Stanford University Press, 1993).
[123] Pipes (n 14), ch II.
[124] ibid chs III–V.
[125] Treaty of Riga: Pipes (n 14) 154; Aviel Roshwald, *Ethnic Nationalism & the Fall of Empires: Central Europe, Russia & The Middle East, 1914–1923* (New York: Routledge, 2001) 162.
[126] Roshwald (n 125) 247–55; Finer (n 109) 397.
[127] 1924 Constitution.
[128] ibid Ch VI.
[129] Finer (n 109, 398.
[130] Suny (n 122).
[131] van de Ven (n 53) ch 13.

Empire was reconquered, save for the fringe territories of Taiwan (Nationalist controlled), Hong Kong (British controlled), Macao (Portuguese controlled) and Outer Mongolia (independence in 1924). China thus remained almost intact and constitutionally unitary without the need of a federal system, and the 1954 Constitution functioned precisely as designed and stabilised ethnic nationalism.

v. Section IV: The Local People's Congresses and the Local People's Councils

The Local People's Councils and Congresses resurrected and modernised the previous post-imperial Republican provincial and municipal state delineations. This installed new administrative structures on top of the old imperial counties and villages that had lain at the bottom of the system.[132] Section IV needs to be read in conjunction with Section V of the 1954 Constitution. This section creates a pyramid of vertically interlocking Local People's Congresses and Local People's Councils that mirrored that of the Central Government in the capital city. The apex of this hierarchy is the NPC in Beijing.[133] The system functions according to the principles of democratic centralism, under which lower bodies are required to observe the decisions of higher ones.[134] This state structure was set out in Chapter 2 of the 1954 Constitution, which was based on the Soviet Constitution as well as the Soviet *nomenklatura* system.[135] Stalin had refined the *nomenklatura* system following Lenin's death in January 1924[136] by shifting political power from the Council of Ministers to the Community Party. With this shift, appointments to the People's Congress were made on the basis of hierarchy and seniority. The Soviet state was thus 'colonised by the instrument of party'.[137]

In China, this system allowed only approved Communist Party members to be appointed to various key administrative positions in the state bureaucracy and industries. Naturally, this allowed the old system of official appointments to continue. Under this model, there were, in both the Soviet Union and China, two operative governments: the Party and the state. However, the Party is *not* the Government, despite very close linkages. The Party might be considered the senior branch of government where policy decisions are made or confirmed. The State Council and the NPC would thus be the junior branches of government.[138] Under this system, the ruling CCP was free to pick and choose the institution best suited to implementing the policy decisions passed by the various

[132] Yang (n 48),281–519; Xu (n 115) 80–88.
[133] Arts 64, 65 and 66, 1954 Constitution.
[134] Schurmann (n 59) 54.
[135] ibid 73 and 74; John P Burns (ed), *The Chinese Communist Party's Nomenklatura System* (ME Sharpe, 1989).
[136] Graeme Gill, *The Origins of the Stalinist Political System* (Cambridge University Press, 1990) chs 2 and 3.
[137] Richard Sakwa, *Communism in Russia* (Palgrave Macmillan, 2010) 100.
[138] Sakwa (n 71) 17.

Party committees.[139] This system of hierarchical congresses merged almost seamlessly into the pre-existing administrative divisions of imperial and nationalist republican China.[140] Under the 1954 Constitution, however, large Autonomous Regions were created out of provinces on the periphery and smaller ones within locales. All are represented through the NPC and Local People's Congresses.[141]

vi. Section II: The President of the People's Republic of China

Chapter Two, Section II covers the office of the President of the PRC. This was the most significant and problematic Chinese addition to the models of the Russian Constitution, and it was to have very serious negative consequences. This section of the Constitution reinstated the equivalent of an emperor, a top-down autocratic ruling personality, in the form of a 'President' with wide governmental, ceremonial and military powers. This upset the carefully constructed constitutional power balance that had been fine-tuned in the Russian model. This was precisely what the RSFSR Constitution sought to eliminate in 1918. The Tsar was replaced by a bottom-up collective of delegates from the soviets across the country, which formed the All-Russian Central Executive Committee.[142] This arrangement was maintained in the Soviet Constitutions of 1924 and 1936.[143] And, as previously noted, the Tsar's traditional constitutional role and his autocratic power were dissolved and replaced by the Presidium of the Supreme Soviet.[144] In the 1954 Chinese formulation, the equivalent of the Presidium of the Supreme Soviet was the NPCSC.[145]

Without understanding the Soviets' historic fear of the Tsar and his despotic power, Western scholars often mistake the Presidium (or the NPCSC) as 'merely' a small proxy or stand-in for the 'full legislature' (Supreme Soviet or the NPC) when the latter is not in session.[146] By presenting the Presidium as akin to an American *collective presidency*, however, Samuel Finer wisely macerated this deliberative body into a conceptually palatable form for Western intellectual consumption:

> In theory this Presidium merely acts on behalf of the Supreme Soviet during the intervals when the latter is not sitting. It is charged with a series of important responsibilities. It issues decrees, it interpret the laws of the USSR, it convenes and dissolves the Supreme Soviet, it releases and appoints ministers, it awards decoration, orders, medals and titles of honour, it exercises the right of pardon, it appoints and removes the high command, and it can even, in the intervals between sessions of the Supreme

[139] Christiansen and Rai (n 28) 88–97.
[140] Yang (n 48).
[141] Arts 23, 54, 55 and 56, 1954 Constitution.
[142] Art 28, 1918 Constitution.
[143] Art 29, 1924 Constitution; Art 49, 1936 Constitution.
[144] Art 45, 1906 Constitution.
[145] Art 30.
[146] Finer (n 109) 408.

> Soviet, proclaim a state of war, or general or partial mobilisation. It ratifies and denounces treaties, appoints ambassadors and receives them, and it can, in an emergency, proclaim martial law. In fact, this Presidium is like the presidency of the USA, but a presidency which is put into commission, a collective presidency rather than an individual one. Effectively, in working practice, the Presidium operates as a small working legislature ...[147]

Mao became the first President under the 1954 Constitution,[148] and the Presidency unambiguously reflected and protected Mao's personal power in the new state. According to Xu Congde of Renmin University, who was a young member of the drafting committee in 1954, the addition of the Presidency and how this should be defined was led by Mao's personal ideas.[149] There was no other rational structural consideration other than the fact that they were at liberty to create the Presidency.[150] The broader historical background, however, sheds important light on the reasons. The CCP's victory in 1949 was a straightforward and successful military conquest. There was no need for the CCP to rely on collective coalitions to gain or maintain power. As such, the power conferred on the President under the 1954 Constitution was real and significant,[151] with Article 42 authorising the President to command 'the armed forces of the country' and appointing him 'Chairman of the Council of National Defence'.[152] Mao's power derived from his chairmanship of the CCP, which controlled the PLA that created the state. Yet the 1954 Constitution exerted little control over the PLA, save through Article 42, and only while Mao remained President.[153] The military otherwise had no representation in the NPC that controlled the bureaucratic state structure.

The balance of powers under the Soviet Constitution relied on membership numbers, attendance arrangements and frequency of meetings to balance and dampen the different aggressive political forces and individual ambitions. This system worked because the military came from within; the armed forces have always been part of the Russian state government structure. This was not the case in China in 1949, however. The CCP had built the PLA from scratch, and in 1954 it lay outside the new state structure created by the Constitution. Unfortunately, the addition of the President in the Chinese system completely upset the stability and equilibrium of the Soviet constitutional model. Having a President with real independent military power was problematic from the start.[154] From the state's point of view, to elect a President who commanded a conquering army meant heaping legal legitimacy on to an already politically

[147] ibid; Unger (n 74) 18.
[148] Xu (n 115) 206.
[149] ibid, ch 7.
[150] ibid.
[151] ibid.
[152] Art 42, 1954 Constitution; Xu (n 115) 206.
[153] Art 42, 1954 Constitution.
[154] Xu (n 115) 206.

powerful personality. In practical terms, it meant that the President could literally push through any policy of his own fancy. Chapter Two, Section II of the Constitution further provided the President with his own personal 'parliament' in the form of the Supreme State Conference, which he could call at will.[155]

During Mao's tenure as President, he consistently used this power to formalise, announce and promote policies decided by himself.[156] The President's constitutional powers (eg in Article 40) overlap with those of the NPCSC to act pursuant to decisions of the NPC or NPCSC (Article 31). Yet this was unlikely to restrain Mao. The only way to stop him was to remove him from office, which was what happened after the disaster of the Great Leap Forward. In July 1955, Mao pushed forward with the infamous Great Leap programme against his colleagues' wishes. This radical policy triggered a famine that left an estimated 27 to 45 million people dead.[157] Mao had to step down as President in April 1959, but continued to hold non-economic power as Chairman of the Communist Party.[158]

The creation of the separate Chinese Presidency upset the important Bolshevik constitutional innovation that should have reposed powers in the NPCSC, which was meant to exercise ultimate 'imperial' power as a 'small working legislature' replacing the Emperor's personal sovereign power. Theoretically, the NPCSC was to dilute the formidable absolutist individual imperial power and place it in a small collective 'parliament'. The establishment of a separate Chinese Presidency immediately created a state role for an individual in the state structure, which was the very antithesis of the original 1918 Soviet design. This destabilised the upper echelons of Chinese politics, triggering power struggles for a non-collective Presidency that empowered an individual on an imperial scale. In post-imperial Russia there was no such problem, because even Lenin was compelled to operate from within this distributive structure by embedding himself in the Council of Ministers (a state position).[159] Stalin also worked within this system without change, moving the locus of political power away from the Council of Ministers only after Lenin's death. He controlled the entire state structure from his position as the General Secretary of the Communist Party (a party position), a post that he personally refined and empowered.[160] Hence, the huge structural tension that the 1954 Constitution generated between Party and state, when Mao and Liu separately occupied the top positions in the Party and in the state, did not occur in the Soviet Union, even at the peak of powerful personality rule. An all-powerful presidency was a purely Chinese creation.

[155] Art 43, 1954 Constitution.
[156] Dietrich (n 21) 63, 95, 106, 117, 121 and 134.
[157] Frank Dikötter, *Mao's Great Famine: The History of China's Most Devastating Catastrophe, 1958–62* (Bloomsbury, 2017); Dietrich (n 21) ch 4.
[158] Dietrich (n 21) ch 5.
[159] Rigby (n 68) chs 1, 2, 3 and 12.
[160] Gill (n 136) chs 2 and 3.

VIII. THE PRC AND STATE BUILDING

Following the CCP's victory, the PRC was established by the Common Programme of the Chinese People's Consultative Conference on 29 September 1949.[161] This was not a formal constitution but a short provisional constitutional document with just 16 Articles, setting out a programme for taking power from the defeated Nationalist regime. This included authorising an interim military takeover (Article 14) and the enactment of the Organic Law of the Central People's Government of the People's Republic of China to exercise state power (Article 13). The Leninist-structured CCP thus ruled China, with Mao as Party Chairman. He was also Chairman of the newly-established Central People's Government by the Organic Law,[162] and this cemented his position as the head of state under direct Communist Party rule in the name of a coalition of eight other pre-existing 'democratic' parties present at the CPPCC of 1949.[163]

With the promulgation of the 1954 Constitution things changed radically, especially on the economic front. State economic intervention now became a state constitutional duty, authorising wholesale nationalisation of the economy in the name of 'socialist transformation':

> Article 4
>
> The People's Republic of China, by relying on the organs of state and the social forces, and by means of socialist industrialisation and socialist transformation, ensures the gradual abolition of systems of exploitation and the building of a socialist society.[164]

Socialist transformation was speedily achieved by 1956. From the economic perspective, the Chinese state could be seen as a gigantic commercial conglomerate or holding corporation that swept up and monopolised all modern economic power. No economic activity was left outside the state structure. Private enterprises were banned and the economy was closed to the outside world. It was at this time that Mao grew increasingly disgruntled with the system. At this

[161] Preamble, 1949 Common Programme of The Chinese People's Political Consultative Conference; Christiansen and Rai (n 28) 84–87.

[162] Tung (n 13) 269–70.

[163] ibid 259–62.

[164] The state created by the 1954 'Constitution of the People's Republic of China' actively absorbed entire industries. By Art 4 of the 1954 Constitution, the Communist Government set about nationalising all commercial businesses. The Editor, 'You zhunbei, you buzhou di tuidong siying gongye shixing quan hangye gongsi heying' ['A well-prepared and methodologically organised establishment of state-private cooperative ventures for private industries in all industrial sectors'] *Renmin ribao* [*People's Daily*] (25 November 1955) collected in Li Qing et al (eds), *Zhongguo Ziben zhuyi gong-shangye de shehui zhuyi gaizao: Zhongyangi juan* [The socialist transformation of capitalist industrial and commercial sector of China: Central government volume] (Zhongguo dangshi chubanshe, 1993) 973; Chen Yun, 'Shehui zhuyi gaizhao jiben wancheng yihou de xin wenti' ['New problems after the near completion of socialist transformation'] *Renmin ribao* [*People's Daily*] (21 September 1956), collected in *Zhongguo Ziben zhuyi gong-shangye de shehui zhuyi gaizao: Zhongyangi juan* [The socialist transformation of capitalist industrial and commercial sector of China: Central government volume] 1199.

time, most of the industries had been absorbed into the NPC state structure. The economic success of those initial years depended on the support of the Soviet Union, then friendly with China. Mao, however, struggled to keep up with economic developments because he had little technical knowledge of complex (often mathematical) but systematic central planning of the economy introduced by Soviet experts.[165] He thus attempted to set the agenda to maintain his power and influence by launching his simpler but more radical alternative development programme: the disastrous Great Leap Forward.[166] By 1958, Mao already detested the state Constitution and wanted to bypass it. He said in a meeting:

> The Constitution was drafted by my participation but I don't remember it anymore … All our present resolutions are now laws; meetings are also laws. We mainly rely on resolutions and meetings. Do it four times a year. To keep order, there is no need to rely on civil or criminal laws.[167]

The removal of Mao from the Presidency set off a series of events that was to devastate China in the coming years. Having lost the Presidency, Mao had no choice but to return to his 'base' to rebuild his power. Employing mass gatherings, street rallies and images of him swimming across the Yangtze River, he built a personality cult amongst the youth to support his violent crusade against 'revisionists' in the state bureaucracy and re-took state power.[168] This resonates with contemporary political sentiments of a popular political figure pledging to 'drain the swamp' in the capital city,[169] albeit in an extremely violent manner.

Whatever euphemistic language was used to soften the impact of Mao's ousting – such as Mao's retreat 'to the second line'[170] – it did not alter the fact that Mao was now out of the NPC state power structure,[171] even if he remained Party Chairman. He was definitely out of economic power, because all economic power by this time was concentrated within the NPC state structure. Even so, as Party Chairman, Mao was able to install an ally, Marshall Lin Biao, as Minister of Defence in September 1959. Mao himself, however, was denied any further role in state economic matters.[172] He had to reinvent himself to regain power.

[165] Shen Zhihua, *Zhonghua Renmin Gongheguo shi* [The History of the People's Republic of China] (Chinese University Press, 2008) vol 3, 113; David M Bachman, *Bureaucracy, Economy, and Leadership in China: The Institutional Origins of the Great Leap Forward* (Cambridge University Press, 1991).

[166] Carl Riskin, *China's Political Economy: The Quest for Development Since 1949* (Oxford University Press, 1988) 82.

[167] Ding Shuzhu, *Yang mou: fan youpai yundong shimo* [Open conspiracy: the complete story of Chinese Communist Party's Anti-Rightist Campaign] (Open Books, 2006) 320.

[168] Dietrich (n 21) ch 6.

[169] It would be a better metaphoric parallel if Beijing were not located on the arid and sandy North China Plain but on a wet and swampy river estuary like Washington, DC.

[170] Immanuel CY Hsü, *The Rise of Modern China*, 6th edn (Oxford University Press, 2000) 690.

[171] Table 12 and Table 13, appendix to Fairbank and MacFarquhar (eds) (n 22) 603–04.

[172] Fairbank (n 25), 306; Dietrich (n 21) 136–38.

By 1956, Mao had mastered the art of wielding real, theoretical and symbolic political power. In 1959, he launched vehement theoretical textual attacks on the Soviet Union's Marxist ideology and its 'revisionist' Communist leadership.[173] This directly contributed to the withdrawal of Soviet industrial and technical support to the new Chinese state structure in 1960.[174] Without Soviet backing, the NPC state bureaucracy under President Liu became vulnerable and exposed. Mao continued his theoretical offensive against the Soviet Union from 1961 to 1964 while he waited behind the 'second line'.[175] In the meantime, the state, but not the Party, was firmly under the leadership of Liu and his colleague Deng Xiaoping. This continued for seven years until 1966.[176] In August 1966, with Lin Biao's support, Mao made a daring comeback by launching the Cultural Revolution. This decade-long movement of destruction and Mao personality cult decimated state bureaucracies and eliminated Mao's perceived enemies. By manipulating the young and rebellious 'Red Guards' in 1966,[177] Mao succeeded in taking control of the whole state structure by appointing revolutionary committees under his direct control. The state bureaucrats were removed, while the NPC was mostly suspended.[178] President Liu was arrested, severely criticised, stripped of all official positions and removed by the Party in October 1968. In November, he died from pneumonia in a state of neglect and isolation while in detention in Henan Province.[179]

After Liu's downfall, Lin Biao vied unsuccessfully for the powerful Presidency, but Mao carefully left the office empty and hanging.[180] After Lin's 1971 failed *coup d'état* and death in a Gobi Desert air crash,[181] Mao and his hard-left supporters sought to revamp the state structure to consolidate power. In the 1975 Constitution, Mao emptied out the state positions and abolished the Presidency.[182] He took no role within the formal state and the Constitution was

[173] Qian Xiangli, *Lishi de bianju: cong wanjiu weiji dao fan xiu fang xiu* [The changing dynamics of history: from rescuing crisis to anti-revisionism and preventing revisionism], *1962–1965* (The Chinese University of Hong Kong Research Centre for Contemporary Chinese Culture, 2008) 331–75.

[174] The rapid success of the new Chinese nation was achieved because of Soviet support for the Chinese Government; Mao admitted that he was confused as to how to construct China economically, and there was no other way but to follow the Soviet methods in their entirety; Shen Zhihua (n 165) 113. See also Nicholas R Hardy, 'Economic Recovery and the 1st Five-Year Plan' in Fairbank and MacFarquhar (eds) (n 22) 178; William C Kirby, 'China's Internationalization in the Early People's Republic: Dream of a Socialists World Economy' in *The History of the PRC (1949–1976): The China Quarterly Special Issues New Series No 7*, ed Julia Strauss (Cambridge University Press, 2007), 30–32; and Lowell Dittmer, *Sino-Soviet Normalization and its International Implications, 1945–1990* (University of Washington Press, 1992) 17–25.

[175] Dietrich (n 21) 162–63.

[176] Ezra F Vogel, *Deng Xiaoping and the Transformation of China* (Belknap Press, 2011) 42–43.

[177] Dietrich (n 21) ch 6.

[178] Christiansen and Rai (n 28) 98.

[179] Dietrich (n 21) 206.

[180] Christiansen and Rai (n 28) 98–99.

[181] Dietrich (n 21) 213–17.

[182] 'Meeting and Leaders, Table 35: State Leaders, 1965–1983,' appendix to John K Fairbank and Roderick MacFarquhar (eds), *The Cambridge History of China*, vol 15: *The People's Republic*

degraded, to the point that it read like a mere litany of ideological dogmas. Mao controlled the state and the economy through the Party. The head of state reverted to the NPCSC (Chairman), similar to the set-up in the Soviet Union.[183] After Mao's death in 1976, however, the 1978 Constitution gradually restored the NPC structure and its formal functions.[184]

When Deng Xiaoping returned to power, he oversaw the establishment of a new CPPCC and the drafting of the 1982 Constitution. This effectively 'rebooted' the 1954 Constitution in an updated version.[185] Deng clearly recognised the problem caused by the 1954 Presidency, because he participated in the drafting of the 1954 Constitution.[186] He also recognised the inefficient and dangerous over-concentration of economic power in the state owing to socialist transformation. While maintaining China as a socialist state, Article 4 was abolished.[187] The 1982 Constitution restored the Presidency, which was transformed into the position of a head of state with ceremonial and nominal powers.[188] Deng and his constitution drafters clearly recognised the insufficiency of the original Soviet model for China and created a new Central Military Commission within the NPC. This gave the military permanent representation in the all-important state structure.[189] The first representative of the military in this office in 1983 was Deng himself.[190] Deng occupied no other constitutional role in the state structure until he stepped down in April 1990.[191]

The 1982 Constitution of the People's Republic of China streamlined the 1954 Constitution. It is designed to constrain and rebalance the aggressive forces and personal ambitions in a way similar to that of the original Soviet model. It also seeks to correct the mistakes made in the drafting of the 1954 Constitution.[192] In Deng's revised formulation, real central power does not lie with the President but is distributed and harmonised among three pillars of the state and Party: the General Secretary of the CCP (Party); the Premier of the State Council (Government); and the Chairman of the Central Military Commission (Military). In this way, the explosive warring forces released by

Part 2: Revolutions within the Chinese Revolution, 1966–1982 (Cambridge University Press, 1991) 887–88; Roderick MacFarquhar, 'The Succession to Mao and the End of Maoism,' in Roderick MacFarquhar (ed), *The Politics of China: Sixty Years of the People's Republic of China*, 3rd edn (Cambridge University Press, 2011) 246, 254–55.

[183] Gasper (n 86) 174; Liu (n 2) 41.

[184] Christiansen and Rai (n 28) 100.

[185] ibid,100–07.

[186] Xu (n 115) 110.

[187] ibid 104.

[188] ibid 102.

[189] Sec IV: The Central Military Commission, 1982 Constitution.

[190] MacFarquhar, 'The Succession to Mao' (n 182) 331.

[191] Joseph Fewsmith, *Elite Politics in Contemporary China* (Routledge, 2015) 56.

[192] The CPPCC was reinstated in a lesser form in 1978, and the ultra-leftist revolutionary 1975 and 1978 Constitutions were discarded and replaced by the 1982 Constitution; see Christiansen and Rai (n 28) 99–101.

imperial collapse could finally be tamed and contained, and order was restored to the lands belonging to the former Chinese Empire.

IX. EPILOGUE: CONSTITUTIONAL FOUNDING

By the turn of the twenty-first century, it was clear that in the big, complex and post-imperial Chinese Empire that is now the PRC, the primary role of its first Constitution was to lay down a foundational framework for continental peace, territorial integrity and political stability, rather than to limit the state's power and protect individual rights. There were many very large-scale destructive wars in China before 1954, and failure after failure to establish a liberal democratic constitutional order between 1911 and 1949. By 1954, Mao's Government succeeded in stopping all wars on Chinese soil. For what it is worth, he and his fellow Communists, many of whom he drove to their death in the Cultural Revolution, reunited China after over a century of invasions, dismemberments and armed upheavals since the Opium Wars that ceded Hong Kong to the British Empire. The creation of this new post-imperial Chinese political order incorporated modern but non-Western Russian constitutional ideas and institutions as the prime component of this founding. As history has shown, this order was not a liberal constitutional democracy.

3

The Making of the Constitutional Order of the Hong Kong SAR: The Role of Sino-British Diplomacy (1982–90)

ALBERT HY CHEN AND MICHAEL NG*

INTRODUCTION

The Hong Kong Special Administrative Region (HKSAR) of the People's Republic of China (PRC) was established in 1997 with the termination of British colonial rule in Hong Kong. The year 2020 marked the 30th anniversary of the enactment of the Basic Law of the HKSAR in 1990. The Basic Law is the constitutional instrument of post-colonial Hong Kong. It not only provides the legal foundation of the HKSAR and defines its relationship with the Chinese central Government; once enacted in 1990, it also paved the way for post-1997 developments in Hong Kong in political, legal, social, economic and other domains. Most of the major incidents and controversies in the history of the HKSAR so far can be traced back to concepts, principles or provisions in the Basic Law. In recent years, faced with increasing tensions and stress generated by the model of 'One Country, Two Systems' (OCTS) as prescribed in the Basic Law, the Chinese authorities have reiterated the authority and importance of the Basic Law together with the Chinese Constitution on which the Basic Law was based, urging the HKSAR Government to promote Basic Law education, and urging the people of Hong Kong to acquire a 'correct' understanding of the Basic Law and of OCTS.[1]

* The authors are most grateful to Prof Kevin Tan and Dr Humphrey Ko for their very helpful comments on an earlier draft of this chapter.

[1] See, eg, President Xi Jinping's speech in Hong Kong on 1 July 2017 at the 'Meeting celebrating the 20th anniversary of Hong Kong's return to the motherland and the inaugural ceremony of the fifth-term government of the HKSAR' at www.locpg.hk/2017-07/01/c_129645318.htm (visited 20 April 2019).

However, the Basic Law does not stand alone. It originated from the Sino-British Joint Declaration (JD) of 1984, which expressly stipulated that the policies set out in the JD regarding post-1997 Hong Kong would be provided for in a 'Basic Law'. The text of the JD itself was a joint product of the two Governments and was only concluded after two years of strenuous negotiations. Approximately half of the provisions of the Basic Law were largely reproduced from the JD.[2] It is therefore impossible to understand the Basic Law fully without taking into account its historical context and the background of the JD, which provided for China's resumption of Hong Kong in 1997.

The British colony of Hong Kong was created by three treaties between the Qing Empire in China and the British Empire in the nineteenth century.[3] By the Treaty of Nanjing 1842, signed by China after its defeat in the Opium War, the island of Hong Kong was ceded to the British. A subsequent war leading to the Anglo-French invasion of Beijing ended with another treaty, signed in 1860, under which Kowloon Peninsula was added to the colony of Hong Kong. In 1898, the third treaty was concluded, providing for a 99-year lease to Britain of the 'New Territories' (north of Kowloon Peninsula).[4] The PRC considered these treaties as 'unequal treaties' and therefore not binding on the PRC.[5] The creation of the British colony of Hong Kong as a result of the Opium War was, from China's perspective, part and parcel of the story of humiliation and shame for the Chinese people in the face of Western imperialism in modern history.

Colonial Hong Kong was ruled by the British on the basis of a rudimentary constitution contained in the Letters Patent and Royal Instructions issued by the British monarch.[6] Power was concentrated in the hands of the Governor appointed by the London Government, who ruled with the assistance of an Executive Council and a Legislative Council appointed by him. Leading members of the local business and professional elite were co-opted into these Councils, whose members included both senior government officials and 'Unofficial' (meaning non-government) members. The government claimed to

[2] This estimate is based on the authors' article-by-article comparison of the text of the Basic Law with that of the JD.

[3] On Hong Kong's history, see GB Endacott, *A History of Hong Kong*, 2nd edn (Oxford University Press, 1964); Steve Tsang, *A Modern History of Hong Kong* (HKU Press, 2004); Frank Welsh, *A History of Hong Kong* (HarperCollins, 1993).

[4] See generally Peter Wesley-Smith, *Constitutional and Administrative Law* (Longman Asia, 1994) 23–30; Peter Wesley-Smith, *Unequal Treaty 1898–1997*, rev edn (Oxford University Press, 1998).

[5] Wang Shuwen (ed), *Introduction to the Basic Law of the Hong Kong Special Administrative Region* (Law Press, 2000) 8.

[6] See Norman Miners, *The Government and Politics of Hong Kong*, 4th edn (Oxford University Press, 1986); Kenneth Roberts-Wray, *Commonwealth and Colonial Law* (Stevens & Sons, 1966); Albert HY Chen, 'From Colony to Special Administrative Region: Hong Kong's Constitutional Journey' in Raymond Wacks (ed), *The Future of the Law in Hong Kong* (Oxford University Press, 1989) 76, 76–79.

practise 'government by consultation';[7] there was no democratic election[8] except to the Urban Council – a municipal council with responsibilities in the domains of public health, environmental hygiene and recreational facilities – on the basis of a limited franchise.[9] The English legal system, based on the common law, the rule of law and judicial independence, was transplanted to Hong Kong.[10] There was no bill of rights in the colonial constitution (until a constitutional amendment in 1991),[11] and laws enacted by the colonial regime placed considerable restrictions on freedoms of speech, publication, assembly and association.[12]

However, by the 1970s, colonial Hong Kong had acquired a fair reputation among Asian jurisdictions in terms of the rule of law and efficiency of government.[13] Controls on civil liberties in Hong Kong as of the 1970s seemed to be more relaxed than those practised by the other three of the 'Four Little Dragons' of East Asia – Singapore, Taiwan and South Korea.[14] By the 1970s, the security of colonial rule in Hong Kong and popular support for its continuation[15] were such that the colonial government could afford to rule without overt repression of civil liberties.

Hong Kong is on the southern coast of mainland China, in which the PRC was established by the Chinese Communists in 1949. Many Hong Kong residents were migrants from the mainland, fleeing to the British colony as civil war raged in China in the late 1940s. The 'Cultural Revolution' in China had a spill-over effect in Hong Kong in the form of the riots against colonial rule in 1967, but the

[7] See Albert HY Chen, 'Development of Representative Government' in Johannes Chan and CL Lim (eds), *Law of the Hong Kong Constitution*, 2nd edn (Sweet & Maxwell, 2015) 245, 252.

[8] For an overview of the colonial political system in Hong Kong, see Miners (n 6), and Steve Tsang (ed), *Government and Politics: A Documentary History of Hong Kong* (HKU Press, 1995). Although members of the Legislative Council were all appointed by the Governor, there existed a constitutional convention in the period 1884–1973 that two LegCo members were elected respectively by the Hong Kong Chamber of Commerce and the unofficial Justices of the Peace in Hong Kong and then appointed by the Governor: see Chen (n 7) 248.

[9] See Fan Zhenru, *Xianggang tebie xingzhengqu de xuanju zhidu* [The Electoral System of the Hong Kong Special Administrative Region] (Joint Publishing, 2006) 39–43.

[10] See Peter Wesley-Smith, *An Introduction to the Hong Kong Legal System* (Oxford University Press, 1987) ch 11.

[11] See Albert HY Chen, 'Constitutional Adjudication in Post-1997 Hong Kong' (2006) 15 *Pacific Rim Law & Policy Journal* 627, 653–55.

[12] See Raymond Wacks (ed), *Civil Liberties in Hong Kong* (Hong Kong, Oxford University Press, 1988); Nihal Jayawickrama, 'Public Law' in Raymond Wacks (ed), *The Law in Hong Kong 1969–1989* (Oxford University Press, 1989) ch 2; Michael Ng, 'When Silence Speaks: Press Censorship and Rule of Law in British Hong Kong (1850s–1940s)' (2017) 29(3) *Law and Literature* 425.

[13] For an overview of the history and the status of rule of law in East and South-East Asian countries, see *The Rule of Law: Perspectives from the Pacific Rim* (Center for Pacific Affairs, 2000); Randall Peerenboom (ed), *Asian Discourses of Rule of Law* (Routledge Curzon, 2004).

[14] For an overview of the history and the present status of human rights in East and South-East Asian countries, see Kenneth Christie and Denny Roy, *The Politics of Human Rights in East Asia* (Pluto Press, 2001); Randall Peerenboom, Carole J Petersen and Albert HY Chen (eds), *Human Rights in Asia* (Routledge, 2006).

[15] See Miners (n 6) ch 3; Lau Siu-kai, *Society and Politics in Hong Kong* (Chinese University Press, 1982); Ambrose YC King and Rance PL Lee (eds), *Social Life and Development in Hong Kong* Chinese University Press, 1981).

overwhelming majority of the population of Hong Kong stood on the side of the colonial government at the time.[16] Since then, and particularly since the introduction in the 1970s of new social policies[17] by Governor MacLehose,[18] it was apparent that the people of Hong Kong supported the continuation of colonial rule, for they realised that the only alternative to colonial rule was integration into Communist China. Thus there was never an independence movement in colonial Hong Kong, despite the growth of a local identity (as 'Hongkongers') among members of the new generation born in Hong Kong after the War,[19] who, unlike their parents who were refugees from mainland China, considered Hong Kong their home and never experienced living elsewhere in China.

Hong Kong's economic development had been spectacular, particularly after the Second World War and the establishment of the PRC, which resulted in capital flight from Shanghai and other Chinese cities to Hong Kong and massive migration from mainland China to the British colony. By the 1970s, Hong Kong had risen to become one of the 'Four Little Dragons' of East Asia. By 1982 – the year when Britain and China started to negotiate on Hong Kong's future, Hong Kong, with its population of 5 million (relative to the population of one billion in mainland China at that time), had a GDP that was 15 per cent that of mainland China's GDP.[20]

As 1997 drew near, the British Government became increasingly concerned about Hong Kong's future. Sino-British negotiations on this subject began in 1982. The Chinese Government considered the issue of Hong Kong's future as a subject to be discussed exclusively between the Chinese and British Governments, and emphatically rejected the idea of the 'three-legged stool'.[21] Advocates of this idea originally suggested that the participants in determining Hong Hong's future should include not only the British and Chinese Governments, but also the people of Hong Kong or their representatives. However, from the point of view of the Chinese Government, the interests of the people of Hong Kong were

[16] Tsang (n 3) 183–90; David Bonavia, *Hong Kong 1997* (South China Morning Post, 1983) ch 3; Richard Hughes, *Hong Kong: Borrowed Place – Borrowed Time* (Andre Deutsch, 1968).

[17] Tsang (n 3) 192; Joe England and John Rear, *Industrial Relations and Law in Hong Kong* (Oxford University Press, 1981) 21–23, 203–05; Nelson WS Chow, 'A Review of Social Policies in Hong Kong' in Alex YH Kwan and David KK Chan (eds), *Hong Kong Society: A Reader* (Writers' & Publishers' Cooperative, 1986) ch 6.

[18] Governor MacLehose also established the Independent Commission Against Corruption (ICAC) to combat the then prevalent corruption: see HJ Lethbridge, *Hard Graft in Hong Kong: Scandal, Corruption and the ICAC* (Oxford University Press, 1985).

[19] See Tsang (n 3) 190–96; David Faure, 'Reflections on Being Chinese in Hong Kong' in Judith M Brown and Rosemary Foot (eds), *Hong Kong's Transitions, 1842–1997* (Macmillan Press, 1997) ch 5.

[20] In 1997 – the year of the handover of Hong Kong to the PRC, Hong Kong's GDP was 18% that of mainland China. However, due to continued rapid economic growth in mainland China since then, by 2020, Hong Kong's GDP was only 3% that of the mainland (and the population figures of the mainland and of Hong Kong are estimated at 1,400 million and 7.5 million respectively).

[21] Li Hou, *Huigui de lichen* [The Journey of Reunification] (Sanlian shudian, 1997) 120; Zhou Nan, *Zhou Nan jiemi Gang Ao huigui* [Zhou Nan on the Secrets of the Reunification of Hong Kong and Macau] (Zhonghua chubanshe, 2012) 130; Percy Cradock, *Experiences of China* (John Murray, 1994) 187, 211.

to be represented by and taken care of solely by the Chinese Government. At the same time, the British Government also purported to speak for the interests of the people of Hong Kong.

After the JD was concluded in 1984, China began to engage in the task of drafting the Basic Law – the 'mini-constitution' of post-colonial Hong Kong under OCTS. In this process, it never recognised publicly that the British Government or the colonial Hong Kong government had any role to play in the drafting of the Basic Law. The Chinese Government considered the making of the Basic Law a purely domestic affair of the PRC. The official policy was to welcome the participation and input of the people of Hong Kong in the drafting of the Basic Law. Thus there were both mainland Chinese and Hong Kong members in the Basic Law Drafting Committee (BLDC), and the larger 180-member Basic Law Consultative Committee (BLCC) consisted entirely of Hong Kong people from different walks of life.[22] Extensive consultation was carried out during the process of Basic Law drafting, which took four years and eight months, culminating in the enactment of the Basic Law by the National People's Congress (NPC) in April 1990 – seven years before the law was to come into effect in Hong Kong.[23]

Although officially Britain had no role to play in the drafting of the Basic Law, both British and Chinese sources published subsequently reveal that London did provide significant inputs during the drafting process via engaging in behind-the-scene diplomacy with Beijing, including detailed article-by-article comments on the draft Basic Law.[24] Such British input was actually welcomed by the Chinese authorities and was taken into account to varying extents. Before the events of 4 June 1989, the British Government was apparently largely satisfied with the text of the draft Basic Law.[25] The Tiananmen incident and the ensuing crisis of confidence in Hong Kong nevertheless led the British Government to press for further amendments.

Drawing partly on archival materials recently made available in Britain and memoirs by persons who participated in the negotiation of the JD and the drafting of the Basic Law, and also relying partly on accounts by journalists, historians and other scholars, this chapter attempts to investigate the one key aspect of the making of the constitutional order of the HKSAR, namely, the role played by Sino-British diplomacy in determining the content of the policies on post-1997 Hong Kong set out in the JD, as well as the British role in shaping or influencing the content of the Basic Law. It argues that the blueprint for the constitutional order of post-1997 Hong Kong is a joint product of the Chinese

[22] Emily Lau, 'The early history of the drafting process' in Peter Wesley-Smith and Albert Chen (eds), *The Basic Law and Hong Kong's Future* (Butterworths, 1988) 90.

[23] See Wang (n 5); *Wen Wei Po* (ed), *Jibenfa de dansheng* [The Birth of the Basic Law] (Xianggang wenhui chubanshe, 1990); Ming K Chan and David J Clark (eds), *The Hong Kong Basic Law* (HKU Press, 1991).

[24] See section IV of this chapter.

[25] See section IV of this chapter.

and British Governments that was shaped not only by publicised negotiation, but also by continuous behind-the-scene Sino-British diplomacy. Actually, the input of colonial Hong Kong's political elite, civil society and public opinion also played a significant role in the drafting of the Basic Law, although this will not be the focus of this chapter. The extent to which the British Government contributed to the shaping of the post-1997 constitutional order of Hong Kong will be the focus of our inquiry.

The use in this chapter of archival materials can enable us to have a fuller picture than ever before of the joint creation of the constitutional order of the HKSAR by the Chinese and British Governments. The case of Hong Kong's transition in 1997 is different from the general pattern of decolonisation in other British colonies.[26] Unlike these colonies, which eventually became independent states with new constitutions drafted primarily either by the British or by local political elites, the British colony of Hong Kong became incorporated into a Communist Party-state as an autonomous city[27] governed by a Basic Law that is to some extent a legacy of British colonial rule in Hong Kong. This chapter seeks to elucidate this particular feature of Hong Kong's present constitution, which is unique from the perspective of comparative constitutional law.[28]

The story of Sino-British interactions in the creation of the constitutional order of the HKSAR can be told as a play in five acts. Apart from this introduction, this chapter consists of five sections, followed by some concluding reflections. The five sections correspond to five periods, the first of which began with the commencement of Sino-British negotiations on Hong Kong's future in 1982, and the last period ending with the enactment of the Basic Law in 1990.

I. THE NEGOTIATION OF THE JOINT DECLARATION (1982–84)

Sino-British negotiations on Hong Kong's future began after Margaret Thatcher's visit to Beijing in September 1982. Shortly before the visit, the Chinese party-state led by paramount leader Deng Xiaoping had already made a firm decision to recover Hong Kong in 1997, and to apply a '12-point policy' to post-1997 Hong Kong,[29] which subsequently found its way into the text of the JD. The policy basically involved a series of measures aimed at preserving Hong Kong's stability and prosperity after the Chinese recovery of Hong Kong. Hong Kong would become a Special Administrative Region (SAR) of the PRC, enjoying a high degree of autonomy, with 'Hong Kong people ruling Hong Kong'.

[26] Norman Miners, 'The normal pattern of decolonisation of British dependent territories' in Wesley-Smith and Chen (eds) (n 22) 44; Roberts-Wray (n 6) 247–301.

[27] For the unique characteristics of Hong Kong's decolonisation, see Lau Siu-kai, *The Practice of 'One Country, Two Systems' Policy in Hong Kong* (Commercial Press, 2017).

[28] For the unique features of Hong Kong's post-1997 constitution, see Yash Ghai, *Hong Kong's New Constitutional Order*, 2nd edn (HKU Press, 1999).

[29] Wong Man Fong, *China's Resumption of Sovereignty over Hong Kong* (Hong Kong Baptist University, 1997); Li (n 21) 70–76, 104–08; Zhou (n 21) 111–17; Cradock (n 21) 179.

Hong Kong's existing economic, social and legal systems would remain basically unchanged. Thus the Hong Kong SAR would continue to practise capitalism, despite the practice of socialism in the Chinese mainland. Hence the expression 'One Country, Two Systems'.

The making of this decision on Hong Kong's future was prompted by the 'British initiative' to raise with China the question of Hong Kong's future.[30] This question was first raised in 1979 when Hong Kong Governor Murray MacLehose visited Beijing, as the 'lease' that Britain acquired in 1898 over the New Territories was due to expire in 1997.[31] In the two years following the visit, the British 'took every opportunity they could find to probe the Chinese attitude further'.[32] It was in these circumstances that Deng decided in 1981 that a policy on Hong Kong's future had to be developed.[33]

At that time, the Chinese authorities were developing a new policy of peaceful reunification with Taiwan on the basis of a 'nine-point policy' announced in September 1981 by Ye Jianying, then Chairman of the National People's Congress Standing Committee.[34] The nine-point statement was largely drafted by Liao Chengzhi, Director of the Hong Kong and Macau Affairs Office (HKMAO) of the PRC's State Council. Liao was now given the task of developing a policy for Hong Kong's future as well.[35]

The proposed policy was discussed at meetings at the Party Secretariat, first in April 1981 and then in December 1981. In December 1981, Deng instructed that a concrete plan for the recovery of Hong Kong and its post-1997 governance should be developed in three months' time.[36] In January 1982, a five-man group led by Liao was established to work on the matter. They submitted a report on a 12-point policy in March 1982.[37] Between March and June 1982, meetings were arranged between Deng and 12 delegations of visitors from Hong Kong, in which they were consulted as regards China's plan for Hong Kong's future.[38] The Hong Kong policy was finalised by Deng at an internal meeting on 16 September 1982[39] – this was one week before Thatcher's visit to Beijing on 22 September 1982. According to the memoirs of Li Hou, Vice-Director of the HKMAO, the 12-point policy was further revised and submitted to the PRC's central authorities in March 1983; it was approved by the Politburo, the PRC's highest decision-making body, in April 1983.[40] After Liao's death in August 1983,

[30] Steve Tsang, *Hong Kong: An Appointment with China* (IB Tauris, 1997) 92.

[31] John Carroll, *A Concise History of Hong Kong* (HKU Press, 2007) 177.

[32] Tsang (n 30) 90.

[33] Wong (n 29) 5–6, 17; Wu Jiping, *Zhong Ying huitan fengyun lu* (*The Story of the Sino-British Negotiations*) (Xingdao ribao, 1997) 159.

[34] Li (n 21) 74.

[35] ibid, 74; Wong (n 29) 12–16, 38.

[36] Li (n 21) 75; Wong (n 29) 17.

[37] Li (n 21) 76; Wong (n 29) 19–20, 37.

[38] Li (n 21) 76–77; Wong (n 29) 71.

[39] Li (n 21) 88–89; Zhou (n 21) 117.

[40] Li (n 21) 105.

the policy was further refined and details were worked out under the leadership of Ji Pengfei, the new director of the HKMAO.[41]

During Thatcher's visit to Beijing in September 1982, Deng told her that he would allow one to two years for the negotiation, and would then make a unilateral announcement on Hong Kong's future even if the negotiation was unsuccessful.[42] Lu Ping, member of the Chinese negotiating team who subsequently became Director of the HKMAO, recounted that the negotiation had been a difficult process, and almost broke down at some points.[43] Both Chinese and British participants at the negotiation have written about it and divided it into three phases.[44] In the first phase, Britain insisted on the continued validity of the three nineteenth-century treaties. In a letter dated 10 March 1983, Thatcher retreated from this position and the second phase of the negotiation began, with negotiating teams formally established by both sides. In this phase, Britain offered to transfer sovereignty over Hong Kong to China in exchange for China's agreement to continued British administration of Hong Kong after 1997. This was firmly rejected by China.

When former British Prime Minister Edward Heath visited Beijing and met Deng on 10 September 1983, Deng expressly ruled out the possibility of exchange of sovereignty for administration. He made it clear that even if the negotiation did not produce any outcome, China would unilaterally announce its plan for Hong Kong's future in September 1984.[45] On 14 October 1983, Percy Cradock, chief negotiator on the British side, brought Thatcher's message to the Chinese authorities that Britain was prepared to consider China's plan for Hong Kong's future as an alternative to the British proposal for continued British administration of Hong Kong after 1997. Thus began the third phase of the negotiation, which proved to be constructive and ultimately resulted in the agreement that took the form of the JD initialled and published on 26 September 1984.

The JD consists of a main text and three annexes that, according to paragraph 8 of the main text, are equally binding as the main text. China's '12-point policy' regarding post-1997 Hong Kong was set out in paragraph 3 of the main text. Annex I, entitled 'Elaboration by the Government of the PRC of its basic policies regarding Hong Kong', is particularly detailed and consists of 14 sections, with each section consisting of several paragraphs. Annex II relates to the 'Sino-British Joint Liaison Group' (JLG) set up to facilitate consultation relating to a smooth transfer in 1997; Annex III relates to the handling of land leases in Hong Kong. Annex I contains significant amounts of detail on the

[41] ibid 106–08.

[42] ibid 92; Geoffrey Howe, *Conflict of Loyalty* (Macmillan, 1994) 365; Margaret Thatcher, *The Downing Street Years* (HarperCollinsPublishers, 1993) 261.

[43] Lu Ping, *Luping koushu Xianggang huigui* [Lu Ping Tells About Hong Kong's Reunification] (Sanlian shudian, 2009) 50.

[44] For information on these three phases as discussed below, see Cradock (n 21) 183; Li (n 21) 87–137; Zhou (n 21) 121–71. See also Tsang (n 30) 94–107. For the letter dated 10 Mar 1983 and the message of 14 Oct 1983 mentioned below, see Li (n 21) 48, 111.

[45] Li (n 21) 103; Wong (n 29) 77–78.

governance of the HKSAR; paragraph 12 of the '12-point policy' states that the policy and its elaboration in Annex I would be stipulated in the Basic Law.

Annex I was drafted mainly by a joint working group set up in June 1984 under the Sino-British negotiation teams. The working group was headed by David Wilson on the British side and Ke Zaishuo on the Chinese side.[46] The provisions of Annex I were drafted after taking into account many working papers produced by the British side on colonial Hong Kong.[47] As already mentioned, the Chinese 12-point policy had been set even before the commencement of the negotiation. The British input into the content of the JD mainly took the form of the joint drafting together with the Chinese side of the detailed provisions of the Annexes to the JD.

The subsequently published writings of both British and Chinese participants in the negotiation reveal that the British input to the drafting of Annex I was actually substantial. Writing about the third phase of the negotiation, Cradock commented that once the British came to accept China's '12-point policy' on Hong Kong's future,

> a surprise awaited us. We had been pushing at the door of a locked room, containing, as we thought, treasures of Chinese painting. Now the door was open and the room was found to be virtually empty. There were some broad prescriptions, little else. This offered us an invaluable opportunity to fill in the void with our essentials for post-1997 Hong Kong.[48]

As regards the eventual product that took the form of Annex I to the JD, Cradock wrote 'The meat of the agreement lay in Annex 1, which was the elaboration, nominally by both sides, but in fact by the British, of the broad Chinese plans for Hong Kong set out in the main agreement.'[49]

Wu Jiping, a young assistant to the Chinese negotiating team at the time, also acknowledged in his memoirs the substantial British input to the drafting of the detailed provisions of the JD.[50] Writing about the third phase of the negotiation, he commented that once the questions of sovereignty and administration of post-1997 Hong Kong had been resolved, the Chinese leadership considered that the negotiation had been largely concluded. As regards 'the remaining technical issues', the Chinese side had only a few liberal policies as regards Hong Kong but it did not have detailed plans. On these issues,

> so long as it was not inconsistent with such policies, the Chinese side basically adopted the British suggestions regarding concrete arrangements for the executive, judicial, legislative, financial and other aspects of post-1997 Hong Kong so as to preserve Hong Kong's existing system as far as possible.[51]

[46] Cradock (n 21) 199; Wong (n 29) 89–90; Wu (n 33) 233–36.
[47] Wu (n 33) 180, 238; Thatcher (n 42) 490.
[48] Cradock (n 21) 192–93.
[49] ibid 208.
[50] Wu (n 33).
[51] ibid 179.

Thus the working documents provided by the British side were heavily relied on.[52] 'The British input on concrete details was substantial. In particular, on topics such as financial system and taxation, the legal system, and multilateral trade agreements, British proposals were basically adopted.'[53]

Cradock considered the JD 'a considerable achievement',[54] given that '[i]t was a highly unequal negotiation' in which '[t]he Chinese held virtually all the cards',[55] and given 'how remote were [the] starting points' of the two sides.[56] Even in the third phase of the negotiation, China would have preferred parallel declarations by the two Governments that were relatively brief, leaving the details of the governance of post-1997 Hong Kong to be settled by the Basic Law to be drafted by the Chinese side. On the other hand, Britain wanted to have a very detailed agreement that was binding on both states in international law.[57] In the end this British objective was achieved.

Thus a process of give-and-take did occur during the negotiation, with some concessions made by the Chinese side. In particular, the provision in Annex I to the JD on the election of the legislature and the accountability of the executive to the legislature was, in Cradock's words, 'one of the last concessions wrung out of the Chinese side'.[58] Geoffrey Howe, Foreign Secretary at the time, recalled that this provision was the result of an exchange of correspondence between him and Chinese Foreign Minister Wu Xueqian in mid-September 1984.[59] Chung Sze-yuen, Senior Unofficial Member of Hong Kong's Executive Council that was privy to the negotiation, disclosed in his memoirs that the Chinese side originally preferred a provision that the legislature would be 'elected or appointed'. When it ultimately agreed to the provision proposed by the British side, it consciously avoided any reference to 'direct election' or 'direct geographical election', and the word 'elections' in the agreed provision was in the plural, implying that multiple modes of election could be used.[60]

II. REPRESENTATIVE GOVERNMENT AND SINO-BRITISH 'CONVERGENCE' (1984–86)

The 1980s was a decade of constitutional change in colonial Hong Kong. Soon after his visit to Beijing in 1979, as mentioned in section I, Governor MacLehose

[52] ibid,239.
[53] ibid 252.
[54] Cradock (n 21) 209.
[55] ibid 211.
[56] ibid 210.
[57] ibid, 197–98, 212; Howe (n 42) 369; David Wilson, 'Learning to Live with China' in Sally Blyth and Ian Wotherspoon (eds), *Hong Kong Remembers* (Oxford University Press, 1996) 175, 179.
[58] Cradock (n 21) 226.
[59] Howe (n 42) 379. The finalised draft of the JD was agreed upon between the Chinese and British sides on 18 September 1984: see Wang (n 5) 13.
[60] Chung Sze-yuen, *Hong Kong's Journey to Reunification* (Chinese University Press, 2001) 111–12; Chung Sze-yuen (Zhong Shiyuan), *Xianggang huigui lichen* [Hong Kong's Journey to Reunification] (Chinese University Press, 2001) 82.

introduced a new system of District Boards, which was advisory in nature but included members elected by universal suffrage in geographical constituencies. The scheme was proposed in a Green Paper on 'A Pattern of District Administration in Hong Kong' published in June 1980, which was followed by a White Paper on the subject in January 1981.[61] The practice of the colonial government was that a Green Paper would be used for public consultation on a proposed policy, and the White Paper that followed would announce the policy decided by the government after such consultation.

During the negotiation on Hong Kong's future, Thatcher at one point in time discussed with her colleagues the possibility of rapid democratisation of Hong Kong. This was January 1983, when the negotiation was deadlocked. Thatcher's memoirs revealed that on 28 January 1983, she 'held a meeting with ministers, officials and the Governor of Hong Kong to review the position', and 'proposed that in the absence of progress in the talks [the British side] should now develop the democratic structure in Hong Kong as though it were [the British] aim to achieve independence or self-government within a short period, as [Britain] had done with Singapore'. She also suggested the British Government might 'consider using referenda as an accepted institution [in Hong Kong]'. However, 'nobody else seemed much attracted by [her] ideas' and they were quickly dropped.[62]

Action was ultimately taken by Britain in the midst of the negotiation to steer Hong Kong in the direction of electoral democracy. On 18 July 1984, the colonial government published a Green Paper on *The Further Development of Representative Government in Hong Kong*,[63] proposing a series of far-reaching constitutional reforms. The objective was 'to develop progressively a system of government the authority for which is firmly rooted in Hong Kong, which is able to represent authoritatively the views of the people of Hong Kong, and which is more directly accountable to the people of Hong Kong'.[64] The consultation exercise stimulated much public interest and discussion on the future of Hong Kong's political system. After consultation, the colonial government published in November 1984 the White Paper on the subject,[65] providing for the introduction of two new types of seats in the Legislative Council (LegCo) in 1985: 12 seats to be elected by electoral colleges comprising members of the District Boards, the Urban Council and the newly established Regional Council, and 12 other seats to be elected by 9 'functional constituencies', such as chambers of commerce, industrialists' federations, banks, trade unions, and professional groups such as engineers, lawyers, doctors, teachers and social workers.

[61] See Joseph YS Cheng, 'The 1985 District Board Elections in Hong Kong' in Joseph YS Cheng (ed), *Hong Kong in Transition* (Oxford University Press, 1986) ch 3.

[62] Thatcher (n 42) 488.

[63] Hong Kong Government, *Green Paper on The Further Development of Representative Government in Hong Kong* (1984).

[64] ibid para 7.

[65] Hong Kong Government, *White Paper on The Further Development of Representative Government in Hong Kong* (1984).

When the Green Paper was first published, the reaction of the Chinese Government was relatively muted. A spokesman of the Foreign Ministry said that the Paper was produced unilaterally by the British, and the Chinese Government did not assume any obligations regarding it.[66] Upon the publication of the White Paper, Xu Jiatun, Director of the Hong Kong branch of the New China News Agency (NCNA) (de facto representative of the PRC Government in colonial Hong Kong) and head of the CCP's Committee on Hong Kong and Macau Work, commented that the political structure of the future HKSAR was to be determined by Basic Law to be enacted by the NPC.[67] At this time, the exercise of the drafting of the Basic Law had not yet begun, but it had been decided that this exercise would commence soon and should be completed by 1990. There is evidence that the Chinese authorities had contemplated earlier that 1993 would be the target date for the enactment of the Basic Law, but Deng decided in mid-1984 to bring it forward to 1990.[68]

Xu wrote in his memoirs about the Chinese authorities' concern and suspicion regarding the British initiative to introduce constitutional change and democratisation in Hong Kong without any prior consultation with the Chinese Government. He contrasted the concepts of 'returning power to the people' (of Hong Kong) and 'returning power to China'.[69] He pointed out that it was not for the colonial government to return power to the people of Hong Kong. Instead the British were obliged to return power over Hong Kong to China, and it was up to the Chinese Government to decide how Hong Kong people were to rule Hong Kong.

Xu also referred to the strategy secretly promoted by some people, of '13 years of big change followed by 50 years of no change'.[70] This meant introducing fundamental changes to Hong Kong's political system in the 13 years preceding 1997, and creating a *fait accompli* by that time so that the system then existing would have to be perpetuated after 1997. This was perceived as an attempt to force the Basic Law to converge with the political system that the British authorities were establishing in Hong Kong.

[66] Mark Roberti, *The Fall of Hong Kong* (John Wiley & Sons, 1994) 103; Wu (n 32) 242.

[67] Nicholas Thomas, *Democracy Denied* (Ashgate, 1999) 163, referring to *Hong Kong Standard* (Hong Kong newspaper), 25 November 1984. See also Roberti (n 66) 120–21.

[68] Zhou (n 21) 152–53; the National Archives (TNA), Kew, London, Records of the Prime Minister's Office (PREM), PREM 19/1796, Youde to Foreign and Commonwealth Office (FCO), Telno. 2804, 11 December 1985. On 19 December 1984, just before the signing of the JD, Premier Zhao Ziyang announced that the Basic Law would be promulgated by 1990: see Gao Wanglai, *Sino-British Negotiations on Democratic Reforms in Hong Kong*, PhD dissertation (Waseda University, 2009) available at http://waseda.repo.nii.ac.jp, accessed 12 April 2020, at 127, referring to *Ming Pao* (Hong Kong Chinese newspaper), 20 December 1984. For a revised version of this dissertation published in Chinese, see *Daguo tanpan moulue: Zhong Ying Xianggang tanpan neimu* (Shishi chubanshe, 2012). See also Martin Lee, 'The fight for democracy' in Blyth and Wotherspoon (eds) (n 57) 233, 236.

[69] Xu Jiatun, *Xujiatun Xianggang huiyilu* [Xu Jiatun's Hong Kong Memoirs] (in 2 vols) (Lianhe bao, 1993), vol 1, 169, 185.

[70] ibid 170–73.

Xu suspected that the ultimate motive of the British was to win the support and allegiance of the people of Hong Kong, by bringing forward and realising in advance the democratic reform that was implied in the JD, and to cultivate pro-British political forces in the course of Hong Kong's political reform, so that British interests in Hong Kong would be well taken care of after 1997.[71] Similar sentiments were expressed by Lu Ping in his memoirs, who remarked that the purpose of the British exercise to develop 'representative government' in Hong Kong was 'to change the existing executive-led system into a legislature-led system, and to turn post-1997 Hong Kong into an "independent political entity"'.[72]

The official position of the Chinese Government to the colonial government's project of representative government was publicised in October 1985.[73] By this time the BLDC had already been established (in June 1985) and the BLCC was in the process of being formed in Hong Kong. On 19 October 1985, Ji Pengfei, HKMAO Director and Chairman of the BLDC, publicly stated that the post-1997 political system of Hong Kong was to be determined by the Basic Law; in the interests of a smooth transition and stability and prosperity in Hong Kong, any political reform during the period of transition before 1997 should 'converge' with what was going to be prescribed in the Basic Law; Hong Kong's political system should not undergo radical change in the meantime.[74] The Chinese Government arranged for the issues of 'convergence' and political reform in Hong Kong to be put on the agenda of the JLG's meeting on 26–29 November 1985.[75] On 21 November 1985, speaking at his first press conference in Hong Kong since assuming the office of the Director of the Hong Kong branch of the NCNA in 1983, Xu Jiatun warned that there existed a trend of 'not acting in accordance with the Joint Declaration'. The statement was made in the context of the Chinese concern regarding the British plan to develop 'representative government' in Hong Kong.[76]

The principle of convergence as advocated by the Chinese authorities soon came to be accepted by the British. It was agreed at the JLG meeting in November 1985 that political reform in Hong Kong before 1997 should converge with the political system of the post-1997 HKSAR.[77] The JLG meeting was followed by Ji Pengfei's visit to Hong Kong in December 1985 and the visit to

[71] ibid 168–73.
[72] Lu (n 43) 66.
[73] Thomas (n 67) 163–65; Gao (n 68) 141–48.
[74] Robert Cottrell, *The End of Hong Kong* (John Murray, 1993) 182–83; Thomas (n 67) 164–65; Li (n 21) 189–90.
[75] Li (n 21) 189–90; Gao (n 68) 146, referring to *Liaowang* magazine (in Chinese), 30 November 1985.
[76] Xu (n 69) 174.
[77] Li (n 21) 190; memorandum from Governor Edward Youde to the Foreign and Commonwealth Office (FCO) Telno 2804, 11 December 1985, TNA (n 69 above), PREM 19/1796, Youde to FCO, Telno 2804, 11 December 1985. See also Roberti (n 66) 159.

Beijing in January 1986 of Timothy Renton, Minister of State at the British Foreign Office with special responsibility for Hong Kong. After meeting with Ji, Renton publicly announced that there was agreement with the Chinese side on the need for convergence between the evolving political system in Hong Kong and the system to be prescribed in the Basic Law. He added a vivid analogy: 'We are creating a set of railway lines that lead up to 1997. The Chinese will be creating a set of railway lines that lead on from 1997. The need is to see that those two railway lines meet together at a crossing point.'[78]

The thinking of the Chinese and British Governments and their diplomatic interaction at the time was revealed by Governor Youde's memorandum to FCO reporting on his meeting with Ji in Hong Kong in December 1985.[79] At the meeting, Youde explained to Ji the Hong Kong government's commitment to the '1987 Review', which was a review promised in the 1984 White Paper of whether and how Hong Kong's political system should further develop in 1988 when the next LegCo election would be held. Youde emphasised to Ji the need to retain the confidence of the professional middle classes who 'had begun to demand a greater degree of participation in their government', hence Hong Kong's need to begin 'a process of evolving a more representative system of government beginning with the District Boards and working up to the latest step in which a proportion of the members of LegCo were indirectly elected'.[80]

Ji agreed, per Youde's meeting record, with 'the need to retain in Hong Kong the professional classes', and confirmed that the Chinese 'were not opposed to the 1987 review'. However, he 'wondered what form the review would take and thought it better to slow things down a little (Ji used the expression "*tuo*" – literally to drag out)'. Although the Chinese side would not by 1987 be able to produce the Basic Law in a concrete form, it would have some 'preliminary ideas, and it would by then be easier for the two sides' ideas to converge'. The Chinese side had 'no objections to elections since these were provided for in the Joint Declaration', but expressed that 'time was needed to judge whether there should be direct, indirect or some other form of election'. Ji mentioned in his meeting with Youde that '[a] fully directly elected system was not necessarily right.' Ji also revealed that '[t]he Chinese side had originally thought of 1993 for the first draft of the Basic Law' and that '[t]hey were now trying to bring this forward to meet the British timetable'. Ji admitted that '[t]he Chinese had not started work on the Basic Law', while 'British ideas were more or less mature.' Hence 'the Chinese side did not know what the future system should be and therefore wondered whether there was a problem of convergence'.[81]

[78] Gao (n 68) 156–57, particularly fnn 359–61.
[79] TNA, PREM19/1796, Youde to FCO, Telno 2804, 11 December 1985.
[80] ibid.
[81] ibid.

III. INFORMAL DIPLOMATIC DIALOGUE AND THE 1987 REVIEW (1986–88)

By the time of the meeting of Governor Youde and Ji in December 1985, mentioned in section II, the newly established BLDC had met only once. This was its inaugural meeting in Beijing in July 1985.[82] The meeting decided on the timetable for the drafting of and consultation on the Basic Law. The first draft of the Basic Law would be completed and released for public consultation in early 1988. After the consultation exercise, a second draft would be prepared and submitted to the NPC Standing Committee in early 1989. There would be a second round of consultation. The final version of the Basic Law would be submitted to the NPC for enactment in early 1990.

The inaugural meeting of the BLDC also decided that research work in preparation for the drafting of the Basic Law would commence immediately. The plan was that at the second plenary session of the BLDC to be held in the first half of 1986, the topics to be covered in the Basic Law would be decided upon, and the drafting work would then begin. It was also agreed that a Basic Law Consultative Committee (BLCC) would be established in Hong Kong to collect the views of Hong Kong people and provide input to the BLDC during the drafting process. After the BLDC's inaugural meeting, preparations were made to set up the BLCC. In December 1985, the BLCC, consisting of 180 members from different walks of life in Hong Kong, held its inaugural meeting.[83]

In April 1986, the second plenary session of the BLDC was held in Beijing. The structural outline of the Basic Law, which was prepared by the BLDC secretariat led by Li Hou and Lu Ping, was adopted. The meeting decided to set up five sub-groups of the BLDC specialising in different topics to be dealt with in the Basic Law. Initial drafts of various chapters of the Basic Law were to be prepared by the relevant sub-groups for consideration by the BLDC at its future plenary sessions.[84]

The period 1986–88, which is covered by this section of the chapter, began with the Sino-British agreement on 'convergence' by the end of 1985, and ended in the first half of 1988 with the publication of the White Paper on *The Development of Representative Government: The Way Forward* in February 1988 and the publication of the first draft of the Basic Law in April 1988. This period

[82] Zhang Jiefeng, Yang Jianxing, Lu Yongxiong and Chen Luqian, *Bubian wushinian? Zhong Ying Gang jueli Jibenfa* [No Change, For Fifty Years? China, Britain and Hong Kong Struggle Over the Basic Law] (Langchao chubanshe, 1991) 40–44; Basic Law Drafting Committee (BLDC) Secretariat, *Zhonghua renmin gongheguo Xianggang tebie xingzhengqu jibenfa qicao weiyuanhui quanti huiyi wenjian huibian* [Collection of Documents of Plenary Sessions of the HKSAR Basic Law Drafting Committee of the PRC] *1985–1990*, available at University of Hong Kong Library 'Basic Law Drafting History On Line' database, http://sunzi.lib.hku.hk/bldho/bldhoSearch.action; and at Library of the Hong Kong Legislative Council electronic resources at https://library.legco.gov.hk.

[83] For the establishment of the BLCC, see Lau (n 22) and Zhang (n 82) 45–53.

[84] BLDC Secretariat (n 82).

saw the simultaneous progress and mutual interaction of two trains of events: (i) the Sino-British discussion relating to the 1987 review of the political system, and (ii) the political debate between different groups and forces in Hong Kong's political spectrum regarding issues arising from both the 1987 review and the drafting of the Basic Law, particularly the design of the political system of the HKSAR and its constitutional relationship with the central authorities in Beijing.[85] This section of the chapter will focus more on the Sino-British discussion on the 1987 review.

Governor Youde visited Beijing from 29 August to 2 September 1986. After the visit, a note was sent on 8 September by the FCO to the Prime Minister's Office reporting on the visit. It was pointed out that the 'continuing process of developing a more representative system of government in Hong Kong has periodically aroused strong Chinese suspicion that we are planning to introduce a full Westminster-style system in Hong Kong before 1997'. The Chinese side expressed during its meetings with Youde 'the firm position that' the British side 'should take no decision on direct elections before the publication of the [draft] Basic Law in 1988'. The Chinese side was concerned that political reform would 'introduce instability in Hong Kong through political infighting' and 'pre-empt the Basic Law which they are now drafting'. The FCO also reported to the Prime Minister that in order to reassure the Chinese side that the British side was mindful of the need to converge with the future Basic Law, they had 'embarked upon a process of *informal dialogue*' with the Chinese Foreign Minister and handed over detailed papers summarising 'the areas where compatibility needs to be achieved between the present system and the structure described in the Joint Declaration' as well as 'the current state of opinion in Hong Kong on the political structure issue'.[86]

The dialogue, embracing formal meetings and confidential exchanges between the British and Chinese Governments on the 1987 review, continued thereafter. According to a note of visit recording the meeting between Renton and Ji in Beijing on 13 October 1986, the Chinese side reiterated that a 'cautious attitude must be adopted' on the issue of direct election and 'hoped that any decision concerning direct election could be delayed'.[87]

In reply, Renton explained that '[t]he review would not be slanted in any particular direction'; as regards the issue of direct election, the review would discuss 'a limited matter only: a proportion of seats perhaps being filled by direct election'. He emphasised that the British side did not have 'any preconceived views about direct elections', and noted that 'opinion in Hong Kong on

[85] Zhang (n 82).

[86] TNA, PREM 19/1796, letter entitled 'Hong Kong: Call by the Governor and Members of the Executive Council' enclosing a briefing to Prime Minister (PM) for the call from RN Culshaw of FCO to Charles Powell, Private Secretary to PM, 8 September 1986 (emphasis added).

[87] TNA, PREM 19/1796, Evans from Peking to FCO, Telno 1989,14 October 1986.

the subject was divided'. He also reminded Ji that '[they] must avoid any suggestion that British responsibility for Hong Kong up to 1997 was being dislodged'.[88]

In December 1986, Governor Youde visited Beijing again but died there in his sleep.[89] In April 1987, David Wilson, who had participated actively in the negotiation on Hong Kong's future as a member of the British team, assumed his new position as Governor of Hong Kong.[90] Shortly after his arrival, the *Green Paper on the 1987 Review of Developments in Representative Government*[91] was published in May, initiating a consultation exercise that would conclude at the end of September 1987. A 'Survey Office' was established to collect public opinions on the issues raised in the Green Paper.

In September 1987, Wilson visited Beijing for the first time in his capacity as Hong Kong's Governor.[92] In the meantime, British Foreign Secretary Geoffrey Howe had the opportunity to meet Chinese Foreign Minister Wu Xueqian in New York. On 2 October 1987, Howe wrote to Prime Minister Thatcher to brief her about the 1987 review:

> [A] significant majority of public opinion supports their introduction [of direct elections] in principle; but ... those in favour are sharply divided on the timing of their introduction, with no clear majority for introduction next year rather than at a later date. A substantial body of Hong Kong opinion believes that direct elections should not be introduced until after 1990, when the Chinese Government will promulgate the Basic Law for post-1997 Hong Kong.[93]

In his letter, Howe also reported that at his recent meeting with Wu and during Wilson's recent visit to Beijing, the Chinese authorities had been briefed 'in strict confidence' about 'the likely outcome of the Review'. The British side had

> proposed that ... the White Paper in early 1988 should acknowledge public support in principle for an element of direct elections, and state, with an appropriate reference to the Basic Law, that these would be introduced in 1991 or 1992.[94]

The Chinese 'replied that if direct elections were not introduced until after the promulgation of the Basic Law', they 'would see that there was appropriate

[88] ibid.

[89] Roberti (n 66) 182.

[90] Wilson (n 57).

[91] Hong Kong Government, *Green Paper on The 1987 Review of Developments in Representative Government* (1987).

[92] Li (n 21) 194.

[93] TNA, PREM 19/2727, secret and personal letter entitled 'Hong Kong: Representative Government' from Geffrey Howe, Secretary of State for Foreign and Commonwealth Affairs to PM, 2 October 1987. After the report of the Survey Office (on the public response to the Green Paper) was released on 4 November 1987, there were criticisms that the report was biased against those who supported direct elections in 1988, and that the relevant data and figures had been 'manipulated to come up with the results which the government wanted': Ian Scott, *Political Change and the Crisis of Legitimacy in Hong Kong* (Oxford University Press, 1989) 294. See also Thomas (n 67) 179 and fn 150 thereof.

[94] TNA, PREM 19/2727, letter dated 2 October 1987 (n 93).

provision for them in the Basic Law'.[95] Thatcher agreed with Howe that 'the outcome is highly satisfactory' and 'attaches particular importance to having secured Chinese agreement to provide for direct elections in the Basic Law'.[96]

Thereafter, the FCO told the Prime Minister's Office that 'the existence of this understanding' regarding China's 'private commitment that if direct elections [were] not introduced until after the promulgation of the Basic Law, there [would] be an appropriate provision for them in the Basic Law' was a 'very sensitive' matter; hence '[n]othing [would] of course be said about [the British] understanding with the Chinese' when MPs and the press were briefed about the outcome of the Review.[97] '[T]he precise wording of the reference in the White Paper to direct elections and the Basic Law'[98] was subsequently a subject of consultation with the Chinese side via the British Ambassador in Beijing.[99]

On 6 January 1988, Howe wrote to the Prime Minister to brief her about the White Paper. Thatcher was informed that 'a private commitment' from the Chinese Government had been obtained, that is, the Chinese Government had 'agreed that the White Paper could state, with an "appropriate reference" to the Basic Law, that direct elections will be introduced in 1991 … in the form of 10 directly elected seats in geographically based single seat constituencies'. Howe reported that the outcome that was then 'emerging [was] a very satisfactory one, both from [the British] point of view and for Hong Kong', and that the British team had '*overcome Chinese resistance to the principle of direct elections*'.[100]

In February 1988, the White Paper was duly published. It dealt with the relationship between electoral reform and the Basic Law in the following passage:

> In considering the development of Hong Kong's system of representative government before 1997, account must therefore be taken of the relevant stipulations of the Sino-British Joint Declaration and the deliberations of the Basic Law Drafting Committee over how those provisions should be implemented after 1997. In this connection, the Government has taken note of the fact that all the options in the *latest draft of the Basic Law* concerning the election of the future legislature include an element of direct elections.[101]

Actually, the first draft of the Basic Law was only published for public consultation in April 1988. The reference in the White Paper to 'the latest draft of the Basic Law' referred to the tentative draft (which had been publicised) considered

[95] ibid.

[96] TNA, PREM 19/2727, Powell to AC Galsworthy, Private Secretary of FCO, 5 October 1987.

[97] TNA, PREM 19/2727, Galsworthy to Powell, 29 October 1987.

[98] ibid.

[99] TNA, PREM 19/2727, Howe to PM, 6 January 1988.

[100] ibid (emphasis added). According to Cradock's memoirs (n 21), the Chinese Government had resisted the idea of direct election to Hong Kong's legislature during the Sino-British negotiation on Hong Kong's future. He wrote (at 249), 'It is also worth noting how slowly and painfully the Chinese came to tolerate the idea of even an element of direct elections. When, in late 1983, I first raised the possibility of direct elections before 1997 the reaction was one of horrified dismissal.'

[101] Hong Kong Government, *White Paper on The Development of Representative Government: The Way Forward* (1988) para 26 (emphasis added).

by the BLDC at its 6th plenary session in December 1987.[102] The provisions in the tentative draft on the political system and election of the legislature were decided upon by the BLDC sub-group on the political system at its meeting at the end of October 1987. In the tentative draft, three different proposals for the election of the legislature were set out for inclusion into the draft Basic Law. All three options contained elements of direct election in the legislature, ranging from 25 per cent to not less than 50 per cent of the seats. The documents of the 6th plenary session stated that within the sub-group on the political system, there was relatively more support for the first option, which provided for 25 per cent of the LegCo's seats being returned by direct election. However, there were a few members who supported either the election of all seats by direct election, or the election of all seats by functional constituencies.[103]

Subsequently, immediately after the 7th plenary session of the BLDC in April 1988, the first formal draft of the Basic Law was published for consultation. It contained four options for the election of the legislature. All options included elements of direct election, with the proportion of directly elected seats ranging from 25 per cent to not less than 50 per cent.[104]

IV. TOWARDS THE SECOND DRAFT OF THE BASIC LAW (1988–89)

The publication of the first draft of the Basic Law in late April 1988 initiated a five-month consultation period ending on 30 September 1988. The discussion and debates in the Hong Kong community and among politicians, political groups, social activists, civil society organisations, and business and professional elites reached a new climax.[105] Such discussion had already begun with the consultative activities launched by the BLCC in 1986, and had further developed during the consultation on the Green Paper on the 1987 review of representative government. There was also continuing dialogue between diplomats and officials of the Chinese and British Governments on issues arising from the drafting of the Basic Law.

During the consultation period, the first draft of the Basic Law was discussed in considerable detail in both the Hong Kong Legislative Council and the British Parliament. LegCo's debate on the draft Basic Law took place on 13–14 July 1988. The British House of Lords' debate on the subject took place even earlier, on 10 June 1988, followed by the House of Commons' debate on the draft Basic Law on 15 July 1988.[106]

[102] BLDC Secretariat (n 82).
[103] ibid.
[104] *The Draft Basic Law of the Hong Kong Special Administrative Region of the People's Republic of China (for Solicitation of Opinions)*, published in Hong Kong by the BLCC, April 1988.
[105] Zhang (n 82) pts 2 and 3.
[106] For extracts from the speeches, see Chan and Clark (n 23) 92–144.

After the end of the consultation period, sub-groups of the BLDC held several meetings to propose revisions to the first draft of the Basic Law. The revisions were finalised and voted upon at the 8th plenary session of the BLDC in January 1989.[107] The second draft of the Basic Law was submitted to the NPC Standing Committee in February 1989 as part of a progress report on the BLDC's work. In accordance with the original timetable for the work of the BLDC, the Standing Committee decided to publish the second draft of the Basic Law for a second round of public consultation scheduled to end on 31 July 1989.[108]

As far as official public statements are concerned, neither the Chinese Government nor the British acknowledged any substantive British input to the drafting of the Basic Law, which after all was a domestic law of China. On the other hand, as the JD itself provided that its provisions would be translated into the Basic Law, Britain naturally had an interest in ensuring that the draft Basic Law would conform 'fully with the spirit as well as the letter of the Joint Declaration'.[109] There is now abundant evidence that the British Government 'worked hard in private discussions with [Chinese officials] behind the scenes'[110] and did contribute substantial numbers of opinions and suggestions during the drafting of the Basic Law, even though it took care not to publicise them.

As early as a few months after the Basic Law drafting exercise commenced in mid-1985, British Foreign Secretary Howe reminded his colleagues that when they responded to press enquiries regarding the British role in the drafting process, it was important to convey a coherent message that 'the drafting of the Basic Law is a matter for the Chinese government'. Howe thought 'it would be most unwise to imply that the UK government (or the Hong Kong government) might have any role (even a secondary role) in the drafting process'.[111]

The British approach to the drafting of the Basic Law was well described by David Wilson in an interview for the British diplomatic oral history programme.[112] He said that at the same time as providing inputs to the Chinese side on such drafting, the British 'were very careful that they should not be public because that would have embarrassed China very much and would have made it harder to achieve what [the British] wanted'. Although the British 'had no direct locus' in the drafting of Basic Law:

> We [the British] had though on their [the Chinese] discussion panels a lot of people from Hong Kong, some of whom were friendly towards the Hong Kong Government,

[107] BLDC Secretariat (n 82).

[108] *Wen Wei Po* (n 23) 34–35, 209–10.

[109] *Hansard* HC 13 July 1989, vol 156, cols 1165–66 (China and Hong Kong: Sir Geoffrey Howe) at http://hansard.parliament.uk/Commons/1989-07-13/debates/; Gao (n 68) 223.

[110] TNA, PREM 19/2727, letter enclosing a paper entitled 'Hong Kong' for PM's meeting with Governor on 22 February 1989 from RN Peirce, Private Secretary of FCO to Powell, 17 February 1989.

[111] TNA, FCO 40/1869, Howe to Hong Kong, Telno. 1501 entitled 'Representative Government and the Basic Law', 8 Oct 1985.

[112] Interview with Lord Wilson, 19 Sept 2003, pp. 51–52, British Diplomatic Oral History Programme, Churchill Archives Centre, GBR/0014/DOHP, referred to in Gao (n 68) 129.

some who were not, so [the British] had lines into that. But [the British] also – more importantly really – made sure that [they] had lines directly into the Chinese Government, using the rubric that these were suggestions [the British] were making informally which might be helpful to [the Chinese].[113]

Other than 'informal' suggestions made through such dialogue, the 'lines' Wilson mentioned included communications via such formal channels as the JLG.[114] Thus Chung Sze-yuen wrote in his memoirs that 'It may be said that the British and the Hong Kong governments had participated in the drafting of the Basic Law.'[115]

Cradock also wrote in his memoirs that '[i]n practice there was consultation [between China and Britain] on the Basic Law and to some degree British views were taken into account.'[116] Xu Jiatun, aforementioned representative of the Chinese Government in Hong Kong, acknowledged in his memoirs that 'the British government participated throughout the whole process of the drafting of the Basic Law, mainly through diplomatic channels such as the foreign ministries of the two governments and the Sino-British Joint Liaison Group', and it 'expressed views on each chapter, each section, each paragraph and even specific wordings'. 'The Chinese government actually welcomed such British input and respected their views.'[117]

On 17 February 1989 – two days after the second draft of the Basic Law was presented to the NPC Standing Committee,[118] the FCO sent to the Prime Minister's Office a letter enclosing an Annex II that summarised changes that had been made to the first draft, 'at least in part in response to our [British] representations and those of the Governor of Hong Kong'.[119] 'Annex II' is a table entitled 'Improvements to Key Articles endorsed by the Basic Law Drafting Committee at its Eighth Plenum (9–15 January) [1989]'. The table consists of two columns: the left-hand column is 'Criticism on consultation draft', and the right-hand column is on 'Improvements in latest draft'. The substantive content of the table is divided into 12 points. In respect of each point, the criticism of a relevant provision in the first draft of the Basic Law is set out in the left-hand column, while the right-hand column describes the improvement made to the relevant provision as evidenced in the second draft adopted by the BLDC in January 1989.

In the letter, the FCO stated that the British 'influence on the drafting process' had been 'extensive and important', and that 'the Chinese [had] made it

[113] ibid.
[114] Chung, *Hong Kong's Journey* (n 60) 161.
[115] ibid 122. Cradock (n 21) also wrote in his memoirs (at 218), 'In practice there was consultation [between China and Britain] on the Basic Law and to some degree British views were taken into account.'
[116] Cradock (n 21) 218.
[117] Xu (n 69) 154–55.
[118] *Wen Wei Po* (n 23) 209–10.
[119] TNA, PREM 19/2727, Peirce to Powell, 17 February 1989.

clear that they value[d] [the British side's] contribution and [had] accepted many of [the British side's] ideas'. The FCO's assessment of the position then was that '*all the provisions of the Joint Declaration [were] reflected in the [second] draft Basic Law*'.[120] Cradock echoed by advising the Prime Minister on 21 February 1989 that '[p]art of the Basic Law simply reproduces the provisions of the 1984 Agreement. Part of it [was] more detailed work, breaking new ground.' He acknowledged that during the drafting process of the Basic Law 'the Chinese [were] in the lead but [had] been responsive to [the British side's] persuasions'. He reckoned that by then there were 'only a limited number of points which cause[d] [British] concern and [it] should be able to deal with these in the next round of consultations before the final version [was] promulgated in 1990'.[121]

Apart from providing detailed comments on the draft Basic Law, the British Government had also negotiated with the Chinese as regards the constitutional arrangement for the transition of government in 1997, particularly what was subsequently known as the 'through train' arrangement for the last colonial legislature, whereby its members could automatically become members of the first legislature of the HKSAR. In fact, after the issues of 'convergence' and the 1987 review were resolved as discussed above, the next major issue discussed between the two Governments was the precise mechanism of the transition and the formation of the first SAR government in mid-1997. This was the main subject of discussion when Governor Wilson visited Beijing in December 1987[122] and again in November 1988.[123] The negotiation on this matter continued throughout the year 1988, resulting in a consensus being reached on the 'through train' arrangement by the end of 1988.[124] The consensus was reflected in the second draft of the Basic Law published in February 1989.[125] As will be discussed, this 'through train arrangement' was further refined just days before the final version of the Basic Law was adopted by the BLDC in February 1990.

V. POST-4 JUNE DEVELOPMENTS (1989–90)

Less than two months after the publication of the second draft of the Basic Law in late February 1989, the student movement sparked off by the mourning of the

[120] ibid (emphasis added).
[121] TNA, PREM 19/2727, confidential memo from Percy Cradock to PM, 21 February 1989.
[122] Li (n 21) 196.
[123] Roberti (n 66) 227.
[124] Li (n 21) 196–97.
[125] *The Basic Law of the Hong Kong Special Administrative Region of the People's Republic of China (Draft)* (Hong Kong, Secretariat of the Consultative Committee for the Basic Law, February 1989). There was an appendix to this draft Basic Law, entitled 'Decision of the NPC of the PRC on the Method for the Formation of the First Government and the First Legislative Council of the HKSAR (Draft drawn up for the NPC)'. Art 6 of this draft 'Decision' provides that the first-term LegCo of the HKSAR will have a term of office of only two years; it also provides for the possibility and procedure of members of the last colonial LegCo becoming members of the first-term LegCo of the HKSAR.

death of Hu Yaobang, former liberal-minded Chinese Communist Party General Secretary, began to engulf Beijing, culminating in the infamous 'June 4th incident' at Tiananmen Square. Hong Kong saw the largest demonstrations in its history, in which hundreds of thousands of people marched in support of the student movement and in protest against the crackdown. The actions taken by the Chinese authorities to quell the protests precipitated an unprecedented crisis of confidence in Hong Kong.[126]

For a while, all activities of the BLCC were suspended;[127] so was a scheduled meeting of the JLG.[128] Szeto Wah and Martin Lee – two members of the BLDC – who led the Hong Kong protests and formed the 'Hong Kong Alliance in Support of Patriotic Democratic Movements in China', were expelled from the BLDC. Two other members – including Louis Cha Leung-yung, co-convenor of the powerful BLDC sub-group on the political system – resigned from it of their own accord.[129]

Generally speaking, the demand in the Hong Kong community for more rapid democratisation grew stronger than ever before.[130] Even some leading members of the 'Business and Professional Group' (BPG or 'Group of 89 persons') of the BLCC now joined forces with the 'moderates' (some civil society groups standing in the middle of the political spectrum) and some of the 'democrats' to propose a new model of the political system known as the '4-4-2 model'. During the Basic Law drafting process, the BPG had represented the conservative wing of Hong Kong's political spectrum, as opposed to the 'democrats' led by Szeto Wah, Martin Lee and others. Compared to the BPG's previous proposals, the new '4-4-2 model' incorporated more directly elected elements (40 per cent in the first HKSAR legislature) and allowed a faster pace of democratisation. At the same time, the Unofficial Members of` the Executive and Legislative Councils jointly promoted a model with even more democratic features.[131]

In an interview conducted long after his retirement, Lu Ping, former director of the HKMAO, discussed the difficult situation faced by the Chinese authorities after 4 June.[132] Lu remarked that before 1989, 'we had fairly good cooperation with the British side, and our policy was also to co-operate with Britain'. But in 1989 there was a '180-degree turn in the British attitude from cooperation to confrontation'. He also disclosed that there was at that time a change of mind on the part of some Hong Kong members of the BLDC, 'which made us very nervous'.[133]

[126] Tsang (n 30) 245–52.

[127] Chan and Clarke (n 23) 19.

[128] Qian Qishen, *Waijiao shiji* (*Ten Records on Foreign Affairs*) (Sanlian shudian, 2004) 31; Cradock (n 21) 222.

[129] Chan and Clarke (n 23) 19; *Wen Wei Po* (n 23) 212–13.

[130] Sing Ming, *Hong Kong's Tortuous Democratization* (RoutledgeCurzon, 2004) 114–22; Alvin Y So, *Hong Kong's Embattled Democracy* (John Hopkins University Press, 1999) 155–82.

[131] *Comments on the Basic Law (Draft)* (Office of Members of the Executive and Legislative Councils, October 1989).

[132] Lu (n 43) 69–72.

[133] ibid, 69.

Several recently released documents in the British National Archives reveal the thinking of the British Government immediately after the 'June 4th incident'. On 7 June, Governor Wilson wrote to the FCO recommending the suspension of 'all formal contact between the two sides both in the JLG and the Land Commission'. He also suggested that 'HMG [Her Majesty's Government] should request the CPG [Central People's Government of the PRC] to defer, by one year, the promulgation of the Basic Law scheduled for spring 1990.' He also advised '[t]o re-establish confidence people [in Hong Kong would] want to look very closely at provisions to safeguard further the HKSAR's high degree of autonomy and the rights and freedoms of Hong Kong people.' Wilson believed that '[s]uch a raising of [the British] profile in the Basic Law drafting exercise would, I believe, be fully warranted in the new circumstances.'[134]

On the same day, Charles Powell, the Prime Minister's Private Secretary, wrote to the FCO with reference to the Prime Minister's meeting the next day with the Foreign Minister, the Home Secretary, the Chancellor of the Exchequer and the Governor of Hong Kong. He told the FCO that '[t]here [were] two principal points which [the Prime Minister] wishe[d] to discuss: the pace of democratisation and nationality', and that on the pace of democratisation the Prime Minister's 'own view [was] that [the British side] should come forward with early proposals for speeding up the introduction of direct elections'.[135]

Powell wrote on the same day to the Prime Minister as follows:

> You have been arguing notably at your last meeting with the Governor – that we should be moving more rapidly to establish representative government based on direct elections, so that such representative government would be in place by 1997 and harder for the Chinese authorities to destroy. ... You will want now to press for very early recommendations on how democratisation can be speeded up, with a larger proportion of LEGCO being directly elected in 1991, and faster progress thereafter ...[136]

A draft 'note for the press' on the Prime Minister's meeting with the Governor of Hong Kong on 8 June contained the following passage, 'The Prime Minister also agreed that the process of developing more representative government in Hong Kong should be advanced and consolidated.' In the final version of the press note, this passage was toned down to become 'The Prime Minister is very willing to look again at the process of developing representative government in Hong Kong in the light of the wishes of the Hong Kong people.'[137]

In a letter entitled 'China and Hong Kong' dated 12 June 1989 to Thatcher, Cradock offered his advice on how to tackle the situation:

> [W]e shall have to strike a fine balance between on the one hand condemnation of the barbarities and on the other the need before long to do business with the [PRC]

[134] TNA, PREM 19/2728, Governor Wilson to FCO, Telno 1887, entitled 'China Internal: Implications of Implementation of the JD', 7 June 1989.
[135] TNA, PREM 19/2728, Powell to Stephen Wall of FCO, 7 June 1989.
[136] TNA, PREM 19/2728, Powell to PM, 7 June 1989.
[137] TNA, PREM 19/2728, various versions of 'Note for the Press'. See also Cradock (n 21) 224–25.

> regime in the interests of Hong Kong and of ourselves. … We must also be clear on the rationale for our signature [of the Joint Declaration]. We did not conclude the Agreement with Deng because we thought he was a liberal. … We concluded it because he ruled China and had in consequence the power to hurt or help Hong Kong. …
>
> It is tempting to announce the acceleration of representative government. There will be further pressures in this direction when the Foreign Affairs Committee reports in July. … We must also take account of the risk that Peking reaction, particularly at the present time, would be hostile. If our announcement of what we do before 1997 was followed by an announcement in the contrary sense from Peking on what they would do afterwards we should have done much more harm than good to Hong Kong. … matters arising from the present crisis … are probably best handled by a quiet approach … A dramatic unilateral gesture on our side could only too easily backfire. … We should ask of each policy move not whether it makes us feel better or appeals to British sentiment, but, as we did throughout the negotiations, whether it will help the people of Hong Kong.[138]

What subsequently transpired between the British and Chinese Governments was revealed by Foreign Minister Qian Qichen's memoirs.[139] In a letter dated 19 June 1989 from Howe to Qian, Howe proposed to postpone the meeting of the JLG originally scheduled to take place in July. Soon afterwards, Howe wrote to Chinese Vice-Premier Wu Xueqian with reference to the crisis of confidence in Hong Kong. He suggested that the Chinese Government should reconsider whether to station troops in Hong Kong after the handover. The letter stated that Britain was reconsidering the arrangements for direct election in Hong Kong in 1991. It also suggested that China should postpone the date of the promulgation of the Basic Law.

In July 1989, John Major succeeded Howe as British Foreign Secretary, a position which Major held until late October 1989, when he in turn was succeeded by Douglas Hurd. In late July 1989, Qian met Major for the first time at an international conference in Paris. Qian recalled that Major 'tried to exert influence on our work on the drafting of the Basic Law, for example, by requesting an amendment to the draft provision on the stationing of troops' in post-1997 Hong Kong. Qian rejected his request by pointing out that 'the Basic Law was China's own business' and 'the stationing of troops was already provided for in the Joint Declaration' and 'should not be re-opened'.[140]

Major met Qian again in autumn 1989 at the United Nations assembly in New York. Major 'mentioned again that Britain planned to accelerate the political reform in Hong Kong and to increase the number of directly elected seats in the Legislative Council'. Qian replied that 'the political reform must converge

[138] TNA, PREM 19/2728, memo entitled 'China and Hong Kong' from Cradock to PM, 12 June 1989. See also Cradock (n 21) 224–25.
[139] Qian (n 128) 286–95.
[140] ibid 287.

with the Basic Law which was to be promulgated; the Chinese side advocated the development of democracy in Hong Kong, but this must be done in a gradual and orderly manner'.[141]

The issues of the stationing of troops and democratisation were by no means the only issues on which Britain expressed views to the Chinese side in 1989. According to a recently released archival document entitled 'Critique of the February 1989 Draft of the Basic Law' dated 20 October 1989 prepared by the British and Hong Kong Governments,[142] detailed comments and suggestions from the British side on the second draft of the Basic Law had been or were to be submitted to the Chinese side through various channels. The document was divided in two parts: part A concerned more substantive issues, while part B 'covers issues largely of a technical nature'. The comments and suggestions in part A relate to 22 articles in the second draft of the Basic Law, as well as its Annexes I and II, the draft resolution on the formation of the first government of the HKSAR, and the draft recommendation on the establishment of the Basic Law Committee. Part B of the document concerns proposed technical improvements to 16 articles.

Unlike the case in the consultation on the first draft of the Basic Law, British comments and suggestions on its second draft actually had little impact in shaping the final version of the Basic Law. As Li Hou, Secretary-General of the BLDC, recounted in his memoirs:

> The British side originally had a fairly positive evaluation of the [second] draft of the Basic Law, except for their reservations on article 106 (regarding the principle of a balanced budget) and article 107 (regarding a low rate of taxation) ... But [in] 1989, the British side ... put forward a large quantity of opinions on the draft provisions on the relationship between the central authorities and the HKSAR and the political system ... The points raised by the British were not new but had already been raised previously ... and rejected by the Basic Law Drafting Committee after repeated deliberations. Therefore, the Chinese side decided not to further consider these British opinions.[143]

The final episodes of the Sino-British interaction in the process of the drafting of the Basic Law took place in December 1989 to February 1990, and were well documented by the memoirs of Cradock, Qian Qichen and Li Hou. In December 1989, Cradock visited Beijing as the Prime Minister's personal representative together with Robin McLaren, Assistant Under-Secretary in the FCO. Issues discussed included Chinese concerns regarding Hong Kong's being used as 'a base of subversion' against the PRC regime and regarding the 'internationalisation' of Hong Kong issues after 4 June, and British proposals for increased

[141] ibid.

[142] TNA, FCO 40/2643. We are grateful to Mr Gary Cheung of *South China Morning Post*, who obtained the document from the archives, for his kindly making it available to us.

[143] Li (n 21) 198.

numbers of directly elected seats in LegCo in 1991 and beyond.[144] The visit was followed by Governor Wilson's visit to Beijing in January 1990.[145]

The issue of the numbers of directly elected seats in LegCo in 1991 and in the first-term legislature of the HKSAR, and other issues relating to the legislature's 'through train' in 1997, were ultimately resolved in a series of seven letters exchanged between Douglas Hurd and Qian in the period 18 January–12 February 1990.[146] The full text of the seven letters has since been publicised[147] – this happened two years later in the course of the Sino-British dispute generated by Governor Chris Patten's political reform proposal of October 1992 on electoral arrangements for the last colonial LegCo in 1995.[148] As Cradock wrote,

> [t]he exchanges [of the seven letters] were certainly secret. There would have been no possibility of achieving any advance had they been public; and the Chinese government could not afford to admit that their Basic Law had been so influenced by British persuasions.[149]

Basically it was agreed that the number of directly elected seats in LegCo in 1991 would be increased from 10 (which was the previously agreed number at the conclusion of the 1987 Review) to 18, and the number of directly elected seats in the first-term legislature of the HKSAR would be increased from 18 (as provided for in the relevant provisions adopted by the BLDC sub-group on the political system in December 1989)[150] to 20, which would also be the number of directly elected seats in the last colonial legislature to be elected in 1995. The Sino-British consensus on the relevant numbers of directly elected seats was reached only one day before the ninth and final plenary session of the BLDC opened on 13 February 1990; in the course of this meeting, the relevant provision in the latest draft of the Basic Law was revised to give effect to this consensus reached during the two-month secret diplomatic negotiation.[151]

VI. CONCLUSION

The blueprint for the constitutional order of the HKSAR was jointly created in a long process of interaction between the Chinese and British Governments in

[144] Cradock (n 21) 229–32; Qian (n 128) 288–91; Li (n 21) 198–99.
[145] Cradock (n 21) 232; Li (n 21) 198.
[146] Qian (n 128) 291–95; Li (n 21) 198–203; Douglas Hurd, *Memoirs* (Little, Brown, 2003) 483–86.
[147] The full text has been re-printed in Ralf Horlemann, *Hong Kong's Transition to Chinese Rule* (RoutledgeCurzon, 2003) 262–74.
[148] Chris Patten, Chris, *East and West* (Macmillan, 1998) 63–66; David Akers-Jones, *Feeling the Stones* (HKU Press, 2004) 210; Hurd (n 146) 484–86.
[149] Cradock (n 21) 232.
[150] *Wen Wei Po* (n 23) 37–38; BLDC Secretariat (n 82) 1990.
[151] Li (n 21) 179.

the period 1982–90. Although the '12-point policy' that ultimately found its way into the JD was unilaterally developed by the Chinese side even before the negotiation on Hong Kong's future began, the detailed provisions on the post-1997 governance of the HKSAR, particularly those in Annex I to the JD, were a joint product of the two governments.

The British side made an important contribution to the drafting of such provisions. It is particularly noteworthy that the 12-point policy did not include any provision on how the legislature of the HKSAR was to be constituted. There were no elected seats in Hong Kong Legislative Council at the time of the negotiation on Hong Kong's future. The British proposal that the HKSAR legislature should be constituted by elections was accepted by the Chinese side only a few days before the text of the JD was finalised and initialled in September 1984.

Two months before the conclusion of the negotiation, the colonial government published the Green Paper on the development of representative government in Hong Kong, initiating a process of constitutional reform and democratisation in Hong Kong. In 1985, elections to LegCo were introduced for the first time in Hong Kong's colonial history. Two modes of elections – elections by functional constituencies and by electoral colleges comprising mainly members of the District Boards – were initiated by the colonial government.

Meanwhile, the Chinese exercise of drafting the Basic Law for the post-1997 HKSAR began with the formation of the BLDC in June 1985. The Chinese Government became increasingly concerned about the colonial government's proceeding with constitutional reform unilaterally, which would have the effect of pre-empting what the Basic Law would decide as regards Hong Kong's future political system. The Chinese side publicly advocated the principle of 'convergence' between the colonial government's political reform and the provisions of the Basic Law. The British accepted 'convergence' as a matter of principle by the end of 1985.

How convergence was to be achieved, particularly in the context of the 1987 Review of the further development of representative government, was the subject of behind-the-scenes Sino-British discussion in 1986 and 1987. In particular, the Chinese side objected to the introduction of direct election by universal suffrage to any LegCo seats before the Basic Law settled the issue of the mode of elections to the HKSAR legislature. By early 1988, a secret compromise was reached whereby the colonial government announced in the White Paper of February 1988 that 10 LegCo seats would be directly elected in 1991.

The first draft of the Basic Law was published for public consultation in April 1988. Comments and suggestions on the draft were submitted by the BLCC, politicians, activists, civil society organisations and members of the public in Hong Kong. The debate between conservatives and democrats, which had been intense during the consultation period for the 1987 review, continued and further developed. The British Government and Hong Kong government provided detailed feedback to the Chinese side on the draft Basic Law, though this was done behind the scenes and not publicised.

A major issue negotiated between the two Governments at this time was the precise mechanism for the transition of government in 1997. By the end of 1988, consensus was reached regarding a 'through train' arrangement for members of the last colonial legislature to become members of the first legislature of the HKSAR. This arrangement was reflected in the second draft of the Basic Law published in February 1989.

Internal documents recently released at the British National Archives suggest that the British Government believed that the second draft of the Basic Law published in February 1989 was consistent with the JD, and most of the concerns expressed by the British side regarding the first draft had been dealt with, as reflected by improved provisions in the second draft. However, as largely similar concerns and suggestions for improvement had also been voiced by various sectors of public opinion in Hong Kong during the consultation period for the first draft, it is difficult to estimate the degree to which the British input (relative to other sources of input) contributed to improved provisions in the second draft.

Two months after the publication of the second draft of the Basic Law, a student movement erupted in Beijing, leading finally to the tragedy of the 'June 4th incident'. This precipitated a severe crisis of confidence in Hong Kong. The consultative activities of the Basic Law Consultative Committee were suspended temporarily, though it was subsequently decided to resume the consultation and to extend the consultation period to the end of October 1989. The climate of public opinion changed considerably in Hong Kong, and there was an upsurge in the demand for democratisation.

Responding to the crisis of confidence in Hong Kong, the British Government decided to negotiate further with the Chinese side regarding the provisions of the Basic Law and political reform in and after 1991. However, at this time the Chinese side was not receptive to proposals for further significant amendments to the draft Basic Law and for an overhaul of the provisions on the political system of the HKSAR. Eventually, by means of the now famous exchange of seven letters in January and February 1990 between the foreign ministers of the two Governments, an understanding was reached regarding the increase in the number of directly elected seats in LegCo in 1991 from 10 to 18, and also regarding the numbers of seats elected by various modes in the last colonial legislature of 1995 and the first HKSAR legislature of 1997.

The British contribution to the shaping of the constitutional order of the HKSAR was not limited to the circumstances summarised above. In particular, the two British initiatives of the insertion of the provision on the election of the legislature in the JD and the project of the development of 'representative government' in Hong Kong launched in 1984 had far-reaching consequences that were not easy to evaluate. But history would most probably have to be rewritten if the JD had not contained a provision that the legislature of the HKSAR should be constituted by elections, or if there had been no Green Paper on the development of representative government in July 1984.

The institution of 'functional constituencies' that originated from the Green Paper of 1984 was subsequently adopted as a key institution in the Basic Law. Moreover, the electoral provision in the JD and the vision of representative government presented by the Green Paper created a 'political opportunity structure' that was unprecedented in Hong Kong's history.[152] They initiated a process of 'top-down' or 'regime-led' democratisation, which in turn stimulated and nurtured demands in the community for 'bottom-up' democratisation.[153] They generated new expectations and nurtured the hope that there would be a new Hong Kong, with elected legislators accountable to the people of Hong Kong.

Thus the genie of democracy was let out of the bottle. For the Beijing side, a Pandora's box of political uncertainties was opened. The 1980s saw the political awakening of Hong Kong people, and the gradual rise of political consciousness, emerging social movements and nascent political parties or quasi-parties. Hong Kong would never be the same again. It was in this new climate of public opinion that the provisions in the Basic Law on the political system of the HKSAR were drafted, expressing the aspirations in Articles 45 and 68 that eventually the Chief Executive and all Hong Kong legislators would be directly elected by universal suffrage. Although this ultimate goal has not yet been realised even today – 30 years after the enactment of the Basic Law and 23 years after it came into operation – it is still very much alive in the minds and hearts of Hong Kong people, as demonstrated by social movements in recent years. The very existence of these idealistic and aspirational Basic Law provisions can be traced back to, and is explicable by, the political and social dynamics initiated by the British project of democratisation of colonial Hong Kong and the Chinese project of the drafting of the Basic Law in the 1980s.

Thus, by negotiating with China the details of the post-1997 governance of Hong Kong and getting them written into the JD, by launching the political reform towards 'representative government' in 1984 and by actively engaging in dialogue with the Chinese side throughout the process of the drafting of the Basic Law, the British Government made a significant contribution to the making of the constitutional order of the HKSAR. In retrospect, the period 1982–90 that saw the birth of the JD and the Basic Law was a unique period in the political history of both China and Britain that provided favourable conditions for Sino-British cooperation in working out Hong Kong's future.

The PRC was in the early experimental stage of the post-Mao era of 'reform and opening'. China's paramount leader was Deng Xiaoping, who, relative to his predecessors, was at the time pragmatic, open-minded and relatively liberal, and had the supreme authority to make decisions without being constrained by factional politics. Britain was under the strong leadership of Thatcher, who was well-advised by China experts such as Cradock. Thatcher stayed in power

[152] Sing (n 130) 66, 69, 70.
[153] ibid, 69–71, 79.

from 1979 until 1990, so that Britain was able to conduct diplomacy effectively with China as regards Hong Kong matters without being adversely affected by any change of government. On the global level, the second half of the 1980s saw Gorbachev's *Perestroika* in the Soviet Union; by the end of the decade China had experienced the trauma of 4 June 1989 and Communism had collapsed in Eastern Europe. If these dramatic developments had occurred earlier, would Deng Xiaoping have been less confident about 'One Country, Two Systems' and less willing to cooperate with Britain to design a constitutional order for post-1997 Hong Kong that is relatively liberal and promises increasing degrees of democratisation after 1997? One wonders. In retrospect, the period covered by this chapter may be seen as constituting a rare window of opportunity that gave rise to the unprecedented political experiment of 'One Country, Two Systems' and the HKSAR.

4

Macao's Constitutional Founding

XIAOBO ZHAI*

INTRODUCTION

LOCATED ON THE southwestern corner of the Pearl River estuary, and an hour's ferry ride west of Hong Kong, Macao,[1] known as the casino capital of the world, is a small city consisting of the Macao Peninsula and Taipa and Coloane islands. The two islands are joined by land reclaimed from the sea and connected with the Macao Peninsula by bridges. Its area of about 33 square km is populated by about 680,000 residents, which is less than one-tenth of Hong Kong's population. According to the 2016 census, more than 88 per cent of its residents were Chinese, 1.4 per cent Portuguese, and 4.6 per cent Filipino. Chinese and Portuguese are its official languages. More than 80 per cent of the population speak Cantonese. Portuguese is spoken by about 2 per cent of the population. English is also commonly spoken.[2] Macao has the highest per capita income in the world. However, its economy is fragile, overwhelmingly dependent on the gambling industry, which is seven times larger than that of Las Vegas.[3] Its residents rely on mainland China for food, water and energy, and its gambling industry almost entirely counts on tourists from mainland China. It had been under the administration of Portugal for hundreds of years, and became a Special Administrative Region (SAR) of China in 1999. Its journey of homecoming to China started in the 1980s.

In October 1984, Deng Xiaoping, China's *de facto* supreme leader, first mentioned to a group of guests from Macao that the solution of the question of Macao was 'no other than "One Country Two Systems"' (OCTS).[4]

*I thank Albert Chen, Kevin Tan and Michael Ng very much for their invaluable detailed comments on an earlier draft of this chapter, and Zeng Binbin for her excellent research assistance.

[1] 'Macao' is the English name, whereas 'Macau' is the Portuguese name.

[2] Macao Government, 'Geography and Population' at www.gcs.gov.mo/files/factsheet/geography.php?PageLang=E, accessed 18 November 2020.

[3] Mingjie Sheng and Gu Chaolin, 'Economic growth and development in Macau (1999–2016): The role of the booming gaming industry' (2018) 75 *Cities* 72, 72.

[4] See *Deng Xiaoping's Speeches: Meetings* (邓小平讲话实录 (会议卷)) (Hongqi Chubanshe, 2018) 260.

This event marked the beginning of Macao's constitutional founding, which was concluded with the promulgation of the Macao Basic Law in 1993. However, when the Drafting Committee started to write the Macao Basic Law in October 1988, the basic policies and principles of the future constitutional order of Macao were already established and widely known. These policies and principles can be called the Hong Kong model of OCTS. Nevertheless, it needs to be added that the Hong Kong model is only one (although the predominant one) among various factors that ultimately contributed to the formation of the regime embodied in the Macao Basic Law. Other important factors include China's *de facto* control of the Macao society from the founding of the People's Republic of China (PRC) in 1949 until the handover in 1999, and the Macao Organic Statute enacted by Portugal in 1976. These complex factors that finally shaped Macao's constitutional founding can be best understood by investigating Macao's history.

This chapter offers, first, a brief narration of how the pre-handover regime of Macao was formed; second, an account of how OCTS and its Hong Kong model had unfolded; and, third, a description of the drafting of the Macao Basic Law from October 1988 to March 1993, and a comparison of Macao and Hong Kong Basic Laws.

I. BEFORE THE HANDOVER: THE HISTORICAL BACKGROUND

A. The PRC's Position and its *de facto* Control (1949–99)

As the preamble to the Macao Basic Law says, the constitutional arrangement of Macao had taken account of Macao's history and realities. 'Macao … has been part of the territory of China since ancient times; it was gradually occupied by Portugal after the mid-16th century.' Portugal's gradual occupation since the mid-sixteenth century culminated in the unequal Sino-Portuguese Treaty of Friendship and Commerce of 1887 (the Treaty of Beijing), which confirmed 'the perpetual occupation and government of Macao by Portugal' and provided that Portugal should never alienate Macao without previous agreement with China. The Treaty of Beijing was different from the Treaty of Nanking of 1842 ceding the Hong Kong island and the Convention of Beijing of 1860 ceding the Kowloon peninsula to the UK: it did not cede Macao to Portugal.

With the end of the Second World War, Portuguese domination in Macao had greatly declined, and the Portuguese from then only governed Macau in the shadow of China. After the Communist Party took over, China's influence on Macao's politics and society further extended and deepened. China did not recognise the validity of the Treaty of Beijing, and stated repeatedly that Macao had always been China's territory, that the pending question of Macao inherited from the past should be settled peacefully through negotiations when the conditions were ripe and that, before the settlement, the status quo should be maintained.[5] The Communist Government was not anxious to take back the capitalist Hong Kong and Macao. Because of the international isolation and blockade imposed upon the Communist China by western powers, China's position towards Hong Kong and Macao was to 'keep a long-term perspective, and make full use of it'(长期打算, 充分利用).[6] At the same time, China started 'a long-term strategy of peaceful penetration', and slowly but effectively increased its *de facto* influence and even control over Macao. For example, China, especially Guangdong province, worked hard to ensure a constant supply of daily necessities (especially foods) for Macao, even when the mainlanders did not have enough to eat. The Chinese Government supported the establishment and operation of many patriotic social organisations, and maintained close contact with Chinese elites in Macao. António de Oliveira Salazar, Prime Minister of Portugal from 1932 to 1968, stated, 'no matter how we resist, Macao will be incorporated into China, because people's everyday life in Macao is completely dependent on China'.[7]

China's *de facto* control was best illustrated by the 12–3 incident in 1966. The incident represented a violent mass campaign against the corrupt, oppressive and racist Portuguese Government in Macao. The direct cause was a clash between Chinese residents and Portuguese officials: the former were constructing a school, whereas the latter blocked the construction for having received no bribes from the former. The clash led to a series of demonstrations and protests, and finally riots on 3 December. The riots were brutally cracked down on by the colonial government: eight Chinese were killed and 212 were injured. The Chinese communities in Macao and Guangdong, and the Guangdong provincial government, responded immediately and effectively to the crackdown, and put forward a number of demands, including punishing those responsible for the violence and crackdown on Chinese residents, permitting the construction of the school, compensating the loss of lives and injuries, releasing the arrested protestors, promising never to supress or beat Chinese residents again and issuing a formal apology to China. After hesitations and struggles, the Portuguese Government yielded to all these demands, and the statement of apology was signed under the portrait of Chairman Mao.[8] The already declined authority of the Portuguese Government over Macao had slumped after the 12–3 incident: it governed Macao only nominally, to the extent that China allowed. Commenting on the incident, Franco Nogueira, then Portuguese Foreign Minister, said,

[5] See Wang Shuwen (王叔文) et al, *Introduction to the Basic Law of Macao SAR* (澳门特别行政区基本法导论) (Zhongguorenmin Gongandaxue Chubanshe, 1993) 10.

[6] Shi Zhe (师哲), *With the Giants in History: a Memoir* (在历史巨人身边 – 师哲回忆录) (Zhongyang Wenxian Chubanshe, 1991) 380.

[7] Cited in Jorge Noronha e Silveira (肖伟华), *Research Materials on the History of Macao's Constitution* (澳门宪法历史研究资料) (Legal Translation Office, 1997) 65.

[8] For the 12-3 incident, see Wu Zhiliang (吴志良), *The History of Macao's Political System* (澳门政治制度史) (Guangdong Renmin Chubanshe, 2010) 197–217.

'we have never possessed sovereignty over Macao, and our presence has been thanks to the goodwill of China: we have always shared sovereignty over Macao with China'.[9]

In 1972, China's Ambassador to the United Nations (UN) wrote to the UN Special Committee on Decolonisation, requesting the UN to remove Hong Kong and Macao from its list of colonial territories:

> The questions of Hong Kong and Macao belong to the category of questions resulting from the series of unequal treaties left over by history, treaties which the imperialists imposed on China. Hong Kong and Macao are part of Chinese territory occupied by the British and Portuguese authorities. The settlement of the questions of Hong Kong and Macao is entirely within China's sovereign right and does not at all fall under the ordinary category of 'colonial territories'. Consequently they should not be included in the list of colonial territories covered by the Declaration on the Granting of Independence to Colonial Countries and People. With regard to the questions of Hong Kong and Macao, the Chinese Government has consistently held that they should be settled in an appropriate way when conditions are ripe.[10]

The UN granted this request.

B. The Macao Organic Statute (1974–76)

In April 1974, a military coup took place in Portugal that brought in a democratic regime with decolonisation as one of its goals. The new democratic regime completed its task of decolonisation by the end of 1975, with the exception of Macao.[11] In June, two months after the coup, Almeida Santos, Minister for Inter-Territorial Coordination, stated:

> Macao is ... a very special case amongst the special ones. ... Once diplomatic relations with China are established – we will do whatever is needed for that purpose – or as soon as a form of actual dialogue is initiated, dialogue will dictate the future of Macao if it has to diverge from its present.[12]

In September, Mario Soares, Portugal's Foreign Minister, pointed out:

> We do not regard Macao as a colony as such, but rather as a trading post. Naturally the status of Macao must be negotiated between the two interested parties, Portugal and China. I feel that there will be good reasons on both sides to reach a good understanding regarding Macao.[13]

[9] Cited ibid 203.

[10] Cited in Christine Loh, *Underground Front: The Chinese Communist Party in Hong Kong* (HKU Press, 2010) 130.

[11] Malyn Newitt, *Portugal in European and World History* (Reaktion Books Ltd, 2009) 219.

[12] Interview with *L'Espresso* (Rome, 27 June 1974), cited in FG Pereira, *Accommodating Diversity: The People's Republic of China and the 'Question of Macao'* (Centro Cientifico e Cultural de Macao, 2013) 155.

[13] SWB/ 4705/A1/1 (17 September 1974), cited in Pereira (n 12) 157.

It is clear that there was a broad agreement between China and Portugal as regards how to solve the question of Macao. What both sides needed was the right time.

The Coup in Portugal had nearly no immediate repercussions on the life of Chinese residents in Macao. However, it made some impact on the Portuguese and Macanese (descendants of marriages or liaisons between Portuguese and Chinese) in Macao. In November 1974, Colonel Garcia Leandro was appointed Governor (1974–78). In response to political disagreements between the conservative and authoritarian Portuguese political groups on one hand, and the radical and democratic ones on the other hand, and also in order to improve the autonomy and efficiency of the administration of Macao, Leandro decided to draft an Organic Statute for Macao (MOS), which was to serve as the foundation of Macao's political system designed by the Basic Law. Yash Ghai wrote, 'This Statute, with a few amendments, constituted an important benchmark when negotiations for the transfer of the exercise of sovereignty began in 1986.'[14] The drafting commission was set up in January 1975, and there were nine members, two of whom were local Chinese leaders, Ho Yin and Chui Tak Kei. According to FG Pereira, Ho Yin and Chui Tak Kei 'played a crucial role in defining the final architecture of the new political institutions'.[15] Governor Leandro preferred a more democratic legislative assembly based on universal suffrage and secret ballot, which met with opposition from the Chinese representatives, who deemed 'inconvenient … the existence of a Chinese majority in the local lawmaking body'.[16] The draft of the MOS was published in July for public discussion. Then, after being revised in the light of feedback from the public, it was sent to the Ministry of Coordination of Inter-regional Territories (MCIT) in Lisbon. With minor revisions by MCIT, it was approved by the Revolutionary Council (*Conselho de Revolucao*) in Lisbon and promulgated in February 1976. The Constitution of Portugal (CP) promulgated in April 1976 confirmed the constitutional validity of the MOS, stating that it and its future amendments 'continue in force' (Article 292 CP). The MOS, with its later amendments, had been the mini-constitution for Macao before being replaced in 1999 by the Basic Law. And the Basic Law's design of Macao's political system had drawn upon the MOS.

The CP and the MOS clarified the constitutional status of Macao: it was 'under Portuguese administration' (Article 292(1) CP) and not part of Portugal's territory (Article 5 CP). In January 1975, the Portuguese garrison was formally replaced by a local security force, which symbolically marked the end of Portugal's sovereignty in Macao.

[14] Yash Ghai, 'The Basic Law of the SAR of Macao: Some Reflections' (2000) 49 *International and Comparative Law Quarterly* 183, 186.

[15] Pereira (n 12) 161.

[16] ibid. Also Wu Zhiliang (n 8) 242.

The MOS granted Macao a high degree of autonomy. Article 2 provided that

> the territory of Macao shall be organized as a corporation which shall have the right of autonomy in administration, economy, finance, and legislation, except as provided otherwise in the Constitution of the Republic Portugal and this organic statute.[17]

It needs to be noted that the right of autonomy here did not apply to the judiciary, which continued to be part of the Portuguese judicial and legal system (Article 51 MOS). The Assembly of the Republic had the power to amend the MOS, but any future amendments to the MOS could only be initiated with the proposal or consent of the Legislative Assembly of Macao or the Governor of Macao; these amendments could only be promulgated after receiving a favourable opinion from the Legislative Assembly of Macao or the Governor of Macao (Article 292 CP; Article 30 MOS).[18] If an issue were 'within the exclusive legislative competence of Macao', national laws would give way to Macao's local laws.[19] The powers to deal with foreign relations and external security belonged to the President, who, however, could and did delegate to the Governor of Macao the powers to deal with matters concerning Macao only (Articles 3 and 12 MOS).

The MOS set up for Macao an executive-led political system, with some moderate internal checks and balances between different branches. The Governing Bodies of Macao were the Governor and the Legislative Assembly; and the Governor was advised by a Consultative Council (Article 4 MOS). The Power of Legislation belonged to the Legislative Assembly and the Governor (Article 5 MOS): while both shared some legislative powers, each had its own exclusive ones. The Governor was the core of the system, and he represented in Macao the sovereignty – except its judicial branch – of the Republic (Article 3 MOS), and was responsible for the implementation of laws (Article 6 MOS).[20] The Legislative Assembly was an organ representing the dominant interests of Macao. Among its initial 17 members, five were appointed by the Governor, six elected by direct universal suffrage and six elected by indirect suffrage. These three ways of producing legislators were later inherited by the Basic Law. The President of the Republic could dissolve the Legislative Assembly upon the advice of the Governor. The Legislative Assembly could pass a no-confidence vote on the Governor's performance, but the no-confidence vote would not have legally binding effect.[21] The judiciary, which according to the MOS still belonged to the Portuguese system, was independent.

[17] The Organic Statute of Macao (澳门组织章程), available at https://bo.io.gov.mo/bo/i/76/09/leiar01_cn.asp, accessed 27 July 2020. My translation draws on the English translation in Steve Shipp, *Macau, China: A Political History of the Portuguese Colony's Transition to Chinese Rule* (McFarland & Company, Inc, 1997) 178.

[18] See Pereira (n 12) 162; RD Cremer, 'A Model for Macau?' (1986/1987) 13 (No 4) *Asian Affairs: An American Review* 41, 45.

[19] Cremer (n 18) 46.

[20] I rely upon the English translation of the Organic Statute of Macao in Shipp (n 17) 178–93.

[21] ibid 95; Pereira (n 12) 164.

The first election for the Legislative Assembly took place in 1976. While, on one hand, there were strict and unfair limitations on the right to vote – those of Portuguese nationality were allowed to vote if they were 18 years old and lived in Macao, whereas those of Chinese or other nationalities must have lived in Macao for at least five or seven years in order to vote – on the other hand, the local Chinese and their leaders were not interested in the direct election. Consequently, only 2,846 people voted and the six direct elected seats all went to Portuguese- or Macanese-dominated associations; the minority of Chinese members were either indirectly elected or appointed by the Governor. This situation only changed during the election of the third Legislative Assembly in the mid-1980s.[22]

C. OCTS for Macao (1980s)

As noted in section I.B, Portugal and China were waiting for the right time to solve the question of Macao. In February 1979, they established diplomatic relations and reached a protocol on Macao, according to which Macao was a Chinese territory under Portuguese administration, and the question of Macao would be solved by negotiations at an appropriate time.[23]

In October 1984, speaking to a group of guests from Hong Kong and Macao, Deng Xiaoping said, 'The question of Macao will be solved in the same way as that of Hong Kong. … The solution of the question of Macao question is no other than "One Country Two Systems".'[24] This was the first time the Chinese Government had revealed the plan of applying the Hong Kong model to Macao. In February 1985, Chinese President Li Xiannian, at a meeting with the Governor of Macao, Vasco Almeida e Costa, formally announced this plan:

> The question of Macao is now not a problem. When China and Portugal established formal relations, an agreement was reached that the question would be solved by means of negotiations … Hong Kong is an example for the future of Macao: 'One country two systems', instead of socialism.[25]

In June, Ji Pengfei, Director of the Chinese State Council's Hong Kong and Macao Affairs Office, when receiving a group of visitors from Macao, explained:

> The principle according to which China solves the question of Macao is to make sure that the interests of all parties be respected and that the handover be peaceful. …

[22] Cai Yongjun (蔡永君), *Macao's Political Elites in Transitional Era* (转型时期的澳门政治精英) (Shehuikexue Wenxian Chubanshe, 2016) 47–50; Pereira (n 12) 164. Cao Qizhen was directly elected as a member of the Portuguese-dominated Associação para a Defesa dos Interesses de Macau (ADIM).

[23] Kang Jimin (康冀民), 'The Journal of Macao's Return' (澳门回归之路) (2009) 3 *Materials of the History of CCP* (中共党史资料) 13.

[24] *Journal 'Va Kio'* (华侨报) (6 October 1984), cited in Wu Zhiliang (n 8) 251.

[25] *Macao Daily* (澳门日报)(8 February 1985, cited in Wu Zhiliang (n 8) 252.

> The Hong Kong model will be largely referenced (参照), but it will not be copied (照搬), because Macao has many concrete problems which are not the same as those in Hong Kong.[26]

The formal negotiations between Portugal and China started in June 1986, and the Macao Basic Law was passed in 1993, but its major principles and contents had been effectively decided first in 1984, when the Sino-British Joint Declaration on the question of Hong Kong was concluded, and then in 1990, when the Hong Kong Basic Law was promulgated. The writing of the Macao Basic Law was to a significant extent applying the Hong Kong model to Macao: the percentage of overlap between the 12 policies in the two joint declarations is 13 per cent, and between two basic laws 82 per cent. If the Hong Kong Basic Law is an *original* mini-constitution then Macao's Basic Law is a typical *derivative* one. Without understanding Hong Kong's constitutional founding, it is impossible to understand that of Macao.

II. THE HONG KONG MODEL

A. OCTS for Hong Kong

The Hong Kong model is the principle of OCTS, which, in Deng Xiaoping's words, means that 'within the PRC, socialism is practiced for the one billion people in mainland China, and capitalism for Hong Kong and Taiwan'.[27] According to Deng,

> OCTS has two aspects. On the one hand, within some regions of a socialist country, capitalism is allowed, not for a while, but for decades and even one hundred years; on the other hand, the main body of the country is socialist.[28]

Deng said in 1984 that

> the principle of OCTS was initially not formulated for Hong Kong, but for Taiwan. The nine-principle proposal announced by Ye Jianying – Chairman of the Standing Committee of the National People's Congress (NPCSC) – on the eve of the national day of 1981 contained the essence of OCTS, although not so called then. Two years ago, when the question of Hong Kong was raised, we decided to apply OCTS to Hong Kong.[29]

[26] *Wen Wei Po* (文汇报)(12 June 1985), cited in Wu Zhiliang (n 8) 254.

[27] Deng Xiaoping, 'One Country, Two Systems' (一个国家，两种制度) (22 and 23 June 1984) at www.hrgps.edu.hk/data/stdpjo/p6web/6g/20/country.htm, accessed 27 July 2020.

[28] Deng Xiaoping, 'A Speech to the Members of the HKBLDC' (会见香港特别行政区基本法起草委员会委员时的讲话) （16 April 1987） at www.locpg.hk/2015-03/18/c_127503257.htm, accessed 27 July 2020.

[29] Deng Xiaoping, 'China will keep its promise' (中国是信守诺言的) （19 December 1984） at www.locpg.hk/jsdt/1984-12/19/c_125955719.htm, accessed 27 July 2020. In fact, the basic idea of OCTS came into being in 1979, see Wang Shuwen et al (n 5) 3.

Put forward as a proposal for the peaceful reunification of the mainland and Taiwan, Ye Jianying's nine principles were as follows:

(1) The Chinese Communist Party and the Kuomintang shall hold reciprocal negotiations on the issue of the reunification.
(2) Direct links or communications shall be established.
(3) After the reunification, Taiwan will become a special administrative region, enjoy a high degree of autonomy, and even can keep its armed forces. The Central Government will not intervene in Taiwan's local affairs.
(4) Taiwan's current social and economic systems, and its way of life remain unchanged; its economic and cultural ties with foreign countries remain unchanged. Private property will not be infringed.
(5) Taiwan people can take leading positions in national political organs, and participate in the management of the state.
(6) The Central Government will help Taiwan if the latter has financial difficulties.
(7) Taiwan people are welcome to settle down in the mainland.
(8) Taiwan people are welcome to invest in the mainland.
(9) All suggestions regarding the unification from Taiwan people are welcome.[30]

The central idea of Ye's proposal was written into the 1982 Constitution, Article 31 of which provides:

> The state may establish special administrative regions when necessary. The system to be instituted in special administrative regions shall be prescribed by law enacted by the National People's Congress in the light of the specific conditions.

When introducing the draft of the Constitution to the NPC, Peng Zhen, Vice Chairman of the Committee for Revision of the Constitution, declared:

> We are absolutely unequivocal on the principle of safeguarding China's sovereignty, unity and territorial integrity. At the same time, we are highly flexible as regards specific policies and measures and will give full consideration to the concrete situation in the Taiwan region and the wishes of the people in Taiwan and those of all personages concerned. This is our basic position in handling problems of a similar kind.[31]

'Problems of a similar kind' include the questions of Hong Kong and Macao. China and the UK started in 1982 the negotiations about the future arrangement for Hong Kong.[32] After the UK reluctantly agreed to give up first sovereignty

[30] Ye Jianying (叶剑英), 'The Policies for Taiwan's Return to the Motherland and the Peaceful Reunification' (关于实现台湾回归祖国，实现和平统一的方针政策) (30 September 1981) in Zhonggongzhongyang Wenxianyanjiushi (中共中央文献研究室) (ed), *Important Documents on OCTS* (Zhongyang Wenxianchubanshe, 1997) 5–7.

[31] Peng Zhen, 'Report on the Draft of the Revised Constitution of the People's Republic of China' (26 November 1982) in *Chinese Documents: Fifth Session of the Fifth National People's Congress* (The Foreign Languages Press, 1983) 100–01.

[32] For a detailed account, see ch 3 of this book by Albert Chen and Michael Ng.

and then administrative rights over Hong Kong,[33] China presented its 12 basic policies for Hong Kong, which formed the basis of the final phase of the negotiations. These 12 policies, as formulated in the Sino-British Joint Declaration, were:

(1) The Chinese Government decided to resume the exercise of sovereignty over Hong Kong as of 1 July 1997.
(2) The Central People's Government (CPG) would establish an SAR in Hong Kong. Hong Kong would be directly under the authority of the CPG and would enjoy a high degree of autonomy.
(3) Hong Kong would be vested with legislative and independent judicial power, including that of final adjudication. The law would remain basically unchanged.
(4) The government would be composed of local inhabitants.
(5) The current social and economic systems in Hong Kong would remain unchanged, and so would the life-style. Freedoms would be ensured in Hong Kong. Private property would be protected by law.
(6) Hong Kong would retain the status of a free port and a separate customs territory.
(7) Hong Kong would retain the status of an international financial centre. There would continue to be a free flow of capital, and the Hong Kong dollar would continue to circulate and remain freely convertible.
(8) Hong Kong would have independent finances.
(9) Hong Kong might establish mutually beneficial economic relations with the UK, whose economic interests in HK would be given due regard.
(10) Hong Kong would have considerable freedom to engage in international activities, and might itself issue travel documents.
(11) The maintenance of public order in Hong Kong would be the responsibility of the Hong Kong government.
(12) The above-stated policies would be stipulated in the Basic Law by the NPC, and they would remain unchanged for 50 years.[34]

B. The Sino-British Joint Declaration

The autonomy allowed to Hong Kong in these policies is less than that for Taiwan: for example, Hong Kong is not permitted to have its own armed forces. Deng insisted that stationing troops in Hong Kong was a necessary element

[33] See Yash Ghai, *Hong Kong's New Constitutional Order* (HKU Press, 1999) 45–48.

[34] See 'Joint Declaration of the Government of the United Kingdom of Great Britain and Northern Ireland and the Government of the People's Republic of China on the Question of Hong Kong' (the Sino-British Joint Declaration) para 3 at www.cmab.gov.hk/en/issues/jd2.htm, accessed 23 July 2020; Ghai, *Hong Kong's New Constitutional Order* 49–50.

of China's sovereignty.[35] These 12 policies were abstract and vague. They were fleshed out by difficult and complex negotiations. Beijing did not like to see the UK-sponsored democratisation in Hong Kong. The UK managed to persuade China to agree, for example, that 'the legislature of the HKSAR shall be constituted by elections. The executive authorities shall abide by the law and shall be accountable to the legislature', and that 'the provisions of the ICCPR ... as applied to Hong Kong shall remain in force'.[36] In December 1984, the heads of government from both countries signed the Joint Declaration: within the framework decided by China, the UK contributed substantially to the detailed arrangements spelled out in Annex I to the Joint Declaration.[37] The Joint Declaration is not called a treaty but it is a legally binding treaty approved by China's NPC and the UK's Parliament, and registered with the UN.[38] It consists of one main text and three annexes. China and the UK had disagreements over the historical question of sovereignty over Hong Kong. This difference was expressed in the Joint Declaration by two parallel statements, through which each stated its own position: the Government of the PRC declared that 'it has decided to resume the exercise of sovereignty over Hong Kong with effect from 1 July 1997', whereas the Government of the UK declared that 'it will restore Hong Kong to the PRC' from the same date. Paragraph 3 of the Joint Declaration recorded China's 12 basic policies towards Hong Kong, which were elaborated in Annex I. These policies were significant, and provided Hong Kong with a degree of autonomy that is much greater than that of China's ethnic autonomous regions.[39] Some powers granted to Hong Kong are even not possessed by states under federalism. For example, 'The power of final judgment of the HKSAR shall be vested in the court of final appeal in the HKSAR, which may as required invite judges

[35] Deng Xiaoping, 'Maintaining Hong Kong's Prosperity and Stability' (保持香港的繁荣和稳定 (3 October 1984) in *Deng Xiaoping on OCTS* (邓小平论一国两制) (Joint Publishing (HK) Co, 2019) 21–22.

[36] Annex I to the Sino-British Joint Declaration, i, para 3; xiii, para 4; Ghai (n 33) 51; Danny Gittings, *Introduction to the Hong Kong Basic Law* (HKU Press, 2016) 15. Also ch 3 of this book by Albert Chen and Michael Ng.

[37] Ch 3 of this book by Albert Chen and Michael Ng. Also Ghai (n 33) 51; Gittings (n 36) 17.

[38] 1399 United Nations Treaty Series 61 at https://treaties.un.org/doc/Publication/UNTS/Volume%201399/v1399.pdf, accessed 23 July 2020. See Wang Tieya (王铁崖), 'The Basic Law Will Not be Changed, Even If the Constitution is Changed' (宪法改了基本法也不会变) in Wenwei Press (ed), *The Birth of the Basic Law* (基本法的诞生) (Wenwei Press, 2018) 61–62; Gittings (n 36) 18; Ghai (n 33) 55.

[39] Gittings even claims that these policies were 'revolutionary' and provided Hong Kong 'a degree of autonomy arguably higher than almost any other place in the world that is not a country in its own right': Gittings (n 36) 16–17. However, as Albert Chen said in his comments on the draft of this chapter, Gittings' is a controversial claim, and it at least does not pay enough attention to the relationship between autonomy and democracy. See also Albert Chen, 'The Development of Constitutionalism in Hong Kong: from a Colony to a Special Administrative Region' (香港的宪治发展：从殖民统治区到特别行政区) in He Zhihui (何志辉) (ed), *Research on Legal Culture: Symposium on Legal Culture of Hong Kong* (法律文化研究：香港法律文化专题) (Shehuikexue Wenxian Chubanshe, 2016) 60.

from other common law jurisdictions to sit on the court of final appeal.' These policies and their elaboration later formed the foundation of the Hong Kong Basic Law.[40]

C. The Drafting of the Hong Kong Basic Law

The drafting of the Hong Kong Basic Law started in 1985, and it took four years. In contrast to the general political indifference of the Macao society, there was a widespread and strong demand across the Hong Kong society for liberal democratisation. This was a crucial feature of the social background against which the Hong Kong Basic Law was drafted. Compared with other laws made in China, the process of drafting the Hong Kong Basic Law is indeed the most careful, open and participatory one: it was reported in a left-wing newspaper as 'a process of democratic negotiation, and the draft is the fruit of democracy'.[41] The major task of drafting was undertaken by the Drafting Committee for the Basic Law (BLDC) of the HKSAR established by China's NPCSC: it was responsible to the NPC, and to the NPCSC when the NPC was not in session. The BLDC's membership was 'unprecedentedly diverse':[42] among its 59 members, 23 were from Hong Kong. Although most of the Hong Kong members were business leaders who were not passionate for democracy, there were also enthusiastic democrats, especially Martin Lee and Szeto Wah. The BLDC's decision was made by a two-thirds majority, which means that the Hong Kong members could veto proposals from the mainland members. Seventeen members were experts on law, including law professors and lawyers. These 59 members were divided into five groups, responsible respectively for drafting provisions in the following areas:

(1) The relationship between the central authorities and the HKSAR;
(2) The fundamental rights and duties of residents;
(3) The political structure;
(4) The finance and economy;
(5) Education, science, technology, culture, sports and religion.

The first meeting of the BLDC decided to set up 'a broadly representative Basic Law Consultative Committee' whose job was to extensively collate opinions and suggestions on the drafting from the Hong Kong public, and to offer consultations to the BLDC.[43] From July 1985 to April 1990, the BLDC held nine meetings,

[40] Xiao Weiyun (肖蔚云), *On Hong Kong Basic Law* (论香港基本法) (PKU Press, 2003) 3; Gittings (n 36) 17.

[41] Lei Jieqiong (雷洁琼), 'The Basic Law is the Fruit of Democratic Negotiation (基本法是民主协调成果)' in Wenwei Press (n 38) 129.

[42] Gittings (n 36) 20.

[43] See Wenwei Press (n 38) 249–50.

and the five drafting groups 73 meetings. There were two stages of public consultations. The first was in 1988, lasting five months, which was regarded as 'a high point of the drafting process with critical opinions being freely expressed and, in many cases, accommodated ... more than 100 changes were made, 80 of them are substantial'.[44] The second was in 1989, lasting several months and leading to 24 revisions. Regarding Beijing's attitude towards dissenting views, the drafting can be divided into two phases, with the 4 June incident as the watershed, before which Beijing was more liberal and accommodative, but after which Beijing became less patient and accommodative, and more distrustful of Hong Kong's liberal and democratic forces.[45]

Many provisions of the Basic Law were directly copied from the Joint Declaration. However, the drafting was not a tranquil and smooth process: 'quarrels were constant, which was not bad, and many problems were solved through quarrels'.[46] Many bitter battles were fought, among which the relations between the Central authorities and the HKSAR and the political system of the HKSAR were the two most contentious subjects.[47] The controversial issues debated and that are of great long-term significance included:

(1) Who should have the residual powers?
(2) How should the power to interpret the Basic Law be allocated?
(3) How would the Chief Executive (CE) and the members of the Legislative Council (LegCo) be selected?
(4) What would be the relationship between the executive and the legislature?

After many debates, the BLDC answered these questions with two principles. First, the HKSAR is a local administrative region with a high degree of autonomy within the unitary Chinese state. Second, the political structure of the HKSAR is executive-led,[48] under which the judiciary is independent, and the executive and the legislature are separate from each other and check each other.

Regarding the remarkable high degree of autonomy granted to Hong Kong, Danny Gittings commented:

> [T]he Hong Kong Basic Law was *the product of a brief window of opportunity* as China began to emerge from decades of isolation during the early 1980s. ... Only with Deng Xiaoping's rise to power in the late 1970s, and the advent of more

[44] Gittings (n 36) 25–26.
[45] See ch 3 of this book by Albert Chen and Michael Ng, section V, 'Post-4 June Developments (1989–90)'.
[46] Wenwei Press (n 38) 17. For the British Government's substantial but behind-the-scenes contributions, see ch 3 of this book by Albert Chen and Michael Ng.
[47] Wenwei Press (n 38) 17.
[48] The term 'executive-led' is now widely used to characterise the political system established by the Hong Kong Basic Law but, as Albert Chen pointed out, the term itself does not appear in the Basic Law, and neither does it appear in Ji Pengfei's official explanations of the Basic Law to the NPC in March 1990. See Albert Chen, 'The Origin of the Concept "executive-led"' ('行政主导'概念的由来) (2 October 2014) at https://www.master-insight.com/category/topic, accessed 18 November 2020.

> pragmatic policies emphasizing economic development, in which Hong Kong was expected to play a major role, did *a brief window of opportunity* to strike a deal securing the city's future emerge. Just how brief that window of opportunity would be is only evident with the benefit of hindsight … from today's perspective, it seems almost inconceivable that Chinese leaders would have agreed to such an extraordinary arrangement for Hong Kong had the same negotiations taken place now, when China has already emerged as an economic power in its own right and Hong Kong no longer plays such a critical role as a conduit for foreign investment.[49]

The window of opportunity and its brevity concerned not just the economic relationship between Hong Kong and China in the late 1970s and early 1980s, but also Deng's brief tolerance of political liberalisation during the same period, when one compares it with China's current return to authoritarianism.

With this brief account of the constitutional founding of the HKSAR, let us now consider how the Hong Kong model, including both the negotiations over the Joint Declaration and the drafting of the Hong Kong Basic Law, was applied to solve the question of Macao, despite many differences between Hong Kong and Macao.

III. THE MAKING OF THE MACAO BASIC LAW

Following the steps of the arrangement for Hong Kong, China – guided by the OCTS – first negotiated with Portugal a Joint Declaration on the question of Macao, and then passed the Macao Basic Law to implement the Joint Declaration.

A. The Sino-Portuguese Joint Declaration

In contrast to the Sino-British negotiations, the Sino-Portuguese negotiations were shorter and smoother, one reason for which was that, unlike the question of Hong Kong, there was no dispute on the issue of sovereignty between Beijing and Lisbon. The negotiations lasted only nine months through four rounds of talks, whereas the Sino-British negotiations lasted two years through 22 rounds of talks. The Sino-Portuguese Joint Declaration was signed in April 1987. Unlike the parallel statements on sovereignty in the Sino-British Declaration, the Portuguese Government and the Chinese Government declared together in the Sino-Portuguese Declaration that the Macao region formed part of Chinese territory and that the Chinese Government would resume the exercise of sovereignty over Macao with effect from 20 December 1999.[50]

[49] Gittings (n 36) 9–10.

[50] See 'the Sino-Portuguese Joint Declaration' (中葡联合声明) at www.zlb.gov.cn/2014-07/21/c_126779272.htm, accessed 27 July 2020; the English version is available at https://treaties.un.org/doc/Publication/UNTS/Volume%201498/volume-1498-I-25805-English.pdf, accessed 27 July 2020.

There were also disagreements, which were not as political as, but more practical and technical than, those in the Sino-British negotiations.[51] The first was about the time of the handover of Portugal's administration. China's original plan was to recover Macao in 1998, one year after Hong Kong's retrocession. Portugal wanted to govern Macao beyond 2000, perhaps until 2003, which would mark the 450th anniversary of Portuguese settlement in Macao, a request China resolutely rejected. China also compromised, though, allowing the handover to take place on 20 December 1999. The second disagreement concerned the nationality of about 130,000 Macao residents with Portuguese passports. China did not allow dual citizenship. Portugal insisted that these residents, apart from having Chinese nationality, continue to have Portuguese nationality. China compromised again and agreed, first, that these residents could still use Portuguese passports as travel documents and, second, that both expressed their disagreements by parallel memoranda in the Joint Declaration: the Portuguese Government declared that 'the Macao residents who are Portuguese citizens and have Portuguese passports on 19 December 1999 can continue to use their passports', whereas the Chinese Government declared that China 'allows Macao Chinese citizens with Portuguese travel documents to continue to use the documents to travel in other countries and regions, and that they do not receive Portuguese consular protection in Macao and other regions of China'.

Beijing's basic policies for Macao were essentially the same as those for Hong Kong, with some minor differences. For example, Macao was not an international financial centre, and there was therefore no point in repeating the policy of 'retaining the status of an international financial centre' found in the Sino-British Joint Declaration. Having not educated the people of Macao in the Portuguese civilisation or values or the Portuguese language, Portugal became upset about its legacy in Macao, and was anxious to keep Portuguese history and culture manifested in their buildings or relics in Macao.[52] The Sino-Portuguese Joint Declaration therefore maintained that 'the Macao SAR shall protect the cultural heritage of Macao in accordance with the law'. Portugal's bargaining power was far weaker than that of the UK. It is widely believed that Macao had benefited from the Hong Kong model: 'Macao has most likely achieved a higher degree of autonomy than it would have without the Hong Kong precedent.'[53]

B. The Transitional Period

The ratification of the Joint Declaration in 1987 marked the beginning of the 12-year transitional period. Following the Hong Kong model, the Sino-Portuguese Joint Declaration set up a Sino-Portuguese Liaison Group, to 'create appropriate conditions for the transfer of power in 1999'.

[51] See Kang Jimin (n 23) 13–15.
[52] Ghai (n 14) 187.
[53] ibid 184.

Macao's mini-constitution before the handover was the MOS that came into effect in 1976. The political system could be characterised as executive-led, with moderate checks and balances between three branches – the executive, the legislature and the independent judiciary. The politics had become more democratic than before. The administrative and judicial branches were still monopolised by the Portuguese. Changes were taking place in the legislative branch. For the election of the third Legislative Assembly in 1984, the people who voted were already more than 10 times those in 1976; two Chinese members were directly elected, and all the six indirectly elected seats went to Chinese candidates. From the fourth Legislative Assembly in 1988 until the handover, Chinese members had dominated both direct and indirect elections. In 1990, the MOS was amended to increase both the directly and indirectly electable seats to eight, and the Governor-appointed seats to seven. These Chinese legislators were mostly successful businessmen: they first became leaders of large business or social organisations, and then entered the Legislative Assembly by direct or indirect election. It is not clear to what extent they really represented the common Macao people. Macao has long been a society full of social organisations. However, except for a few large and powerful ones, most other social organisations rarely participated in politics. Besides, the majority of Macao people did not belong to any social organisation.[54]

During the transitional period (1987–99), 'three big problems' were solved by the Liaison Group's hard work.[55] The first concerned the status of the Chinese language. Under Portugal's rule, Portuguese was the official language, but Portugal, unlike the UK in Hong Kong, did not teach the Portuguese language to the majority of people in Macao. The huge gap between a small group of officials using Portuguese as a working language and the overwhelming majority of people who were ignorant of Portuguese had caused huge difficulties in people's lives, and to the resolution of another two problems: the localisation of the civil service, and that of the law and legal profession. The Sino-Portuguese Joint Declaration of 1987 stipulated that 'in addition to Chinese, the Portuguese language may be used in government agencies, in the legislative body, and in the courts of the Macao SAR'. In 1989, the Legislative Assembly passed a law requiring that 'legislation must be proposed in both Chinese and Portuguese from 2 June 1989'. In January 1992, the colonial government formally recognised Chinese as official language in Macao, having the same legal status as Portuguese.

The second problem was the localisation of the civil service. In colonial Macao, the civil service was dominated by the Portuguese at the high level, and by the Macanese in the middle. Local Chinese were excluded from any role in

[54] See Cai Yongjun (n 22) 50–60; Wu Zhiliang (n 8) 263–66; Zhidong Hao, *Macau: History and Society*, 2nd edn (Hong Kong University Press, 2020) 45.

[55] See Kang Jimin (n 23) 16–22.

governing. After 1999, most officials were required to be local residents. The education and training of capable officials could not be done overnight. From the late 1980s, under pressure from and with the help of Beijing, the colonial government had adopted a series of measures to localise the civil service, such as recognising degrees from Chinese universities, prohibiting the hiring of civil servants overseas, and setting up colleges to educate local youth, etc.

Differently from Hong Kong, the law in force in colonial Macao was Portuguese law in the Portuguese language, and the legal profession (including judges and lawyers) was monopolised by the Portuguese. Macao only had courts of first instance, which were extensions of the Portuguese judicial system. The third big problem was therefore the localisation of the law and legal profession, and the establishment of an autonomous judiciary. Before the handover in 1999, all important laws had been translated into Chinese. The Macao government took vigorous measures to educate legal professionals. There had been more than 100 local bilingual legal professionals, over 20 of whom had become judges or procurators. As part of the transitional arrangement, Portugal's Constitution was amended in 1989, providing that 'Macao shall have its own judicial organizations, [which are] autonomous and adapted to the specificities of Macao' (Article 292(5) CP). In 1990, Portugal's parliament revised the MOS accordingly, granting Macao judicial autonomy.[56] The Macao government then severed links with the appellate courts in Portugal, and established an autonomous system of courts. In 1993, Macao High Court was established, which, although officially an appellate court, would work as a *de facto* court of final appeal until 1999.

C. The Drafting of the Macao Basic Law

The drafting of the Macao Basic Law followed the same procedures as the Hong Kong Basic Law. The drafting committee was established by the NPC in September 1988. The Macao Basic Law Drafting Committee (MBLDC) was composed of 'persons and experts from all walks of life, including Macao compatriots'.[57] Among its 48 members, 14 were leading officials from relevant government departments, six were famous and influential figures from all walks of life, six were experts on law; 19 were from Macao, including two Macanese; 16 members, including four law professors, were also members of the HKBLDC. Like the HKBLDC, these members were divided into five subgroups. In October 1988, the MBLDC set up the Macao Basic Law Consultation Committee (MBLCC) of 90 members, which was regarded as 'the largest and the

[56] Ghai (n 14) 187; Wang Shuwen et al (n 5) 295–98.

[57] 'NPC's Decision on Establishing the Macao BLDC' (全国人民代表大会关于成立中华人民共和国澳门特别行政区基本法起草委员会的决定) (13 April 1988) at www.npc.gov.cn/wxzl/gongbao/2000-12/05/content_5004503.htm, accessed 26 July 2020.

most representative non-governmental consultation organization in the history of Macao'.[58] Starting from September 1988, after 70 sub-group meetings, nine MBLDC plenary meetings and two rounds of public consultation, the Macao Basic Law was finally passed by the eighth NPC in March 1993. According to Ji Pengfei, Chairman of the MBLDC:

> The draft of MBLDC was the fruit of the common endeavour of all drafting members and of the active participation and support of all classes of Macao society and the relevant sections of the mainland. The whole drafting process was guided by the principle of openness and democratic deliberation. The MBLCC composed of people of all walks of life of Macao had offered great assistance to the drafting: … they had collated a great number of opinions and suggestions for the MBLDC.[59]

The drafting of Macao Basic Law followed that of Hong Kong Basic Law, procedurally and substantively. It was much more harmonious and less contentious than that of Hong Kong Basic Law. There were also controversies:[60]

(1) The Preamble to the Macao Basic Law states that Macao 'was *gradually occupied* by Portugal after the mid-16th century'. Some Macanese residents wanted this sentence to be deleted, whereas the majority of the MBLDC and Macao residents thought that it was a correct description of the history.
(2) Some argued that the Basic Law should explicitly stipulate that the Central People's Government (CPG) would not station military troops, whereas others suggested that the Basic Law should state that expenditure for the garrison should be borne by the CPG. Considering, first, that the Sino-Portuguese Joint Declaration did not mention stationing military troops in Macao, second, that there was no practical need to station troops since Macao was geographically surrounded by Zhuhai and, third, that the prohibition on stationing troops was not in conformity with the principle of sovereignty, the MBLDC adopted a more flexible and elastic formulation, providing in Article 14 that 'the CPG shall be responsible for the defense of the Macao SAR. The Government of the Macao SAR shall be responsible for the maintenance of public order in the Region.'
(3) Article 23 of the Macao Basic Law provides that

> the Macao SAR shall enact laws, on its own, to prohibit any act of treason, secession, sedition, subversion against the CPG, or theft of state secrets, to prohibit foreign political organizations or bodies from conducting political activities in the Region, and to prohibit political organizations or bodies of the Region from establishing ties with foreign political organizations or bodies.

[58] Wang Shuwen et al (n 5) 18.
[59] Ji Pengfei (姬鹏飞), 'Some Explanations of the Drafting of the Macao Basic Law and other Relevant Documents' (关于《中华人民共和国澳门特别行政区基本法（草案）》和有关文件及起草工作的说明) at www.npc.gov.cn/wxzl/gongbao/2000-12/28/content_5002899.htm, accessed 27 July 2020.
[60] See He Li (何力), 'The Birth of the Macao Basic Law' (《澳门基本法》的诞生) in *Documents on the Macao Basic Law* (澳门基本法文献集) (Macao Daily Press, 1993) 97–98.

Some people were worried that this article might threaten or reduce political freedom in Macao, especially that the meaning of 'political' might be vague and expansive. The MBLDC assured these sceptics that the CPG would not interfere regarding the issues set out in this article, stressing that the meaning of 'political' would be defined by Macao and that the legislation would be completed by Macao's LegCo.

(4) Although the Macao Basic Law set up a political system that was essentially the same as that for Hong Kong, the political system, as in the drafting of the Hong Kong Basic Law, was a topic attracting many quarrels. Some wanted to have more democracy, and more checks and balances between the three branches.

D. Two Basic Laws Compared

Overall, the Macao Basic Law followed the Hong Kong Basic Law in its process of preparation, structure and content. As Ji Pengfei, Chairman of the Drafting Committees of both Basic Laws, stated,

> the country's basic principles and policies for Hong Kong and Macao are the same. The two basic laws were made according to article 31 of the Constitution, the general policy of OCTS, and the country's basic policies for Hong Kong and Macao, and the Macao Basic Law's general structure and main principles are the same as the Hong Kong Basic Law.[61]

These main principles are as follows:

(1) The general principles of both Basic Laws are the same, and the percentage of overlap in content between them is 93 per cent. Both Basic Laws in provide Chapter One that the SAR is an inalienable part of the PRC; that the SAR is authorised to exercise a high degree of autonomy and enjoy executive, legislative and independent judicial power, including that of final adjudication; that the executive authorities and legislature shall be composed of permanent residents of Macao; and that the previous capitalist system and way of life shall remain unchanged for 50 years.

(2) Chapter Two of the Macao Basic Law is entitled 'Relationship between the Central Authorities and the Macao SAR', which follows the Hong Kong Basic Law almost verbatim, except for Article 14 on stationing military troops. The percentage of overlap in content is 94 per cent. This chapter provides that the Macao SAR is a local administrative region of the PRC with a high degree of autonomy; that the CPG is responsible for foreign affairs, and the CPG authorises the Macao SAR to conduct relevant external affairs on its own; that the CPG shall appoint or remove the

[61] Ji Pengfei (n 59).

Chief Executive and the principal officials of the government; that the Macao SAR shall conduct the administrative affairs of the Region on its own; that the Macao SAR has legislative power, but shall report its laws to the NPCSC for the record; that some national laws relating to defence and foreign affairs shall be applied in Macao SAR; that the NPCSC can exercise the powers of war or emergency in exceptional situations; that, subject to the previous restrictions, the Macao courts have jurisdiction over all cases except acts of state; that the power of interpretation of the Basic Law belongs to the NPCSC, who authorises the courts of the SAR to interpret the provisions within the limits of the autonomy of the Region,

> however, if the courts of the Region, in adjudicating cases, need to interpret the provisions of this Law concerning affairs which are the responsibility of the Central People's Government, or concerning the relationship between the Central Authorities and the Region, and if such interpretation will affect the judgments on the cases, the courts of the Region shall, before making their final judgments which are not appealable, seek an interpretation of the relevant provisions from the Standing Committee of the National People's Congress through the Court of Final Appeal of the Region.

(3) The political structure of Macao is similar to that of Hong Kong. Chapter Four of both Basic Laws specifies the powers or functions of the Chief Executive (CE), the government, the legislature and the judiciary, which are based upon the principle of the leadership of the executive, and the principle of cooperation and checks and balances. The composition and the decision-making procedure of the legislature were designed to privilege the business community. As Ghai pointed out, this type of political structure had a common foundation in the colonial past of both Hong Kong and Macao, which was characterised by strong executives and weak legislatures, bureaucracy-dominated systems, top-down administration, the dominance of the business community and little political activism.[62]

(4) The chapters of both Basic Laws on Foreign Affairs and Interpretation and Modification are entirely the same.

Despite its overwhelming and important similarity with the Hong Kong Basic Law, the Macao Basic Law also has its own distinguishing features, based on its own history and political realities. For example, regarding land and natural resources, unlike in Hong Kong, where the only freehold private land was possessed by the Anglican Church, there were some pieces of land belonging to private persons in Macao. The Macao Basic Law therefore, after copying the basic principle from the Hong Kong Basic Law that the land and natural resources are state property and the SAR government shall be responsible for their management, added a proviso, 'except for the private land recognized as

[62] Ghai (14) 184, 189.

such according to the laws in force before the establishment of the Macao SAR' (Article 7).

Regarding the basic rights and duties of the residents, the Macao Basic Law and the Hong Kong Basic Law are essentially the same, but there are differences. First, perhaps thanks to drawing upon relevant provisions of the Portuguese Constitution, the Macao Basic Law's provisions on this subject were much better written: the rights and interests of women, minors, the aged and the disabled received special mention. Second, the interests, customs and cultural traditions of the residents of Portuguese descent were highlighted. Third, there is a major difference regarding the acquiring of permanent residence: Article 24(2) of the Macao Basic Law says that the children of Macao's permanent residents of Chinese nationality are Macao's permanent residents only if they are born after their parents have become Macao's permanent residents. The Hong Kong Basic Law did not mention the time of birth of these children, which was a defect remedied only by an interpretation from the NPCSC.

The chapter on the economy has the smallest percentage of overlap (ie 58 per cent) with its counterpart in the Hong Kong Basic Law, which is easy to understand: Hong Kong is an international financial centre, and a global shipping and aviation hub: it has a diverse and vibrant economy, whereas Macao's economy is overwhelmingly dependent upon tourism and recreation. The Hong Kong Basic Law has four sections and 31 articles on the economy, but there are only 18 articles on the economy in the Macao Basic Law. Inheriting Portugal's Continental legal tradition, Macao's legal system is different from Hong Kong's common law system.

The most important differences concern the future development of democracy in the two SARs,[63] especially relating to how the CE and the LegCo are produced. The basic arrangement regarding the selection of the CE is the same for both: the CE shall be selected by election or through consultations held locally and be appointed by the Central People's Government. However, Article 45(2) of the Hong Kong Basic Law adds that

> the method for selecting the CE shall be specified in the light of the actual situation in the HKSAR and in accordance with the principle of gradual and orderly progress. The ultimate aim is the selection of the CE by universals suffrage upon nomination by a broadly representative nominating committee in accordance with democratic procedures.

There is no such aim in the Macao Basic Law. Similarly, regarding the constitution of the LegCo, Article 68 of the Macao Basic Law says that 'the majority of its members shall be elected', which means that some of its members will be appointed by the CE. In contrast, Article 68 of the Hong Kong Basic Law provides that the LegCo of the HKSAR shall be constituted by election, and

[63] ibid 191–93.

then it stipulates the ultimate aim of the election of all its members by universal suffrage.

Due to the disagreements and distrust between the Hong Kong democrats and Beijing, nobody knows when this ultimate aim will be achieved, although 23 years have passed since the handover. However, the absence of the aim of ultimate suffrage shows that the enthusiasm and forces for democracy in Macao were negligible, compared with the general passion and strong forces for democracy in Hong Kong.[64] The Organic Statute of Macao allowed direct election of the members of the Legislative Assembly in 1976, far ahead of Hong Kong, but the election then was mainly a game between the Portuguese and the Macanese, and the majority Chinese were not interested in it, and therefore did not get involved. With the return of Macao to China, the Portuguese and the Macanese united into one force, who might have wanted more democracy but were a tiny minority in Macao.

E. The Question of Democracy

Since the mid-1980s, Chinese Macao residents have gradually dominated the elections (both direct and indirect) of the legislature. Currently, 14 seats are directly elected, 12 indirectly elected (by social sectors) and 7 appointed by the CE. Within the LegCo, business sectors are excessively represented. The CE is elected by an Election Committee of 400 members: among them, 120 are from industrial, commercial and financial sectors; 115 from cultural, educational sectors and other professions; and 115 from labour, social services, religious and other sectors. For the first election committee in 1999, the candidates were more than the legally required number of the Committee members. For the third one in 2009, the number of the candidates was the same as the latter. There were two candidates for the CE election in 1999; and since then there has been one candidate for the CE election: every time, the CE was elected with over 95 per cent of the votes.[65] There have occasionally been campaigns or protests for democracy in Macao. An anti-corruption demonstration in 2007 saw hundreds of people take to the streets.[66] The year 2014 saw thousands of people taking to the streets to protest against a government bill granting lavish retirement packages to top officials. Cao Qizhen, who had been Chairwoman of the LegCo for 10 years, said that the LegCo was incapable of carrying out effective supervision over the government.[67] However, Stanley Ho, Macao's casino tycoon and billionaire,

[64] ibid 192.

[65] See Zhidong Hao (n 54) 46–47.

[66] 'Protesters demand Macau democracy' (20 December 2007) at http://news.bbc.co.uk/2/hi/asia-pacific/7153771.stm, accessed 18 November 2020.

[67] Cao Qizhen (曹其真), 'A Review of My Ten Years as Chairman of the LegCo' （立法会主席十年工作的总结报告） at www.al.gov.mo/uploads/attachment/2016-12/26900584690d4e22d7.pdf, accessed 18 November 2020.

disagreed with the pro-democracy activists, arguing that 'Macau is democratic and free enough ... It is prosperous enough. Why do people need to do this (that is, protesting for democracy)?'[68] This shows that perhaps there are two radically different types of understanding of democracy in the Macao society: Ho's democracy versus Cao's democracy.

IV. A SUMMARY

Macao's constitutional founding was a process lasting for about 15 years, from 1984, when China decided to apply the Hong Kong model to Macao, until the handover in 1999. For China, the question of Macao was essentially the same as the question of Hong Kong: it was a question that the socialist China inherited from its humiliating modern history. As the result of unequal treaties, China was forced to give up the exercise of sovereignty over Hong Kong and Macao, and both territories had flourished under capitalism. Essentially the same question called for essentially the same solution. China determined to resume its exercise of sovereignty, and at the same time maintain the stability and prosperity of Hong Kong and Macao. China's solution was OCTS: Macao and Hong Kong would be local regions of China, with a high degree of autonomy. The questions of Macao and Hong Kong were part of China's internal affairs, but with a strong international dimension. China needed the cooperation of the UK and Portugal. The different attitudes and strategies of the UK and Portugal led to some differences in the solutions. Since Portugal and China had no disagreement on the sovereignty over Macao, since Portugal did not have such strong bargaining ability as the UK, and since the Macao society was not as plural, diverse, and democratic and politically active as that of Hong Kong, the resolution of the question of Macao was much easier, and more dominated by China's will, than the resolution of the question of Hong Kong. As a result of the UK's pre-handover efforts at democratisation and the enthusiasm of the Hong Kong society for democracy, China promised universal suffrage in due course to Hong Kongers. However, due to the similarities in the political arrangements in pre-handover Macao and Hong Kong, China designed an executive-led system for both.

It has been suggested that 'the preoccupation with the Hong Kong model perhaps meant that insufficient consideration was given to the specific historical and contemporary circumstances of Macao'.[69] There is perhaps some truth in this suggestion, which is at least supported by the fact that the two Basic Laws seem to play very different roles in both societies: a more political role in Macao versus a more legal role in Hong Kong.

In the society of Hong Kong, nearly all major problems have been formulated as or transformed into debates of the Basic Law in the courts; debates on

[68] 'Protesters demand Macau democracy' (n 66).
[69] Ghai (n 14) 184.

the application and meanings of the Basic Law are constant and frequently very intense, and have an immediate and important impact on people's everyday lives. The actions of the CE, the government, the LegCo, even of the central authorities, are frequently tested and evaluated against the Basic Law in the courts. As Chen and Ng have pointed out, the Basic Law

> not only provides the legal foundation of the HKSAR and defines its relationship with the Chinese central Government; once enacted in 1990, it also paved the way for post-1997 developments in Hong Kong in political, legal, social, economic and other domains. Most of the major incidents and controversies in the history of the HKSAR so far can be traced back to concepts, principles or provisions in the Basic Law.[70]

However, the Macao Basic Law operates in a very different way. Macao's authorities are structured according to the Basic law. There are many events and activities every year teaching and publicising the Basic Law, emphasising the greatness, wisdom and importance of the Basic Law. However, it is rarer in Macao than in Hong Kong that the Basic Law works as a ground for people's rights claims, and for people's legal challenges against the arrangements of the central authorities. In contrast to Hong Kong, which continues to hanker after the freedoms it enjoyed under the British, Macao has always respected the decisions or arrangements of the central authorities, and has been hailed by the central Government as a successful example of OCTS.

[70] See ch 3 of this book by Albert Chen and Michael Ng.

5

The Birth of the Constitution of the Republic of China

CHIEN-CHIH LIN

INTRODUCTION

IF THE ENACTMENT of a constitution can be likened to the conception, gestation, birth and growth of a human being then the experience of the Constitution of the Republic of China (ROC) has been rather miserable. In what should have been its years of growth and development, it was under threat from confinement. Not until it was well into its fifties was it sincerely accepted and welcomed. Still, its legitimacy is questioned by some and there are still attempts to ostracise it.

This chapter fleshes out the fraught gestation and life of the ROC Constitution from its birth in mainland China to its later move to Taiwan. In particular, I will introduce two supreme laws in the ROC after the Nationalist Party (Kuomintang or KMT, known as GMD in China) had formally unified China in 1928:[1] the Provisional Constitution of the Political Tutelage Period, and the ROC Constitution. The former had considerably affected the contents of two draft constitutions that ultimately became the ROC Constitution after a constellation of negotiations and compromises.

With a population of 23 million people, Taiwan is a developed economy and fully-fledged liberal democracy in East Asia. Officially known as 'the Republic of China (ROC)', but normally referred to as 'Taiwan', its sovereign status is

[1] It should be emphasised at the outset that many competing constitutional thoughts and constitutional movements, which are beyond the scope of this chapter, had surfaced since the late Qing Dynasty. For instance, some prominent intellectuals had proposed a constitutional monarchy, while others advocated republicanism. See Guido Mühlemann, 'China and Constitutional Monarchy: Four Short Encounters Around 1900' in Antje Flüchter and Susan Richter (eds), *Structures on the Move Technologies of Governance in Transcultural Encounter* (Springer, 2012) 105, 115–22. After the demise of Yuan Shikai in 1916, however, the call for a constitutional monarchy in the ROC had essentially dissipated. Moreover, there were debates on the choice between a unitary system, a federal one and, arguably, a confederate state. Unsurprisingly, the last two options were off the table after the KMT unified the ROC in 1928 and launched its own constitution-making project. Therefore, the discussion in this chapter will inevitably be KMT-centric to some extent.

contested by the People's Republic of China (PRC). Since 1971, it has not been a member state of the United Nations.

The ROC Constitution, enacted in Nanjing, China in 1946, is the apex law in Taiwan.[2] Having been amended seven times, the main text of the ROC Constitution comprises 175 articles and amendments of 12 articles. Even though it was suspended from 1948 to 1991, the Constitution has never been replaced and remains one of the most enduring constitutions in Asia.[3] Paradoxically, even though it is the first permanent modern constitution in Chinese history – there have been numerous provisional constitutions – it functions and thrives *only* in Taiwan and not in mainland China. To some in Taiwan, it is a political totem that symbolises the ROC as the legitimate Chinese Government.[4] To others, it is 'an instrument of annexation'[5] that should be repealed whenever possible.

The ROC Constitution is paradoxical in many ways. During its drafting process, it drew from the 1936 Stalin Constitution, the Weimar Constitution and the American Constitution.[6] Although the KMT controlled a supermajority of seats in the Constituent Assembly, the most important framer of the ROC Constitution was the leader of a minor party. To explain these paradoxes, this chapter will consider the apparently disparate threads of law, history and politics.

Before the ROC Constitution took effect, the Provisional Constitution of the Political Tutelage Period (1931–47) was the Basic Law in China. As its name suggests, it was meant to be temporary and transitional. In 1932, the KMT commenced the constitution-making process, knowing that the Provisional Constitution could not be the supreme law of China for too long. Indeed, constitution-making is a project the KMT had long wanted to launch to fulfil the political agenda of the KMT President and ROC founder, Sun Yat-sen. Therefore, immediately after the promulgation of the Provisional Constitution, the KMT started working on the drafts of the ROC Constitution. The ROC Constitution is partly drawn from the May Fifth Draft Constitution (1936) and partly from the Political Consultative Conference Draft Constitution (1946). The former was single-handedly put together by the KMT, while the latter was a collaborative effort between several and even mutually antagonistic parties, including the Chinese Communist Party (CCP). Both drafts have virtues and

[2] The Constitution of the Republic of China (Taiwan) (1947) at https://english.president.gov.tw/Page/93.

[3] Wen-chen Chang et al (eds), *Constitutionalism in Asia: Cases and Materials* (Hart Publishing, 2014).

[4] Jiunn-rong Yeh, *The Constitution of Taiwan: A Contextual Analysis* (Hart Publishing, 2016) 5; Chien-Chih Lin, 'Constitutions and courts in Chinese authoritarian regimes: China and pre-democratic Taiwan in comparison' (2016) 14 *International Journal of Constitutional Law* 351.

[5] Jiunn-Rong Yeh and Wen-Chen Chang, 'The Emergence of East Asian Constitutionalism: Features in Comparison' (2011) 59 *The American Journal of Comparative Law* 805, 820.

[6] Wen-Chen Chang, 'Comparative Discourse in Constitution-Making: An Analysis on Constitutional Framers as Dialectic Agent' in Chang-fa Lo et al (eds), *Legal Thoughts between the East and the West in the Multilevel Legal Order* (Springer, 2016) 95.

vices peculiar to them. In the process of constitution-making, both domestic power struggles and foreign constitutional jurisprudence shaped the contour of the ROC Constitution. Despite the acrimonious disagreements and strife in the Constituent Assembly, some issues the framers considered to be of prime importance eventually turned out to be constitutionally trivial. In contrast, other issues to which the framers paid less attention sowed the seeds for future constitutional change, precipitating constitutional court decisions, leading at times to constitutional amendments. These constitutional changes encapsulate the political cataclysm – such as the changes in political conditions, national identity and the governmental system – after 1949 when the ROC retreated to Taiwan.

I. THE ROC CONSTITUTION AND THE DRAFT CONSTITUTIONS

A. The Provisional Constitution of the Political Tutelage Period

The collapse of the Qing Dynasty (1911) at the hands of revolutionaries – who organised themselves into the KMT later – led to the establishment of the ROC in 1912. With this, there was an immediate call for a modern and progressive constitution to be constructed. During this period, many draft constitutions were attempted and circulated.[7] For example, Wang Chung-hui, the first Chinese to receive a doctorate from Yale Law School and an eminent jurist in China, penned a draft constitution in 1913. Nonetheless, the constitution-making project was curtailed and suspended because of political instability and fragmentation of central authority following the death of Yuan Shikai in 1916. In this light, most of the draft constitutions were neither fully developed, nor considered for adoption.

After Marshal Chang Hsueh-liang surrendered at the end of the Northern Expedition, the KMT-led political unification of China was completed in 1928. With this, the ROC entered a period of 'Political Tutelage.' This was in line with Sun Yat-sen's (1866–1925) vision of a three-stage political journey for China – the military stage, the political tutelage stage, and the constitutional stage.[8] To Sun, this was essential, because a stable democracy could not be established overnight in a country with two millennia of dynastic rule and no democratic tradition to speak of. 'Political Tutelage' was thus necessary for constitutionalism to take root and flourish in China.

[7] Charles Gamba, 'Constitution-Making in China' (1950) 1 *University of Western Australia Law Review* 409, 424; Jerome Alan Cohen, 'China's Changing Constitution' (1978) *China Quarterly* 794, 795–96; Note, 'Dr Wu's Constitution' (2019) 132 *Harvard Law Review* 2300, 2305–07. See also ch 2 by Humphrey Ko in this volume.

[8] Audrey Wells, *The Political Thought of Sun Yat-sen: Development and Impact* (Palgrave, 2001) 54–55.

Guided by this vision, Generalissimo Chiang Kai-shek proposed that a constitution be drafted in accordance with Sun's last wishes. After Wang Chung-hui prepared the draft,[9] the seven-day People's Convention was convened on 5 May 1931. Five hundred delegates from every province, and also Mongolia and Tibet, attended this Convention.[10] As a Japanese colony, Taiwan did not attend the conference. On 12 May 1931, the Provisional Constitution of the Political Tutelage Period was eventually ratified. It took effect on 1 June 1931 and became China's supreme law, until the promulgation of the ROC Constitution on 1 January 1947.

The Provisional Constitution comprised a preamble and eight chapters. The preamble stated that the Provisional Constitution was enacted so that 'the realization of constitutional government may be accelerated and political power restored to a popularly elected government'.[11] Subsequently, many articles in the Provisional Constitution–such as the bill of rights and the provisions regarding people's livelihood, education and labour protection–were transplanted to draft constitutions in future.

The embedding of basic rights aside, the Provisional Constitution was repugnant to modern constitutionalism from many perspectives. For instance, Article 30 stated that 'during the period of political tutelage, the National Congress of Kuomintang delegates shall exercise the governing powers on behalf of the National People's Congress'.[12] Furthermore, Article 85 stipulated that 'the power of interpretation of this [Constitution] shall be exercised by the Central Executive Committee of the Kuomintang of China'.[13] In other words, the KMT monopolised all political powers. There were no checks and balances. From this perspective, the Provisional Constitution was enacted to layer the KMT's absolute political power with a veneer of constitutional legitimacy. Though the Political Tutelage stage was intended to last for six years, it only ended 16 years later when the ROC Constitution was formally passed. In the move from the political tutelage to constitutional governance, two draft constitutions were particularly noteworthy – the May Fifth Draft Constitution and the Political Consultative Conference Draft Constitution.

B. The May Fifth Draft Constitution

To prepare for the transition from 'Political Tutelage' to constitutional rule, a permanent constitution had to be drafted and enacted. The impetus for this

[9] Pan Wei-Tung, *The Chinese Constitution: A Study of Forty Years of Constitution-making in China* (Catholic University of America Press, 1945) 48.

[10] See John A Fairlie, 'Constitutional Developments in China' (1931) 25 *American Political Science Review* 1016, 1016–17.

[11] CL Hsia, 'China's People's Convention: National Constitution and Ten-Year Plan' (1931) 4 *Pacific Affairs* 779, 793.

[12] ibid 794.

[13] ibid 798.

came from Sun Fo, son of Sun Yat-sen, at the third plenary session of the fourth Central Executive Committee of the KMT in 1932.[14] Following his proposal, he convened and chaired a constitution-drafting committee. The next year, 1933, John Jingxiong Wu, one of the vice chairmen, prepared the first tentative draft. A year later, after further revisions in the light of feedback received, it was released to gather public opinion.[15] The draft was approved by the Legislative Yuan after three readings and became the Legislative Yuan Revised Draft.

On one hand, this was a progressive draft, as it provided extensive protection for rights. It had a bill of rights that extended beyond civil and political rights to cover social and economic rights. It obliged the Government to pay special attention to the rights of labourers, farmers and children. These reflected the influence of the Provisional Constitution. In terms of the separation of powers, on the other hand, it reflected Sun Yat-sen's political legacy,[16] including his five-power constitutional theory. This reflected his borrowing from imperial Chinese systems, and resulted in the creation of the Control Yuan and Examination Yuan.[17] Both branches were founded on the Confucian theory of good governance.[18] On top of the five Yuans, this draft established the National Assembly, which resembled the All-Russian Congress of Soviets.[19] It was also characterised by a strong legislative branch vis-à-vis a weak executive branch.[20]

The Legislative Yuan Revised Draft was transmitted to the Central Executive Committee of the KMT for endorsement. The KMT, however, was not satisfied with this version. In particular, it took issue with the clauses regarding central government structure, because they constrained the executive power, then in the hands of the KMT, excessively.[21] Further revisions ensued, and it was accepted and promulgated by the Government on 5 May 1936. Known as the May Fifth Draft Constitution, it provided for a strong presidency in line with the wishes of the KMT. To ratify this draft, the Government had held elections to elect

[14] CL Hsia, *Background and Features of the Draft Constitution of China* (Nanking, Council of International Affairs 1937) 195, 200.

[15] ibid 201.

[16] Herbert HP Ma, 'American Influence on the Formation of the Constitution and Constitutional Law of the Republic of China: Past History and Future Prospects' in Lawrence Ward Beer (ed), *Constitutionalism in Asia: Asian Views of the American Influence* (University of California Press, 1979) 35, 44–45.

[17] Roughly speaking, the Examination Yuan aims to enhance the impartiality and quality of the civil service system, while the Control Yuan, modelled on the imperial Censorate, is functionally equivalent to ombudsmen. See Ernest Caldwell, 'Widening the Constitutional Gap in China and Taiwan' (2017) *University of Illinois Law Review* 739, 746–47.

[18] Baogang He, 'Confucianism and Democracy' (2016) 12 *Taiwan Journal of Democracy* 59, 72–73; Arthur N Holcombe, 'Chinese Political Thought and the Proposed New Constitution' (1946) 8 *Journal of Politics* 1, 12–15.

[19] Hsia (n 14) 208–09; Woodbridge Bingham, 'Review: The Chinese Constitution: A Study of Forty Years of Constitution-Making in China by Pan Wei-Tung' (1946) 14 *University of Chicago Law Review* 146, 147.

[20] Lloyd E Eastman, *The Abortive Revolution: China under Nationalist Rule, 1927–1937* (Harvard University Press, 1990) 167.

[21] ibid 176.

representatives of the Constituent Assembly in early 1937, in preparation for its convening in November 1937. The outbreak of the Second Sino-Japanese War on 7 July 1937 effectively put the constitution-making plan on hold. For the next eight years, China would be embroiled in a conflict that eventually become the Second World War. Despite being extensively revised later, the May Fifth Draft Constitution was highly influential in determining the structure of the final ROC Constitution.

C. The Political Consultative Conference Draft Constitution

Although the May Fifth Draft Constitution never passed, it served as the prototype for the next draft constitution. After the Japanese surrender in August 1945, open warfare soon broke out between the KMT and the CCP. The American President, Harry S Truman, soon sent Secretary of State, George C Marshall, to lead the Marshall Mission to negotiate a settlement between the two sides.[22] In a rare show of comity, the KMT and the CCP agreed to convene a cross-party committee to discuss post-war national affairs such as democratisation, the formation of a united government, general elections and the nationalisation of the military.

On 10 January 1946, the KMT, the CCP and smaller political parties gathered in Chongqing to hold the Political Consultative Conference, chaired by Lei Chen who served as its Secretary General. In all, there were 38 participants – eight from the KMT, seven from the CCP, five from the Chinese Youth Party, nine from the China Democratic League and nine independents – who represented the Chinese political mainstream. While the China Democratic League was generally sympathetic to the CCP, most of the independents were selected by the KMT. These participants were divided into five panels looking, amongst other issues, into government structures, policy guidelines, the military, the national assembly and, most importantly, the draft constitution.[23] Each panel included representatives of different parties.

Sun Fo, whose proposal in 1932 gave birth to the May Fifth Draft Constitution, was the KMT representative on the draft constitution panel. The panel used the May Fifth Draft Constitution as the blueprint and submitted 12 principles regarding how the future Constitution should be refined.[24] These 12 principles outlined the structures of the National Assembly, the five Yuans, the Presidency,

[22] US Department of State, *United States Relations with China: With special reference to the period 1944–1949* (US Government Printing Office, 1949) 132–36; Daniel Kurtz-Phelan, *The China Mission* (Norton, 2018) 50–98.

[23] ibid 138.

[24] Compilation Commission of the Record of the National Assembly, *Record of the National Assembly* (Secretariat of National Assembly 1946) 278–81(in Chinese).

local autonomy, rights and duties of the people, guidelines for fundamental national policies, and the process and the power to amend the Constitution.[25] To revise the draft constitution according to these principles, the panel also suggested convening another committee comprising 35 members. This would be made up of five representatives from each party and 10 constitutional experts.[26]

These 12 principles thoroughly rewrote the May Fifth Draft Constitution. The National Assembly was significantly remodelled and its new institutional structure had deviated from Sun Yat-sen's original plan. Many of its powers, enshrined in the May Fifth Draft Constitution, such as the power to elect and impeach the President, the Presidents of different Yuans and legislators, and the power of initiative and referendum, were transferred to other branches.[27] In contrast, legislative power was expanded and legislators would be generated through popular election. Furthermore, the Judicial Yuan became the apex court in China instead of serving as a judicial administrative agency. Moreover, the 12 principles emphasised the independence and impartiality of judges – this was significant as the KMT had politicised the judiciary extensively in the Political Tutelage era. Most importantly, the central governmental structure was changed from presidentialism to a parliamentary system.[28] Previously, the Executive Yuan was accountable to the President, but it now answered to the Legislative Yuan instead. The Presidency would be akin to a nominal head of state as its power had shrunk greatly. Finally, the principles provided for federalism in the sense that each province should enact its own constitution.[29] Provincial governors would be elected directly by the people. This was a marked departure from the centralisation of power preferred by the KMT. Hence, if fully implemented, the 12 principles would produce a brand-new Constitution that had diverged remarkably from Sun Yat-sen's political theory.

After the Political Consultative Conference, a committee to draft a constitution was formed immediately. Chaired by Sun Fo, this committee included Carsun Chang (Chang Chun-mai) of the China Democratic League. Chang was instrumental in drafting the ROC Constitution. Originally, the committee had recommended seven persons to be the framers of the Constitution, who included, inter alia, Sun Fo, Wang Chung-hui, John Wu, Carsun Chang, Zhou Enlai (who later became the first Premier of the PRC) and others. Eventually,

[25] For a detailed content of the 12 principles, see Mou Quan-Ji, *The Compilation of Materials Concerning the Constitution-Making in China* (Academia Historia Office, 1989) 591–94 (in Chinese).

[26] For a full list of these 35 members, see Lee Ben-Nan, *The Political Consultation Conference and the KMT-CCP Negotiations* (Yong Ye Publishing, 1993) 309 (in Chinese).

[27] Mou (n 25).

[28] ibid. It should be emphasised that both draft constitutions adopted a hybrid system that could not be perfectly categorised as either 'presidentialism' or 'parliamentary system'. The difference was that the May Fifth Draft Constitution included more elements of presidentialism, while the Political Consultative Conference Draft Constitution had more features of a parliamentary system.

[29] ibid.

Carsun Chang singlehandedly drafted the Constitution, given his knowledge about constitutional theory and foreign constitutional jurisprudence and his willingness to do so.[30] It certainly helped that Chang represented a minority party, making him acceptable to both the KMT and the CCP. Two other constitutional experts, Wang Chung-Hui and John Wu, also sat on this committee. But they were, given their KMT affiliations, reluctant to draft a constitution on the basis of the 12 principles that substantially changed the May Fifth Draft Constitution preferred by the KMT.

In February 1946, Chang quickly submitted a draft for discussion. In response, there were comprehensive and robust debates on the institutional design of the National Assembly, the central government system and local self-government. It is notable that in these debates, the constitutional theories and designs of the United States, the United Kingdom, Germany and France were invoked and compared. Responses were polarised. The CCP and the minority parties welcomed the draft because it curtailed the powers of the Presidency and the central Government in favour of the parliamentary system and federalism. In contrast, the KMT was infuriated by this and provoked into vehemently attacking the draft and demanding revisions. Eventually, both sides relented and concessions were made. The Political Consultative Conference Draft Constitution was penned in April 1946, notwithstanding that the CCP had made some critical reservations.[31] It was eventually submitted to the Legislative Yuan for approval in November 1946, after its wording was finessed further by Wang Chung-hui, John Wu and Lei Chen. The trio did not make substantive changes and the final product was faithful to the version penned by Carsun Chang.

To ratify the Draft Constitution, the Government revised and promulgated the National Assembly Organization Act and the Supplemental Act for the National Assembly Election in November 1946 to elect representatives of the National Assembly. According to the Acts, the would be 2,050 seats in the Constituent Assembly. Of these, 1,200 were allocated to regional and occupational representatives (such as those of workers or businessmen), 700 to representatives of political parties and independents, and 150 to Taiwan and the northeast part of China,[32] which had been ceded to or occupied by the Empire of Japan before the Second World War. Of the 700 seats, 220 went to the KMT, 190 to the CCP, 120 to the China Democratic League, 100 to the China Youth Party and 70 to independents. All participating parties ostensibly agreed to this allocation of seats.

[30] Lei Chen, *History of Constitution-making of the Republic of China* (Daw Shiang Publishing, 2010) 105–08 (in Chinese).

[31] ibid 325–27.

[32] After the end of the Second World War, the ROC reclaimed Taiwan, which was ceded by the Qing Dynasty to the Empire of Japan in 1895 in the Treaty of Shimonoseki after Japan's victory in the First Sino-Japanese War.

Table 5.1 The Composition of the Constituent Assembly

Category	**Designated Number**	**Registered**	**Absent**
KMT appointees	220	216	4
CCP appointees	190	0	190
China Youth Party appointees	100	99	1
China Democratic League appointees	80	0	80
Social Democrat (split from China Democratic League) appointees	40	39	1
Independent	70	64	6
Regional Election	770	735	35
Occupational Election	437	406	31
Special Election[33]	143	142	1
Total	2,050	1,701	349

Source: Ching, Chih-jen, *History of China's Constitution-Making* (Linking Publishing, 1984) 452–53.

As mentioned previously, the KMT Government had already held elections to the National Assembly in most provinces in 1937. Although the elections were suspended because of the outbreak of war, most provinces had already elected their representatives. For the few provinces and municipalities that had failed to elect their representatives in time, the KMT Government had appointed representatives to fill these vacancies.[34] Whether these representatives should all be subject to fresh elections became a matter of controversy in 1946. The opposition parties contended that they should be freshly elected. Having been elected a decade ago, they no longer represented their constituencies legitimately. Some of these representatives were KMT appointees and not elected. The election itself was in question – corruption, bribery, vote-buying and other electoral shenanigans were rampant because most Chinese people were extremely poor and ignorant, if not illiterate. They could not care less about elections, let alone constitution-making, and hence the voter turnout was low.[35] Moreover, the household registration system had not been fully founded and properly maintained. In many places, local officials simply made up the number of people in

[33] Special elections were held to elect representatives in certain circumstances, such as in Mongolia and Tibet, for overseas Chinese and for those in the military.

[34] Yuxian Lang and Wen-Chun Chen, *History of the Elections in the Republic of China* (Central Election Commission, 1987) 230–31 (in Chinese).

[35] Chang Peng-yuan, *The Dilemma of Chinese Democracy 1909–1949: Legislative Elections Since the Late Qing* (Linking Publishing, 2007) 178–89 (in Chinese).

their jurisdictions.[36] As a result, the democratic legitimacy of these representatives was seriously questioned.[37]

Moreover, parties in the Political Consultative Conference had agreed to form a cross-party united Government. In this regard, the CCP and its ally, the China Democratic League, insisted that they should occupy at least one-third of the seats – this would give them a power of veto over major policies.[38] Predictably, the KMT refused to compromise on this. This political stalemate paralleled the protracted armed conflict between the KMT and the CCP. Consequently, the KMT decided to hold the Constituent Assembly without the participation of the CCP. In response, the CCP and most members of the China Democratic League refused to participate in the Constituent Assembly and, by extension, the making of the Constitution.[39] Eventually, only 1,701 out of 2,050 representatives (roughly 80 per cent) were present in Nanjing, most of them having been elected before the second Sino-Japanese War in 1937. Given that most representatives were members of the KMT (Nationalist Party) or its satellite parties, the National Assembly was ridiculed as a 'Nationalist Assembly'.[40] It is not without irony that despite its boycott of the Constituent Assembly, the CCP actually consulted the ROC Constitution when it wrote the first PRC Constitution in 1954.[41]

Some statistics should be mentioned. Only 80 representatives out of the 1,701 (4.7 per cent) were female.[42] Most representatives were in their forties and fifties.[43] Representatives from the southern provinces, which were under the firm control of the KMT, formed the majority in the Constituent Assembly.[44] Finally, there were 18 representatives that came from what was then Taiwan Province.

D. The Constitution of the Republic of China

To enact the ROC Constitution, the Constituent Assembly was convened on 15 November 1946. Procedurally, the constitution-making process took place over four phases: the preparation stage, general discussions, panel discussions and the readings.

In the first stage, Sun Fo, President of the Legislative Yuan, chaired all four preparation meetings that focused on the procedural issues of the Constituent

[36] ibid 171–72.

[37] Shin-Min Chen, *Constitutional Jurisprudence* (self-published, 2015) 41 (in Chinese); but see Wang Yun-wu, *Hsiulu Lun Kuoshih* (Commercial Press, 1965) 177 (in Chinese).

[38] Chen Chih-Mai, 'The Post-War Government of China' (1947) 9 *The Journal of Politics* 503, 510.

[39] ibid 506.

[40] Qianfan Zhang, *The Constitution of China: A Contextual Analysis* (Hart Publishing, 2012) 33.

[41] See Glenn D Tiffert, 'Epistrophy: Chinese Constitutionalism and the 1950s' in Stéphanie Balme and Michael W Dowdle (eds), *Building Constitutionalism in China* (Palgrave Macmillan, 2009) 67.

[42] Lang and Chen (n 34) 238–39.

[43] ibid 240.

[44] ibid 241.

Assembly, including the election of chairmen. On 25 November 1946, the general discussions commenced when Chiang Kai-shek, head of the KMT Government, formally proposed the draft constitution to the Constituent Assembly. Sun Fo then presented and made clear the contents of the draft constitution to the entire Constituent Assembly, focusing specifically on the difference between the final draft and the May Fifth Draft Constitution.[45] Held over nine sessions from 25 November to 5 December 1946, the purpose of the general discussions was to collect questions, comments and suggestions for revisions.

On 5 December, the Constituent Assembly decided to begin the panel discussions. In all, nine panels discussed different chapters of the draft constitution. In their deliberations, they took into consideration the views collected from the general discussions. Panel I discussed Chapter 1 of the draft constitution, which stipulated the general provisions. Beyond the issues of citizenship, territory, the national flag and the capital city, this chapter recognised Sun Yat-sen's 'Three Principles of the People' as fundamental or bedrock principles of the constitution. Panel I also looked into Chapter 2, which protected fundamental rights, such as equality, freedom of expression, freedom of religious belief, the right to work, due process of law and property, among other things. On top of these rights, there was a catch-all clause that protected unenumerated rights. It also stipulated the duty of performing military service. Panel II discussed the chapter regarding the National Assembly and the implementation of the Constitution after ratification. This was particularly controversial, because the structure of the National Assembly in the Political Consultative Conference Draft Constitution, preferred by other small parties, was significantly different from that in the May Fifth Draft Constitution preferred by the KMT. Panel III discussed the power of the executive, including the President and the Executive Yuan, and the power of the legislature. The debate in this panel was robust as well, because the KMT preferred the presidentialism in the May Fifth Draft Constitution while other small parties preferred the parliamentary system in the final draft constitution. Panel IV discussed the other three branches of government, that is, the Judicial Yuan, the Examination Yuan and the Control Yuan. Panel V discussed the vertical separation of powers between the central Government and local governments. Panel VI discussed the institutional design of local governments, including both provinces and counties. Panel VII discussed fundamental national policies, such as national defence, foreign policy, economic policy, social security, and education and culture. Panel VIII discussed the special local governments in Mongolia and Tibet. The last Panel was responsible for an overall review and the final round of legal wordsmithing.[46]

The panel discussions lasted 11 days. After that, the panellists reported to the General Assembly, which completed the first reading of the draft constitution

[45] Compilation Commission (n 24) 392–99.
[46] ibid 400–01.

on 18 December 1946. After the first reading, however, a few controversial questions remained heatedly contested. Chairman Chiang Kai-shek personally explained the disputes and proposed compromise solutions at the beginning of the second reading. After he spoke, the Constituent Assembly began the second reading, clause by clause. Some clauses that passed the first reading, such as the location of the capital city, failed to survive the second reading on 24 December. The next day, on 25 December, the Constituent Assembly completed the third reading, and the Constitution of the ROC was born. It is not a coincidence that the Constitution was promulgated at Christmas. Being a devout Christian, Chiang had compared the protection of rights and freedoms by the Constitution to the blessings of Christianity.

Generally speaking, the newly-born ROC Constitution may be seen as a revolutionary constitution,[47] one that marked a clean break from the Qing Dynasty. The Constitution attempted to consolidate the achievements of the decades-long struggle, first against monarchical rule and then against warlord rule, by enshrining basic rights and entrenching the separation of powers. Both provisos were alien to China in its long past. More specifically, those rights extended beyond civil and political rights to cover socio-economic rights. And there was a catch-all clause that protected unenumerated fundamental rights, which could not be infringed upon without due process of law. Moreover, governing powers were to be exercised by five branches of equal standing: the Executive Yuan, the Legislative Yuan, the Judicial Yuan, the Control Yuan and the Examination Yuan. In addition, there was the National Assembly and a President. This intricate system of checks and balances was aimed at ensuring that there was no absolute power or personal ambition that could override any branch of government. The ruler's legitimacy came not from the mandate of heaven, but from the consent of the ordinary people.

Having said that, there was some institutional continuity with the past. The Control Yuan and the Examination Yuan are two paradigmatic examples. As mentioned in section I.B, Sun borrowed from imperial Chinese systems and created the two Yuans. Although he passed away long before the promulgation of the Constitution, his political legacies were inherited by the framers and entrenched in the Constitution.

II. CONSTITUTIONAL QUESTIONS CONSIDERED BY THE DRAFTERS AND THEIR AFTERMATH

As already discussed, many controversial questions had been intensively debated in the Constituent Assembly, partly because the KMT's ideal version differed considerably from that of minority parties. Since the framers discussed

[47] Bruce Ackerman, *Revolutionary Constitutions: Charismatic Leadership and the Rule of Law* (Belknap Press, 2019).

numerous issues in the Constituent Assembly, this section introduces some of the most important issues that continued to affect constitutional developments in Taiwan.[48] Some of them sowed the seed for future constitutional evolution, while others were unresolved for decades. In hindsight, some mundane issues turned out to be major issues later, while some fiercely contested questions turned out to be minor issues after the promulgation of the Constitution. The major issues include the political ideology of the nascent Constitution, the territory of the new republic after the Second World War, the structure and power of the National Assembly, the choice between presidentialism and the parliamentary system, the vertical separation of powers and the role of the Judicial Yuan.

A. Sun Yat-sen's Three Principles of the People

Sun Yat-sen was the founding father of the ROC and the first chairman of the KMT. Because of his unrivalled status in modern China, his political thought had a profound impact on the framework of the Constitution. In fact, his political thought, which combines traditional Chinese political philosophy and Western constitutional theory,[49] epitomises the formation of modern China and the ROC Constitution.

In honour of his contribution, the preamble to the Constitution states unequivocally that the ROC was established 'in accordance with the teachings bequeathed by Dr Sun Yat-sen'.[50] Whether or how to tightly weave his 'Three Principles of the People'[51] into the fabric of the Constitution was hotly debated in the Constituent Assembly. The Provisional Constitution provided that 'The Three Principles of the People shall be the basic principles of education in the Republic of China.'[52] Article 1 of the May Fifth Draft Constitution stated that 'The Republic of China was a republic of the Three Principles of the People.'[53] This was strongly opposed by other political parties in the Political Consultative Conference for various and antithetical reasons. Some believed it was too ideological and partisan to be enshrined in the Constitution, while others maintained that it was too vague. Eventually, Carsun Chang submitted a compromise version,

[48] Other examples not discussed in this chapter include eminent domain. See Yun-chien Chang, *Eminent Domain Compensation in Taiwan: Theory and Practice* (Angle, 2013) 22–36.

[49] Paul Myron Anthony Linebarger, *The Political Doctrines of Sun Yat-sen: An Exposition of the* Sun Min Chu I (Greenwood Press, 1973).

[50] Constitution of the Republic of China (Taiwan) (1947) at https://english.president.gov.tw/Page/94.

[51] The Three Principles refer to the Principle of Nationalism, the Principle of Democracy and the Principle of People's Livelihood. See Sun-Yat-sen, *The Three Principles of the People*, tr Frank W Price (China Publishing, 1981). For an introduction to the Three Principles, see Arthur N Holcombe, 'Political Thought and the Proposed New Constitution' (1946) 8 *The Journal of Politics* 1, 10–12.

[52] Hsia (n 11) 796.

[53] Compilation Commission (n 24) 242.

which stated that 'The Republic of China, founded on the Three Principles of the People, shall be a democratic republic of the people, to be governed by the people and for the people',[54] emphasising the democratic dimension of Sun's political thought. Although this formulation had substantially altered the meaning of the Three Principles, it was accepted by all participating parties, including the KMT and the CCP.

Nevertheless, in the Constituent Assembly, many KMT representatives proposed reinstating the phrasing of the May Fifth Draft Constitution. Some even wanted to make it explicit that the Three Principles of the People referred to were the Principle of Nationalism, the Principle of Democracy and the Principle of People's Livelihood.[55] Of course, these proposals were strongly objected to by representatives of minority parties and rejected. Eventually, Carsun Chung's formulation was adopted as Article 1 of the ROC Constitution.

Although this ideological clause was seriously debated in the constitution-making process, it did not receive much attention after democratisation in Taiwan. Nevertheless, it was invoked by the Government in a case that involved prior restraint on the freedom of expression in 1998. In Judicial Yuan Interpretation ('JY Interpretation') No 445 (1998), Article 4 of the Assembly and Parade Act prohibited any assembly or parade that advocated Communism or secession. Interestingly, the KMT Government argued that 'this provision is grounded on the finding that communism is by nature antithetical to the Three Principles of the People'.[56] Still, the Constitutional Court ruled against the Government on the grounds of the freedom of assembly and parade.

B. The Territory and the Capital of the Republic of China

One politically sensitive issue during the constitution-making process involved the capital and territory of the ROC. Nanjing was designated as the capital in the draft constitution because most KMT members, including Chiang Kai-shek, came from southern China. Indeed, Nanjing was already designated as the capital city in the Provisional Constitution. However, there were 23 proposals in the Constituent Assembly as to the location of the capital, and some even called for the creation of a second capital. Beijing (northern China, the capital of imperial China for 700 years), Xi'an (western China, the capital of imperial China for 500 years) and Wuhan (central China, where the Wuchang uprising that ultimately overthrew the Qing Dynasty began) were also nominated as possible locations of the capital. In the first reading, 700 representatives successfully

[54] Art 2 of the Constitution of the ROC (1947).

[55] Compilation Commission (n 24) 1039.

[56] JY Interpretation No 445 (1998) (Taiwan) [3] at http://cons.judicial.gov.tw/jcc/en-us/jep03/show?expno=445.

replaced Nanjing with Beijing as the capital because of historical and military concerns. However, Chiang Kai-shek insisted on Nanjing as the capital given the CCP's military preponderance in northwest and northeast China.[57] Eventually, the KMT compromised during the second reading and proposed not to specifically designate any city as capital in the Constitution. This was welcomed by the Constituent Assembly and the clause was subsequently deleted.

After the KMT lost the Chinese Civil War and retreated to Taiwan in 1949, the location of the ROC's capital became a politically embarrassing question. In 2013, while the KMT was the ruling Government, the Ministry of Education required that all textbooks for high schools, junior high schools and elementary schools name Nanjing – which had belonged to the PRC since 1949 – as the capital of the ROC in Taiwan.[58] The instruction, which was at once anachronistic and mirth-inducing, was heavily criticised by the opposition parties. Within a day, the Government withdrew the policy and apologised.[59]

As for the territorial issue, Article One of the Provisional Constitution stipulated that 'The territory of the Republic of China consists of the various provinces and Mongolia and Tibet.'[60] It stipulated that both Mongolia and Tibet were part of China, but did not spell out what the other provinces were. By contrast, the May Fifth Draft Constitution specified the territory of the ROC, enumerating each province the ROC controlled at that time, such as Jiangsu and Zhejiang, and including Mongolia and Tibet. Note that Taiwan was not included because it was a Japanese colony when the May Fifth Draft Constitution was published in 1936. This framing was rejected in the Political Consultative Conference Draft Constitution, which provided a general description that stipulated 'The territory of the Republic of China according to its existing national boundaries shall not be altered except by resolution of the National Assembly.' Eventually, the Constituent Assembly rejected enumerating the provinces and instead adopted the version in the Political Consultative Conference Draft Constitution. There were three reasons for this change. First, most constitutions in the world do not specify their territory. Second, it was too inflexible to enumerate every province in the Constitution. Using Mongolia and Taiwan as examples, Sun Fo explained to the representatives why enumeration was unfeasible:[61] the former achieved independence from China in 1921, while the latter was returned in 1945. Finally, and perhaps most interestingly, some representatives were aware of the fact that Hong Kong and Macau were

[57] Kuo Ting-Yee et al, *The Reminiscences of General Pai Chung-Hsi*, vol 2 (Institute of Modern History, Academia Sinica, 1984) 849–50.

[58] Chris Wang, 'Schools to teach Nanjing is ROC capital: ministry' *Taipei Times* (4 December 2013) at www.taipeitimes.com/News/front/archives/2013/12/04/2003578264?fb_comment_id=1395403210703608_37979.

[59] Staff writer, with CNA, 'Interior minister reaffirms Taipei is ROC's capital' *Taipei Times* (5 December 2013) at www.taipeitimes.com/News/taiwan/archives/2013/12/05/2003578356.

[60] Hsia (n 11) 793.

[61] Compilation Commission (n 24).

still administered by the United Kingdom and Portugal in 1946.[62] It would take another 50 years or so for China to reclaim these territories. Therefore, it would be awkward to either include or exclude the two territories in the Constitution.

In hindsight, this was an astute and practical move. Still, this unexpectedly resulted in another constitutional decision in 1993. At that time, the ROC had already moved to Taiwan and controlled only Taiwan and its neighbouring islets. Although the constitutional amendments separated the mainland area (ie China, or PRC) from the liberal area (Taiwan), what constituted the territory of the ROC became a tricky question constitutionally. Many legislators of the opposition parties petitioned the Constitutional Court, requesting it to delineate the boundaries of the ROC's territory. The Justices of the Constitutional Court demurred, arguing in JY Interpretation No 328 (1993) that the boundary of the territory was a 'political question and thus it (was) beyond the reach of judicial review'.[63]

C. The National Assembly

The most contested provisions in the Constitution were those involving the structure and functions of the National Assembly. As mentioned in section I.B, the institutional design of the National Assembly was derived from Sun Yat-sen's political thought, to which the CCP and minority parties were vehemently opposed. In the May Fifth Draft Constitution, the National Assembly was much more powerful. It had the power to elect/recall the President, Vice President, Presidents of the Legislative Yuan and the Control Yuan, legislators and members of the Control Yuan, amongst other things. Representatives of the National Assembly were to be elected from each county and there would be around 2,500 representatives. However, in the draft Constitution, the power to elect/recall Presidents of the Legislative Yuan and the Control Yuan and their members was removed. Moreover, it provided that these representatives should be elected from among the legislators and members of the Control Yuan – this was because the CCP and other small parties wanted to restrict the scale of central government.[64] In fact, this was already a compromise, because they argued the National Assembly should be abolished entirely![65]

In the Constituent Assembly, these two points – the function and the organization of the National Assembly – were heavily disputed. In terms of its function, many representatives complained that under the draft Constitution,

[62] ibid 1215.

[63] JY Interpretation No 328 (1993) (Taiwan), available at http://cons.judicial.gov.tw/jcc/en-us/jep03/show?expno=328.

[64] Lei (n 30) 158.

[65] ibid 157.

the National Assembly was too weak, and there were 20 proposals calling for a more powerful National Assembly. In addition, some even suggested granting the National Assembly more powers. This included the power to interpret the Constitution,[66] to declare war and make peace,[67] to conclude treaties,[68] to issue bonds,[69] to elect/recall the President of the Judicial Yuan,[70] to decide the budget[71] and so on. These calls reflected the fundamentally different understanding and expectations for the National Assembly between the KMT – that accepted and espoused Sun Yat-sen's political thought – and the minority parties that rejected it.[72] Eventually, the minority parties prevailed and the institutional structure of the National Assembly generally followed the Political Consultative Conference model.

As to the organisation of the National Assembly, many proposals were advanced to restore the regulations contained in the May Fifth Draft Constitution. This was attained in the final version, which did not require the representatives of the National Assembly to be elected from the legislators and members of the Control Yuan. Nonetheless, it remained unclear whether legislators and members of the Control Yuan could serve simultaneously as representatives of the National Assembly. This constitutional puzzle led to two Constitutional Court decisions, JY Interpretation No 15 (1953)[73] and JY Interpretation No 30 (1954).[74] In both decisions, the Constitutional Court maintained that neither members of the Control Yuan nor legislators could serve as representatives of the National Assembly.

The existence of the National Assembly has engendered further constitutional crises. One of these was over the so-called 'old thieves',[75] referring to the first-term congressmen who were elected in China in November 1947 and then continued to exercise power in Taiwan until December 1991. This constitutional anomaly arose because of the ROC's geopolitical reality. After the ROC retreated to Taiwan in 1949, and in so doing lost 97 per cent of its territory, it was no longer possible for it to hold 'national elections' in mainland China. These first-term representatives were useful to symbolically justify the KMT's naive claim that the ROC was the only legitimate Chinese country in the world

[66] Compilation Commission (n 24) 819.
[67] ibid 804.
[68] ibid 862.
[69] ibid 862.
[70] ibid 1036.
[71] ibid 1051.
[72] Lei (n 30) 156–57.
[73] JY Interpretation No 15 (1953) (Taiwan), available at http://cons.judicial.gov.tw/jcc/en-us/jep03/show?expno=15.
[74] JY Interpretation No 30 (1954) (Taiwan) at http://cons.judicial.gov.tw/jcc/en-us/jep03/show?expno=30.
[75] Tom Ginsburg, 'Confucian Constitutionalism? The Emergence of Constitutional Review in Korea and Taiwan' (2002) 27 *Law & Social Inquiry* 763, 770.

because they were popularly elected from China.[76] In JY Interpretation No 261 (1990),[77] the Constitutional Court held that the KMT Government must hold fresh national elections for all representatives of the National Assembly to be re-elected in Taiwan.

Even though its democratic legitimacy was bolstered via popular election in Taiwan, the National Assembly remained problematic as it monopolised the power to amend the Constitution and did so to its own advantage.[78] The most notorious example of this was when the National Assembly prolonged its own term of office through the 1999 constitutional amendments. This constitutional rent-seeking infuriated most of the Taiwanese people, leading to the intervention of the Constitutional Court. In delivering JY Interpretation No 499 (2000),[79] the Court declared the 1999 constitutional amendments to be unconstitutional and void. To add to this political spectacle, a bipartisan consensus was reached in 2005 to completely abolish the National Assembly by way of a constitutional amendment.

In hindsight, the National Assembly created more constitutional problems than it solved. It would have been better to adhere to the 12 principles of the Political Consultative Conference and not to institutionalise the National Assembly at the very beginning.

D. Central Government Structure

One of the recurring questions for the framers of the ROC Constitution was whether a nascent republic should adopt presidentialism or a parliamentary system, given that most of its citizens were poor and illiterate. On one hand, given China's long monarchical tradition, a presidential system that concentrated all political power in the hands of one charismatic leader could easily result in the replacement of one autocratic system with another. On the other hand, given the above-mentioned chaos in electing the representatives of the National Assembly, it appears clear that Chinese society was not mature or sophisticated enough for a parliamentary system. Therefore, the structure of the central Government, as contained in the draft Constitutions, moved back and forth between these two models. The May Fifth Draft Constitution

[76] Jiunn-rong Yeh, 'The Cult of Fatung: Representational Manipulation and Reconstruction in Taiwan' in Graham Hassall and Cheryl Saunders (eds), *The People's Representatives: Electoral Systems in the Asia-Pacific Region* (Allen & Unwin, 1997) 23, 24–26.

[77] JY Interpretation No 261 (1990) (Taiwan) at http://cons.judicial.gov.tw/jcc/en-us/jep03/show?expno=261.

[78] Jiunn-rong Yeh, *Democratic Transition and Constitutional Change* (Angle, 2003) 131–34 (in Chinese).

[79] JY Interpretation No 499 (2000) (Taiwan) at http://cons.judicial.gov.tw/jcc/en-us/jep03/show?expno=499.

appeared to have adopted presidentialism because the Premier (President of the Executive Yuan) was accountable not to Congress but to the President, who had the unilateral power to appoint the Premier, President of the Judicial Yuan and the President of the Examination Yuan. It was widely believed that this draft adopted presidentialism because of Chiang Kai-shek's desire to monopolise political power. In opposition to Chiang's dictatorial desires, most participants in the Political Consultative Conference favoured a parliamentary system. In their draft Constitution, the Premier was accountable to the legislature, which could cast a vote of no confidence against the former. Furthermore, the President could appoint the Premier only with the consent of the legislature.

In the Constituent Assembly, some representatives proposed redefining the relationship between the executive and the legislative powers, expanding the former at the expense of the latter.[80] These proposals, however, did not garner a majority vote and the ROC Constitution retained many elements of a parliamentary system. The President could appoint the Premier but only with the consent of the legislature, with the latter serving as a check on the former. Unfortunately, Chiang Kai-shek promulgated the Temporary Provisions Effective During the Period of National Mobilisation for Suppression of the Communist Rebellion in 1948 – this dramatically expanded the President's emergency powers and effectively suspended the ROC Constitution. After this, the Temporary Provisions were amended several times, each amendment only expanding the presidential power further. These Temporary Provisions, which were enacted by the first-term National Assembly following the constitutional amendment procedure, were not lifted until 1991.

Since democratisation in Taiwan in 1987, the Constitutional Court has delivered two rulings regarding when the Premier is obliged to resign. Because the Premier was appointed by the President with the consent of the legislature before 1987, the Constitutional Court ruled in JY Interpretation No 387 (1995) that

> Since the premier has to receive consent from and be politically accountable to the Legislative Yuan, the premier has to resign before the first session of each new Legislative Yuan so as to fulfill the doctrine of government by the people and his/her political accountability.[81]

In a similar vein, the Constitutional Court argued in JY Interpretation No 419 (1996):

> That the Premier tenders the general resignation [of the entire Cabinet] on the occasion of the new President's inauguration is a matter of courtesy in deference to the nation's leader, not an obligation under the Constitution.[82]

[80] Compilation Commission (n 24) 817, 1168, 1184, 1345.

[81] JY Interpretation No 387 (1995) (Taiwan) at http://cons.judicial.gov.tw/jcc/en-us/jep03/show?expno=387.

[82] JY Interpretation No 419 (1996) (Taiwan) at http://cons.judicial.gov.tw/jcc/en-us/jep03/show?expno=419.

The key foundation of both rulings is that the Premier must receive consent from the legislature before appointment.[83]

Nevertheless, this foundation has changed. Since 1997, the constitutional amendments have granted the President the power to appoint the Premier without legislative consent.[84] On this score, the current central government structure reverted to that of the May Fifth Draft Constitution, which preferred presidentialism over the parliamentary system.

E. The Role of the Judicial Yuan

Compared with the institutional design of the coordinate branches, the role of the Judicial Yuan was not the most important issue during the founding period of 1911–12. Nonetheless, the structure of the Judicial Yuan changed several times, alternating between the American and German models. Wang Chung-hui had imitated the judicial review system in the United States in his draft Constitution in 1913. In that draft, he noted that although courts in most European countries did not have the power of judicial review, the nascent ROC should imitate the United States in this respect in order to safeguard the Constitution and constitutionalism.[85] Consequently, his draft stipulated that the courts should have the duty and power of judicial review.[86] It is noteworthy that he used the word 'courts' rather than 'constitutional court' or 'supreme court', meaning that the power of judicial review should be granted to every court rather than being monopolised by an apex court. This is typical of diffuse judicial review practised in the United States and many other common law jurisdictions.

The May Fifth Draft Constitution provided that, being the highest *judicial organ* of the state, the Judicial Yuan should have charge of civil, criminal and administrative cases and *oversee judicial administration*. It should be noted that prior to the enactment of the ROC Constitution, high courts and district courts were under the control of the Ministry of Judicial Administration, which was part of the Executive Yuan, because the latter exercised the power to oversee judicial administration. To eradicate this anomaly, the May Fifth Draft Constitution explicitly allocated the power to oversee judicial administration to the Judicial Yuan.[87] Also, it required the President of the Judicial Yuan, who was unilaterally appointed by the President, to be accountable to the National Assembly. However, Carsun Chang believed this institutional design would undermine

[83] Sec 1, Art 55 of the Constitution of the ROC (1947).

[84] Sec 1, Art 3 of the Additional Articles of the Constitution of the ROC (2005).

[85] Wang Chung-hui, *Wang Chung-hui Fahsueh Wenchi*, ed Zhang, Ren-Shan (Law Press China, 2008) (in Chinese).

[86] Chuan-Chi Miao, *Chungkuo Chihhsienshih Tzuliao Huipien* (Academia Historia, 1989) (in Chinese).

[87] Compilation Commission (n 24) 960–61.

judicial independence.[88] As a result, the Political Consultative Conference Draft Constitution provided that the Judicial Yuan itself should be the highest *tribunal* of the state, having general jurisdiction over all civil, criminal and administrative cases and constitutional interpretation. Moreover, the President of the Judicial Yuan should be appointed by the President with the consent of the Control Yuan, which, in the minds of the framers, was roughly equivalent to the Senate in the United States. Through the prism of institutional design, the Judicial Yuan was modelled after the Supreme Court of the United States.

In the Constituent Assembly, two questions regarding the judiciary were discussed: the power to consent and the power to oversee judicial administration. Some representatives suggested that instead of the Control Yuan, either the Legislative Yuan or the National Assembly should exercise the power to consent. These proposals were rejected – the main text of the ROC Constitution still grants the power to consent to the Control Yuan.[89] Others suggested that the Constitution should explicitly grant the power to oversee judicial administration to the Judicial Yuan, instead of the Executive Yuan, because the executive power was more vulnerable to partisan interests. In fact, the power to oversee judicial administration had been transferred back and forth from the executive to the judiciary and back to the executive multiple times before the ROC Constitution from 1928 to 1942.[90] Ultimately, it is not crystal clear in the constitutional text[91] whether the Judicial Yuan should have the power to oversee judicial administration and whether the Judicial Yuan itself was the apex court in the ROC.[92] In practice, the Judicial Yuan only had jurisdiction over constitutional controversies, while the Supreme Court and the Supreme Administrative Court were the final appellate tribunals for civil, criminal and administrative cases. Worse still, the administration of high courts and district courts was discharged not by the Judicial Yuan, but by the Ministry of Judicial Administration, Executive Yuan.

These two problems resulted in two Constitutional Court rulings in Taiwan: JY Interpretation No 86 (1960) and JY Interpretation No 530 (2001). In the former case, the controversy was whether high courts and district courts should affiliate with the Judicial Yuan. After the promulgation of the Constitution, high

[88] Chun-Mai Carsun Chang, 'Political Structure in the Chinese Draft Constitution' (1946) 243 *Annals of the American Academy of Political & Social Science* 67, 72–73.

[89] Art 79 of the ROC Constitution reads 'The Judicial Yuan shall have a President and a Vice President, who shall be nominated and, with the consent of the Control Yuan, appointed by the President of the Republic.'

[90] Chao-Lung Yang, 'Powers of Chinese Courts' (1947) 1 *Vanderbilt Law Review* 16, 18–19.

[91] Art 77 of the ROC Constitution reads 'The Judicial Yuan shall be the highest judicial organ of the State and shall have charge of civil, criminal, and administrative cases, and over cases concerning disciplinary measures against public functionaries.'

[92] Yen-tu Su, 'Regime Unchanged: The Organization and Failed Reorganization of Taiwan's Judicial Yuan' in Neil Chisholm (ed), *Judicial Reform in Taiwan: Democratization and the Diffusion of Law* (Routledge, 2020) 104, 108.

courts and district courts continued to affiliate with the Ministry of Judicial Administration, rather than the Judicial Yuan.[93] The Constitutional Court ruled that 'the high courts and their subordinate courts, being vested with the power to adjudicate civil and criminal cases, should be organizationally placed under the Judicial Yuan'.[94]

Furthermore, according to the original intent of Carsun Chang, who was the most influential framer of the ROC Constitution, the Judicial Yuan itself should be the apex court, just like the Supreme Court of the United States.[95] This original intent was never implemented because of the resistance of the then Supreme Court. In 1999, the Government convened a national judicial reform committee that was aimed, among other things, at implementing this original intent by reorganising the Judicial Yuan. In 2001, moreover, the Constitutional Court delivered JY Interpretation No 530 (2001), maintaining, *inter alia*, that 'the separation of the highest adjudicative organ from the highest judicial administration' is unconstitutional and the Government should revise related statutes 'to be consistent with the intent of the framers of the Constitution that considered the Judicial Yuan as the highest judicial adjudicative organ'.[96] Unfortunately, the reorganisation project was aborted and the decision never implemented because of entrenched and long-standing resistance, and the constitutional mandate has been blatantly ignored, without enforcement for two decades.[97]

F. Local Autonomy

The vertical separation of powers between central and local governments has always been a thorny issue in the constitution-making process. Should a state adopt federalism or become a unitary state? To what extent should local governments have autonomy? What powers could they exercise? These questions, already complex in themselves, become even more so in the ROC context. Given China's geographical vastness and ethno-linguistic and cultural diversity, a one-size-fits-all system would be difficult to adapt to myriad local needs. The fragmentation of centralised political authority from 1916 to 1928 meant that many provinces, ruled by warlords, had enacted their own constitutions and

[93] Yueh-Sheng Weng and Chien-Liang Lee, 'Separation of the Judiciary and the Public Prosecution' in Neil Chisholm (ed), *Judicial Reform in Taiwan: Democratization and the Diffusion of Law* (Routledge, 2020) 89, 94.

[94] JY Interpretation No 86 (1960) (Taiwan) at http://cons.judicial.gov.tw/jcc/en-us/jep03/show?expno=86.

[95] Wen-Chen Chang, 'Courts and Judicial Reform in Taiwan' in Jiunn-Rong Yeh and Wen-Chen Chang (eds), *Asian Courts in Context* (Cambridge University Press, 2015) 143, 146.

[96] JY Interpretation No 530 (2001) (Taiwan), available at http://cons.judicial.gov.tw/jcc/en-us/jep03/show?expno=530.

[97] Su (n 92) 105–06.

favoured some sort of federalism.[98] Even after ostensible political unification in 1928 following the Northern Expedition, the KMT was reluctant to give local governments too much power and autonomy. As such, in the May Fifth Draft Constitution, the provincial governments remained very much subject to the fiat of the central Government given the KMT's sceptism regarding federalism. The KMT feared that federalism would spur the revival of local militarism. This fear was deepened with the rise of the CCP, which in practice controlled a few provinces in northwest and northeast China. As a result, the provincial governor was to be appointed by the central Government and was in charge of executing the laws passed by the central Government. The county, rather than the province, is the highest unit of local self-government.

This separation of powers between central and local governments was rejected by opposition parties in the Political Consultative Conference. Hence, the 12 principles adopted federalism – every province could enact its own constitution as long as it did not contradict the ROC Constitution. As a result of the KMT delegates' strong opposition, the Political Consultative Conference Draft Constitution drove a middle way between the May Fifth Draft Constitution and the 12 principles. It provided that provincial governments could elect their governors and enact self-government regulations rather than constitutions. In the Constituent Assembly, several KMT representatives proposed curtailing provincial power,[99] but to no avail. Therefore, the vertical separation of powers in the ROC Constitution is akin to that in the Political Consultative Conference Draft Constitution, which gave the provincial governments some substantive powers without adopting federalism.[100]

Following its retreat to Taiwan at the end of the Chinese Civil War in 1949, the ROC effectively controlled only Taiwan and its neighbouring islets. Its territory and population largely overlapped with that of Taiwan Province. After 1996, this created an embarrassing situation: both the Governor of the Taiwan Province and the President of the ROC are democratically elected and their constituencies are almost the same. Who represents the will of the Taiwanese people? Does the ROC in Taiwan still need a Taiwan provincial government? To solve this problem, the 1997 constitutional amendments suspended the constitutional provisions regarding the election and the power of a province. After this constitutional revision, the Constitutional Court also delivered JY Interpretation No 467 (1998) to further clarify the legal status of the Taiwan provincial government, which 'no longer has jurisdiction over matters regarding local self-government'.[101]

[98] In 1921, for example, the Zhejiang province enacted its own constitution. See R Keith Schoppa, 'Province and Nation: The Chekiang Provincial Autonomy Movement, 1917–1927' (1977) 36 *Journal of Asian Studies* 661, 667–68.

[99] Compilation Commission (n 24) 1349.

[100] Roscoe Pound, 'The Chinese Constitution' (1947) 22 *NYU Law Quarterly Review* 194, 218–19.

[101] JY Interpretation No 467 (1998) (Taiwan) [1] at http://cons.judicial.gov.tw/jcc/en-us/jep03/show?expno=467.

III. THE IMPACT OF INTERNAL AND EXTERNAL FACTORS

A. External Factors

Because of their educational backgrounds, many Chinese constitutional drafters were heavily influenced by foreign constitutional jurisprudence, particularly those of the United States and Germany.[102] As mentioned before, Wang Chung-hui had attended both the University of California at Berkeley and Yale University, which accounts for his draft Constitution to some extent.

More importantly, John Wu, the key drafter of the May Fifth Draft Constitution, had studied at Michigan Law School after graduating from Soochow University in China. He was mentored by Harvard Law Professor Felix Frankfurter and was a friend of Justice Oliver Wendell Holmes of the US Supreme Court.[103] Soochow University itself was a product of the American Methodist Episcopal Church, which explains its strong connections with American law schools and legal education model.[104] Indeed, even before entering Soochow University, Wu had been exposed to both Chinese and Western education in primary school.[105] In addition to the United States, Wu had also studied in France and Germany. He also maintained a good friendship with Roscoe Pound, Dean of Harvard Law School, and Benjamin Cardozo, Associate Justice of the US Supreme Court. All these relationships and training made Wu more liberal than most of his KMT comrades, and this was reflected in the chapter of rights and duties in his draft Constitution.[106] Furthermore, Wu had researched many written constitutions in different jurisdictions, including the United States, Germany, France and Japan, as well as the treatises of legal philosophers and

[102] In addition to this kind of indirect foreign impact, some foreign counsellors had directly proposed their draft constitutions in the 1910s when China was under the control of the Beiyang Government before the KMT unified China 1928. For example, Yuan Shikai, who was the first President of the ROC, had invited several foreign legal consultants to assist in drafting his Constitution, which aimed to build a constitutional monarchy in which he would be anointed as the emperor. Nagao Ariga, a well-known constitutional law professor in Japan, had modelled Yuan's 1914 Constitution on the Meiji Constitution. In a similar vein, Frank Johnson Goodnow, who was the President of Johns Hopkins University, had also provided a draft Constitution for Yuan's 1914 Constitution. See Daw-Yih Jang and Kuo-Ching Hsu, 'Lorenz von Stein and Chinese Constitutional Movement: A Reexamination of Legal History' (2015) 10 *National Taiwan University Law Review* 1, 4; Jedidiah Kroncke, 'An Early Tragedy of Comparative Constitutionalism: Frank Goodnow and the Chinese Republic' (2012) 21 *Pacific Rim Law & Policy Journal* 533, 558; Noel Pugach, 'Embarrassed Monarchist: Frank J Goodnow and Constitutional Development in China 1913–1915' (1973) 42 *Pacific Historical Review* 499.

[103] 'Dr Wu's Constitution' (n 7) 2300; John CH Wu, *Beyond East and West* (Mei Ya Publishing, 1969) 87–132.

[104] Li Xiuqing, 'John CH Wu at the University of Michigan School of Law' (2008) 58 *Journal of Legal Education* 545, 548–50.

[105] ibid 551.

[106] Thomas E Greiff, 'The Principle of Human Rights in Nationalist China: John CH Wu and the Ideological Origins of the 1946 Constitution' (1985) 103 *China Quarterly* 441, 441–42; Charles Sumner Lobingier, 'The *Corpus Juris* of New China' (1944-1945) 19 *Tulane Law Review* 512, 514–15.

political theorists, such as Montesquieu and Rousseau, before preparing for the May Fifth Draft Constitution.[107] Wu's understanding of constitutional rights, albeit liberal in general, was circumscribed not only by the social and political environment the draft was embedded in, but also by his desire to syncretise Western concepts with China's needs at that time.[108] Therefore, all the fundamental rights provisions in his draft included a caveat that the exercise of these rights might be restricted by statute. This design was criticised by the opposition parties because the legislature was basically controlled by the KMT. This partly explains why the Political Consultative Conference Draft Constitution had greatly overhauled the May Fifth Draft Constitution

The drafter of the Political Consultative Conference Draft Constitution, Carsun Chang, was no less familiar with Western constitutional and political institutions. Born in Shanghai, a city where Western influence was particularly evident in China, he was immersed in Chinese classics and Western studies throughout his early education.[109] In 1906, funded by the Qing Government, he studied law, political science and German in Waseda University in Japan. It was there that his studies of Western political philosophies, such as those of John Locke and John Stuart Mill, 'laid the foundations for his lifelong attachment to constitutional democracy'.[110] In 1913, he studied politics in the University of Berlin, and returned to China in 1916. Comparing the stumbling China with the post-First World War Germany (which Chang believed had successfully been rehabilitated from the ashes), he once advocated that China adopt the German constitutional model.[111] Later on, he was gradually influenced by American constitutional jurisprudence. Inspired by Alexander Hamilton and James Madison, he published several essays in China that advocated and elaborated on what constituted ideal constitutional design, before drafting the Constitution.[112] These essays were compiled as a collection entitled *Ten Essays on the Chinese Democratic Constitution*, which he compared to *The Federalist Papers* in the prologue.[113] As already mentioned, the Judicial Yuan in his draft was modelled on the US Supreme Court. Intellectually, he was also deeply influenced by neo-Confucianism, and had published widely on the relationship between Confucianism, liberalism, socialism and (Chinese) Communism.[114]

[107] Xiaomeng Zhang, 'John CH Wu and His Comparative Law Pursuit' (2013) 41 *International Journal of Legal Information* 196, 215–16.
[108] Greiff (n 106) 456–58.
[109] Roger B Jeans Jr, *Democracy and Socialism in Republican China: The Politics of Zhang Junmai (Carsun Chang), 1906–1941* (Rowman & Littlefield Publishers, 1997) 73–74.
[110] ibid 13.
[111] ibid 32–38.
[112] Chun-Mai Chang, *Chunghuaminkuo Minchu Hsienfa Shihchiang* (The Commercial Press, 1971) 97–98.
[113] ibid.
[114] See, eg, Carsun Chang, 'Confucianism and Chinese Communism' (1961) 4 *American Behavioural Scientist* 15; and Carsun Chang, *The Development of Neo-Confucian Thought* (Bookman Associates, 1957).

It is noteworthy that, while he was aware of the 1924 Soviet Constitution, he nevertheless saw it as 'a farce' because of his confidence in Western democracy.[115]

Beyond these prominent figures, many representatives in the Constituent Assembly were familiar with foreign constitutional law as well. For example, several representatives, inspired by the US Constitution, proposed imitating the Third Amendment of the Constitution of the United States, which prohibits quartering soldiers in any house in peacetime, and inserted a similar clause into the ROC Constitution.[116] The Political Consultative Conference Draft Constitution included an identical clause, because military seizure and expropriation of civilian houses was common in China after decades of military conflict. Although this clause was removed during the Constituent Assembly upon the request of KMT representatives,[117] the impact of American constitutional law was vividly demonstrated. Notably, there seems to be no evidence that suggests the United States had pressured the KMT to adopt a particular type of constitution.

B. Internal Factors

There are many reasons to explain why a country would decide to enact a constitution – for instance, to secure basic rights, to constrain state power, or to build national identity.[118] The ROC Constitution was less inspired by these exalted ideals than by the power struggle between the KMT, the CCP and minority parties. Many would perhaps find it surprising to know that the KMT's nemesis, the CCP, played a significant role in the process of constitution-making, Indeed, it even shaped the contours of the ROC Constitution to some extent.

As mentioned previously, the ROC Constitution is a compromise that encompasses both the May Fifth Draft Constitution and the Political Consultative Conference Draft Constitution. Although the KMT unilaterally drafted the May Fifth Draft Constitution, this was revised considerably in the Political Consultative Conference, in which the delegates of the CCP and minority parties outnumbered those of the KMT. Before this Conference, the CCP delegates had proposed several guidelines as to how to build China peacefully from the ashes.[119] Some of these became part of the Political Consultative Conference Draft Constitution and were eventually enshrined in the ROC Constitution.

[115] Jeans (n 109) 138–44.
[116] Compilation Commission (n 24) 1199.
[117] Lei (30) 142.
[118] Tom Ginsburg, Terence C Halliday and Gregory Shaffer, 'Constitution-Making as Transnational Legal Ordering' in Tom Ginsburg, Gregory Shaffer and Terence C Halliday (eds), *Constitution-Making and Transnational Legal Order* (Cambridge University Press, 2019) 1, 3.
[119] Fei-Ling Wang, *The China Order: Centralia, World Empire, and the Nature of Chinese Power* (SUNY, Press 2017) 173.

For instance, Article 7 of the ROC Constitution (emphasis added) provides that 'All citizens of the Republic of China, irrespective of sex, religion, race, *class*, or *party affiliation*, shall be equal before the law.' These signifiers, which were not present in the May Fifth Draft Constitution, were added in the Political Consultative Conference. Studies have averred that 'class' and 'party affiliation' were added at the request of the CCP,[120] which is understandable given the Communist ideology and political atmosphere at that time.

Another example relates to the military. Article 138 of the ROC Constitution (emphasis added) provides 'The land, sea, and air forces of the whole country shall be above personal, regional, and *party affiliations* …'. And Article 139 stipulates 'No political party and no individual shall make use of armed forces as an instrument in the struggle for political powers.' Absent in the May Fifth Draft Constitution, both articles aimed to curtail the military power of the KMT,[121] which had its own military from 1924 to 1947 when the ROC Constitution was promulgated.

A third example is Article 80 of the ROC Constitution (emphasis added), which provides that 'Judges shall be above *partisanship* and shall, in accordance with law, hold trials independently, free from any interference.' In the May Fifth Draft Constitution, the same article read 'Judges shall, in accordance with law, hold trials independently.' The requirement 'shall be above partisanship' was added to the Political Consultative Conference Draft Constitution because of the KMT's notorious 'politicization of the judiciary'[122] and its use of the judiciary to oppress political dissidents.[123]

The last example is Article 168, which reads 'The State shall accord to various racial groups in the frontier regions legal protection of their status and shall give special assistance to their local self-government undertakings.' This provision appeared as Article 5(2) of the Political Consultative Conference Draft Constitution. Proposed by the CCP, this article was ostensibly aimed at protecting the Uyghurs in Xinjiang Province, because the May Fifth Draft Constitution mentioned only Mongolia and Tibet.[124]

Nonetheless, this gives rise to the question why the KMT representatives accepted these proposals made by the CCP. Remember that the CCP boycotted and was completely absent from the Constituent Assembly. Although the minority parties might be sympathetic to the CCP's proposals, the KMT still controlled a supermajority of seats in the Constituent Assembly. Why did the KMT compromise, and even succumb to the CCP and other parties' insistence, at least to some extent? The answer involves the function of a

[120] Lei (30) 134.
[121] ibid 356–57
[122] Heng-Wen Liu, 'The Politicization of the Judiciary in Post-war Taiwan: The KMT's Control of Judicial Personnel before 1990 and Its Aftermath' (2019) 24 *Academia Sinica Law Journal* 1, 6–23.
[123] Lei (30) 270–76.
[124] ibid 130.

constitution – regime reinforcement. At that time, the CCP and the China Democratic League had boycotted the Constituent Assembly, which meant that the KMT had almost absolute control over it. This was actually a liability instead of an asset to the KMT, which had intended to give its reign a veneer of legality by enacting a democratically-passed Constitution. Given that the CCP and the China Democratic League had refused to attend, the KMT had to ensure that other minority parties remained in the Constituent Assembly. This gave the minority parties a semblance of leverage to bargain with the KMT. Moreover, the spectre of civil war against the CCP loomed over the constitution-making process. In light of these considerations, KMT Chairman Chiang Kai-shek openly supported Carsun Chang's Political Consultative Conference Draft Constitution, despite many hardline KMT representatives' preference for the May Fifth Draft Constitution.[125] Although the final version of the ROC Constitution was a hybrid of the two drafts, the KMT had actually made a substantial concession with regard to the substance of the Constitution to expedite the process of constitution-making.[126] In other words, Chiang Kai-shek cared more about the passage than about the content of the ROC Constitution, given that the KMT essentially controlled the central Government. In short, the power struggle and political calculation between participating political parties, rather than constitutional theories and ideals, determined the content of the ROC Constitution.

IV. THE IMPACT OF THE ROC CONSTITUTION ON TAIWAN'S STATE BUILDING

So far, we have identified the lingering effects of the constitutional issues debated in the Constituent Assembly in 1947. This section will analyse the impact of the ROC Constitution as a whole on state building in Taiwan.

To begin with, the bill of rights enshrined in Chapter II of the ROC Constitution laid down a solid foundation for the protection of basic rights in Taiwan. Enacted seven decades ago, the bill of rights in the Constitution is still fairly liberal and progressive, even by today's standards, as it explicitly protects not only civil and political rights but also socio-economic rights, including the right of existence, the right to work, the right to receive an education and so on. To fully protect these rights, the power of judicial review has explicitly been granted to the Judicial Yuan, which has exercised this power continuously and without interruption since its inauguration. Furthermore, Chapter XIII of the

[125] Wen-Chen Chang, *Transition to Democracy, Constitutionalism and Judicial Activism: Taiwan in Comparative Constitutional Perspective* (June 2001) (unpublished JSD dissertation, Yale Law School) 87–90 (on file with the author).

[126] ibid.

Constitution, which prescribes fundamental national policies, also provides for a social security system, national health insurance and free elementary education, amongst other things. Admittedly, most of the provisions, including a catch-all clause,[127] are terse and subject to interpretation. Still, Justices of the Judicial Yuan have repeatedly invoked these articles to build an impressive and outstanding constitutional rights regime. Many rights that are not explicitly enumerated in the Constitution have been recognised as fundamental rights in Taiwan. Moreover, the Constitutional Court has creatively relied on Article 23[128] as the textual peg on which to hang a requirement of proportionality.[129] These efforts have made the ROC (Taiwan) one of the Asian countries that best protects human rights.

On the flip side, Taiwan's nation building as an independent country has been shackled by the ROC Constitution since the KMT retreated to Taiwan in 1949. It has been argued that the ROC Constitution was a part of the modernisation project for the Chinese people[130] and an instrument for national inclusion for the Taiwanese people,[131] given that Taiwan was a Japanese colony when the early draft constitutions were promulgated. Nonetheless, the original constitutional framework is too complicated to cater to Taiwan's context. Although 18 representatives in the Constituent Assembly came from the then Taiwan Province, they were a token presence[132] because the contents of the Constitution were basically a negotiation between political elites in China. This is clear when one considers that these 18 Taiwanese representatives advanced only four proposals[133] out of a total of 427,[134] all of which were rejected in the Constituent Assembly. Many constitutional provisions in the ROC Constitution thus look ridiculous in the context of Taiwan after 1949, such as those regulating Mongolia and Tibet. In this light, the key problem of constitutional politics in contemporary Taiwan is that the supreme law of the land was not designed for the people of Taiwan. Nor do Taiwanese people share the same memory embodied in the ROC Constitution by its Chinese framers.[135] It is thus unsurprising

[127] Art 22 of the Constitution of the ROC reads 'All other freedoms and rights of the people that are not detrimental to social order or public welfare shall be guaranteed under the Constitution.'

[128] Art 23 of the Constitution of the ROC reads 'All the freedoms and rights … shall not be restricted by law except such as may be necessary …'

[129] Chien-Chih Lin, 'Proportionality in Taiwan' in Po Jen Yap (ed), *Proportionality in Asia* (Cambridge University Press, 2020) 60, 62.

[130] Yeh and Chang (n 5) 819.

[131] Wen-Chen Chang, 'East Asian Foundations for Constitutionalism: Three Models Reconstructed' (2008) 3 *National Taiwan University Law Review* 111, 132–33.

[132] Chao-Ju Chen, 'A Feminist Critique of History and Traditions in Judicial Review' (2010) 7 *Academia Sinica Law Journal* 81, 90–91.

[133] They were proposal no 187, proposal no 203, proposal no 234 and proposal no 420. See Compilation Commission (n 24) 1065–66, 1077–80, 1127–31, 1350–51.

[134] Compilation Commission (n 24) 685.

[135] Catherine Dupré and Jiunn-rong Yeh, 'Constitutions and Legitimacy over Time' in Mark Tushnet, Thomas Fleiner and Cheryl Saunders (eds), *Routledge Handbook of Constitutional Law* (Routledge, 2013) 45, 46–47 (arguing that the enactment of a constitution constructs a memory).

that about one-fifth of the original constitutional provisions have been either suspended or revised.[136]

Indeed, for those supporting Taiwan's pursuit of its own state building as an independent country, the ROC Constitution may be regarded as an imposed constitution for the Taiwanese people for three reasons. First, the ROC Constitution contains the one-China policy that has been discarded by most Taiwanese. The preamble to the constitutional amendments clearly states that the purpose of constitutional revision is 'To meet the requisites of the nation prior to national unification.'[137] This assumes that China and Taiwan belong to different parts of the same country and would be reunited eventually. Indeed, this interpretation has been confirmed by both the KMT and the CCP. Former President Ma Ying-jeou claimed in 2015 that the ROC Constitution does not tolerate 'two Chinas', 'one China and one Taiwan', or 'Taiwan independence'.[138] One year later, Wang Yi, the Foreign Minister of China, took advantage of this constitutionalised one-China policy to force President Tsai Ing-wen to recognise that there is only one China in the world.[139] Second, as Taiwanese national identity has gradually shifted in Taiwan,[140] so has its constitutional identity.[141] Long-term public opinion polling organised by the National Cheng Chi University has suggested that, as recently as December 2020, when asked about cross-Strait relations, 54.3 per cent of Taiwanese preferred maintaining the status quo, 32.4 per cent of Taiwanese chose independence and only 7.6 per cent opted for unification.[142] More crucially, the trend – as indicated by the same poll – is clear – over the past two decades, more and more Taiwanese people have preferred Taiwan to be independent while fewer and fewer hoped for unification.[143] So long as the trend continues, the ROC Constitution is repugnant to the will of most people inasmuch as it embodies the one-China policy. Finally, although constitutional amendments in Taiwan have better mirrored the political reality and reinforced the democratic legitimacy of the

[136] Yeh (n 78) 151.

[137] Additional Articles of the Constitution of the Republic of China (1947) at https://english.president.gov.tw/Page/95.

[138] Mainland Affairs Council, Republic of China (Taiwan), 'Full text of ROC President Ma Ying-jeou's remarks in meeting with mainland Chinese leader Xi Jinping' (9 November 2015) at www.mac.gov.tw/en/News_Content.aspx?n=2BA0753CBE348412&sms=E828F60C4AFBAF90&s=4F225A4BA95218E4.

[139] William Lowther, 'China touts Taiwan Constitution' *Taipei Times* (27 February 2016) at http://www.taipeitimes.com/News/front/archives/2016/02/27/2003640311 accessed 30 January 2020.

[140] Lung-chu Chen, *The US-Taiwan-China Relationship in International Law and Policy* (Oxford University Press, 2016).

[141] Chien-Chih Lin, 'We the Taiwanese People' in Richard Albert, Menaka Guruswamy and Nischal Basnyat (eds), *Founding Moments in Constitutionalism* (Hart Publishing, 2019) 179–99.

[142] Election Study Center, National Cheng Chi University, 'Changes in the Unification/Independence Stances of Taiwanese (1994~2020.12)' at https://esc.nccu.edu.tw/PageDoc/Detail?fid=7805&id=6962.

[143] ibid.

Constitution domestically,[144] they also set an excruciatingly high quorum for future constitutional change. To amend the Constitution requires the consent of three-fourths of the legislators and the majority of votes of the total electors.[145] This unchangeability will perpetuate and aggravate the imposition,[146] because it deprives the Taiwanese people of any possibility of autonomous constitutional change.

In short, the ROC Constitution plays a Janus-faced role here: for people who regard themselves as Chinese in Taiwan, the ROC Constitution marks the culmination of decades of constitution-making and state building; for those who regard themselves as Taiwanese, however, the ROC Constitution is, at least in part, a straitjacket that constrains their state-building project.

V. CONCLUSION

The road to constitutionalism in Taiwan was long and arduous. Like many other constitutions in the world,[147] the ROC Constitution was born in a period that was the least favourable for constitution-making. Domestically, the ROC had been devastated by decades of armed conflicts and rebellion; internationally, it had been embroiled in two World Wars. In hindsight, nevertheless, this prolonged period of gestation has made the Constitution more progressive and inclusive, in such a way that many socialist ideas have been incorporated into the supreme law. Even though the warfare did not prevent the nascent republic from enacting a modern constitution, the new Constitution did not survive in China after the Chinese Civil War (1945–49) and was instead brought over to Taiwan by the KMT. Somewhat surprisingly, it has not only endured but also thrived in Taiwan:[148] in the name of the ROC Constitution, Taiwan has become the first Asian country to legalise same-sex marriage. Also, the freedom of the press is

[144] Yeh (n 78) 164–75.

[145] Art 12 of the Additional Articles of the Constitution of the Republic of China reads 'Amendment of the Constitution shall be initiated upon the proposal of one-fourth of the total members of the Legislative Yuan, passed by at least three-fourths of the members present at a meeting attended by at least three-fourths of the total members of the Legislative Yuan, and sanctioned by electors in the free area of the Republic of China at a referendum held upon expiration of a six-month period of public announcement of the proposal, wherein the number of valid votes in favor exceeds one-half of the total number of electors …'

[146] Xenophon Contiades and Alkmene Fotiadou, 'Imposed Constitutions: Heteronomy and (un)amenability' in Richard Albert, Xenophon Contiades and Alkmene Fotiadou (eds), *The Law and Legitimacy of Imposed Constitutions* (Routledge, 2019) 15, 31–32; David Landau, 'Constitution-Making Gone Wrong' (2013) 64 *Alabama Law Review* 923.

[147] Jon Elster, 'The Political Psychology of Constitution-Making' in Jon Elster et al (eds), *Constituent Assemblies* (Cambridge University Press, 2018) 207, 216–17.

[148] Zachary Elkins, Tom Ginsburg and James Melton, *The Endurance of National Constitutions* (Cambridge University Press, 2009) 171–74; Chien-Chih Lin, 'Survival of the Fittest(?): The Endurance of the ROC Constitution and the Constitution of Japan' (2014) 62 *The American Journal of Comparative Law* 775.

best protected in Taiwan among Asian countries,[149] and so is gender equality.[150] Ironically, this was probably not expected by either the drafters or the framers of the ROC Constitution, who did not care much about the island. Contrasting the constitution-making process in China with the constitutional development in Taiwan vividly suggests how difficult it is for constitutional framers to enact a constitution 'for faithful and perpetual observance by all'.[151]

149 Reporters without Borders, 'Media independence on hold' at https://rsf.org/en/taiwan.

150 World Bank, Women, 'Business and the Law 2019' at https://openknowledge.worldbank.org/bitstream/handle/10986/31327/WBL2019.pdf?fbclid=IwAR0QXlhwhSy_AD1r_umEKupqZPgoQKgMWObiU_kxvKvn77GFy-b16rQCbGc.

151 Prologue of the Constitution of the ROC (Taiwan) (1947).

6

The Meiji Constitution and Japan's Emergence in the International Order, 1853–1905

KENTARO MATSUBARA

INTRODUCTION

In the Entrance Hall of the American Museum of Natural History in New York City, there is a mural that depicts the signing of the Portsmouth Treaty, which brought an end to the Russo-Japanese War of 1904 to 1905.[1] It is part of a celebration of the life of President Theodore Roosevelt, who won the Nobel Peace Prize for brokering this treaty. From the viewpoint of the Japanese Government of the time, the treaty concluded a successful diplomatic campaign to enlist the help of the United States and its President in a difficult negotiation of peace.[2] One individual in particular is credited with having achieved this success: this was Baron Kaneko Kentaro, who resided in the United States throughout the war, charged with the mission of lobbying the President and influencing American public opinion in favour of the Japanese.

Prior to the peace conference Roosevelt was brokering at the Japanese Government's request, Kaneko wrote Roosevelt a letter in which he thanked the President for having received him at the Roosevelt family's summer house.

[1] The figures depicted in the mural, alongside a presiding Theodore Roosevelt himself, are the Japanese envoys, Foreign Minister Komura Jutaro and Ambassador Takahira Kogoro, as well as three of the Russian envoys, Count Sergei Witte, who was the chief Russian envoy, JJ Korostovetz, whose diary provides a first-hand account of the negotiation process, and Konstantin Nabokov, whose celebrated nephew would later depict this mural in his own memoir (Vladimir Nabokov, *Speak, Memory: An Autobiography Revisited* (Penguin Twentieth Century Classics, 1969) 49).

[2] Transcription of a telegram received from the Minister of Foreign Affairs, Theodore Roosevelt Papers, Library of Congress Manuscript Division at www.theodorerooseveltcenter.org/Research/Digital-Library/Record?libID=o284604, Theodore Roosevelt Digital Library, Dickinson State University; telegram from Kogoro Takahira to Theodore Roosevelt, Theodore Roosevelt Papers, Library of Congress Manuscript Division at www.theodorerooseveltcenter.org/Research/Digital-Library/Record?libID=o49486, Theodore Roosevelt Digital Library, Dickinson State University.

In this thank-you note, Kaneko commends the President for his home life, describing it as one of 'simple living and high thinking',[3] which he further writes is an 'ideal life of Japanese Samurai'.[4] Such a reinterpretation/reformulation of traditional Japanese ideals in the light of Western concepts is not atypical of Japanese social thought in the Meiji era, and more specifically of Kaneko, who was one of the three drafting committee members of the Meiji Constitution.

Born in 1853 to a low-class samurai family, Kaneko Kentaro distinguished himself as a gifted student, and was selected to join the Iwakura Mission of 1871 to pursue his studies in the United States. While he began attending a primary-level grammar school at the age of 18, he was admitted to study at Harvard Law School in 1876, just five years later.[5] His legal education prepared him to participate, a decade later, in the drafting of the Meiji Constitution. Moreover, his Harvard affiliation was to prove useful in his later mission during the Russo-Japanese War,[6] and in a 1904 letter to Kaneko, Roosevelt mentions how delighted he was to learn how well his friend, Justice Oliver Wendell Holmes, knew Kaneko.[7]

Roosevelt's correspondence, both with Japanese such as Kaneko and with others around this time, shows how he came to accept Japan as an emerging world power in East Asia, and was optimistic about how it would coexist with American interests in the region.[8] Kaneko was born the year the Perry expeditions ended 200 years of Japan's – albeit relative – self-isolation. In both his trajectory and outlook, Kaneko is an excellent representation of how Japan integrated itself into a new and different international order during the half-century between 1853 and 1905, in close relationship with the United States.

It is well-known that the Meiji Constitution is based on the Prussian/German constitutional model and was favoured for its centralisation of power in the Emperor. However, this was a path chosen amidst various internal tensions within Japanese society. Influences from, and interactions with, the United States

[3] The words are typically traced back to William Wordsworth's sonnet *Written in London, September 1802*, and the line 'Plain living and high thinking are no more.'

[4] Letter from Kentarō Kaneko to Theodore Roosevelt, 5 July 1905.

[5] Kaneko Kentaro and Takase Nobuhiko (eds), *Kaneko Kentaro Jijo-den* [Autobiography of Kaneko Kentaro] 金子堅太郎自叙伝 [金子堅太郎著] ; 高瀬暢彦編 (研究叢書 / 日本大学精神文化研究所 [編], 11–12) 日本大学精神文化研究所, 2003.3-2004.3第1 集第 2 集

[6] Masayoshi Matsumura, Baron Kaneko and the Russo-Japanese War (1904–05): A Study in the Public Diplomacy of Japan, tr Ian Ruxton (Lulu Press, 2009).

[7] Letter from Theodore Roosevelt to Kaneko Kentarō, Theodore Roosevelt Papers, Library of Congress Manuscript Division at www.theodorerooseveltcenter.org/Research/Digital-Library/Record?libID=o187802, Theodore Roosevelt Digital Library, Dickinson State University.

[8] Letter from Theodore Roosevelt to Sir Cecil Spring Rice, Theodore Roosevelt Papers, Library of Congress Manuscript Division at www.theodorerooseveltcenter.org/Research/Digital-Library/Record?libID=o188381, Theodore Roosevelt Digital Library, Dickinson State University; Letter from Theodore Roosevelt to Theodore Roosevelt, Theodore Roosevelt Papers, Library of Congress Manuscript Division at www.theodorerooseveltcenter.org/Research/Digital-Library/Record?libID=o187366, Theodore Roosevelt Digital Library, Dickinson State University.

formed an important part of these multi-layered tensions. This chapter attempts to reconstruct some of the ideological and political conflicts that underlay these tensions. It aims to understand the Meiji Constitution and the formation of the modern Japanese state in the context of these oppositions that were couched in heavily transnational terms.

I. JAPAN'S INTRODUCTION TO A NEW INTERNATIONAL ORDER: INTERNATIONAL LAW AND THE JAPANESE *ANCIEN RÉGIME*

A. The American Expeditions and Japanese Exposure to a New International Order

The unequal treaties that were signed in 1854 and 1858 as a direct result of Commodore Perry's expeditions in 1853, had a defining impact on both the diplomacy and domestic politics of Japan over the following half-century. On one hand, the Shogunate's policy of placating the Western powers was met with strong resistance – the resultant political divide became a major driving force behind fundamental regime change, which led to the Meiji Restoration (1868). On the other hand, the Japanese became highly cognisant about the importance of being well-versed in international law, which was the corpus of rules followed by the international community as defined by the Western powers.

Japan's integration into the international community, which can loosely be termed the Westphalian system of sovereign states, was a radical departure from Japan's centuries-long participation in the Sinocentric regional order. In successfully keeping a distance from the Sinocentric tributary system that integrated neighbouring entities such as Korea and the Ryukyus, Japan restricted its relationships to trading with the Chinese and the Dutch, limited diplomatic relations with Korea and imposing Japanese rule through the Satsuma domain over the Ryukyus whilst allowing the Ryukyus to maintain its tributary relations with China. The Japanese were thus acutely aware of the affairs in its wider world. China's defeat in the first Opium War (1839–42) caused much consternation in Japan and triggered a change in its policy toward foreign ships. Further, there were larger forces of change that triggered a realisation of Japan's vulnerability – it was impossible for Japan to hold on to the theoretical constructions of its international order in the light of the arrival of the Perry expeditions (1853–54) and their demands for unequal treaties. The consequences were many. Japan's physical borders as a sovereign state were defined. In 1855, the border with Russia was established just north of Iturup in the Kurile Islands, recognising the whole of Hokkaido as Japanese territory. A later treaty of 1875 ceded the whole of Sakhalin Island to the Russian Empire, while Japan extended its rule over the Kurile Islands. Following this in 1879, the Ryukyu kingdom was forced to give up its tributary relations with the Qing Empire, and became Okinawa prefecture.

When the American textbook *Elements of International Law* by Henry Wheaton was translated by the Qing Government and published as *Wanguo Gongfa* in 1864, there was little impact. Its publisher, the *Zongli Yamen*, was established in 1860, under British and French pressure in the Treaty of Peking, to centrally manage China's foreign affairs, acknowledging a major shift away from the tributary system.[9] Essentially, the *Zongli Yamen* became a component in the *Yangwu yundong*, or Western Affairs Movement. This movement was characterised by the principle of *Zhongti Xiyong*, or 'Chinese substance, Western application'. Western learning (such as the principles of international law) was seen as a means to an end, to be used in accordance with traditional Chinese values and learning. In this light, the *Wangguo Gongfa* and the principles of international law did little to fundamentally alter the state apparatus of the Qing Government. Its reception (and impact) in Japan was radically different, however.

In 1865, the Japanese edition was released, having been made more accessible to its readers. Its impact on future lawmakers was immediate, among them such future jurists as Nishi Amane and Tsuda Mamichi, who were sent to Europe to study international law. This was not entirely surprising. The Japanese *ancien régime* of the Tokugawa Shogunate was much less committed to Confucianism than the Qing Government. The Chinese defeat in the First Opium War (1839–42) had also triggered a shift in their worldview. The merits of Western institutions had also been debated, albeit in Confucian terms, and the ruling samurai class was pragmatically ready for a radical ideological shift toward a westernised legal order, including the notion that this order had universal value.[10] It is well known that the Meiji Restoration maintained a certain duality. It retained the form of the Shogunate 'returning' rule over the islands to the Emperor, and many new institutions drew their names from ancient texts. At the same time, the newly minted 15-year old Emperor began his rule with a manifesto (the Charter Oath) that was explicitly committed to abolishing 'malign customs of the past' and following the 'public way of Heaven and Earth'. This 'public way' is thought to have been conceptualised with an understanding of 'universal' values that had been learned from the West.[11] In this sense the 'Restoration' was the introduction of a radically new regime, and not a return to the past.[12]

[9] The Qing Government previously had no centralised bureau for diplomacy. Relations with tributaries such as Korea were handled at the Board of Rites 礼部, affairs with such regions with a non-Han majority that would be incorporated into China as a modern state (Tibet, Inner Mongolia, Xinjiang, etc) and Russia were managed at the *Lifanyuan* 理藩院, and trade with the West through the Canton system was regulated by the Governor General of Guangdong and Guangxi 両廣総督.

[10] See Kentaro Matsubara, 'East, East, and West: Comparative Law and the Historical Processes of Legal Interaction in China and Japan' (2019) 66 *The American Journal of Comparative Law* 769, 773–75.

[11] It has been argued that this phrase had its origins in a reading of the *Wangguo Gongfa*. Maruyama Masao and Katô Shûichi, *Honyaku to Nihon no Kindai* [Translation and Japanese Modernity] (Iwanami Shoten, 1998) 120.

[12] Watanabe Hiroshi, *Nihon Seiji Shisôshi: 17–19 Seiki* [A History of Japanese Political Thought from the 17th to the 19th Century] (University of Tokyo Press, 2010) 382–84.

B. The *Ancien Régime* and its Affinity with Constitutional Government

Some aspects of the old Tokugawa administration were already congruent with this vision of a new regime. This eased the introduction of novel institutions and influenced the creation and development of a political culture in the decades following the Restoration. This evolution culminated in the promulgation of the Meiji Constitution in 1889.

One such congruence was how the deliberative committees were central to the Tokugawa administration's decision-making process. Two to six individuals, each holding official titles as Rôjû 老中 (Elder), Waka-doshiyori (Junior-Elder), Ô-metsuke (Senior Censor) and Kanjo-bugyo (Commissioner), were appointed to each committee, whose officials were compelled to deliberate on any decision it was assigned. Designed to prevent power from being appropriated by a particular individual or faction, this system helped preserve the authority of the Shogun, but also instilled a culture of debate and deliberation in the administrative process.[13]

Moreover, a meticulous separation of powers, between the Rôjû managing the Shogunate and the Daimyo of the Domains, between the power of the Shogun and the authority of the Emperor, between the Elders and the Censors, was key to Tokugawa governance. Even Fukuzawa Yukichi, a leading Meiji-era thinker and a sharp critic of the Tokugawa regime, acknowledged in 1890 that the opening of a parliamentary body only 23 years into the Meiji was largely due to Japan's experience of deliberative government and separation of powers under the Tokugawa regime.[14]

As such, the Shogunate's actions in the 1850s segued into the existing administrative culture perfectly. Faced with the crisis of an internal rift, particularly between the Shogunate's policy to negotiate the unequal treaties on the one hand, and the critics/rebellious samurai who advocated expelling the foreign barbarians on the other, the Shogunate chose to form a deliberative body involving Daimyo on both sides of the divide in order to discuss policy. Moreover, in a bid to consolidate its legitimacy in pursuing its own policies, the Shogunate sought to receive permission in the form of an imperial edict, effectively placing itself in a governmental structure involving separate powers.

In this process, notions of public discussion (*Kôgi* 公議) and discussion amongst the people (*Shûgi* 衆議: although in this case the 'people' engaged in discussion were mainly the Daimyo class) were employed to legitimise the Shogunate's policies. While the Shogunate's attempts at stabilising its rule by forming a coalition of Daimyo failed, and the ensuing armed conflict between the Shogunate and an alliance of the Domains led to the Meiji Restoration, it is worth noting that both sides resorted to the notion of *Kôgi* to legitimise their

[13] Mitani Taichiro, *Nihon no Kindai toha Nani de attaka* [What was Japanese Modernity?] (Iwanami Shoten, 2017) 43–48.

[14] Fukuzawa Yukichi, 'Kokkai no zento' [future of the Diet], serialised in *Jiji Shinpô* (10–13 December 1890).

respective visions of government.[15] These notions of *Kôgi* and *Shûgi*, having emerged during the Tokugawa era, subsequently became part of the constitutional debates of modern Japan.

C. Japan's Early Meiji International Experiences and the Constitution

i. Socio-Political Tensions and the West in the Meiji Restoration

Despite the Shogunate's attempts to secure an imperial edict that would empower it to sign the 1858 Treaty of Amity and Commerce between the United States and the Empire of Japan, it failed to do so and the signing of the Treaty met with fierce domestic resistance. Consequently, much of the political tension leading up to the Meiji Restoration revolved around the issue of *Kaikoku* 開国 ('opening the country') versus *Jôi* 攘夷 ('expelling the western barbarians'). Samurai from the domains Satsuma and Chôshû advocated the latter policy strongly, and they would later lead the Meiji Restoration. Former samurai from these two domains came to dominate positions of power in the Meiji Government. However, although they garnered much the support because of their policy of expelling the foreigners, their stance toward foreigners had been significantly tempered by the time of the Meiji Restoration. Both Satsuma and Chôshû were in armed conflict with foreign powers in 1863 – both were heavily defeated. By the time they came to power in the Meiji Government, the attitude of the leaders was one of 'learning' from the West, not only in technology, but also in its institutions. They aimed for recognition as a civilised nation through the renegotiation of the unequal treaties, which denied Japan tariff autonomy and allowed the Western powers extraterritorial consular jurisdiction, as a major goal.

Fukuzawa argued that while the leaders behind the Meiji Restoration advocated revering the Emperor and 'expelling the western barbarians', neither of these goals was fundamental to the movement. According to him, these policies were 'branches and leaves', and the real objective of the 'Japanese people' was their liberty. By liberty, Fukuzawa meant liberation from the hereditary system of status, where one's livelihood, be it in agriculture, mercantile activities or a post in the domain's government, was determined at birth. This system was essentially one of primogeniture (the family professions was capable of accommodating only one of the sons), which meant that many samurai's sons were destined to be unemployed, without a government post to inherit, but also without property or the right to engage in commerce. Such lower-class samurai were the main drivers of the *Jôi* movement, and then of the Meiji Restoration. In this respect, one might say that the Meiji Restoration originated in a constitutional issue, regarding the rights of the individual and his place in the state apparatus.[16]

[15] Mitani (n 13) 61–65.
[16] For an analysis of the psychology of such samurai, see Watanabe (n 12) 398–402.

Another socio-political tension that had long-term consequences concerned Japan's relations with the rest of Asia. Confucianism formed the intellectual backbone of the early Meiji intellectuals, and the Government would be divided on how to engage, in particular, with China and Korea. While geopolitical concerns continued to dominate the discourse, the 1880s saw a rise in the notion of *Kô-A*興亜, the Rise of Asia as a whole, and engagement with modernising factions in China and Korea. As these efforts faltered in the face of the conservative forces in these countries, the opposing idea of *Datsu-A*脱亜, Leaving Asia, emerged. The name typically associated with this idea is that of Fukuzawa – his case was that it was dangerous to wait for other Asian nations to modernise, and Japan needed to modernise independently.[17] However, the importance of the *Kô-A* idea endured and provided the ideological basis (and justification) for the continental military expansion that began in the late nineteenth century, which eventually developed into the Great East-Asian Co-Prosperity Sphere. While the Meiji Constitution was drafted in view of Japan's particular modernisation context, it was eventually hijacked by military expansionists, particularly in domestic politics involving the notion of *Kokutai*国体. This will be touched upon at the end of this chapter.

ii. The Iwakura Mission and the Turn Towards Constitutionalism

The early years of the Meiji Government were marked by profound political tensions in the ruling elite – civil wars persisted until 1877. Drastic reforms were being implemented, one of the most radical being the abolition of Domains in 1871, effectively depriving the entire samurai class of the stipends on which they depended. Amid these tensions, however, a group of government leaders left Japan from 1871 to 1873 on a mission visiting the United States and Europe. The Mission consisted of over 100 members, many of whom were young students who remained abroad afterwards. These included the 18-year-old Kaneko Kentaro, and 6-year-old Tsuda Umeko, who became a pioneer of Japanese female education. One of the Mission's main diplomatic objectives was to postpone the renegotiation of the unequal treaties – its members saw that the negotiations were disadvantageous for Japan, given the state of Japan's ostensible modernisation. Another objective was to learn, and to obtain advice from these countries, in order for Japan to organise its laws and civic institutions in a manner that would allow it to be recognised as a 'civilised' nation.[18]

[17] A common misconception is that Fukuzawa wrote *Datsu-A Nyû-Ô*脱亜入欧 (Leaving Asia and Entering Europe). Whereas Fukuzawa himself never wrote the term *Nyû-Ô*, the slogan would gain a life of its own. Maruyama Masao, *Fukuzawa Yukichi no Tetsugaku* [The Philosophy of Fukuzawa Yukichi] (Iwanami Shoten, 2001) 280–85.

[18] Iokibe Kaoru, *Jôyaku Kaiseishi* [Meiji Treaty Revision: The Prospect for a Unified Jurisdiction and Nationalism] (Yuhikaku, 2010) 13–15.

The Mission statement indicates clearly how Japanese leaders situated Japan's place in a transnational order:

> The revision of these treaties will have to be based on the Public Law of the Nations (Rekkoku Kôhô 列国公法). Based on the Public Law of the Nations, any of our state laws, civil laws, trade laws, criminal laws, and tax laws, etc, if among these there are any that are in opposition to this Public Law, they must be changed and revised. It is imperative to formulate an approach and method for bringing about this change.

The Mission's objective was to 'report to and consult with' foreign governments. In his work that attempts to place the Meiji Constitution in the context of the history of civilisations, Takii Kazuhiro remarks on the optimism shown in this document, regarding the goodwill on the part of the Western powers to treat Japan fairly.[19]

Whether or not the leaders of the Meiji Government, with their experience of conflict with Western powers and civil war, maintained the naive optimism implied in this Mission statement, it is clear that they chose to accept the universality of international law, and wanted to revise their own laws in accordance with it, in the hope that they would be accepted as a civilised nation worthy of full membership of the transnational order.

While the Mission's negotiations over the treaty revision ended in chaos, records also indicate that members of the Mission were alert to the diversity among the Western powers, the *realpolitik* of international politics (especially involving the politics of international law), and the importance of a written constitution.[20] In particular, the Mission's meetings with German Chancellor Otto Von Bismarck and jurist Rudolf Von Gneist in the recently unified Germany (1871), highlighted the importance of tailoring a legal system suited to the particular context of a nation. Kido Takayoshi, who returned from the Mission in July 1873, submitted a proposal to establish *Seiki* 政規, a term that denotes basic norms of the polity. Okubo Toshimichi, another leading member of the Mission, stressed the importance of deliberating on the *Kokutai*国体, the basic formation of the state. To do so, it was imperative to institute *Kokuho* 国法, laws of the state, that would delineate and define the rights of the monarch and of the people.[21]

The Iwakura Mission appears to have brought about a change in the attitude of the Japanese establishment regarding legislation. There was a shift from the abstract principle that Japanese laws should be aligned with international law to enable the renegotiation and revision of the unequal treaties, to a more realistic and concrete strategy that involved strengthening the power of the state to ensure its survival in a potentially hostile international environment. This led to a clearer vision of the type of laws to be legislated – laws (including, but not limited to, the Constitution) that were suited to Japan's context. This, in turn,

[19] Takii Kazuhiro, *Bunmeishi no naka no Meiji Kenpo* (Kodansha, 2003) 21–27.
[20] ibid 54–80.
[21] ibid.

would lead to defining what 'Japanese-ness' meant, and this reformulation took place amid various political tensions.

II. LEGAL MODERNISATION AND THE REFORMULATION OF TRADITION

A. The Beginnings of the Liberty and Civic Rights Movement

One of the political tensions that emerged in the 1870s was between the government establishment, dominated by former Satsuma and Choshu samurai, and a coalition of former samurai who had either been ousted from, or never had the opportunity to participate in, the Meiji Government. The latter rallied around the notion of liberty and people's rights and pushed for wider participation in government. In January 1874, shortly after the return of the Iwakura Mission and Kido's proposal for *Seiki*, a proto-written constitution, a proposal to the Government on the establishment of an elected parliamentary body was submitted by a group led by Itagaki Taisuke and Goto Shojiro, statesmen who had recently been ousted following controversy over the Government's continental policy. This group, which became the Patriotic Public Party 愛国公党, was influenced by thinkers of the late Edo and early Meiji periods, who in turn introduced ideas such as social contract, universal human rights and the Enlightenment to the Japanese. These ideas, synthesised with Confucian ideas, informed constitutional debate in the Meiji period.[22] The proposal criticised the Japanese administration as one of bureaucratic despotism (*Yushi Sensei* 有司専制). Neither the Emperor nor the people had any real power. The proposal demanded the establishment of an elected parliamentary body to invigorate 'Public Discussion under Heaven'(*Tenka no Koron* 天下之公論), invoking the notion of *Koron* once more.[23]

On one hand, this proposal attracted immediate attention. Kato Hiroyuki, who would later become the first president of the University of Tokyo, argued controversially that it was too early to introduce such a parliamentary body. Controversy aside, this proposal is widely perceived to be the genesis of a major political movement – the Liberty and Civic Rights Movement. It produced over 60 draft constitutions between 1872 and 1887, until such work was prohibited by law in 1887.[24] On the other hand, the Government began initiatives to

[22] On the notion of the Enlightenment in Japan during the 1860s and 1870s, see Matsumoto Sannosuke, *Meiji Seishin no Kozo* [Structure of Meiji Thought](Iwanami shoten, 1993) 33–36. For a striking example of how Western political ideas were synthesised with Confucian thought, see Nakae Chomin's attempt to understand Rousseau's notion of *liberté morale* as an equivalent of *Kozen no ki* (*haoran zhi qi* 浩然之), a concept found in Mencius. Watanabe (n 12) 461–71.

[23] Minsen Giin Setsuritsu Kenpakusho 民選議院設立建白書 [Proposal for a Parliamentary Body Chosen from Among the People].

[24] *Hoan Jorei* 保安条例 (Security Ordinance) Edict no 67 of 1887（明治20年勅令第67号）.

codify. In 1873, Gustave Émile Boissonade, who produced the first Civil Code of Japan, arrived in Japan.

Moreover, the Meiji Government had more to worry about than the Liberty and Civic Rights Movement and codification of laws. Some former members of government, having left following the controversy on the continental policy (sending troops to Korea), were not contented with such reform proposals. Triggered by long-standing criticism and grievances against the Meiji Government, they resorted to civil war and rebellion. Eto Shinpei, one of the signatories of the proposal on a parliamentary body, eventually led an uprising in Saga the month after doing so. Saigo Takamori, one of the heroes of the Meiji Restoration, returned to Kagoshima in 1877 and led a rebellion that became known as the Southwestern War or the Satsuma Rebellion.

B. Kaneko Kentaro and the Drafting Process

In 1877, Kaneko Kentaro was completing his studies at Harvard Law School. His autobiography recounts that Oliver Wendell Holmes Jr, his constitutional law teacher, became worried that he was overworking. As a distraction, Holmes Jr brought Kaneko to meet members of Boston's high society – amongst those whom he met was Oliver Wendell Sr, the renowned physician and poet.[25] Returning to Tokyo the following year, Kaneko was offered a position at the Ministry of Justice at a salary equivalent to that of a graduate of the University of Tokyo. He refused this position on the grounds that a Todai graduate was hardly the peer of a Harvard graduate.[26] He collaborated with activists such as Baba Tatsui, and became engaged in a particular group of the Liberty and Civic Rights Movement. He was also employed as a part-time lecturer in law at the University of Tokyo. In 1880, however, he was employed by the Chamber of Elders, and began advising government leaders on how to engage the critics of the Government in debate. In particular, he is known to have introduced a conservative strand to the debate – the ideas of Edmund Burke.[27]

In 1881, the debate on the constitution took centre-stage on the political scene, when Okuma Shigenobu, a government councillor, produced a radical proposal calling for the introduction of a parliament and a British-style cabinet system, within two years. Ito Hirobumi, who had amassed immense power following the death of Kido Takayoshi in 1877 and Okubo Toshimichi in 1878, opposed this. Instead, he favoured a Prussian-style constitution with power concentrated in the hands of the Emperor. However, Ito (and his principal adviser Inoue Kowashi) did not have a concrete alternative. While Ito succeeded

[25] *Kaneko Kentaro Jijoden* Dai 1 shu [Autobiography of Kaneko Kentaro, vol 1] (Nihon University, 2003) 99.

[26] ibid 114–15.

[27] ibid.

in his political manoeuvres to oust Okuma from government, he also became acutely aware of the necessity for him to acquire a solid theoretical grounding and a proposal for a constitution.[28]

In 1882, Ito returned to Europe with his close adviser, Ito Miyoji. He would meet with leading jurists in Berlin and Vienna, among them Rudolf von Gneist and Lorenz von Stein. This experience boosted Ito's confidence. He saw that German jurisprudence had developed differently from the seventeenth- and eighteenth-century traditions on which his political opponents in Japan based their arguments. Stein in particular, who had made his own enquiries regarding Japan's context, left a strong impression on Ito. Ito wrote that having heard from Stein, whose arguments were based on history and evidence, he had nothing to fear from mediocre Japanese thinkers such as Okuma in particular. They had simply drawn the terms from this and that constitution, or this and that governmental function, without giving due consideration to their historical context or how they might operate in the context of Japanese society.[29]

Back in Japan, Inoue Kowashi, who was on the Iwakura Mission, and the most influential adviser on constitutional matters to both Iwakura and Ito, reached out to Kaneko Kentaro, requesting a meeting. In his autobiography, Kaneko recalls his frequent visits to Inoue's home, and in the course of exchanging views on political matters, they found that they had much common ground and deepened their friendship.[30]

In 1884, Inoue informed Kaneko that Ito Hirobumi wished to meet him. Soon after the pro forma introductions, Ito quickly asked Kaneko to become his official secretary – the Emperor had ordered him to draft a constitution and he needed Kaneko. After this, Kaneko joined the (then) 11-man division created in the Imperial Household Ministry, the *Seido-torishirabe-kyoku* (division for the investigation of institutions).[31]

At this point, it is instructive to outline the structure of government in early Japan. Prior to the drafting of the Constitution, the Meiji Government operated on the *Dajôkan-seido* system of the Grand Council of the State. With the Meiji Restoration, the Shogun 'returned' rule to the Emperor – the new Government employed official titles and basic notions from ancient aristocratic governments. After 1875, the Grand Council took charge of the executive, the *Genrô-in* (Senate) and *Chihôkan-kaigi* (Committee of Provincial Officials), the legislature, the *Dai-shin-in* (Supreme Court) and the judiciary. Much of the executive power was vested with four to 11 *Sangi*, whose number varied over

[28] Takii (n 19) 84–87.

[29] Hiratsuka Atsushi (ed), *Ito Hirobumi Hiroku* (Hara Shobo, 1982) 307. The perceived dichotomy between the historical school of jurisprudence, with its origin in 19th-century Germany, and the preceding natural law tradition would inform later debate in Japanese jurisprudence regarding the codification of the civil law. Matsubara (n 10) 775–76.

[30] Kaneko (n 25) 152.

[31] ibid 159–62.

time. Ito himself held this title until its abolition in 1885. There were also *Dai-jin* (Ministers), who were nominally superior to the *Sangi* councillors. These posts were held by former aristocrats with close ties to the Emperor. Ito saw them as neutral and plausibly useful in maintaining a balance of power.[32] Government ministries, being part of the executive, were controlled by the Grand Council, and consequently by the *Sangi*.

Following Kaneko's appointment to the *Seido-torishirabe-kyoku*, important changes were made to the formation of government institutions, with a view to incorporating them into the constitutional framework that was being drafted. In 1884, an aristocracy was instituted, with the intention of forming a 'House of Lords' type of upper house in a bicameral system. Finally, in 1885 the *Dajôkan* system itself was abolished. This move freed the executive from the control (albeit nominal) of the *Dai-jin* from the former aristocracy, in turn establishing a cabinet system. In 1886 the University of Tokyo was reorganised as the Imperial University, with the explicit aim of training the human resources necessary for the state. In the same year, Kaneko became the first person to teach constitutional and administrative law in this University.[33]

From May 1886, three members of the *Seido-torishirabe-kyoku* – Kaneko Kentaro, Inoue Kowashi and Ito Miyoji – were assigned to aid Ito in the actual drafting of the Constitution. They began to meet frequently at an inn in Yokohama. Ito would join them in these meetings, away from political opponents such as the Liberty and Civic Rights activists. In this relatively safe place, he would debate the Constitution with them, point by point. But the prevailing political tensions were never far from them. Once, Ito Miyoji had his papers stolen by a thief in this inn. This led to a major political scare – the drafting committee members construed this as a hostile act by opposing activists seeking information on the discussions. Partly in reaction to this incident, Ito built a house on a remote island off the Yokosuka Bay in May 1887, where members could meet and discuss in peace.[34] However, incidents continued to happen. Materials used in drafts were leaked. Armed activists showed up and demanded to see Ito. These incidents led to the enacting of the Security Ordinance in December 1887.[35] Under this law, over 500 activists were banished from Tokyo (3 *li*, that is, approximately 12 km, from the Imperial Palace). The law also was interpreted in such a way that private drafting of constitutional proposals was prohibited.[36] The drafting continued apace under Ito's leadership – public opinion was excluded, especially from the Liberty and Civic Rights Movement.

[32] Chuo Shimbunsha, *Ito-ko, Inoue-haku, Yamagata-ko Genkun-dan* [Conversations of Elder Statesmen Marquis Ito, Count Inoue, and Marquis Yamagata] (Bunbu-do, 1900).

[33] Kaneko (n 25) 177.

[34] ibid 177–85.

[35] ibid 187–95.

[36] Hoan Jorei保安条例 (Security Ordinance) Edict no 67 of 1887 (明治20年勅令第67号).

The final Constitution is well known for its incorporation of principles such as the separation of powers between the executive, legislature and the judiciary, and the enumeration of numerous civic rights, such as the right to a trial by law, liberty of speech and freedom of religion, which would be protected under specific legislation. These civic rights were, however, the rights of *Shinmin* 臣民, subjects, allowed by the sovereign, the Divine Emperor.[37] Most significantly, the Emperor's divinity, holiness and inviolability were explicitly written into Article 3 of the Constitution. The concept of sovereignty of the Emperor, who descended from a mythical unilineal line of descent for all generations, underpinned this entire structure of rules.[38]

C. The Divine Emperor as a Western Concept

The emergence of the idea of the Divine Emperor can be interpreted as part of the wider legal trend of recasting Japanese tradition in Western terms. In doing so, a tradition is invented or updated, and can in turn be incorporated in a 'civilised' society accepted by the prevailing international order of the time. For Ito Hirobumi, who had studied from thinkers as Rudolf von Gneist and Lorenz von Stein, it was important that the Constitution was tailored to the context of Japanese society. Yet one aspect of Japanese society troubled Ito – there was an absence of organised religion.

The early American missions to Japan explicitly observed that in Japan, 'the higher and better educated are indifferent to all religions' (from the Perry expeditions), or that 'all the higher classes are in reality *atheists*' (Townsend Harris). The American journalist and merchant Francis Hall wrote that even Confucianism was treated with disbelief. Furthermore, British diplomat Sir Rutherford Alcock described how the educated classes scoffed at such notions as an eternal soul or life after death, as notions that the ignorant lower classes subscribed to. Even Fukuzawa Yukichi evinced the view that the Japanese 'gentlemen' *shijin* 士人 did not believe in any religion. For the educated Japanese, what struck them most in their initial encounter with the West was how religion flourished, despite beliefs that they regarded as superstitious. Somewhat counterintuitively, the richness of religious life was deemed more impressive than the 'rational' or 'scientific' ethos.[39]

Ito, who was drafting the Constitution, was similarly impressed by how religion provided an 'axis' around which society revolved in Europe. In 1888,

[37] These included the right to be tried before a judge according to the law, the (inviolable) right to property, liberty of abode, freedom of religion, liberty of speech, publication, association and public meetings, to name but a few.

[38] This notion of mythical unilineal descent is expressed in the term, *Bansei Ikkei* 万世一系, which appears in Art 1.

[39] Watanabe Hiroshi, *Higashi Ajia no Oken to Shiso* [Monarchic Power and Thought in East Asia] (enlarged new edn) (University of Tokyo Press, 2016) 271–73.

Ito mentioned how religion permeated the depths of the human mind, and how minds coalesced around it. In his search for such an 'axis' in Japanese society, Ito drew a blank. Indeed, Mitani Taichiro speculates that Ito's meetings with Gneist on his European trip between 1882 and 1883 influenced his thinking on these matters.[40] Gneist stated in an 1885 lecture that the promotion of religion and the support of churches were important in creating a strong nation – religion brought people together through their belief, and caused them to sacrifice themselves for a higher purpose, for a nation that loved and protected them. He even went on to recommend that Japan use Buddhism as a means to achieve such ends.[41]

Ito, however, diverged significantly from Gneist in search of the functional equivalent of Christianity in Europe. He was inclined to believe that only the Imperial Household could be the 'axis' for Japanese society. In that sense, the Divine Emperor was an invented tradition stemming from the reception of a Western idea and not a tradition indigenous to Japan. The subsequent deification of the Emperor in the written Constitution, especially its interpretation through the notion of *Kokutai* 国体 (fundamental body/substance of the state), a notion that was at once all-powerful and yet semantically ambiguous, had long-lasting effects on Japanese politics, down to the end of the Second World War (1939–45).

In this process, a belief system known as State Shintoism was established. This involved the situating of the diverse shrines throughout Japan in a hierarchy – the Ise Shrine, which was the Shrine for the Imperial Household, was at its apex. Yet, for all its trappings, this form of Shintoism was not legally regarded as a religion. The Meiji Constitution guaranteed the imperial subjects' freedom of religion 'within limits not prejudicial to peace and order, and not antagonistic to their duties as subjects' (Article 28). State Shintoism was defined legally in terms of state rituals, with legislation providing for these rituals and the Emperor himself holding the supreme right to lead such rituals. The shrines, rather than being religious corporations (as they would become in the post-war world), were state institutions, and the priests were state employees.[42] Whether participation in these rituals was seen as comprising 'duties as subjects' was open to interpretation, with scholars on opposing sides, but it was clearly accorded a special status. This formulation eventually led to incidents, such as the one when Catholic students from Sophia University, a Jesuit institution, created a national scandal by refusing to pay their respects at the Yasukuni shrine in 1932. To them, these rituals at the Yasukuni shrine were seen as a curb on their religious freedom.[43]

[40] Mitani (n 13) 213–16.

[41] ibid, *Gneist-shi-danwa* [Conversations with Mr Gneist] (on file at the Center for Modern Japanese Legal and Political Documents, University of Tokyo, Graduate School of Law and Politics).

[42] The *Jingu Saishi-rei* 神宮祭祀令and the *Jinja Saishi-rei* 神社祭祀令, Minobe Tatsukichi *Kaitei Kenpo Satsuyo* [Compendium of the Constitution, rev edn] (Yuhikaku, 1946) 204ff.

[43] Kate Wildman Nakai, 'Patriotic Duty or Religious Rite? The 1932 Yasukuni Shrine Incident and the Issue of "Reverence at Shrines"', Japanese Studies Association of Australia Fifteenth Biennial Conference, The Australian National University, Canberra (2007).

III. THE CREATION OF THE MEIJI FAMILY

The drafting of the Constitution proceeded concurrently with codification in other areas of the law. Gustave Émile Boissonade spent the decade between 1879 and 1890 drafting the first civil code, while also advising the Government on international law, the renegotiation of the unequal treaties and the codification of criminal law. Hermann Roesler, who arrived from Germany in 1878, was tasked with drafting the commercial code, but also assisted by providing his insights (and at least one draft) on the Constitution.[44]

This is not the place to go into the details of the controversy regarding the civil code, but to illustrate the point of how Japanese tradition was reinterpreted and reformulated in the course of legal modernisation, we will briefly touch upon the creation of the legal entity of the Meiji family.

The draft civil code, much of which was written by Boissonade, was enacted in 1890. The original plan was for the code to come into effect in 1893, but a controversy arose regarding its content, and its enforcement was postponed and extensive redrafting carried out.[45]

One of the most vocal critics of the code was Hozumi Yatsuka, who had recently returned from Germany (and hence was not Kaneko's student) and was appointed professor of public law at the Imperial University. Hozumi's often-cited dictum was 'Civil Law emerges, and Loyalty and Filial Piety Perish.' What sounded like a defence of traditional Japanese values against Western influence, however, turned out to be a comprehensive reinterpretation of Japanese history in specifically Western terms:

> Ours is a country of Ancestral religion, the home of the family system … [W]hen we talk of the clan or of the state, it is but an extension of the family system … in short, the practices and rules particular to us are very similar to those of pre-Christian Europe. However, our jurists appear to take as a standard the jurisprudence developed in Europe after Christianity, and to have forgotten that we are not a Christian nation. This is regrettable.[46]

The characterisation of Japanese society as one of 'ancestral religion', a term that did not exist in pre-Meiji Japanese language, and equating it with the pre-Christian European state, is taken straight from Fustel de Coulange's *La Cité antique* of 1864, in which Fustel sees the Greek and Roman city-states as being formed with the family as their basic units, and that the family in turn

[44] Roesler's draft was used as material in the actual drafting by Ito, Inoue, Kaneko and Ito (Miyoji). On the incident in which Boissonade's proposal for treaty revision and Roesler's draft for the Constitution were leaked to the press in 1887, see Kaneko (n 25) 188–90.

[45] It is worth noting that the family law section was written not by Boissonade but by a group of Japanese jurists, in order to take account of Japanese 'customs'. On the significance of fitting traditional Japanese elements into the (westernised) legal debate by characterising such elements as 'customs', see Matsubara (n 10) 774–78.

[46] 'Minpo idete Chuko horobu', *Hogaku Shinpo*, vol 5 (1891).

was brought together in ancestral worship. The disintegration of the city-states came with the downfall of this ancestral religion and the rise of Christianity.[47]

Partly due to such criticism, the code was redrafted and the Meiji family system was created. The traditional (pre-Meiji) family was basically defined by its occupation. The family functioned as a building-block of the state (in this case the state would primarily be the Domain (*Han*) ruled by a Lord (*Daimyo*)), and being born into a family meant either inheriting the family occupation or having to fend for oneself. Property, to the extent one was allowed to hold it (the samurai were famously prohibited from owning land, their stipend being paid in rice), belonged primarily to the family unit and was basically inalienable.[48] After this system was abolished following the Meiji Restoration, with much greater freedom to choose one's occupation and newly instituted property rights that involved alienability, the traditional family unit became obsolete, especially in relation to a capitalist economy that involved market transactions of land.[49]

The new family system thus needed to be compatible with a new order of civil law, and this led to the the creation of the *Koshu*, the family head. He was the individual owner of the property that belonged to the family, but also had legal obligations towards other family members. This, again, was a reformulation of Japanese tradition in a primarily western legal framework, which tried to reconcile the need to preserve aspects of family unity that had hitherto functioned in a completely different social environment.

IV. THE CHANGING PLACE OF JAPAN IN THE INTERNATIONAL ORDER AND THE MEIJI CONSTITUTION

A. Japan between Anglo-American and Continental European Influences

As we have seen, Japan's initial opening to the world was brought about by the United States, and Japan's integration into the international order through the unequal treaties was also led by the United States. Given these origins of modern Japan, it might seem a little odd that it was legal advisers such as Boissonade and Roesler who played a dominant role, with American influence being much less visible. While European influence was quick to arrive at the end of the Tokugawa period, and while the Shogunate sought military advice from France, American influence on the various aspects of modernisation was in no way negligible. Takayanagi Kenzo, who was professor of Anglo-American law at the Tokyo Imperial University, writes of the early days of the University, when Japanese

[47] La Cité antique (1864).

[48] This system has been described as *kashoku kokka* 家職国家, Nation of Family Businesses, Watanabe (n 12) 70–87.

[49] Kentaro Matsubara, 'The Meiji Land Reform and the Formation of Modern Land Rights in Japan' in Sui-wai Cheung (ed), *Colonial Administration and Land Reform in East Asia* (Routledge, 2017) 37.

laws were still nascent and the study of law consisted of studying foreign law. Students would be divided into those learning French law in French and English law in English, and the two schools eventually formed antagonistic camps:

> The most prominent foreign teacher of the French school was Gustave Emile Boissonade de Fontarabie … The most eminent scholar of the English school was an American, Professor Henry T Terry, who came to Japan in 1877 and devoted a major part of his life to the study and teaching of common law at Tokyo University … If the French school advocated the universal validity of civilized jurisprudence, the English school stressed that the law is and ought to be an embodiment of national customs … However, in view of the strong national aspirations to abolish extraterritoriality, the English school as well as the French had to recognize the necessity of codification of law along occidental lines. It was codification as a political exigency which brought about the defeat of the English school.[50]

Other than Henry Terry, American legal advisers such as John Henry Wigmore and George W Hill certainly influenced Japanese legal thinking, especially in relation to the use of 'custom'. However, American influence on early Meiji Japanese society was more pronounced in the area of education, which influenced generations of Japanese at the grassroots level. American education expert David Murray of Rutgers College lived in Japan from 1873, advising the Ministry of Education for more than five years, influencing the curriculum and school architecture.[51] English became the most popular foreign language for students, and English loan words in Japanese tended to be American rather than British.

B. William Smith Clark and the Christian Intellectuals of Modern Japan

Another influential American in early Meiji Japan was William Smith Clark, one of the agricultural experts who aided in the founding of an agricultural college in Sapporo. This later developed into Hokkaido Imperial University. Clark stayed in Sapporo only for a few months, and hence taught only the first graduating class. However, his teaching of 'ethics' with the Bible profoundly influenced this class, and they all converted to Christianity. When the second class arrived, this first class of students enthusiastically tried to convince them to convert as well. In this second class were two of the most influential Christian intellectuals of Meiji Japan – Uchimura Kanzo and Nitobe Inazo. While Christianity did not necessarily attract a very large number of converts, it was clear that it succeeded in recruiting many intellectuals of former samurai background.[52]

[50] Kenzo Takayanagi, 'Contact of the Common Law with the Civil Law in Japan' (1955) 4 *The American Journal of Comparative Law* 60, 60–61.

[51] James C Thomson Jr , Peter W Stanley and John Curtis Perry, *Sentimental Imperialists: The American Experience in East Asia* (Harper Torchbooks, 1985) 71.

[52] ibid 77.

Uchimura and Nitobe both went to study in the United States in 1884, and eventually returned to teach at the First High School, an elite institution where most of the students went on to Tokyo Imperial University. Uchimura oversaw and taught a Bible study group, whose members included many of the leading intellectuals of twentieth-century Japan. To name but three, these included Nanbara Shigeru, the President of the University of Tokyo in the early post-war era, Tanaka Kotaro, later Chief Justice of the Supreme Court and a Judge at the International Court of Justice, and Yoshino Sakuzo, leader of the Taisho Democracy Movement of the 1910s and 1920s. Many of these students were recommended to Uchimura by Nitobe, who became headmaster of the High School after Uchimura was fired from the school in 1891 for not paying sufficient respect to the Imperial Rescript on Education that was decreed by the Divine Emperor.

Nitobe, in addition to being an influential teacher and academic (he became Professor of Colonial Administration at Tokyo Imperial University), became known as an international statesman of stature – he was eventually appointed Under-Secretary General of the League of Nations in 1920. His lasting fame on a more global scale, however, stemmed from a book he wrote in 1900. *Bushido: the Spirit of Japan*, a work originally written in English and published in Philadelphia for a non-Japanese audience, is a prime example of Japanese traditions that were reformulated in a Western context, which then became dogma in the Japanese understanding of such traditions.

The book's Preface starts with a conversation between Nitobe and a Belgian jurist. The latter asks Nitobe whether it is true that Japanese schools offer no religious education, and Nitobe replies that indeed they do not. The Belgian jurist exclaims 'No religion! How do you impart moral education?' This caused Nitobe to conclude that notions of right and wrong came to him through Bushido, the Way of the Samurai.[53] The first chapter then opens with the very word that Nitobe cited in order to explain the concept:

> Chivalry is a flower no less indigenous to the soil of Japan than its emblem, the cherry blossom; nor is it a dried-up specimen of an antique virtue preserved in the herbarium of our history.

Nitobe then went on to unpack the historical layers of the concept, freely citing Caesar, Tacitus and Thomas Hughes (*Tom Brown's Schooldays*), referring to the value system of his own Quaker beliefs.[54] The basic programme of each subsequent chapter picked concepts or institutions that appear characteristic of Bushido ('politeness', 'loyalty' or 'institutions of suicide and redress', to cite but a few), and explained them by setting them in a context of discourse based on Western concepts. Indeed, in the Preface to a later edition, Nitobe regretted being unable to include a chapter on filial piety, not because he could not articulate his views on the (Japanese) notion itself, but because he did not know

[53] Inazo Nitobe, *Bushido: the Soul of Japan* (The Leeds & Biddle, 1900) Preface, v–vi.
[54] ibid 1–7.

enough of the 'Western sentiment' regarding the subject to draw satisfactory comparisons.[55]

Nitobe's book enjoyed remarkable success and was translated into numerous languages, including Japanese. The Preface to the 10th and revised edition, written in May 1905 during the Russo-Japanese War (remarkably, four days before the Battle of Tsushima), recounted how a Russian officer held in captivity in Japan had prepared a Russian translation.[56]

Bushido was but the first of a distinguished line of works by Western-trained Japanese intellectuals, presenting their views on Japanese traditions within a Western conceptual framework, *The Book of Tea* by Okakura Kakuzo (Okakura Tenshin), *Zen Buddhism and its Influence on Japanese Culture* by Daisetz Teitaro Suzuki, and *The Structure of Iki* by Kuki Shuzo being other prime examples.

Coming back to the Meiji Constitution, an episode illustrates how such an American-trained intellectual as Nitobe viewed the Constitution, which was widely known to have adopted a Prussian model. Having studied in Johns Hopkins University from 1884, Nitobe was continuing his studies in Berlin when the Meiji Constitution was promulgated in February 1889. A German who invited Nitobe to a dinner criticised the Japanese Constitution as being a copy of the German Constitution. He further opined that it was strange for Japan, with its different historical background, to simply copy the German model. Initially trying, and then failing, to convince this interlocutor that the Japanese Constitution was *not* a carbon copy of the German, Nitobe turned around and said:

> If so, it is similar to the German constitution itself being a copy of the American constitution. The German constitution just changes the term 'President' into 'Emperor', replaces 'Republic' with 'Empire', and translates 'Congress' into Reichstag (Imperial Diet), but otherwise just copies the Constitution of the United States. If Japan is similar to Germany in its constitution, it is not surprising, since both are copying from the same American model.[57]

Whether or not Nitobe actually believed this to be the case, it does appear to reflect the thinking of a Japanese whose first exposure to Western culture was through the United States.

C. The Formation of Japan as a Modern Nation State in its Interaction with the United States

Shortly after the promulgation of the Meiji Constitution in 1889, Kaneko Kentaro was sent on a mission to Europe and America. Primarily, this was to survey the

[55] Inazo Nitobe, *Bushido: The Soul of Japan*, 13th edn (Eight Winds Books, 2016) 9–10.
[56] ibid.
[57] *Nitobe Inazo Zenshu* [The Complete Works of Nitobe Inazo], vol 6 (Kyobunkan, 1969) 47ff.

functioning of parliamentary bodies prior to opening the Imperial Diet. Its other aim was to present the English translation of the *Kenpo Gikai* 憲法義解, a text incorporating official commentaries and explanations of the Meiji Constitution, to jurists and scholars for their evaluation. These jurists and scholars included Herbert Spencer and Henry Sidgwick in England, Rudolf von Jhering and Rudolf von Gneist in Germany, Lorenz von Stein in Austria, and Oliver Wendell Holmes Jr in the United States.[58] Having codified its laws with the objective of being recognised as a 'civilised' nation, and the ultimate objective of eventually revising the unequal treaties, such an evaluation mattered greatly to the Meiji Government.[59]

While the evaluation was largely positive, especially regarding how characteristics particular to Japan were incorporated, the renegotiation of the unequal treaties took much longer. For this necessitated not only the codification of other laws, including the civil and commercial codes, but also the emergence of more favourable conditions in international politics. In the 1890s, with the building the Trans-Siberian Railway, Britain feared Russian encroachment on British interests in the Far East. To secure Japan as an ally in the region, Britain agreed to a partial renegotiation with the Japanese. This eventually resulted in the abandonment of extraterritorial consular jurisdiction in 1894. This was signed shortly before the Sino-Japanese War (1894–95). Japan's rise as an imperial power ultimately coincided with the process of treaty renegotiation, which finally bore fruit in 1911. Throughout the crucial period of negotiations, one of the most influential legal advisers in the Foreign Ministry was American lawyer Henry Willard Denison, who provided both legal advice and draft treaties from 1880 to 1914. One of his important long-term contributions was to nurture a culture within Japanese diplomacy that would generally try to maintain good relations with Britain and the United States. As a result, in the years leading to Japan's war with these powers, when most of the Government became increasingly hostile toward them, the Foreign Ministry would continue its efforts to minimise tensions.[60]

In the meantime, Japan's relations with the United States were largely cordial. For the Japanese, the United States did not have competing interests in geopolitically important areas of East Asia, and thus appeared to be less of a threat than the European powers. For the United States, the emergence of modernising Japan as a regional power and its victory over imperial China in 1895 were welcomed. They appeared to confirm the American sense of superiority and of

[58] Kaneko Kentaro (with annotations by Obuchi Kazunori), *Obei Giin Seido Torishirabe Junkaiki* [Record of travelling mission to survey parliamentary institutions in Europe and America] (Shinzansha, 2001).

[59] Kaneko would meet with Thomas Erskine Holland, professor of international law at Oxford, and receive detailed advice on a strategy for revising the treaties. Ito Takashi, *Nihon no Uchi to Soto* [Inside and Outside in Japanese Modernity] (Chuo-koron, 2001) 120ff.

[60] Thomson, Stanley and Perry 1985 (n 51) 134–35.

mission, that the westward course of empire reached one point of culmination, with America positively influencing Japan in its civilising mission.[61]

American public opinion, partly influenced by the efforts of Kaneko, was also generally pro-Japanese during the Russo-Japanese War (1904–05), and Japan was happy to find a mediator in Theodore Roosevelt for the peace negotiations at Portsmouth. Nitobe's *Bushido* appears to have played a part in securing Roosevelt's support, as one of Roosevelt's letters to Kaneko mentions the book with appreciation.[62] Nitobe's 1905 Preface to the 10th edition also noted that the President was distributing copies of the book among his acquaintances.[63]

The content of the Portsmouth treaty, however, was a disappointment for the Japanese public. The result – gaining just the southern half of Sakhalin Island and the failure to secure an indemnity – was at odds with great military victories that the Government had portrayed. A major riot occurred in Tokyo, and sentiments toward the United States also began to cool.

At the same time, Japanese and American interests in the region were beginning to cause tensions between the two nations. When Japan protested against the removal of a Hawaiian queen by local whites and the restriction of Japanese immigration in 1893, the McKinley administration responded by beginning the process that resulted in Hawaii's formal annexation in 1898. In the same year the Spanish-American War broke out, and following the Philippine declaration of independence, the United States would occupy the Philippines and precipitate the Philippine-American war. On the American side, there was a fear that if they did not occupy the Philippines, the Japanese might. On the Japanese side, while there was long-running sympathy for Philippine independence activists, some of whom eventually based themselves in Japan and collaborated with other Asian activists as Chinese revolutionaries, this can be seen as a response towards renewed American imperialism.[64]

In July 1905, shortly before the commencement of the peace talks at Portsmouth, Prime Minister Katsura Taro and United States Secretary of War William Howard Taft held talks in Tokyo, and signed a memorandum on the points agreed. This was the Katsura-Taft Agreement. Japan confirmed it had no territorial interests in the Philippines, while Taft in return concurred that the establishment of a Japanese protectorate over Korea would directly contribute to stability in East Asia. While the agreement may have been a reiteration of the positions previously held by the two powers, it consolidated the geopolitical landscape of the western Pacific in the early twentieth century.[65]

[61] ibid 78, 81, 137.

[62] Letter from Theodore Roosevelt to Kentarō Kaneko, Theodore Roosevelt Papers, Library of Congress Manuscript Division at www.theodorerooseveltcenter.org/Research/Digital-Library/Record?libID=o187994, Theodore Roosevelt Digital Library, Dickinson State University.

[63] Nitobe (n 55) 9–10.

[64] Philippine representative to Japan Mariano Ponce to President Emilio Aguinaldo, 8 June 1899.

[65] Raymond A Esthus, 'The Taft-Katsura Agreement – Reality or Myth?' (1959) 31 *The Journal of Modern History* 46.

The first decade of the twentieth century would also see hostilities in the United States against Japanese immigration, which was partially seen as a state-sponsored expansion by Japan into American territory. Moreover, after the Japanese victory in the Russo-Japanese War, its military was soon regarded as a strategic threat, and while it was still over 30 years before the outbreak of open warfare in 1941, the seeds for that outcome had been sown.[66]

While Japan's military successes were largely responsible for its acceptance in the world as a modern nation state and regional power, the Meiji Constitution certainly played a major role as well. The process of drafting and promulgating the Constitution was not a purely domestic one but one that was in constant interaction with the dynamics of the international order, into which Japan was integrating itself. In the course of this integration, the Japanese would reinterpret and reformulate what it was to be Japanese: such reinterpretation and reformulation, consciously or unconsciously, used Western concepts and frameworks, thereby creating new notions of what was traditional, and what was particular, to the emergent nation. In the legal sphere, the Anglo-American legal tradition of seeing law as developing in concrete, particular social contexts, as well as the German school of historical jurisprudence, was important in causing the Japanese to critically examine their own traditional practices, reformulate them and incorporate them into the law. Moreover, the integration of Japan into the Eurocentric international order was itself initiated by the Americans, and it is evident that in the period described above, the development of Japanese society involved rich and diverse interaction with Americans at various levels, be they advisers to various Japanese institutions, teachers, missionaries or government officials pursuing American national interests. Such interactions are an important part of the story of how Japan found its place as a modern nation state in the international order, and this chapter has attempted to tell part of that story.

V. EPILOGUE

The Meiji Constitution was the first Western-style constitution in East Asia. It incorporated both Western legal principles that were deemed universal and elements that the drafters perceived as particularly suited to Japan. In looking at the historical traditions, the constitutional politics and the legal formulations at work, this chapter made the somewhat counterintuitive point that the notion of the separation of powers was easier to adopt because of its affinity with Tokugawa institutions, while the Divine Emperor, with its reference to the mythical unilineal line of descent for all generations (萬世一系 *bansei ikkei*), was a conscious creation designed to replicate the function of Western religion in a Japanese setting.

[66] Thomson, Stanley and Perry (n 51) 144–45.

This divinity of the Emperor having been written into the Constitution meant that the Constitution did not have a 'secular' nature, or a clear separation from what might be regarded as 'sacred' in society. Moreover, the Emperor held the supreme power of command regarding the military. In other words, the military came under the direct control of the Emperor.

In discussions of constitutional structure, the term *Kokutai* 国体was used throughout the era. However, while its semantic meaning was somewhat ambiguous, its political significance changed drastically before and after the promulgation of the Constitution. Literally, this term means the Body of the State, or the Fundamental Body/Substance of the State. When Okubo Toshimichi, on his return from the Iwakura Mission, stated that a debate on *Kokutai* was needed, it meant that a fundamental debate was necessary on what the basic formation of the Meiji State should look like. When Kaneko Kentaro was participating in the drafting of the Constitution, he distinguished between *Kokutai* 国体 and *Seitai* 政体, the latter translatable as Polity. His argument was that *Seitai* was something that changed according to how the state or government was organised. *Kokutai* was not changeable in that way but fundamental to each nation, and not something that a constitution could alter. Kaneko used Edmund Burke's notion of the 'fundamental political principle of England' as his understanding of *Kokutai*.[67]

Once the Divine Emperor was created, and given its place as Sovereign in the Constitution, the already ambiguous term *Kokutai* was conferred with a layer of sacredness in its meaning. Consequently, if any statement, or legal/political argument, was deemed to show insufficient reverence or respect that was due to a supreme divinity, that is the Divine Emperor, anyone seeking to attack that statement or argument simply needed to characterise it as being against the *Kokutai*. There would come a time in the 1930s when the entire Law Faculty of Tokyo Imperial University was accused of peddling anti-*Kokutai* ideology.[68]

Mitani Taichiro has argued that Japan's road to the Second World War was caused by a decentralisation of the regime. Rather than seeing the outcome as one driven by how the military (or certain factions therein) monopolised power, he instead focuses on how successive civilian governments were destabilised by their loss of control of the military, which was capable of staging coups and assassinations on one hand, and then emerging as the only entity capable of containing such activities on the other.[69] In the Meiji Constitution, with the Divine Emperor and the ambiguity of the notion of *Kokutai*, those wishing to destabilise any particular regime or government had found an ideal weapon.

[67] Kaneko (n 5) 166–69.

[68] Tachibana Takashi, *Tenno to Todai* [The Emperor and the University of Tokyo], vol 2 (Bungei Shunju, 2005) 112–15.

[69] Mitani Taichiro, *Kindai Nihon no Senso to Seiji* [War and Politics in Modern Japan] (Iwanami Shoten, 2010).

The Controversy on the Violation of the Right of Supreme Command (which claimed that the Government, negotiating naval disarmament in 1930, without the explicit endorsement of the naval command, had violated the Emperor's right of supreme command) and the Emperor as Organ Theory Controversy (where a constitutional theory was criticised as anti-*Kokutai* and treasonous because it used the term 'organ' for the Emperor – which lacked respect for the deity – and successfully staged a *de facto* coup d'état in the bureaucratic establishment) were two such examples.

A further development would be how the Meiji Constitution would eventually connect to the Post-war Constitution. Kaneko Kentaro wrote that Ito Hirobumi made the point that the Meiji Constitution should be limited to the large framework of imperial rule, with simple articles and a high degree of adaptability in accordance with the nation's development.[70] This characteristic was inherited by the Post-war Constitution, which is known for being extremely short – roughly a quarter in length of the global average of approximately 200 constitutions. It has been argued that this was largely due to many provisions' stipulating that certain aspects of the constitutional order would be 'provided for by law'.[71] The Meiji Constitution thus provided the backdrop for, in turn, an authoritarian regime dominated by former samurai of particular domains, a two-party system that functioned in the 'Taisho democracy' period, and the militarist governments of the 1940s.

However, the history of these events, which would unfold again in close conjunction with Japan's attempts first at finding its place in the prevalent international order and then at building an alternative transnational order, must be left for another paper.

[70] Oguma Eiji, 'Senro to Juyo: Nihonkoku Kenpo no Seitei katei to sono Seikaku' [Occupation and Acceptance: The Formation Process of the Japanese Constitution and its Characteristics] (2020) 34 *Quarterly Jurist* 128.

[71] Kenneth Mori McElwain (with Christian Winkler), 'What's Unique about Japan's Constitution? A Comparative and Historical Analysis' (2015) 41(2) *Journal of Japanese Studies* 249.

7

*Thirty-Years-Old at Birth? The Constitutional Founding of the Republic of Korea**

CHAIHARK HAHM**

INTRODUCTION

THE INDEPENDENCE OF the South Korean state became official on 15 August 1948, three years to the day after Korea's liberation from Japanese colonial rule. A ceremony was held in Seoul at a specially-constructed platform in front of the former Japanese Governor-General's headquarters. In addition to the members of the newly formed government of the Republic of Korea, the event was attended by Douglas MacArthur, the Supreme Commander for the Allied Powers, who had flown in from Tokyo, and John R Hodge, the commanding officer of the US Armed Forces in Korea that had been occupying the southern part of the Korean Peninsula since Japan's surrender. Also participating were some members of the United Nations Temporary Commission on Korea, which had overseen Korea's very first general election three months earlier. The National Assembly that was created by the election had adopted Korea's 'Founding Constitution' on 12 July 1948. The first President of the Republic, Syngman Rhee,[1] elected according to that constitution, opened his commemorating address with these words 'On this day, we are gathered at this ceremony to celebrate our liberation and simultaneously the

* The substance of sections I and III of this chapter were drawn from ch 1 of the author's *The Constitution of South Korea: A Contextual Analysis* (Hart Publishing, forthcoming).

** The author would like to thank Marie Seong-hak Kim and other participants in the workshop for their helpful comments. Sung Ho Kim, my collaborator in an earlier work on constitutional founding, also provided valuable insights, for which I am grateful, as always.

[1] According to the McCune-Reischauer system, the name of the first President of South Korea (李承晩) would be romanised as: 'Yi Sŭng-man'. This chapter, however, will follow the conventional usage and refer to him as Syngman Rhee. All other personal names will be romanised according to the McCune-Reischauer system and will follow the Korean convention of placing the family name before the given name.

renewed birth of our Republic.' At the end of his address, Rhee marked the date as 'Fifteenth of August, Year Thirty of the Republic of Korea.'

In a way, this event nicely captures the multiple layers of meaning with which Korea's constitutional founding was imbued. Deliberately held on the third anniversary of the end of Japanese rule, it was a marker for national independence regained. As such, it signified the rejection of imperialism and foreign subjugation. It also meant the end of the three years of American occupation since liberation. Yet restoration of independence did not mean the resurrection of the pre-colonial dynastic order. As ordained by Article 1 of the Founding Constitution, the new Korean state would be a 'democratic republic', founded on the principle of popular sovereignty and self-government. At the same time, as Rhee sought to underscore, the new state would be understood as the 'renewal' of a previous 'republic' established in 1919. This reference to a supposed indigenous republican tradition, during colonial times, was actually enshrined in the Constitution's preamble. Also, as illustrated by the presence of foreign dignitaries, Korea's constitutional founding took place under the auspices of the United Nations, in a context marked by the onslaught of the Cold War and the looming presence of the United States. Rhee's address noted that the celebration could not but be dampened by the fact that 10 million fellow Koreans in the northern half of the peninsula were prevented from taking part in the founding due to interference by the Soviet Army. In fact, barely a month later, a separate communist government would be proclaimed in the north under the patronage of the Soviet occupying forces.[2] In sum, South Korea's constitutional founding was a true milestone in the history of the Korean nation, in that it saw the establishment of a republic based on popular sovereignty and the rejection of colonial bondage, and yet it was also a process inescapably coloured by deep ideological tensions and geopolitical anxieties.

This chapter will start with some historical background by focusing on how the ideal of constitutionalism became an integral part of Korea's struggle for independence. It will next describe the geopolitical setting after liberation from Japanese rule, particularly the division of Korea and its occupation by the Allied Powers, and how Koreans sought to implement a constitutional government even in such constricted circumstances. Then the chapter will turn to the process of drafting the first constitution of South Korea and highlight certain themes and topics that were prominently discussed in the National Assembly. The last section will be a reflection on the legacy the Founding Constitution for the later development of South Korean constitutionalism.

[2] While the establishment of the Democratic People's Republic of Korea followed the founding of the Republic of Korea, preparations for creating a separate regime in the north began much earlier, when Stalin issued a directive to that effect in September 1945. The formation in February 1946 of the Provisional People's Committee of North Korea, under Soviet supervision, was in fact celebrated as the establishment of a full government.

I. PRE-HISTORY: CONSTITUTIONALISM UNDER COLONIAL OCCUPATION?

The last decades of the nineteenth century saw the Chosŏn (朝鮮) Dynasty, which had been ruling Korea since 1392, make feeble attempts to transform itself from a 'hermit kingdom' to a modern state by adopting a few Western-inspired legal and administrative reforms. Its penultimate monarch Kojong proclaimed himself an emperor and adopted a new name for the state – *Taehan Cheguk* (大韓帝國) or 'Great Han Empire'. Yet the Japanese Empire's annexation in 1910 turned Korea into a colony and shattered all hope of instituting a form of constitutional monarchy. With the loss of sovereignty, however, the ideal of constitutional government became all the more urgent and attractive for the Korean people. No longer a means to limit the power of the monarch, constitutionalism was now perceived as an essential means for re-establishing the state. Constitutional founding would be the process by which Korea regained independence. Indeed, less than a decade after annexation, the goal of the independence movement became the establishment of a republic.[3] Rather than restoring the defunct monarchy, most agreed that, with independence, Korea should be governed by the people through their representatives. 'Korea is an independent state and Koreans are a self-governing people' – these were the words commencing the 'Declaration of Independence', proclaimed on 1 March 1919, which sparked a months-long peaceful protest for independence throughout the nation.[4]

Although the protests were suppressed by the Japanese authorities, they became the symbol of the Korean people's resolve for independence. And although most of the organisers and participants in the March 1st Movement were imprisoned, the movement for independence and constitutional founding only intensified, albeit outside Korea. In April 1919, as many as eight groups purporting to 'represent' the Korean people came forward, all announcing a 'constitution' designed to set up a republican government. Some of these were no more than a list of cabinet members of a 'government' of the Korean people, and they often featured the same individuals (sometimes for different posts). Others were more substantive, having the form of a legal document. Yet all of them took for granted popular sovereignty as the foundational principle of the new Korean state. The authors of these documents, most of whom remained anonymous, apparently regarded themselves as agents of the Korean people who had expressed, through the March 1st Movement, their sovereign will for independence and constitutional government.

For example, on 11 April 1919, a 'Provisional Charter (*Imsi Hŏnjang* 臨時憲章) of the Republic of Korea', consisting of 10 articles, was proclaimed

[3] Kim Do-Hyung, *Taehan Chegukki ŭi Chŏngch'i Sasang Yŏn'gu* [A Study of Political Thought During Taehan Empire] (Chisiksanŏpsa, 1994) 426–34.

[4] 'Son Pyŏnghŭi and others: Declaration of Independence' in Peter H Lee (ed), *Sourcebook of Korean Civilization*, vol II (Columbia University Press, 1996) 432.

by a group based in Shanghai. Article 1 declared that Korea 'shall be a democratic republic' and Article 3 affirmed the equality of all people regardless of sex, class and wealth. Article 4 provided for various civil and political rights. Perhaps influenced by the Republican Chinese Government, a new republican calendar was adopted, according to which 1919 would be 'Year I of the Republic' (*Min'guk wŏnnyŏn* 民國元年). Aside from this group in Shanghai, two others – one based in Seoul and the other in the Russian Far East – had enough personnel and structure to act as the basis of an actual government.[5] These three groups agreed to merge and establish a united 'Provisional Government of the Republic of Korea' (KPG) with its headquarters in Shanghai. This resulted in a more comprehensive 'Provisional Constitution' (*Imsi Hŏnpŏp* 臨時憲法) (11 September 1919), consisting of 58 articles.[6] Article 2 of this document explicitly stated that the sovereignty of Korea resided in the entire people of Korea. For the time being, the exercise of sovereignty was delegated, 'within the limits of the constitution', to the Provisional President, who would be the head of state and oversee political affairs. At the same time, the document was intended to be the basis for a more permanent government based on the principle of separation of powers, and provided for three different branches of the government. The executive branch (State Council) would be headed by a Prime Minister, but his relationship to the Provisional President was not clearly spelled out.[7] Also, perhaps more critically, no term of office was specified for the Provisional President, who was to be elected by the legislative branch (Provisional Legislative Council). These points would be the source of a major crisis in the KPG.

At the time of the merger of the three groups, Syngman Rhee was already regarded as a natural leader for the united KPG and was elected Provisional President. Having been educated in the United States, however, Rhee's primary mode of operation was to lobby the American government to lead international opinion and exert pressure on the Japanese to grant independence to Korea. He was therefore away in Honolulu or Washington, DC most of the time, and scarcely seen at the KPG headquarters in Shanghai. This led to internal discord within the KPG leadership in the early 1920s, which nearly brought the 'government'

[5] The others turned out to be 'paper governments' without any real membership or organisation. The lists of their cabinet members often included the names of the same individuals, usually those who had acquired a nationwide reputation as leaders in the independence movement.

[6] One scholar regards this Provisional Constitution as a 'regression' from the Provisional Charter because it merely declared equality of all Koreans without specifically forbidding discrimination based on 'sex, class, and wealth', and because it omitted the provision banning capital punishment, bodily punishment and public brothels. Han In-sup, 'Taehan Min'guk ŭn Minju Konghwaje ro ham' [Republic of Korea shall be a Democratic Republic] (2009) 50(3) *Sŏul Taehakkyo Pŏphak* 167.

[7] According to one constitutional historian, the earlier Provisional Charter was a more original product of Cho So-ang, arguably the most intellectually creative member of the KPG, whereas the Provisional Constitution was a more hodge-podge of ideas and terms taken from the early Chinese constitution-drafting experiences of 1912–14. Shin Woo-cheol, 'Chungguk ŭi Chehŏnundong i Sanghae Imsijongbu Hŏnpŏpchejŏng e mich'in Yŏnghyang' [Influence of Chinese Constitution-making Movement on Korean Constitutionalism during Shanghai Provisional Government] (2004) 29 *Pŏpsahak Yŏn'gu* 5.

to a collapse. The crisis was exacerbated by the fact, mentioned above, that the Constitution did not specify a term for the President. Rhee finally left the KPG in acrimonious circumstances and resumed his own work for independence from his base in the United States.[8] After Rhee's departure, the KPG Constitution was revised in 1925 with a view to clarifying the institutional uncertainties. The office of the Provisional President was abolished and a position called 'Premier' was created, to be both head of state and the chief executive, who would serve for a fixed term and be responsible to the Provisional Legislative Council. The resulting constitution was considerably shorter (35 articles) than its predecessor. Provisions on individual rights and duties and on the judiciary were deleted, which probably reflects the reality that, being located overseas, the KPG could not offer protection for or adjudicate the rights of most Koreans. The provisional nature of the Constitution was also apparent in the provision that stated that the entire Korean people would be represented by 'activists in the independence movement' (*kwangbok undongja* 光復運動者).

Despite the revision of the constitution, the KPG was still far from a working government. Not only did it not exercise any effective control over Korea, it found it increasingly difficult to hold together the various factions that had developed within. This is not surprising given that the KPG was originally formed through a merger among various groups with different visions and approaches to the goal of independence. The situation was exacerbated by the emergence of 'political parties' among the independence leaders. Some of these even questioned the relevance of the KPG for the future of the independence movement. To accommodate the demands of these different factions, the constitution was revised once more in 1927. The office of Premier was abolished and a system of collective decision making was adopted, in which the State Council was the sole repository of executive power. The Chairman of the State Council was simply to be *primus inter pares*. Rejecting the idea of a strong executive, the new government was to be led by the Provisional Legislative Council. One interesting feature of this revision was the idea that the political party that united all independence activists would exercise the highest power of the state, if and when such a national party came into being. This of course reveals the emergence of political parties as an important part of the constitutional discourse at the time. It also reveals the influence of the Republican Chinese idea of 'party leadership', which in turn was inspired by Leninist notions of revolutionary vanguardism. Although the constitution declared that sovereignty of the Republic of Korea resided in the people, it also specified that before independence, sovereignty would reside in the 'entirety of independence activists'.

The next revision of the KPG Constitution was in 1940, after the KPG moved its headquarters, for the last time, to Chongqing in southwest China. Beginning

[8] Yun Tae-wŏn, 'Imsi Chŏngbu Pŏpt'ongnon ŭi Yŏksajŏk Yŏnwŏn kwa Uimi' [Historic Origins of KPG Succession Debate and Its Meaning] in Ko Jung-hyu et al, *Taehan Minguk Imsi Chŏngbu ŭi Hyŏndaesachŏk Sŏngch'al* (Nanam, 2010) 91.

with the Japanese invasion of China in 1931, the KPG had to relocate frequently in search of a safer base of operation. Between Shanghai and Chongqing, there had been six other cities where the KPG had set up shop. Constantly on the run, the KPG had to undergo a period when its survival could not be taken for granted. It was always strapped for operating funds, and it had to rely on meagre donations from overseas Korean organisations (including Syngman Rhee's in the United States)[9] and the Nationalist (KMT) Government of China under Chiang Kai-shek. At the same time, it continued to be plagued by internal dissention. Numerous 'political parties' sprouted under its umbrella, which constantly clashed with one another. The 'national party' that could unify all independence activists, anticipated in its constitution, never materialised. After relocating to Chongqing, under the leadership of Kim Ku (金九), the KPG was transformed to better serve as a base for military action against the Japanese Empire. Under the revised Constitution, the powers of the Chairman were bolstered to allow for a strong executive, who could issue executive orders and emergency decrees. The Chairman even had the power to command military forces. Accordingly, a 'Korean Restoration Army' was established, with support and training from Chiang Kai-shek's government. This became the umbrella under which various militias could join forces, which had been engaging in armed resistance against the Japanese in Manchuria and elsewhere. The KPG actually declared war against Japan in 1941 and made plans to fight as part of the Allied Powers.

The last revision of the KPG Constitution was in 1944. By way of shoring up its reputation as the leading organisation for independence, the KPG sought to prepare for a full-scale permanent government, to be established after liberation, by adopting a more complete constitution. As such, the 1944 Constitution featured a preamble and a chapter on the judiciary, both of which had been absent since the 1919 Provisional Constitution. The preamble pledged to inherit the 'blood and tears' of the countless patriots, and reaffirmed the nation's will as manifested in the 'March 1st Great Revolution'. The 62-article document also specified the territory of the Republic of Korea (Article 2), provided for a list of rights and duties of the people (Articles 5–7), and included a separate chapter on state finances (Articles 57–60). The bill of rights included the right to request education, work and livelihood assistance (Article 5, item 3). The powers of both the Chairman and the State Council were strengthened to make the government more workable. To underscore the KPG's claim to be the leader of the independence movement, the constitution stressed the role of 'independence activists' in government by requiring at least three years of experience in that role for members of the Provisional Legislative Council (Article 11), and 10 years for the Chairman and members of the State Council (Article 34).

[9] Rhee was eventually given the title of the leader of the KPG's legation to the United States and Europe, although he was also known to have represented himself as the 'President' of the Republic of Korea.

How effective the KPG was in the overall pursuit of independence, or whether it actually functioned as a 'government', may be the subject of debate among historians.[10] What is clear is the fact that its leadership was dedicated to the principle that a republic must be governed in accordance with the constitution. Even when it appeared less like a government than a group of underground independence activists, the KPG sought to justify its activities and its existence by reference to the principle of popular sovereignty enshrined in its constitution.[11] Despite the constant internal rivalry that threatened to tear it apart, it accepted as a given that its mandate and structure should be set out in a constitution. And despite the fact that it was never recognised by the international community, the KPG continually sought to ground its legitimacy in the ideals of popular sovereignty and republicanism. It may be that having a republican constitution was thought to be all the more necessary in this regard, given the repeated failure to win international recognition despite the persistent efforts of such KPG members as Kim Kyu-sik (金奎植).[12] The numerous revisions of its constitution may be regarded as a reflection of the conviction among its leaders that constitution-making must be an integral part of the process of founding a new independent republic.

Constitutional founding was needed not only for rejecting colonial oppression and undoing Japan's 'unnatural and unjust' subjugation of Korea.[13] It was also necessary for rejecting the pre-colonial dynastic order. The goal of independence was not to revive the defunct monarchy but to establish a new democratic republic. The dynastic order was as much the target of repudiation as the colonial regime. Constitutionalist ideas during the colonial period were in fact premised on the negation of 'double tyranny' – Japanese imperialism and pre-colonial dynastic rule.[14] This perspective is most visible in a 1941 KPG document called *Kŏnguk Kangnyŏng* (建國綱領), or 'Essential Points for Establishing a New State', which was to serve as a roadmap for the ultimate constitutional founding of an independent state after liberation.

[10] It is undeniable that the KPG was not the only actor in the independence movement, and its activities were carried out without the participation of the vast majority of the people in Korea.

[11] Oh HyangMi, 'Taehan Minguk Imsi Chŏngbu wa Iphŏnjuŭi: 'Hŏnpŏpkukka' rosŏŭi Chŏngdangsŏng Hwakpo wa Tillema' [Korean Provisional Government and Constitutionalism: Its Legitimation and Dilemma as Constitutional State] (2009) 49 *Kukche Chongch'i Nonch'ong* 277, 293–96.

[12] Even before the official formation of the KPG, Kim Kyu-sik led a Korean delegation to the Paris Peace Conference in 1919 to plead the case for Korea's independence, but was unsuccessful due to Japanese interference. Kim, who once pursued graduate studies at Princeton, was appointed the KPG's Foreign Minister during his stay in Paris. The KPG later sought to join the League of Nations but was similarly rejected. In 1920, the founder of the Republican Government of China, Sun Yat-sen, went so far as to acknowledge the need for mutual recognition, but the status of Sun's own Government at the time was rather precarious. Under Chiang Kai-shek, the KMT Government provided occasional financial assistance but never extended official recognition.

[13] 'Declaration of Independence' in Lee (ed) (n 4) 433.

[14] Yun Ch'i-ho, '25 October 1905', *Yun Chi-Ho's Diary, 1903–1906*, vol 6 (National History Compilation Committee, 1976) 179.

Invoking the 'Great Revolution' that brought about the Republic of Korea, it describes the March 1st Movement not only as having toppled 'despotism by a foreign nation', but also as having destroyed the 'five-thousand year-old encrustation of monarchic rule'. Overcoming the double tyranny was the first step towards the establishment of democratic institutions and the abolition of class distinction.[15]

II. LIBERATION, NATIONAL DIVISION AND CONSTITUTIONAL DEBATES

The KPG's experience in drafting and revising constitutions notwithstanding, constitutional founding of the South Korean state would not come about as a direct offshoot of those efforts. The KPG was actually only one of many overseas organisations that had been working toward independence, all of whom claimed to have a stake in the creation of a new state. Moreover, the project of founding a Korean state was made even trickier by the fact that liberation from Japan's colonial rule on 15 August 1945 was accompanied by the division of the Korean Peninsula along the 38th parallel. Originally conceived as a temporary military measure to facilitate the Japanese troops' surrender to the Allied Powers, the division ensured that Korea's post-colonial founding would be deeply coloured by various layers of external influence. With the arrival of the Soviet Union's Red Army in the northern part and the US Armed Forces in the south,[16] it became clear that any effort to create a new Korean state would be characterised by deep foreign involvement. At the time of their arrival, however, neither side appeared to have a clear plan or directive about what to do in Korea once the Japanese military had been neutralised and the colonial governing structure removed. The American troops in the south, in particular, seemed interested only in maintaining order until further instructions came from Washington, DC. They established the US Army Military Government in Korea (USAMGIK), which declared itself to be the only lawful authority in the territory. As a result, a group called 'People's Republic of Korea', which had been created in Seoul by local leaders such as Yŏ Un-hyŏng (呂運亨) prior to the arrival of American forces, was not given any recognition.[17] Similarly, when leaders of the KPG such as Kim Ku and Kim Kyu-sik returned from China, they were allowed to do so only

[15] Chaihark Hahm and Sung-ho Kim, *Making We the People: Democratic Constitutional Founding in Postwar Japan and South Korea* (Cambridge University Press, 2015) 174–75.

[16] The Red Army arrived in Pyŏngyang around 24 August 1945, whereas the US military arrived in Seoul on 6 September.

[17] A left-leaning founding member of the KPG, Yŏ Un-hyŏng initially trained to become a Christian pastor in Korea, before leaving for China where he attended the University of Nanking (Chinese: Jinling University). He later turned to socialism and was involved with Korean Communist groups in China, but was arrested in Shanghai by Japanese police and sent back to Korea in 1929. At the time of liberation, he was one of a few local leaders with a national reputation.

as individuals and not as members of any 'government'. According to its own self-understanding, the USAMGIK had come to occupy a legal 'no man's land' to create a new state where none existed.[18]

A. From the Moscow Plan to the United Nations

Further instructions on how to manage the Korean situation finally came in late December 1945, as part of the larger Allied plan for the post-war world order. It was decided at the Moscow Conference of the Foreign Ministers of US, UK and Soviet Union that a four-power (US, UK, China and Soviet Union) trusteeship would be established in Korea under the new United Nations framework. This arrangement could last up to five years, during which a 'Provisional Korean Democratic Government' should be set up, which in turn would prepare for a permanent government for a fully independent Korea. This process was to be overseen by a 'US–Soviet Joint Commission', which was to consult with local 'democratic parties and social organizations'. As soon as this plan was reported in Korea, however, protests erupted throughout the country. For most Koreans, who had expected to create an independent state of their own as soon as the Japanese were defeated, a trusteeship plan smacked of another form of foreign domination. Massive demonstrations were organised by various Korean groups demanding immediate and complete independence.[19] The leftist groups, however, soon changed their position and started supporting the trusteeship plan, presumably on the instructions of the Soviet authorities in the north. In the south, the American military government allowed the protests to continue, and silently sat by as one local newspaper reported (incorrectly) that the trusteeship idea was a Soviet plan.

The first meeting of the US–Soviet Joint Commission was convened in March 1946. As soon as they met, however, the negotiators on both sides disagreed over which local groups qualified as 'democratic parties and social organizations' that should be consulted in the process of creating the 'Provision Korean Democratic Government' according to the Moscow Plan. The Soviets insisted that anyone who opposed or criticised the trusteeship plan should not be allowed to participate. This was evidently unacceptable to the Americans, because that meant only the leftist groups would participate in the process. They countered with the argument that the Korean people's freedom of expression should be respected. This standoff between the Americans and Soviets effectively prevented the Joint Commission from making any progress on the trusteeship plan. After almost two years of posturing and mutual finger-pointing, the United

[18] Ernst Fraenkel, 'The Structure of United States Army Military Government in Korea' (1948), repr in (1985) 2 *Journal of Modern Korean Studies* 69.

[19] Sang-Yong Choi, 'Trusteeship Debate and the Korean Cold War' in Bonnie BC Oh (ed), *Korea Under the American Military Government, 1945–1948* (Praeger, 2002).

States finally decided in September 1947 to abandon the trusteeship idea and to refer the Korean question to the United Nations.

On 14 November 1947, the United Nations General Assembly (UNGA) adopted a resolution, over the Soviet Union's objections, to create a commission that would 'facilitate and expedite the attainment of the national independence of Korea and withdrawal of occupying forces'.[20] It also recommended that elections be held in Korea immediately so as to form a National Assembly, which would consult with the commission in establishing a National Government of Korea. Accordingly, a United Nations Temporary Commission on Korea (UNTCOK) was formed, consisting of delegates from eight member states,[21] which arrived in Seoul in January 1948. When it tried to travel to the northern part, however, the Soviet authorities refused to allow entry, which made it impossible for the Commission to fulfil its mission of holding an election throughout Korea. After being instructed by the Interim Committee of the General Assembly to oversee a general election 'in such parts of Korea as are accessible to the Commission', UNTCOK proceeded to observe and certify a general election held only in southern Korea. The historic election of 10 May 1948 established the National Assembly, comprising 200 'Representatives of the Korean People', whose first order of business was the drafting of a new constitution. After the election, UNTCOK submitted a report to the General Assembly, which said:

> The result of the ballot was a valid expression of the free will of the electorate of those parts of Korea which were accessible to the Commission and in which the inhabitants constituted approximately two-thirds of the people of all Korea.[22]

In terms of legal authorisation, the United Nations thus played a significant role in the establishment of Korea's modern constitutional order.[23]

It would appear that almost three years were wasted that could have been used to start Korea's process of constitutional founding. If only the superpowers had granted immediate independence and allowed the Korean people to engage in self-government, a democratic republic would have been set up much earlier. Or so goes the nationalistic narrative in South Korea. While it is quite impossible to know what would have happened if Koreans had taken over immediately after the departure of the Japanese colonial rulers, the likelihood is quite high that a left-leaning, if not outright communist, regime would have come into being. More importantly, the period between liberation and the UN-sponsored general election need not be seen as wasted time. It was indeed during this period that numerous constitutional drafts were produced by various political groups in

[20] UNGA Resolution 112(II), 14 November 1947.

[21] According to the resolution, the Commission was originally to have nine members, but the representative of the Ukrainian Soviet Socialist Republic refused to participate, arguing that the whole process is being directed by the United States.

[22] Following this logic, one-hundred seats in the National Assembly were to be filled by representatives from the northern part of the peninsula, when free elections could be held there.

[23] Hahm and Kim (n 15) 109.

Korea. When the US–Soviet Joint Commission asked local social organisations to submit outlines for the government of a new Korean state, over 400 proposals were submitted. It was a period marked by great uncertainty and volatility, but it was also a time when the Korean people of various political stripes engaged in constitutional politics of the highest sort to debate and argue about the future Korea state.

B. Constitution-making Efforts under American Occupation

The Soviet authorities in the north quickly quelled criticism of the trusteeship plan and set up in February 1946 an Interim People's Committee for North Korea consisting of supporters of the Moscow decision. In 1947, a permanent People's Committee was established, which began preparing a constitution for a separate northern regime. In the south, by contrast, anti-trusteeship demonstrations continued to rage, and the US authorities wavered between carrying out the decision of the Moscow Conference through the US–Soviet Joint Commission and preparing for a separate, pro-American South Korean government. As its goal was not clear, the USAMGIK showed relatively little interest in the constitution-making process.

For Koreans under the USAMGIK, however, adopting a constitution was one of the most urgent orders of business, and they chose to begin the process regardless of the official position of the occupying authorities. A case in point is a group called Emergency National Assembly, originally formed under Kim Ku for the purpose of maintaining the KPG as the basis of the new government of independent Korea. With the support of members of the newly formed right-wing Korean Democratic Party, this group in February 1946 appointed a committee to draw up a draft constitution. This group would soon merge with another one led by Syngman Rhee, called the National Society for the Rapid Realization of Korean Independence. The combined group then delegated to Rhee and Kim the power to appoint a 'supreme political commission'. This 28-member body was renamed the Korean Representative Democratic Council of South Korea (*Nam Chosŏn Taehan Kungmin Taep'yo Minju Uiwŏn*) and was given semi-official status by being made an advisory group to General John Hodge, the head of the US occupying forces. This was clearly not an elected body, nor was it expected to replace the military government. Regardless, it immediately started acting as if its job was to be a transitional government. It established numerous committees, among which was a committee to draft a constitution.

Another early attempt to draft a constitution was made in January 1946 by a group consisting mostly of Koreans who had served in various positions in the colonial bureaucracy. Although these individuals feared being branded 'collaborators' in the post-liberation context, their experience and expertise were sought out by Shin Ik-hee (申翼熙), a member of the KPG, who brought them together to form the Administration Research Association (*Haengjŏng Yŏnguhoe*).[24] Ostensibly a 'private' group, this organisation had committees including experts to prepare the basic laws and policies on a host of issues that the new Korean state would soon be facing. Most significantly, it produced a draft constitution, which would later play an important role during the eventual constitution-making process after the National Assembly was finally formed by the UN-sponsored general election of 10 May 1948.[25]

As mentioned, the meetings at the first session of the US–Soviet Joint Commission essentially stalled over the issue of which local 'democratic parties and social organizations' would be allowed to participate in the process of forming the 'Provisional Korean Democratic Government'. The Soviet position that anyone who opposed the trusteeship be excluded was eminently unacceptable to the Americans, because that would effectively eliminate all political groups in the south except for the Communists. As a compromise, the Joint Commission promised participation to any group that pledged to cooperate with it. Despite this, the meetings were adjourned indefinitely in May 1946, with right-wing political leaders in the south refusing to cooperate with the Joint Commission. Kim Ku, for example, persisted in protesting the trusteeship and arguing for immediate independence and creation of a government based on the personnel and institutions of the KPG. Syngman Rhee, though appearing to be cooperating with the US military authorities, actually wished to directly engage their superiors in Washington, DC, and began suggesting the inevitability of a 'southern' government in light of the developments in the Soviet-zone towards a separate government. The only group that seemed cooperative to the USAMGIK was a small circle of 'centrist' politicians led by Yŏ Un-hyŏng and Kim Kyu-sik.

By way of showing that it had broad-based local support in preparation for the next round of the US–Soviet Joint Commission, the US authorities chose to cultivate this centrist group. This plan resulted in the establishment in December 1946 of the Korean Interim Legislative Assembly (KILA, *Nam Chosŏn Kwado Ippŏp Uiwŏn* 南朝鮮過渡立法議院) as a legislative arm of the USAMGIK. This 90-member body (half of whom were elected and half appointed by the US military governor) was to formulate policy and legislative bills that would become law upon the 'concurrence' of military governor. What is noteworthy is the fact that as soon as it was convened, KILA also began drafting a constitution, even though its mandate was much more limited. For its members, the most urgent task was to jump-start the process of state formation by adopting a constitution so that Korea might become a fully independent nation.

[24] A graduate of Waseda University in Japan, Shin is also reputed to be the main author of the KPG's Provisional Constitution of 1919, adopted after the merger of the three overseas independence groups. After independence, he would be elected the Speaker of the National Assembly after that position became vacant with the election of Syngman Rhee as the first President of the Republic.

[25] Hahm and Kim (n 15) 184.

In fact, KILA produced three draft constitutions, although only one was formally adopted by it. First was an 'outline' of a constitution prepared for the purpose of providing a legal basis for the administration of the territory under US control. Despite being labelled a 'transitional' charter, this document provided for a full-fledged government consisting of legislative, executive and judicial branches, as well as local governments and a state fiscal system. From the USAMGIK's perspective, this was clearly beyond the competence of KILA, in view of the fact that no decision had been made yet to create a separate government in the south. In response, another draft constitution was prepared by KILA encompassing the whole of Korea, which might later be used when a unified Korean government was established. Yet this was also problematic for the US military government. It was beyond the competence of KILA, an assembly with only limited representation of half of Korea, to draft a constitution for the future unified Korean state. The third draft was intended to be a compromise of sorts between the first two, and was actually passed by KILA. The 'Temporary Constitution of Korea', however, never went into effect because the US military governor refused to give his concurrence, on the ground that whatever constitution was made for a unified Korea, it should be drafted when the provisional government for such a unified Korea came into being. Also, by this time, it had been decided in Washington that the Korean question would be dealt with at the United Nations.

III. ENACTING THE FOUNDING CONSTITUTION

On 31 May 1948, the 198[26] elected 'Representatives of the Korean People' convened for the historic opening ceremony of the National Assembly, whose first order of business was the drafting of a constitution.[27] In terms of political orientation, the National Assembly was dominated by rightist politicians who were affiliated with either the Korean Democratic Party, widely seen as representing land-owning interests, or an unofficial group led by Syngman Rhee, who was elected interim Speaker of the National Assembly. Leftists had been purged from the political scene by the US military authorities before the election, and centrists such as Kim Kyu-sik and even a few rightists like Kim Ku chose not to participate in the election.[28] On 3 June 1948, a Constitution Drafting Committee

[26] The National Assembly had 200 seats, but two representing Cheju Island could not be filled due to irregularities during the election.

[27] The National Assembly regarded itself as both a constituent assembly and a regular legislature. As such, it also set up other drafting committees for the purpose of enacting a variety of statutes regarding the organisation of the Government.

[28] Both Kim Kyu-sik and Kim Ku boycotted the election on grounds that an election limited to the southern part would make the hope of overcoming national division more difficult to realise. Yŏ Un-hyŏng, the other 'centrist' politician in the south, had been assassinated in July 1947, before the election.

was formed comprising 30 members of the National Assembly and 10 'expert advisors'. After 16 meetings, the committee presented a final draft to the plenary session of the National Assembly on 23 June 1948. The draft was then debated by the entire membership, during which time numerous changes were made. The final bill was passed on 12 July, and with the Speaker's signing on 17 July, it was promulgated and went into effect immediately.

The fact that the constitution was made in only six weeks may be a sign of the haste that marked the drafting process.[29] Yet it is also a reflection of the accumulated experience in constitution-making since the KPG period and under the US military government. Even before the process formally began, numerous draft constitutions were submitted to the National Assembly for consideration. When the drafting committee met, it adopted two drafts as 'base texts' to frame the discussions. The 'primary text' is commonly known as the 'Yu Draft', after Yu Chin-o (兪鎭午) who was at the time a law professor at Bosung College (later renamed Korea University). A graduate of Keijo Imperial University, the only university in Korea during colonial times, Yu was one of a handful of legal scholars in Korea at the time with some knowledge of public law, and was thus appointed one of the expert advisers to the Drafting Committee. According to his memoir, he had already been commissioned by the Justice Department of the US military government in the fall of 1947 to prepare a draft constitution. Around the time he completed the draft in early May 1948, Yu was also asked by Shin Ik-hee to collaborate with members of the Administration Research Association on drafting a constitution.[30] As mentioned, this group had already prepared a draft constitution in 1946, and so when they met with Yu in mid-May, each side already had complete drafts from which to prepare a joint draft, which was finished literally on the eve of the opening of the National Assembly. It was this joint draft that came to be known, somewhat inaccurately, as the 'Yu Chin-o Draft'.[31]

The other draft adopted by the drafting committee as a 'reference text' was known as the 'Kwŏn Draft', bearing the name of a Korean jurist, Kwŏn Sŭng-nyŏl (權承烈), who at the time was the deputy chief of the Justice Department in the US military government and also an expert adviser to the Drafting Committee.[32] This draft is sometimes seen as the work of the 'Code Drafting Commission'

[29] The new National Assembly decided early on that 15 August, the anniversary of Japan's surrender, would be the date for the inauguration of the new Government of the Republic of Korea. As a result, the members of the Assembly were under enormous pressure to finish the drafting process and to form the Government by that deadline.

[30] Yu Chin-o, *Hŏnpŏp Kich'o Hoegorok* [Recollections on the Drafting of the Constitution] (Ilchogak, 1980)

[31] Members of the Administration Research Association seem to have preferred not to be identified as authors of the draft constitution due to their previous careers in the colonial government.

[32] Kwŏn was educated at Chuo University in Japan. Having passed the Korean (Chosen) bar exam, he was one of a handful of practising attorneys during the colonial period and was known to provide pro bono legal service for Korean defendants prosecuted by the colonial authorities. He would later serve as the first Prosecutor-General of the Republic.

within the Justice Department of the USAMGIK, but there is scepticism as to whose views it reflects and whether it should count as a separate text from the one that Yu Chin-o had submitted to the US military government.[33] Despite substantial overlap between the two texts, there were some significant differences that apparently justified using the Kwŏn Draft as a 'reference'.

When Yu first embarked on his drafting project, he decided on four guiding principles for the constitution of the new Korean state: (i) a bicameral legislature; (ii) a parliamentary-cabinet system of government; (iii) farmland reform; (iv) state control and/or ownership of major economic enterprises.[34] These were maintained in the so-called Yu Draft jointly prepared with the Administration Research Association members. In the end, only two of them would be reflected in the Founding Constitution.

A. Hybrid Form of Government

During deliberations in the Constitution Drafting Committee, the legislature was changed to a unicameral system on grounds that electing an upper house would be too costly and time-consuming. It was argued that, having just gone through a general election, holding another round of election to create the House of Councillors would cause too much turmoil and delay. One of the more progressive members of the Assembly also argued that it would end up being the bastion of privileged aristocratic interests. This unicameral system was passed without much change at the plenary deliberations.

The issue that caused the most controversy during the drafting process was the choice between parliamentary and presidential systems. Here, the role of Syngman Rhee was pivotal in the decision to adopt a presidential system. At the time, Rhee's stature and reputation were such that there was near universal agreement that he would become Korea's first head of state, but the office of the President as envisioned by the Yu Draft comprised merely a figurehead with ceremonial functions.[35] Yu firmly believed that a presidential system was more inefficient and prone to gridlocks between the executive and legislative branches,

[33] Yu Chin-o claimed that he too had prepared his original draft as a member of the Justice Department's Code Drafting Commission and that the Kwŏn Draft was substantially the same as his own draft, except for some minor alterations. By contrast, Kwŏn argued that he and his colleagues at the Code Drafting Commission had never heard of Yu's draft. It is conceivable, however, that Yu's original draft submitted to the Code Drafting Commission was given to Kwŏn and others for further refinement and elaboration. Kim Su-yong, *Kŏnguk kwa Hŏnpŏp: Hŏnpŏp Nonŭi rŭl t'onghae bon Taehan Minguk Kŏnguksa* [Founding and the Constitution: History of Korean Founding as Seen Through Constitutional Debates] (Kyŏngin Munhwasa, 2008) 241–42.

[34] Yu (n 30) 19.

[35] In the Kwŏn Draft the baseline was also a parliamentary system, but by comparison it envisioned a stronger executive branch under a president with veto powers over legislation and a stricter separation of powers than in the Yu Draft.

and that the experience of the United States was an exceptional case. This suited the Korean Democratic Party, which was fast becoming Rhee's primary rival in the National Assembly and which expected that a parliamentary-cabinet system would provide a better chance of furthering their interests. By contrast, Rhee, though not a member of the Drafting Committee, repeatedly made known his preference for a presidential system. He argued that a parliamentary system would be more inefficient due to endless bickering among different political parties in the legislature, and that the head of state should have the proper powers befitting the position, especially in a country, like Korea, that was faced with so many urgent, state-building tasks.[36] Ultimately, he prevailed by threatening to withdraw his participation from any government to be established unless the constitution provided for a presidential system. The Korean Democratic Party's leadership had to relent, because they knew that without Rhee's support, the new government's legitimacy would suffer greatly. Alterations were made to the committee's final draft just before submitting it to the entire floor of the National Assembly. Yu Chin-o protested that such a change required much more than the mere deletion and relocation of a few articles, but had no choice other than to acquiesce.[37] The changed draft was passed with very little modification during plenary deliberations.

The result was a hybrid regime of sorts, which provided for a strong presidential system with elements of the parliamentary system. In addition to the President and the Vice-President, the Founding Constitution provided for a Prime Minister, who was appointed by the President with the consent of the legislature and who was to 'assist' the President and serve as the vice-chair of the State Council (cabinet). Major decisions of the President had to be approved by the cabinet, but all members of the cabinet were appointed by the President. And while cabinet members could retain their seats in the legislature, the legislature could not dismiss the Prime Minister or hold the cabinet accountable. The system inevitably caused confusion as to the real locus of power in the government, but in a way it was also a return to the familiar attempt, going back to the KPG constitutions, at power-sharing among different political groups.[38]

The locus of the power of judicial review was also a point of contention during the drafting process. Even before the Founding Constitution was adopted, a fully operating court system was already in place, because the US military government had preserved the colonial court structure by filling the vacancies created by repatriating Japanese judges with Korean jurists. Despite initial

[36] Lew Young-Ick, 'Yi Sŭngman Kukhoe Uijang kwa Taehan Minguk Hŏnpŏp Chejŏng' [Speaker of the National Assembly Syngman Rhee and the Making of the Korean Constitution] (2006) 189 *Yŏksa Hakpo* 101, 124–25.

[37] Yu (n 30) 74–80.

[38] Sung Ho Kim and Choi Sun, '1948 nyŏn Kŏnguk Hŏnpŏp e Nat'anan Honhapchŏk Kwŏllyŏkkujo ŭi Kiwŏn' [Origins of the Mixed Power Structure of the 1948 Founding Constitution] in Hanguk Mirae Hakhoe (ed), *Chehŏn kwa Kŏn'guk* (Nanam, 2010) 13–15, 25–29.

problems due to the severe shortage of Koreans who had been trained as lawyers during the colonial occupation, most courts were filled by Koreans by the time the National Assembly began drafting the constitution. As such, Korean jurists were becoming an interest group on their own. This was facilitated by the idea, recently imported from the United States, of judicial independence. The draft constitution of the Administration Research Association reflected this by adopting the American system, in which judicial review was exercised by the Supreme Court.[39]

By contrast, Yu Chin-o was adamant that Korean judges, trained as they were under the colonial regime, had neither the experience nor the expertise needed to adjudicate constitutional issues. The rather tenuous nationalist credentials of judges were another reason why he thought it politically inadvisable to have them review the constitutionality of laws.[40] The 'Yu Draft' picked up by the Drafting Committee, however, provided for US-style judicial review, because members of the Administration Research Association insisted on that system. While Yu had no choice but to relent, he still attached a caveat indicating his reservations on the issue. During the Drafting Committee's deliberations, however, one member pointedly challenged the wisdom of granting the Supreme Court the power of judicial review, to which Yu promptly agreed that such a system was problematic. The Committee members apparently agreed that judges 'did not have sufficient credibility and authority' to strike down legislation.[41] In the final draft, the power of reviewing the constitutionality of laws was given to a special agency called the Constitutional Committee. This would be chaired by the Vice-President and comprise five members each from the Supreme Court and the National Assembly.[42]

During deliberations at the plenary meetings, judges made one final attempt at a US-style judicial review system. On behalf to the entire judiciary, the Chief Justice sent an official letter to the National Assembly that argued for the

[39] The same was true for the Kwŏn Draft, which is understandable if it was indeed the handiwork of Korean jurists in USAMGIK's Justice Department.

[40] Despite this, judges apparently exercised the power of judicial review, even before the adoption of a formal constitution. In 1947, the Supreme Court rendered a decision precluding the application of provisions of the Japanese Civil Code according to which a married woman could not file a lawsuit unless she obtained her husband's permission. Most laws left behind by the Japanese colonial government were still being used until they could be replaced by Korean laws. Faced with the question whether a wife had no legal capacity to sue, the Supreme Court invoked the fact that Korea had been liberated from the Japanese and was in the process of establishing a state based on the ideal of democracy, which was inconsistent with all forms of discrimination based on sex. Even with no explicit authorisation and even in the absence of a constitution, the Court apparently thought it justified to engage in what amounted to *de facto* judicial review. Yang Chang Soo, 'Urinara Ch'oech'o ŭi Hŏnpŏpchaep'an Nonŭi' [Korea's First Debate on Constitutional Adjudication] (1999) 40(2) *Sŏul Taehakkyo Pŏphak* 125.

[41] Yu (n 30) 53.

[42] The same method was to be used in the Constitution to constitute the Impeachment Tribunal, which became necessary because the legislature was changed to a unicameral system.

superiority of the American system, but it was largely ignored by the members of the Assembly.[43] The system involving the Constitutional Committee was adopted without much debate.[44]

B. Problem of the Past: Inheriting, Disowning and Reimagining

As mentioned, there was universal agreement that the new Korean state should be a democratic republic. There was, however, no consensus on its proper name. For most Koreans, 'Chosŏn' was the more common denomination for their country, but the drafters of the constitution could not but be ambivalent toward that name. For one thing, it had been the name of a monarchy that ultimately failed to preserve its sovereign independence. Second, the Japanese colonial authorities had used *Chōsen* (Japanese pronunciation of Chosŏn) as the label used to discriminate against and oppress Koreans. Further, the emerging communist regime in the north was using Chosŏn to refer to itself. As an alternative, some proposed 'Koryŏ Republic'. Koryŏ was the name of an even older dynasty before Chosŏn, and was the source of the Western name 'Korea'. It had the merit of being less weighed down with historical memory than Chosŏn, but it too was unsuitable for a democracy. Another proposal was to call it 'Hanguk'. Being more colloquial and perhaps more neutral, this was the name adopted in the Yu Draft. In the end, the Drafting Committee rejected all these and settled on 'Taehan Republic', or *Taehan Minguk* (大韓民國) in Korean. The immediate source was the Kwŏn Draft, but in fact Taehan Minguk had been the KGP's official name since its establishment in 1919. It thus had an obvious aura of respectability. Indeed, the rallying cry of the March 1st Movement had been '*Taehan Tongnip Mansae* (大韓獨立萬歲 [Long Live Taehan's Independence])!'

At the plenary session debates, the choice was retained, but not without some controversy. Dissenters objected that the name Taehan actually came from *Taehan Cheguk*, the name of the ill-fated empire proclaimed during the last years of Chosŏn, when Korea was pillaged by foreign imperial interests. One assemblyman even claimed that this so-called empire was a 'congenital deformity' born of the 1895 Treaty of Shimonoseki, which marked the beginning of Japan's takeover of Korea. For the drafters of the Founding Constitution in 1948, however, the reference to the spirit of independence manifested in the

[43] The letter also suggested other changes that would have enhanced the power of the judiciary, such as allowing the Supreme Court to propose legislative bills and requiring the consent of the Supreme Court for the exercise of the President's power to issue pardons and commute sentences.

[44] Regarding the constitutionality or legality of executive decrees and administrative regulations, the Supreme Court was granted the power to make the final decision. This compromise made at the founding has been maintained throughout the later constitutional revisions and has become a source of tension in the current system of constitutional adjudication.

March 1st Movement and the KPG was more important than any negative association with the short-lived empire that brought on colonisation.[45]

This awareness that constitution-making signified the restoration of independence was also expressed in the discussions on the preamble. Whereas the Kwŏn Draft had no preamble, the Yu Draft began with a preamble that emphasised, amongst other things, the 'indomitable spirit of independence' and the 'great footsteps and hallowed sacrifices of the March 1st Revolution'. During the plenary session, Syngman Rhee insisted that the preamble also include reference to the fact that the Republic of Korea was not a new entity created through the generosity of foreign powers but rather a continuation, or 'reconstruction', of the democratic state that had been proclaimed after the March 1st Revolution.[46] As a result, the final version stated that Taehan Minguk had been established and proclaimed throughout the world by the March 1st Movement, and that the Korean people were 'presently engaged in the re-establishment of the democratic independent state'. Although the reference to 'revolution' was taken out, the preamble appeared to proclaim that the Republic of Korea had already been established in 1919.

This, however, created an interesting tension within the text, which reflected the uneasy relationship between the KPG and the drafters of the Founding Constitution. Despite the invocation of the 'Spirit of March 1st' and the insistence that a 'democratic independent state' had already been created as a result, the preamble did not specifically mention the Provisional Government of the Republic of Korea. This was understandable since, in the post-liberation context, the KPG was considered just one of many political groups that had fought for independence. Moreover, Kim Ku, who had led the KPG as its Chairman during its final days in Chongqing, had boycotted the general election that created the National Assembly, and refused to take part in the process of constitution drafting and government formation. So, in the minds of many members of the National Assembly, neither the 'Republic of Korea established through the March 1st Movement' nor the 'democratic independent state' being re-established in 1948 referred to the specific group of independence activists who had fought in various places in China under the KPG banner. It was more an abstract concept or a principle of legitimation than a historical entity. This is supported by the fact that, during plenary discussion at the National Assembly, the idea of revising or amending the KPG constitutions was proposed, only to be rejected summarily by most of the lawmakers. They were only interested in inheriting the 'spirit' of the KPG, not its institutions or charters. As for Syngman Rhee, even though he used the republican calendar at official events, he insisted

[45] The original choice of Taehan by Emperor Kojong was also meant to signal a move away from the Sino-centric world order and to emphasise the deep roots of nationalist consciousness, going back to the ancient Three Han Kingdoms.

[46] Hahm and Kim (n 15) 167.

that his reference was to the provisional government that had been proclaimed in Seoul on 23 April 1919, rather than the group formed in Shanghai.[47]

Aside from inheriting the glorious republican tradition, the founding of a new Korean state also involved a dimension of repudiating the past – the shameful and more palpable past of colonial subjugation. That meant that some form of punishment had to be meted out for the traitors of the nation who had enriched and ennobled themselves under Japanese rule. A process of lustration was needed to cleanse the soul of the nation. Indeed, for many Koreans, that was the most urgent task facing the entire nation. In the summer of 1947, even before the UN General Assembly's decision to hold an election, KILA had drafted a bill for the 'Special Act on National Traitors, Pro-Japanese Collaborators, and Crafty Profiteers', but it had been vetoed by the US military governor. Yet the election law enacted by the USAMGIK for the general election of 10 May incorporated the definition and classification of collaborators that had been adopted in the KILA bill. Certain individuals, in other words, who were deemed to have benefited from the Japanese occupation, were barred from participating in the historic election that would lay the foundation for the new Korean state.

This was not sufficient for most Koreans, however, who demanded actual punishment of such traitors and collaborators. Proposals were made during the constitution-making process for instituting a process for meting out what would now be called transitional justice. While the Yu Draft contained no such provision, the Kwŏn Draft had a specific article for punishing those who committed 'traitorous acts prior to the enactment of the constitution' and specifically stated that punishment would be applied 'retroactively to the time of the acts'. Drawing on this, the final draft prepared by the Drafting Committee included a supplemental provision that read 'The National Assembly which enacted this Constitution may establish a special law dealing with the punishment of malicious anti-national acts committed prior to 15 August 1945.' A few lawmakers objected that such a provision violated the basic principle of criminal justice, enshrined in the main body of the constitution, that no one should be prosecuted for acts that did not constitute a crime at the time they were committed. By contrast, some right-wing members wished to expand this to allow for the punishment of 'anti-national' leftists who attempted, after liberation, to derail the constitutional founding of the South Korean state. After extended discussion on the scope and the cut-off date of anti-national acts, the provision was passed without change.

C. Structuring a 'Socialistic' Economy to Oppose Communism

The Founding Constitution's provisions for regulating the economy are an example of how forces from the outside as well as the past left their mark on a

[47] Yun Tae-wŏn (n 8) 101.

constitution. They also show how changes in the geo-political environment can quickly render obsolete what was considered the norm at the time of drafting. Immediately following its adoption, the Constitution's economic regime was described as 'socialistic' by one American observer.[48] This was not only because the opening article of the chapter on economy declared that the basic goal of the Republic's economic order was 'the realization of social justice, whereby every citizen's basic needs in life can be met, and the development of a balanced economy'. It also stated 'Each individual's economic freedom shall be guaranteed within these limits.' The following articles then mandated that natural resources would be owned by the state, which could license their use to private citizens. Important enterprises that had a 'public nature', such as transportation, communication, finance, insurance, electricity, water power and gas, were placed under state or public management. Foreign trade was put under state control. Private enterprises could be transferred to state or public ownership, in accordance with law, in the event of an urgent need for national defence or citizens' livelihood. There was even a provision for the redistribution of land.

This might be explained as a reflection of the *zeitgeist*. It is a fact that during the colonial period, many Koreans intellectuals, including Yu Chin-o, had been drawn to socialist ideas as a way of refuting imperialist Japan. Both politically and economically, many stressed the importance of equality (over freedom). A prime example would be the 'Principle of Three Equalities' (*Samgyunjuŭi* 三均主義), formulated by one of the KPG leaders, Cho So-ang. Arguably the theoretical backbone of the KPG's constitutional projects, this principle taught that there should be equality in the three realms of politics, economy and education. It also taught that there should be equality at the three levels of relationship comprising the world: individuals, nations and states.[49] It is important to note, however, that such egalitarian/socialistic ideas that stressed the role of the state in the economic realm were not perceived to be 'revolutionary' in the immediate post-liberation context. When the Japanese occupation ended, there were hardly any private economic actors in Korea, because almost all economically usable resources had been conscripted by the colonial authorities to support Japan's war efforts. Eighty-five per cent of all assets in Korea had been controlled by the colonial government. Even after liberation, the USAMGIK found it necessary to continue the war-time rationing system for basic foodstuff, which had been left behind by the Japanese. Given such background, prescribing a state-centred economic order was in a way a reflection of the status quo.[50]

In addition, the emergence of a communist regime in the northern part at the time of the drafting had the effect of reinforcing, to an extent, the egalitarian/socialistic tendency of the economic regime of the new Republic. The insertion

[48] Paul S Dull, 'South Korean Constitution' (1948) 17(7) *Far Eastern Survey* 207.

[49] Noriko Kokubun, 'The Rise of Korean Constitutional Thought (1875–1945): An East Asian Perspective' in Marie Seong-Hak Kim (ed), *The Spirit of Korean Law: Korean Legal History in Context* (Brill, 2016) 119–26.

[50] Hahm and Kim (n 15) 102.

of a constitutional mandate for land redistribution is a case in point. At the time, it was known that the Soviet authorities in the north had already carried out land reform by confiscating farmland from landowners and distributing it to tenant farmers. To win the hearts of the peasants in the south, who constituted more than 80 per cent of the population, it was necessary for the new Republic to promise a similar measure. Even before the general election was held on 10 May 1948, the USAMGIK hurriedly started distributing to peasants land that had belonged to Japanese owners during colonial times. When the election was held, many candidates, some of whom were landowners, pledged to carry out land reform. When the National Assembly met to deliberate on the constitution, both the Yu Draft and the Kwŏn Draft already had provisions for farmland redistribution. It was simply beyond dispute that the new South Korean state should institute land reform, and indeed this was one of the first measures taken by the Rhee Government.

Another egalitarian/socialistic feature of the economic regime was a provision on the workers' so-called 'right to equal share in profits' (*iik kyunjŏmkwŏn* 利益均霑權). It should be noted, however, that this too was an attempt to win the hearts of the South Korean populace in the face of communist propaganda. Given that the North Korean regime, as well as the leftists in the south, was promising collective ownership of all economic enterprises by the workers, this right was a means to assuage the concerns of labourers in the south about the potential evils of *laissez-faire* capitalism. In other words, despite its 'socialistic' appearance, this right presumed that there would be profit-making private businesses in the new Republic. It was only intelligible, in other words, in an economic regime that recognised private enterprises. As such, it was advocated by labour groups affiliated with right-wing politicians at the time.[51] After much discussion, the Drafting Committee decided against including it in the final draft, but it was revived during plenary deliberations. The right to an equal share in profits was incorporated into the final text and became part of Article 18 of the Founding Constitution on labour rights.

Having a separate chapter on the economy is commonly seen as an influence of the Weimar Constitution, which is widely considered the first to have provided the constitutional basis for a welfare state. Yet the fact that it was more egalitarian and 'socialistic' than most (non-communist) constitutions of the time is probably due to the Doctrine of Three Equalities, and more specifically the 'Essential Points for Establishing a New State', which represented the KPG's attempt to constitutionalise the Doctrine. The Essential Points actually provide for state ownership of land and all means of production. Of course, a heightened economic role for the state could be also justified in terms of a New Deal-type ideology aimed at mitigating the excesses of the pure form of capitalism. For Yu Chin-o, the goal of the constitution was to achieve 'economic

[51] ibid 103–05.

and social democracy'. The chair of the Drafting Committee, Sŏ Sang-il, chose to characterise it as realising a 'national socialist state' (民族社會主義國家).[52] Though the label used may be different, there was a consensus that the new Republic would not be a classical free-market economy. As will be seen, however, the overly 'socialistic' elements would be removed following the Korean War, the first hot conflict of the Cold War, when it became clear that South Korea had to embark on the path of development by embracing a more market-oriented economy based on private initiatives and individual creativity.

D. A Bill of Rights for the 'State-People'

That the Founding Constitution should contain a bill of rights that protected not only civil and political rights, but also social and economic rights was taken for granted by the drafters. Only a few controversies that reflect the political and intellectual environment of the founding period will be mentioned here.

The right to education featured prominently in both the Kwŏn Draft and the original draft by the Administration Research Association, both of which devoted a separate chapter to education. Yu Chin-o, by contrast, thought that it was enough to include a single article on the right to education in the general bill of rights. During plenary deliberations at the National Assembly, objections were raised that a single article failed to do justice to the importance of education. This was perhaps another reflection of the effect of the aforementioned Principle of Three Equalities. Some of the Assembly members argued that the constitution should declare that all costs of education, not merely tuition, would be borne by the state. Others insisted on including secondary education within the scope of constitutionally-mandated compulsory education. The final version declared that 'at least' primary education would be both free and compulsory.

Regarding the rights of the criminally accused, the Yu Draft had originally included a separate clause banning torture and cruel punishments. The National Assembly's drafting committee deleted the clause, but during the plenary deliberations some members proposed to put it back in. The proposal was defeated on the grounds that there was no need for a specific ban because the constitution already had a general provision on 'freedom of the person'.[53]

Aside from the list of rights to be given constitutional protection, whether foreigners were entitled to those rights was a subject of some debate during the drafting process. To be sure, no one sought to exclude foreigners. Yet whether they could, as a matter of course, avail themselves of constitutionally-enumerated

[52] This is unfortunate given that, in English, National Socialism is the name for Hitler's ideology. The Korean term for Nazism, however, would be rendered in English as 'state socialism' (國家社會主義).

[53] The prohibition of torture would become part of the Constitution after the revision in 1962. To this day, no reference is made in the Constitution to cruel punishments.

rights became an issue when members of the National Assembly argued over the proper designation to be employed for the bearer of such rights. In the Yu Draft, the bill of rights section had employed the word *inmin* (人民) to refer to the holder of constitutional rights. This was changed by the Drafting Committee to *kukmin* (國民). The former term literally meant 'human-people', whereas the latter meant 'state-people' or members of the state. Adoption of *kukmin* thus implied that only Korean nationals were entitled to constitutional rights, which raised the question of the status of foreigners and the extent of their rights. By way of addressing this issue, some lawmakers proposed during plenary deliberations that *kukmin* be replaced with the more inclusive *inmin*. Yu Chin-o promptly agreed, stating that the rights given constitutional cognisance were basically 'human rights' (*inkwŏn* 人), which pre-exist the establishment of any state. The term *kukmin*, it was argued, was inappropriate as it suggested that the people's interests were always aligned with those of the state, when the whole point of guaranteeing rights was that the interests of the people and the state could not be assumed to coincide. Against this, another expert adviser and putative author of the 'reference draft', Kwŏn Sŭng-yŏl, argued that since the constitution was an agreement between the state and its members, the use of *kukmin* was proper. Indeed, explicit reference to the state was actually felicitous, argued one lawmaker, given the people's decades-long yearning for an independent state. Besides, the Communists in the north were using *inmin* when referring to 'people's democracy', which made it particularly inappropriate as the designation for the citizens of a free republic.[54] The final decision to retain *kukmin*, however, necessitated the addition of a separate provision for addressing the rights of foreigners. Article 7 stated that foreigners' legal status would be protected in accordance with international law and treaties. This was justified on grounds that showing respect for international law would be meaningful given the international community's interest in the process of constitutional founding in Korea.

That the framers of the Founding Constitution chose 'state-people' as the proper title for the people under the new constitution may be a consequence of their preoccupation with the formation of an independent state. Given the experience of colonial oppression, perhaps it was natural for them to regard the state as the primary protector of, rather than a potential threat to, people's rights. While this may be a common phenomenon in former colonies, it shows that constitution-making in the South Korean context was identified more with the task of founding a new independent republic than with safeguarding individual rights.

[54] Chaihark Hahm and Sung Ho Kim, 'To make "We the People": Constitutional Founding in Postwar Japan and South Korea' (2010) 8(4) *International Journal of Constitutional Law* 800, 843–44.

IV. LEGACY OF THE FOUNDING CONSTITUTION

In the short run, Korea's first constitution might be deemed an utter failure because, immediately following its adoption, the South Korean state was in mortal danger, literally on the brink of annihilation. The constitution was tampered with and treated with disrespect by the very government formed under it. One might even argue that the Founding Constitution was bound to be short-lived due to the internal inconsistency and instability of its power structure. A contrast may be drawn with countries like the United States, where the same constitution has been in force since the founding (albeit with numerous amendments) and has become an object of reverence. In Korea, the constitution was never given the chance to enjoy 'that veneration which time bestows on every thing, and without which perhaps the wisest and freest governments would not possess the requisite stability'.[55]

It may, however, be argued that the Founding Constitution succeeded admirably in achieving what it was intended to achieve, namely, independent statehood recognised by the international community. After all, for generations of independence activists, constitution-making had been the pathway to regaining independence as a democratic republic. Following the establishment of the Republic of Korea Government, the United Nations recognised it in December 1948 as the only legitimate government of Korea (at least in the territory in which the general election had been held).[56] Creating a thriving liberal democracy with robust protection for individual rights was at best a secondary objective.

Moreover, a proper assessment of the Founding Constitution should perhaps pay heed to the role it played in the longer-term project of 'founding'. After all, constitutional founding is an open-ended, future-oriented project, even as it is accompanied by efforts to reject and close off the past. Its full significance can only be grasped if we consider the possibilities opened up by it, as well as the contestations it occasioned.

A. Continuing Pressure from External Forces

As seen, the South Korean state was born in 1948 under a constitution adopted by the representatives of the Korean people. Although there was no direct foreign involvement in the drafting process, the presence of outside forces was unmistakable. It was the United Nations that decided to hold the general election that created the National Assembly, in a territory occupied by foreign

[55] James Madison, 'Federalist No 49' in Terrence Ball (ed), *The Federalist with Letters of 'Brutus'* (Cambridge University Press, 2003) 246.

[56] UNGA Resolution 195(III), 12 December 1948.

troops and in a context defined by the emerging Cold War. The members of the National Assembly were keenly aware that their actions and decisions were being closely watched by the international community. As mentioned, during the drafting process, Syngman Rhee wished to emphasise the spirit of the March 1st Movement as a way of showing the outside world that the founding of the Korean state was the fruition of efforts by the Korean people. Yet this also underlined the extent to which external forces were a crucial part of the founding process.

Outside actors were critical not only for the birth of this new fledgling state, but also for its continued survival. It was by no means clear that the South Korea would survive without the sustained support and commitment of its foreign allies. Less than a month after the establishment of the government under the Founding Constitution, on 9 September 1948, the North Korean regime was set up across the 38th parallel in Pyŏngyang under the supervision of the Soviet occupying forces. Despite the growing instability on the Korean Peninsula, the United States was already making plans to exit Korea, being of the view that America had no long-term strategic interest there. On 15 September, the US armed forces began withdrawing from South Korea. In October, a mutiny led by leftists in the military erupted in southwestern regions of Yŏsu and Sunch'ŏn. On the island of Cheju, violent clashes that had been ongoing between the nascent police force and leftist guerrillas since before the inauguration of the Republic finally resulted in the declaration of martial law on 17 November. In sum, immediately after its birth, the Republic of Korea was under siege, with mortal threats from both within and without.[57] The threat became a reality when North Korean troops, armed with Soviet tanks and artillery, crossed the 38th parallel on 25 June 1950, starting the Korean War. The Republic would have been annihilated had it not been for the intervention of the United Nations forces, composed of military personnel and equipment from 16 member states, under the command of General Douglas MacArthur. As the South Korean military and the UN forces pushed back north, China's 'People's Volunteer Army' crossed the Yalu River into Korea, thereby prolonging the war until July 1953, when a cease-fire agreement was signed.[58]

Given such precarious circumstances, it is perhaps not surprising that the implementation of Korea's constitution would continue to be affected by outside forces and configurations. Soon after the conclusion of the war, for example, the constitution was amended in 1954, for the purpose of changing the provisions on the economic order. With the hostilities now over, it became clear that rebuilding the country would be possible only with massive support from the United States.

[57] For background, see Bruce Cumings, *Origins of the Korean War*, vol II (Princeton University Press, 1991) chs 7 and 8.

[58] Between South Korea's founding in 1948 and the outbreak of the Korean War in 1950, the Chinese Communist Party led by Mao Zedong won the civil war against the Republican Government under Chiang Kai-shek and took control of mainland China, thereby creating an entirely different geopolitical environment for South Korea.

As the leader of the 'free world', the United States insisted that Korea be integrated into the East Asian regional economic order buttressed by American aid and investment. To achieve this, however, Korea's economic orientation needed to be transformed to be more hospitable to foreign investors and supporters. The argument was that in a country where private property could easily be nationalised, or be put under public management, foreigners would be reluctant to make investments. The United States thus openly pressured South Korea to amend its constitution to remove the state-centred and 'socialistic' provisions that were likely to deter foreign investors. Syngman Rhee acquiesced and pushed through an amendment bill, which toned down the emphasis on equality and reduced the possibility of state control or management of the economy.[59] In a fledgling Republic whose economy had been ravaged by war and whose political lot had been cast with the United States in a rapidly changing post-war global order, speedy economic reconstruction through international cooperation had to be the order of the day.

Anti-Communism became the defining feature of the South Korean polity, and this meant that its economy had to be reoriented towards a more free-market system. External forces continued to exert pressure on Korea's constitutional order, quickly making its original economic commitments outdated and unrealistic. It may thus be more accurate to understand South Korea's constitutional founding as having been completed only with the post-war adjustment of its economic order.

B. Continuity Amidst the Ruptures?

From its adoption in 1948, South Korea's constitution would subsequently be changed a total of nine times until 1987, when the transition to democracy finally began and the current constitution was adopted. Until then, the average lifespan of the constitutions was a little over four years. This is but a reflection of the turbulent conditions that characterised Korean politics for the first four decades of the Republic. With the constitution altered so often, mostly to provide legitimation for authoritarian governments, the ideal of a 'democratic republic' enshrined in the Founding Constitution would largely remain a dream and an aspiration for many years. In fact, the constitution would be amended twice during Syngman Rhee's presidency, both times in a direction away from that ideal.

In 1952, while the war was still raging, in the temporary capital city of Pusan, Rhee pushed through an amendment, the main purpose of which was to ensure his own re-election. Realising that his autocratic ways had made him unpopular with the lawmakers in the National Assembly, Rhee changed the system of

[59] Hahm and Kim (n 15) 115–25.

election from one in which the National Assembly chose the President to one in which the general public elected the President. He declared martial law prior to the National Assembly's meeting and allowed practically no deliberation of the proposed amendments. The 1954 amendment, mentioned in section IV.A, also undermined the ideal of a democratic republic. This is because the procedure was marred by irregularities and an absurd way of vote-counting. More importantly, in addition to the changes to the economic provisions of the constitution, the amendment bill also included an article that specifically exempted the sitting President from term limits. Rhee would go on to be re-elected for a third and fourth time, before he was forced into exile in 1960 following a nationwide protest sparked by allegations of election fraud.

The subsequent history of constitutional change in Korea is one marked by frequent ruptures such as military coup d'états. After Rhee's resignation, the constitution was completely rewritten to change the form of government to a parliamentary system. The new government was called the Second Republic as a way to differentiate itself from the Rhee administration. This democratically elected government, however, did not last a year, as it was overthrown in 1961 by a coup led by General Park Chung-hee, who changed the constitution, without following the amendment rules, back to a presidential system, thus bringing about the Third Republic. Emulating Rhee, Park pushed through another amendment in 1969 that exempted him from term limits. Then, in 1972, Park totally revamped the whole government structure by dissolving the National Assembly and adopting an entirely new constitution via a national plebiscite. This period (Fourth Republic) is widely regarded as the low point of Korea's constitutional history, because the new constitution, called the *Yushin* (維新 Revitalisation) Constitution, provided for a government led by an indirectly-elected President with extraordinary powers, who was practically ensured of staying in office indefinitely. After Park's assassination in 1979, another military coup d'état, led by General Chun Doo-hwan, resulted in prolonging authoritarian rule in South Korea. A new constitution for the Fifth Republic was adopted in 1980 and Chun became President through another system of indirect election (albeit slightly different from the Yushin system). Toward the end of Chun's term, nationwide demands for democratic reform, especially for direct public election of the President, became too powerful to be repressed. The government agreed to revise the constitution in accordance with the amendment rules. The result was the current Constitution of 1987, which was Korea's first constitution made in a relatively peaceful manner with the participation of opposition parties in the National Assembly.[60]

As can be seen from this brief summary, South Korea's history of constitutional change has been marked by ruptures and repeated efforts to make a new

[60] For more on the convoluted history of constitutional revisions in South Korea, see Dae-Kyu Yoon, *Law and Political Authority in South Korea* (Westview Press, 1990) 96–108.

beginning. At least two of the changes were unlawful replacements, rather than amendments, in that no effort was made to maintain continuity by following the procedural rules for amendment. Even when the amendment procedure was followed, many of the changes involved total revisions of the text. Further, it may be argued that changes that seemed limited to only a few articles – such as the two amendments under Rhee – also occasioned a significant break from the previous order. Preservation of continuity has not been a hallmark of Korean constitutional history.

It is interesting to note, in this context, that throughout South Korea's turbulent history since the adoption of the Founding Constitution, the preambles to all the subsequent versions stated that they were 'revisions' of that original constitution. Of course, the preambles show variations in the ideals or the mandate invoked to justify the amendment or the making of a new constitution. They even reveal different understanding as to how many times the Korean constitution has been 'revised'. Nevertheless, they have uniformly proclaimed that 'We the People of Korea' are currently 'revising' the Founding Constitution that was first ordained and established in 1948. Despite the all the discontinuity and ruptures, the drafters of the preambles apparently all felt the need to preserve the fiction that the first constitution was not being replaced *in toto* but was somehow kept alive, if only in name. Put differently, the Founding Constitution seems to function as the source of legitimacy, which must be maintained and secured even as the substance of the constitution is being transformed – indeed, even as the spirit of a democratic republic is being undermined. Similarly, the invocation of 'We the People of Korea' in all of the preambles suggests an awareness that constitutions will be deemed legitimate only so long as they can be linked to that original exercise of constituent power by the sovereign people.

At a different level, there is one institutional legacy of the Founding Constitution that is often the target of criticism from politicians and pundits. It is the office of the Prime Minister, who is appointed by the President and whose job description is 'to assist the president'. In other words, the Korean Prime Minister is, despite the name, neither the leader of the governing party in the National Assembly nor accountable to the legislature. This has been a consistent feature of South Korean constitutions ever since the Founding Constitution (except for the short-lived Constitution of the Second Republic, which provided for a parliamentary form of government). In terms of its provenance, this was the result of a 'compromise' during the drafting of the Founding Constitution. As mentioned, the power structure was rather hastily altered from a parliamentary system to a presidential system just before plenary discussions, which resulted in a somewhat inconsistent 'hybrid' form of government that had elements of both systems. A remnant of this compromise, the office of the Prime Minister has remained part of Korea's constitution ever since.

For some politicians and commentators, this suggests that the Korean constitutional order should be operated, if not amended, to approximate a 'semi-presidential' system with a 'dual executive', such as the one found in France.[61] In reality, however, since the Korean Prime Minister is clearly subordinate to the President and owes his/her position solely to the President, it is practically impossible for him/her to be an equal partner in a 'dual executive' system. Presidents have often fired the Prime Minister when faced with politically embarrassing events, as a way of deflecting criticism from the public and the opposition. An ongoing criticism of the power structure has thus been that the Prime Minister is merely an expendable pawn for the President, or a 'fall guy' who can take the blame in the event of an outcry from the general public.[62] The argument is that this institution only contributes to an 'imperial presidency' that allows the President to act without any accountability to the sovereign people. Whether the persistence of the office of the Prime Minister in Korean constitutions is the result of deliberate choice on the part of the drafters is difficult to know. It is, however, commonly regarded as an unfortunate and perhaps unwitting legacy of the Founding Constitution.

C. When was the Republic Founded?

The label 'Founding Constitution' is obviously premised on the view that the drafting and adoption of the constitution in 1948 was a crucial part of the founding of the Republic of Korea. In recent years, however, there has been some debate as to the propriety of this label. More precisely, different views have been expressed by politicians and scholars regarding when to count as the founding of the Republic.

This may be surprising given that a celebration attended by foreign dignitaries was held, as mentioned in the introduction to this chapter, on 15 August 1948, to mark the beginning of the newly independent Korean state. Yet, officially, Korea still does not have a date designated as 'foundation day'.[63] When the National Assembly met in September 1949 to enact a law specifying national holidays for the newly established republic, 15 August was originally designated in the bill as 'Independence Day' (*Tongnip Kinyŏmil* 獨立紀念日). During floor deliberations, the name was changed to *Kwangbokchŏl* (光復節), literally 'Glorious Restoration Day'. Despite the name change, the implicit understanding among

[61] eg, Chang Yŏng-su, 'Punkwŏnhyŏng Chŏngbuhyŏngt'ae esŏ Taet'ongnyŏng-Ch'ongni ŭi Yŏkhalpundam e kwanhan Yŏn'gu' [A Study on the Functional Division between President and Prime Minister under Dual Executive Form of Government] (2017) 46 *Yurŏp Hŏnpŏp Yŏn'gu* 121.

[62] In the Korean political parlance, a somewhat misleading term 'bullet-proof Prime Minister' (*pangt'an ch'ongni* 防彈總理) has been used, because he/she often acted as a shield or a 'bullet-proof vest' for the President.

[63] The date 3 October is celebrated as 'National Foundation Day' in Korea, but the reference is to the mythical founder, Tan'gun, who is said to have inaugurated the first state for the Korean nation in 2333 BC.

lawmakers was that the day was meant to commemorate the inauguration of an independent Korean state the previous year.[64] After the Korean War, however, the media and the public started to use, arguably incorrectly, 'glorious restoration' to refer to liberation from Japanese colonial rule in 1945, such that nowadays the day is marked by remembering the national suffering under foreign domination rather than celebrating the founding of an independent state. Starting around 2006, some historians and politicians began a campaign to change that day's name to *Kŏn'gukchŏl* (建國節), or Foundation Day, so as to make clear that the Republic of Korea was founded on the same date but three years later in 1948. While acknowledging the dual significance of the date, they argued that the founding of the new Korean state should be given priority. Besides, it was odd, they claimed, that a state should not celebrate its own founding. This sparked a controversy, still ongoing, about the proper birthday of the Republic of Korea.

Critics argue that the ceremony in 1948 was for marking the inauguration of a Korean 'government' rather than the founding of a new 'state'. On this view, the Republic of Korea was already founded in 1919, when the Provisional Government was proclaimed in Shanghai by the leaders of the independence movement. The critics point to the fact that the 1948 Constitution itself explicitly states in the preamble that the Republic was established by the March 1st Movement in 1919 and that the project in 1948 had been one of 're-establishment'. Moreover, they invoke the preamble to the current constitution, adopted in 1987, which contains the claim that 'We the People of Korea' are inheriting the 'rightful line of succession' (*pŏpt'ong* 法統) that comes from the Provisional Government of the Republic of Korea.[65] The argument is that the KPG is not only the source of legitimacy, but also the actual government of a real state that has been in existence since 1919. To assign 1948 as the birth year of the Republic would be to neglect and dishonour the numerous independence activists who toiled against the Japanese colonial authorities, at great personal cost. On this position, it would be a mistake to refer to the charter adopted by the National Assembly in 1948 as the 'Founding Constitution'.

For those who see the events of 1948 as the constitutional founding of the Republic, however, the KPG established in 1919 was really the work of a handful of activists who, despite their precious sacrifices, cannot claim to have 'represented' the Korean people. By contrast, the National Assembly that drafted the constitution in 1948 was the result of a historic general election based on universal franchise, and thus could claim democratic legitimacy. Besides, given

[64] Records show that an official ceremony was held on 15 August 1950, during war time, to commemorate the second anniversary of 'independence'.

[65] This passage was inserted during the drafting of the 1987 Constitution at the suggestion of a member of the National Assembly with close affiliation with the KPG and with the organisation that seeks to honour its members and their descendants.

that the KPG was never recognised by the international community, and that it exercised effective control over neither the territory nor the people of Korea, it is at best wishful thinking to claim that the Republic was founded in 1919. Also invoked to support this view is the aforementioned KPG document called *Kŏn'guk Kangnyŏng*, in which the KPG leadership drew a clear distinction between 'restoring a state' (*pokkuk* 復國) and 'founding a state' (*kon'guk* 建國); the former refers to the work of independence activists toward repelling the Japanese occupation and the latter to the subsequent task of establishing the actual organs of the government and adopting a constitution. Indeed, for the generation that experienced the end of the Japanese rule and lived through the US military occupation, the most urgent task was to engage in *kŏn'guk*, that is, 'founding', which is what the members of the National Assembly set themselves to do in 1948.

To be precise, this debate is not per se about the 1948 Constitution. Nevertheless, to the extent that there is a controversy regarding the timing and definition of the Republic's 'founding', the label 'Founding Constitution' is bound to be controversial. Even if that label is to be avoided, it is not clear that all the activities that took place in 1948 can be captured under the rubric of 'establishing a government' (*chŏngbu surip* 政府樹立). It is not clear, in other words, if that coheres with the sense of excitement and the degree of solemnity that attended the whole process that began with the historic election that chose the representatives of the Korean people, to the National Assembly's drafting of the constitution and other basic laws of the country, to the election of the president of the Republic and the appointment of cabinet ministers – a process that was consummated with the ceremony described at the beginning of this chapter.

Interestingly, regardless of the view one takes on this debate, there is a sense in which the controversy was foreshadowed, and is being fuelled, by the Founding Constitution itself. Its ambivalent stance toward the KPG and the nationalistic motivation to locate a 'useable past' in the earlier struggles toward independence may have sown the seeds of disagreement that have sprouted into a political controversy. In that regard, the controversy itself may be seen as a legacy of the Founding Constitution.

V. CONCLUSION

The Founding Constitution failed to give immediate birth to a flourishing liberal democracy in Korea. In fact, it began to be altered and distorted shortly after its adoption, by both internal and external forces. Given that later constitutions became a façade to legitimate the government of whoever was in power, it might even be tempting to conclude that South Korea's first constitution was of very little practical consequence. Yet it should be recalled that adopting a constitutional text comprises only a small part – albeit a very important part – of the larger process of constitutional founding, which can only be understood properly by expanding our scope of vision to include a wider timespan.[66] The Founding Constitution should thus be seen as the culmination of the Korean people's decades-long struggle for constitutional self-government, as well as the template, or a reference point, for South Korea's later constitutional development. It is an important lens through which Korea's past efforts to regain independence through constitutional founding were given official recognition. It has also served as the cornerstone of South Korea's constitutional edifice, however distorted it may have turned out to be, at least in the sense that no regime or ruler has deemed it proper to flatly repudiate the Founding Constitution or replace it with an entirely new constitution.

It should also be borne in mind that constitutional founding is never an isolated domestic affair. The Korean case is perhaps especially more convoluted in the sense that it had to proceed after the nation was initially divided by external forces that had been mutual allies during the Second World War, and then kept apart by the same superpowers who soon became adversaries in the emerging Cold War. The United Nations' attempt to resolve the deadlock between the United States and the Soviet Union added another layer of international involvement in Korea's constitutional founding. Competition between the two nascent Korean states was also a key factor during the constitution-making process. To this day, South Korea's constitution declares that all of the Korean Peninsula and its adjacent islands constitute the territory of the Republic of Korea. The North Korean regime is but an illegal 'anti-state organization' that is unlawfully and coercively occupying the northern territory.[67] In that sense, many South Koreans regard the project of constitutional founding as still a work in progress. To them, the ideal of full independence through constitutional self-government has not been attained to the extent that the nation remains divided. On this view, both founding and independence will be completed when the two Koreas are finally united to form a single state. Even Syngman Rhee insisted that the Korean War, although it started as an unlawful invasion by the North, should not be concluded until the South Korean military, with the help of the UN armed forces, defeated the Communists and the entire Korean Peninsula was under the control of the Republic of Korea. He thus resisted the US pressure to sign the cease-fire agreement, because he believed that true independence would not be achieved until national division was overcome.

This should lead us, finally, to re-examine our understanding of the concept of constitutional founding. What the South Korean case shows, at the least, is the difficulty in deciding when constitutional founding starts and when it ends. Should the proclamation of an overseas provisional government be seen as the starting point of the process? Should the discursive practice of invoking the

[66] Hahm and Kim (n 15) 56–57, 61–62.

[67] According to South Korea's National Security Law, an 'anti-state organization' is defined as any group that 'fraudulently uses the title of a government'.

principles of popular sovereignty and separation of powers be enough to mark the beginnings of a constitutional order? How much weight should be given to the issue of effective control over the territory and the actual population?

If the constitution is modified shortly after its promulgation, as was the case with the economic provisions of the Founding Constitution, does this signify that founding was not yet complete with the initial drafting of the text? If a certain segment of the territory and the population is excluded from the process of constitution-making, does that imply that the founding is incomplete and remains so until that segment is brought under the purview of the constitution? To be sure, these are questions that can be raised, and are probably raised, in other countries around the world. And it is certainly beyond the scope of this chapter to attempt a definitive answer to any of them. From the perspective of comparative constitutional scholarship, however, the South Korean experience in constitutional founding will have been meaningful if it succeeds in spurring further reflections and deeper theorising on the meaning, scope and utility of 'constitutional founding'.

8

Constitutional Founding in the Democratic People's Republic of Korea

ERIK MOBRAND

INTRODUCTION

THE PROMULGATION OF the Democratic People's Republic of Korea (DPRK) Constitution on 8 September 1948 marked the formal beginning of a new state, which was officially established the following day. A young, former guerilla, Kim Il Sung, was at the helm. By September 1948, three years had already passed since the end of Japanese rule on the Korean peninsula. A lot had transpired in those three years. Japan's surrender in the Pacific War led not to a division of the aggressor nation, as happened in Germany's case, but to carving up Korea, a former colony. Southern Korea, including the capital in Seoul, came under the United States' control, while the Soviet Union gained influence in the northern portion. Under the tutelage of Soviet advisers, Kim eventually emerged as the top leader. He drove forward a programme of revolution and, by 1948, had re-made political and social institutions. Americans and Soviets viewed each other suspiciously across the Demilitarized Zone (DMZ) that divided the peninsula. Koreans in the north and south wanted unity. These considerations made security a top priority. As the division of the peninsula hardened, North Koreans prepared for their own constitution. With the chances of unification declining precipitously, it became clearer that distinct states would be declared on either side of the DMZ.

The Constitution laid claim to a territory the Government in Pyongyang did not control. The DPRK was defined in territorial terms as the whole Korean peninsula, never mind that everything south of the 38th parallel was held by the newly-formed Republic of Korea (ROK). The Constitution put the DPRK's capital in Seoul, even as that city, the political hub of Korea since the late fourteenth century, was beyond the Government's reach.

Seventy years later, the DPRK still exists and tension persists on the Korean peninsula. Koreans in both the North and South imagine themselves as part of a unified nation. Meanwhile, the United States has retained its presence for geopolitical reasons. The DPRK Constitution has been amended multiple times since 1948, but none of these amendments signifies a moment of new constitutional founding. Although later amendments brought substantial change to the Constitution, these were never full moments of constitutional founding. A major revision in 1972 introduced the language of a shifting ideological landscape and laid out changes in the institutional structure. Further revisions have helped post-Kim Il Sung leaders settle in. The 1948 Constitution could not predict the many changes that followed in subsequent decades, but it did mark the starting point for a regime that continues to exhibit similarities with the past.

Numerous reference points can help make sense of North Korea's constitutional founding. Given the revolutionary context, it can be discussed alongside other socialist constitutions. It can also be placed among authoritarian constitutions. The DPRK can also be studied in its region, for similarities with or differences from others in Asia. While those comparative reference points indicate a field against which the DPRK Constitution can be placed, the Constitution was written in particular historical circumstances – circumstances that were both local and global, as great powers played inordinately large roles in shaping the Korean peninsula. In order to understand how the Constitution was founded, it is important to first establish how the peninsula was divided and why the makers of the Constitution gained power in the first place.

I. THE ROAD TO THE CONSTITUTION

The north-south division of the Korean peninsula had little basis in Korea itself. Old Korea had not known geographic divisions corresponding to the north-south separation that emerged in 1945. Ruling from Seoul, the kings of the Choson period (1390–1905) had managed to limit or ward off foreign incursions until the 1870s. As external pressure mounted in the late nineteenth century, the monarchy failed to build a centralised response and adapt to changing conditions.[1] Japanese influence crept in. Starting in 1895, various Japanese 'advisers' held greater sway in public affairs. Reforms advocated by Japan were undertaken. In 1910, Japan annexed Korea. Under Japanese rule until 1945, Korea saw tremendous repression and transformation. None of this implied a major divide on the peninsula between north and south. The Korean resistance movement, which gathered pace after 1919, similarly lacked a regional basis. Many resistance figures left the peninsula, for Manchuria or China, or further afield to the United States. Nationalist activities were easier in those places than back in Korea.

During the Second World War, the Allied Powers formulated plans for post-war Japan. Following the Cairo Conference in 1943, the decision was made

[1] James B Palais, *Politics and Policy in Traditional Korea* (Harvard University Press, 1975).

that Korea would be taken from Japan, in the event of Japanese defeat, and made an independent country at some point. With the Cairo Declaration stating that independence would occur 'in due course', the notion of a period of trusteeship preceding independence became the expectation. The Cairo Declaration would hold huge significance for Korea. For the participants at the meeting, Korea was not an especially important topic. Neither did the United States have much information about Korea. This instance was only the first of several for Korea in which a far more powerful external actor, with only some interests in Korea and little understanding, acted in ways that had a huge impact. As this transitional period was phrased vaguely, wartime decisions on Korea left substantial uncertainty about the peninsula's fate.

The dropping of nuclear bombs on Hiroshima and Nagasaki in early August 1945 made the Korea issue pressing. This was even before Japan's surrender on 15 August. As the war drew to a close, the great powers approached Korea in the space of this uncertainty. The Americans proposed a division at the 38th parallel. The Allies hastily agreed that control over Seoul and southern Korea would be given to the Americans, while the Soviets would have northern Korea. Even as this partition was made, the expectation was made that a period of unified government, in a trusteeship arrangement, would follow. Post-war, great power politics intervened. Anticipating the Cold War (or helping to create it), Americans in southern Korea orientated their administration to eliminating alleged Communists. In 1945, Korea was on the frontlines of a looming confrontation between the world's superpowers.

Soviet forces arrived in Korea starting on 14 August, some three weeks before their American counterparts. The Soviets respected the boundary drawn at the 38th parallel and remained in the north. The departing Japanese turned over control of government in Seoul to a group of Koreans who had been based in Korea but had not worked for the Japanese, and who were willing to work with expatriate Korean nationalists. This group was led by Yŏ Un-hyŏng, who established the Committee for the Preparation of Korean Independence (CPKI). In Pyongyang, Cho Man-sik, a Christian, sat atop the local people's committee, a form of organisation that emerged mostly spontaneously as the Japanese left. The Pyongyang people's committee was part of the CPKI. When the Soviets arrived, they worked with the CPKI and initially kept Cho in place.

This separation of north and south became entrenched as the Americans and Soviets selected distinct sorts of figures for leadership on either side of the 38th parallel. In the south, the US Army Military Government in Korea (USAMGIK) sought to suppress the movements. Spontaneously formed people's committees, which chased away collaborators and formed new policies where they gained control over government offices, were viewed with the utmost suspicion. Fearing that agents of Moscow organised people's committees, USAMGIK set about dismantling them. The Americans revived key colonial-era institutions and restored personnel. They identified a set of landlords, industrialists and administrators who they believed could be reliably anti-Communist, and backed them for leadership in the country. These moves put beneficiaries of colonialism in positions of power.

In the north, the people's committees became the grassroots base for the new regime. Even as factional division characterised the leadership, local activism was embraced rather than rejected. The principle was to eliminate those who had worked for the Japanese and replace them with Koreans who were not tainted. While this principle was not always possible to follow,[2] it stands in stark contrast to southern Korea, where many of those who had worked for the Japanese were re-employed. Indeed, much of the American approach in south Korea was to rebuild what the Japanese had established. Doing so was easier for keeping order and seemed like a surer way to fight communism. Thus, the two regimes came to have distinct social bases. While this division eventually set the regimes on the Korean peninsula on course for civil war,[3] they also formalised their separate public orders.

The central role that Kim Il Sung came to play was not obvious at the start. A few groups vied for power in Pyongyang from August 1945. Cho Man-sik's group was one of these. Cho was not a Communist, but the Soviets were keen to tap into the influence he already wielded. In October, Cho was made head of a Five Provinces People's Committee. However, the Soviets were displeased with Cho not only because he was not a Communist, but also because he opposed trusteeship.[4] Korea-based communists formed a second group, one that included many based in the south. A set of Koreans who returned from the Soviet Union made up a Soviet faction. They were educated and versed in ideology. Having close ties to the Soviet advisers, they were in a strong position to gain power. Another group, the Yan'an faction, comprised Koreans who had fought in China alongside the Chinese Communist Party (CCP). Since the CCP struggle against the Kuomintang was ongoing, many in this faction were still in China. Other Koreans had been fighting against the Japanese in Manchuria, and they had now returned to Korea. Kim Il Sung was a leader in this group.

By 14 October 1945, the Soviets had chosen Kim Il Sung as the top leader. In December, Kim became chair of the North Korea branch of the Korean Communist Party. As the Party evolved, next into the North Korean Workers' Party and then into the Korea Workers' Party, Kim remained at the top. With Cho out of contention, the Soviets may have preferred Kim because he was younger than other possible leaders, and hence maybe easier to control.[5] In truth, the precise reason why Kim was chosen instead of a Soviet faction or Yan'an faction figure is unknown. Still, multiple factions coexisted in the early

[2] Patricia Goedde, 'Law of Our Own Style: The Evolution and Challenges of the North Korean Legal System' (2004) 27 *Fordham International Law Journal* 1265, 1269.

[3] Bruce Cumings, *The Origins of the Korea War*, vol I (Princeton University Press, 1981).

[4] Robert A Scalapino and Chong-Sik Lee, *Communism in Korea, Part I: The Movement* (University of California Press, 1972) 338–39.

[5] ibid 326.

years after liberation.[6] It was the Soviets in coordination with Kim and the other factions that prepared for the new state, a project that came alongside carrying out the revolution.

II. PREPARING THE 1948 CONSTITUTION

The mythical story of the 1948 Constitution is that it was outlined by Kim Il Sung in 1932 when he was a guerrilla fighter near the Tumen River. It is unlikely to have been at an advanced stage so early. Most of the work began in late 1947, under close Soviet supervision. With the end of Japanese colonial rule in 1945, the hope had been for the formation of a unified Korean government. Plans for a period of trusteeship over the entire peninsula, which would lead eventually to an independent and unified state, cracked in October 1947. On both sides of the 38th parallel, groups began to prepare for separate constitutions.

On 18 November 1947, the Third Session of the North Korean People's Assembly adopted a resolution to start the Constitution. It elected a Provisional Constitutional Commission. The head of the Commission was Kim Tu-bong, the leader of the Yan'an faction of North Korea's Communists. The USSR's 1936 Constitution was understood to be the primary source of inspiration. North Korean Workers' Party members had translated that Constitution and studied it, amongst others, in preparing their own. The Commission drafted a provisional constitution, the first version being completed in December.[7]

In February 1948, the Commission circulated a draft of the Provisional Constitution. The circulation was intended to gather input from people, following the Soviet practice.[8] The draft then underwent processes out of Korean hands, which have been described by historian Andrei Lankov who has used Soviet sources. In April 1948 in Moscow, the Soviet Central Committee examined it and, according to Lankov, evaluated it negatively.[9] The Committee proposed 12 changes to the document. However, these changes were not made. Instead, the draft went to Stalin and the Politburo. Stalin was less critical of the document than the Central Committee had been. On 24 April, Stalin held a meeting on Korean matters, with General Terenti Shtykov, the Soviet military leader in Pyongyang, in attendance. In that midnight meeting, the North Korean Draft Constitution was discussed, as were other aspects of the Korean situation.

[6] Chong-Sik Lee, 'Politics in North Korea: Pre-Korean War Stage' (1963) 14 *The China Quarterly* 3.

[7] Pak Sŏn-yŏng, 'Chosŏn minjujuŭi inmin konghwaguk hŏnbŏp ŭi chejŏng kwa kaejŏng kwajŏng ŭl t'onghae pon pukhan hŏnbŏp-e kwanhan yŏn'gu' ['The process of constitutional enactment and revision in the Democratic People's Republic of Korea'] (2015) 16 *Kongbŏphak yŏn'gu* [Public law studies] 27.

[8] Kim Hyŏng-sŏng and Cho Chae-hyŏn, 'Pukhan hŏnbŏp pyŏnhwa ŭi t'ŭkching kwa chŏnmang' ['Characteristics and outlook for changes in the North Korean constitution'] (2012) 24 *Sŏnggyun'gwan pŏphak* [Sŏnggyun'gwan legal studies] 1.

[9] Andrei Lankov, *From Stalin to Kim Il Sung: The Formation of North Korea, 1945–1960* (Rutgers University Press, 2002) 42.

Stalin personally re-wrote Article 2, which states that sovereignty lies with the people, and demanded that 'Provisional' be excluded from the Constitution's name. When the document returned to Pyongyang, only three articles had been altered.[10] On 28 April, back in Pyongyang, a Special Session of the People's Assembly approved the Draft Constitution. The approved document was thus one that had been written by Koreans, inspired by the Soviets and then partly amended in Moscow.

Before the Constitution could be promulgated, a legislative body needed to be formed to adopt it. In the South, United Nations-sponsored elections were held in May 1948. The North did not participate, and most who identified as leftists anywhere boycotted the election, which they saw as an effort to exclude them. South and North were headed down a path of not recognising each other. In July, Pyongyang ruled that the Constitution would apply only to the North until the peninsula was unified.[11] This move indicated a separation of regimes. The elections in the South produced a Constitutional Assembly that drafted a Constitution for the ROK, and then selected Syngman Rhee as President. The ROK was proclaimed on 15 August, the third anniversary of liberation from colonial rule.

The North organised separate elections for the legislative body, the Supreme People's Assembly (SPA). These elections took place across the peninsula, including in the South where they were deemed illegal. Voters in the South chose delegates, who met in late August to cast votes for the Assembly. The body featured representatives from provinces in the South. The North Korean Workers' Party and the South Korean Workers' Party held the largest bloc of seats, though well less than a majority.[12] The SPA approved the Constitution on 8 September. The DPRK was formally established the following day.

III. DESCRIPTION OF THE 1948 CONSTITUTION

The first Constitution of the DPRK contains 104 articles in 10 chapters. The absence of a preamble is a distinctive feature of the 1948 DPRK Constitution. However, the statements that usually are found in a preamble can be found throughout the Constitution's articles. The Constitution can be read mostly as an exercise in setting out the legitimising formula. While this function may be allocated mostly to the preamble in other contexts, in North Korea the entire Constitution takes on this role. The lack of a preamble can therefore be thought of not as an absence of something, but as reflecting the fact that the purpose of the Constitution as a whole is to lay out collective values, as a preamble might do in other contexts. The aspiration to rule the whole Korean peninsula infuses

[10] ibid 43.
[11] ibid 44.
[12] ibid 47.

the Constitution. Residents of South Korea are not treated as citizens of another country. Seoul is named as the capital of the DPRK.[13]

Property features strongly in the opening articles of the Constitution. Private property was permitted,[14] but formerly Japanese-held properties belonged to the state.[15] Land reform was announced for any localities that had not yet experienced it.[16] Tenancy farming was outlawed and limits were placed on the amount of land owned by individuals.[17] These articles reflected the concerns of a society rectifying the injustices of colonial rule. Establishing a fully collectivised society was less the stated aim than was redressing colonial-era inequities.

The 1948 Constitution grants a range of rights to individuals. These include rights to free expression and organisation,[18] to pay[19] and rest,[20] and even to run enterprises.[21] Work is a duty.[22] Women and men have equal status.[23]

Chapters 3 through 6 address governing and representative organs. The SPA, which is the people's conduit for exercising power,[24] is the subject of the first section of Chapter 3. The body is made the highest organ of power.[25] Executive power, covered in Chapter 4, rests with the Cabinet; the premier is head of government.[26] People's assemblies are the local organs of power.[27] Chapter 6 details judicial institutions. The Supreme Court and the prosecutors are appointed by the SPA. Trials include people's assessors alongside judges.[28]

To what extent does the 1948 Constitution follow a Soviet model? Some observers have seen the document as largely a variation of the 1936 USSR Constitution.[29] The main evidence for this view would seem to be the parallels in state structure with the Soviet Union. The SPA, for instance, is a counterpart to the Supreme Soviet.[30] As in the USSR, democratic centralism was also the guiding principle for appointments. On the other hand, the concerns of post-colonialism and national division permeate the Constitution.

[13] Constitution of the Democratic People's Republic of Korea 1948, Art 103.
[14] ibid Art 5.
[15] ibid Arts 5 and 8.
[16] ibid Art 7.
[17] ibid Art 6.
[18] ibid Art 13.
[19] ibid Art 15.
[20] ibid Art 16.
[21] ibid Art 19.
[22] ibid Art 30.
[23] ibid Art 22.
[24] ibid Art 2.
[25] ibid Art 32.
[26] ibid Art 59.
[27] ibid Art 68.
[28] ibid Art 84.
[29] Ilpyong L Kim, 'Constitutional Development in North Korea' (1973) II *Journal of Korean Affairs* 31.
[30] Dae-Kyu Yoon, 'The Constitution of North Korea: Its Changes and Implications' (2004) 27 *Fordham International Law Journal* 1289.

IV. CONSTITUTION AND STATE MAKING

Where does the Constitution fit in relation to other public institutions and the process of state making? In 1948, North Korea was consumed by its revolutionary project. The DPRK was a new country with big ideas for its future. North Korea's leaders did not face the same problems seen by those in South Korea. Leaders in Seoul faced legitimacy problems because of the continuities they represented from the colonial period. Kim Il Sung and other leaders in Pyongyang, with their anti-Japanese credentials, did not have these same problems. Guidance from the Soviet Union also strongly shaped the revolutionary project in the DPRK. Soviets dispatched to the DPRK helped with technical aspects of building a Communist economy and society. It was in this context of foreign-assisted socialist state making that the Constitution was announced.

In North Korea, again as in other Communist regimes, the state was only one part of public authority. The Party was another. In the PRC, the CCP clearly rivalled the state as a source of authority. Party and state were grafted onto each other. The North Korean Workers' Party was as important to the authority structure as the state. In the North Korean party-state, Party and state were entwined at the top, in functional departments, and across the hierarchy. In 1949, the Party merged with its southern counterpart to form a unified Korean Workers' Party (KWP). Commands coming from the KWP stood above the Constitution. Furthermore, in a context where Kim Il Sung had not yet attained the level of personal control he would later command, the Party as an organisation was a more important source.

Yet the KWP should not be seen as the same as, for example, the CCP. The KWP carried out revolution in North Korea but it was not the equivalent of the Soviet version or the CCP across the Yalu. The KWP and its predecessors had not fought their way to power. They had been given it. While the Soviets came to power through the Russian Revolution and Mao led a successful civil war campaign with the CCP, Kim had not led the KWP through a battle for power. The end of colonialism had happened to Korea. This is not to say that the KWP was not a party or that it was insignificant. The Party was a crucial network of Soviet-supported leaders, buttressed by a mass membership. However, by 1948, the Party had not gained the significance it had later on. Neither had Kim Il Sung developed the personal authority he would later be known for.

The KWP would endure as a major component of the North Korean political system. The principles guiding the organisation rivalled those of the DPRK's Constitution. In the context of a party-state like North Korea, it should not be surprising that the Party's rules would be of similar importance to the state Constitution.

V. CONTEXTS OF CONSTITUTIONAL FOUNDING

There are multiple ways to think about the primary conditions in which the DPRK's constitutional founding occurred. The DPRK was established between, at one end, post-liberation division and occupation of the Korean peninsula and, at the other, a war that only consolidated that division. This statement points to key contexts for understanding constitutional founding in the DPRK: a revolutionary movement established the state against the backdrop of colonial rule, national division and foreign influence after the Second World War.

First, Korea was a post-colonial entity led by a nationalist movement. Japanese colonial rule had sown deep divisions between ordinary Korean farmers and workers, on one hand, and those who had thrived under colonial rule, on the other hand. Most Koreans were furious with those who had sold out their compatriots by working for the police, serving in high administrative positions or running business in close cooperation with Japanese. Within Korea, during the Japanese period, there was little that could be done politically to mobilise opposition. In Manchuria, some fought against the Japanese. In China, some joined the CCP's revolutionary struggle. Elsewhere overseas, expatriate Koreans pushed for their nation's independence. Liberation on the peninsula on 15 August 1945 saw the immediate mobilisation of popular forces. This mobilisation was an effort at self-governance, as well as at wresting control away from those who had worked for the Japanese.

Those who suffered under colonial rule gained influence in North Korea afterwards, unlike in South Korea. While the leadership group in the North was initially diverse, Kim Il Sung and the core came from the anti-colonial struggle. That struggle gave their authority legitimacy and was the most crucial component in the nationalist story they told. As a post-colonial polity, the leading concerns related to opposing and overturning colonial structures. Expelling collaborators was a priority. Article 5 of the Constitution stated that assets held by Japanese and collaborators would be nationalised; Article 6 stated that Japanese-held land would be confiscated.

Second, and more specifically, it was a post-colonial *revolutionary* context. Revolutionaries sought to overturn the existing social order and make a new one. Local-level people's committees, formed in the immediate aftermath of the Japanese relinquishing power, were the building blocks of the revolutionary regime. People's committees took control of local affairs after 15 August 1945. In 1946 and 1947, a centralised structure took shape, with people's committees at the base. In 1945–46, this force was not a single party but a constellation of groups that sought revolution. By 1946–47, the core group consisted of veterans, like Kim Il Sung, of resistance fighting in Manchuria. This revolutionary force had Soviet support as well as a grassroots base. The Korean Workers' Party, even though it had not led in the seizing of power, was crucial in the context of socialist revolution.

Third, foreign guidance characterised aspects of decision-making. While Koreans ran the Government in Pyongyang even before the DPRK's establishment, Soviet 'advisers' in Korea were influential in decision making. These advisers, and their bosses in Moscow, could shape the course of events in North Korea. Since Koreans had to consult the Soviets, the Korean leadership had a limited autonomy. These limits were visible in constitution-making. Should the

Constitution – and the regime – be considered a Korean creation or a foreign imposition? Scholars take different positions on this question. Lankov writes that 'North Korea was created as a Soviet puppet state.'[31] Assessing the level of Soviet input into the Constitution is not straightforward. Koreans looked to the Soviet model in preparing their Constitution. The Constitution was amended in Moscow and required Stalin's approval. At the same time, the Constitution has themes that reflect the situation in Korea and the concerns of Korean revolutionaries. The emphasis on land reform and struggling against the Japanese were rooted in the experience and visions of Koreans. The Constitution also had clauses that were surprising for a socialist bloc country. Rights to individual property were guaranteed, for example. The constitutional founding involved a mix of local and Soviet influences.

The name of the country is also a subject of debate about the extent of Soviet influence. Lankov suggests that the name had possibly been proposed by a Soviet general.[32] The more familiar reference would be the People's Republic of Korea (PRK), established in Seoul a day before the American arrival in 1945 and dismantled soon after.

Fourth and finally, it was a setting of national division with growing tension with the south. It is difficult, if not impossible, to think about the period of North Korea's establishment without considering both the prior hopes for unification and the war that followed. Indeed, the period from 1945 to 1950 is now understood as setting the basis for the Korean War (1950–53). The formation of separate regimes in the north and south, led by distinct social bases, provided the foundation for war.[33] While North Korean forces invaded on 25 June 1950, both sides had considered military engagements for a long time prior. Those who gained power on either side of the 38th parallel wished to use their states to gain complete control of the peninsula.

This condition had a profound influence on constitution-making in both the north and south. In the north, founding the Constitution was a declaration of intent not to cooperate with the south. When, in November 1947, work began on the Provisional Constitution, that decision meant that Pyongyang was not going to cooperate with Seoul. Yet the move was subtler than that. In the course of preparing the Constitution, the North Korean leadership maintained the public position that they opposed foreign control and desired a government across the whole Korean peninsula.[34] Anti-trusteeship could be a basis for Korean unity, but actors on both sides prepared for separate governments.

The DPRK's founding was also a response to the ROK. The DPRK was established just three weeks after the ROK. The interactive state-building process can be seen from multiple angles. Any posture taken on one side of the 38th parallel

[31] Lankov (n 9) ix.
[32] ibid 47.
[33] Cumings (n 3).
[34] Lankov (n 9) 46–47.

was known to produce a response on the other side. This situation meant that both Governments were well aware of how their actions would be perceived by the other side. They anticipated each other's moves, and this anticipation shaped state building. The path to war, too, was opened through both sides preparing to attack the other and wondering if the other would attack.

North Korea's founding Constitution was concerned not only with building a new society, but also with the ambition to control the peninsula, an ambition seen in the South Korean Constitution too. Developed in a period of growing hostility, these Constitutions refused to recognise each other. Further, they sought to demonstrate their superiority in order to win popular support in the portion of the peninsula they did not control. Both claimed to be rightful representatives of the Korean nation, agreeing only that the nation was one and should be led by a single force. State making in North Korea, as in South Korea, was a statement of hostility, as well as an appeal, with unification under the regime the goal.

The relative significance of these contexts is the subject of debate among historians of the DPRK. Is North Korea best understood as a creation of the Soviet Union? Or as a post-colonial revolutionary country? Answers to these questions point to distinct reference points. The former suggests comparing North Korea with Eastern European countries, while the latter indicates placing North Korea alongside China. These debates inform positions on issues that are closer to questions of fact: Was Kim Il Sung the paramount leader in 1948, or not until 1956? Did Koreans or Soviets have more influence on state formation? Even on these issues, different views can be found.

An analysis of constitutional founding in North Korea has to consider these divergent understandings of the period. While these perspectives cannot be fully reconciled, it is possible to take insights from both. Just because there is evidence that Pyongyang and Moscow made plans for a separate regime, that does not preclude the possibility that North Koreans were also responding to events in Seoul. Those plans were formed, most likely, because of an understanding of what the South Koreans and Americans were preparing. This strategic interplay drove events on the peninsula between 1945 and the outbreak of war in 1950. One side anticipated what the other would do, and made preparation in response to what was anticipated, or else sent signals that sought to mislead the other side. Such interaction between the North and South fundamentally shaped what happened on either side of the 38th parallel. The revolution in North Korea could be both a response to what happened in the South and something influenced by the Soviets.

VI. ENDURANCE AND REVISION: THE 1972 CONSTITUTION

After 1948, the North Korean Constitution has been revised a number of times. In 1972, a revised 'socialist constitution' was introduced. It has, at times, been treated as an entirely new Constitution. Why did the 1948 document not endure further? Should the 1972 Constitution be considered a second founding constitution? These questions can be answered by examining the political changes after 1948 that led to the constitutional revision.

A. Political Transformation

While the establishment of a state might, under most conditions, produce a unity or coherence, on the Korean peninsula it was quite the opposite. Since the DPRK, like the ROK, laid claim to the entire Korean nation but held effective control over only part of it, tension was at the heart of the state's founding. From the South Korean perspective, the DPRK was not a state but an illicit organisation. Tension within the ROK and between the DPRK and ROK simmered in 1948 and 1949. Border skirmishes broke out. Syngman Rhee made overtures regarding forcible unification of the peninsula, a point that worried policymakers in Washington. In June 1950, the conflict came to a head with the outbreak of war. The DPRK forces stormed through Seoul, making South Korean authorities retreat to the southeast corner of the peninsula. After the landing of American troops, the North Koreans were pushed back north of Seoul and then beyond, as the ROK occupied northern Korea. With the PRC entry into the Korean War, Americans and Chinese fought each other, US bombing of North Korea continuing relentlessly, contributing to an enormous toll in lives and suffering. When in 1953 an armistice agreement was signed by the DPRK and the United States (but not the ROK), little had been resolved.

War had an enormous impact on North Korea. As a result of ROK occupation and American bombing, the physical infrastructure had been destroyed. It was necessary to rebuild. Food was another problem. The valleys of southern Korea had always had better conditions for agricultural production, especially compared with the mountainous northern regions. North Koreans were cut off from the traditional circulation of food. Land reform had ensured that farmers had their own land for growing food, but they had no access to the nation's bread basket. After the war, the DPRK shifted towards Soviet-style collectivisation of agriculture. Returning the land to farmers and redistributing some of it had been the priorities in the late 1940s. In the mid-1950s, the main trend was toward collectivisation. Centralisation and mass mobilisation were themes throughout the economy, not just in agriculture. An intensive reconstruction campaign saw the country expand industry in the immediate post-war years, as output grew rapidly. Investment continued to focus on heavy industry into the 1960s, helping North Korea to maintain a higher level of per capita production than South Korea.

The year the Korean War armistice was agreed, 1953, also saw the death of Stalin. The Soviet Union began a project of de-Stalinisation. This project involved criticising the personalisation of power. Soviet satellite states followed suit. Kim Il Sung, fearing a resurgence in Soviet influence in Korea, resisted de-Stalinisation.[35] Looking more to China, he intensified efforts for mass mobilisation and called increasingly for personal loyalty. These moves set the DPRK apart from most eastern bloc countries. Straying from the Soviet Union was possible at this time, in part, because of China's role in the war. Commands came from Beijing, not from Moscow or Pyongyang. Soviet influence declined in relation to China's, and the North Korean leadership found a measure of latitude.

The next decade and a half saw these nascent patterns of independence and power personalisation grow. What had once been a more collective leadership became increasingly the domain of Kim Il Sung. Days after the armistice in 1953, Kim initiated a purge of the domestic Communist faction. One of Kim's main rivals, Pak Hŏn-yŏng, was eliminated. Four years later, Kim went after leading figures in the Soviet and Yanan factions. Exercising his independence from Moscow, Kim purged the Koreans with Soviet experience. After the campaigns that began in 1957, Kim had fully sidelined most other power groups in North Korea. Another purge occurred in 1967, targeting the Kapsan Group of fighters who had supported the guerillas in Manchuria.

As Kim consolidated his own control, the leadership also became cut off from outside connections. The Soviet faction had been important for providing technical assistance in the revolution and in carrying out economic planning. The Yanan group brought their experience from mobilising peasants in China. With those sources of knowledge cast aside, Kim and the shrinking leadership group around him had to do more on their own.

These developments set the stage for the emergence of *juche* (*chuch'e*) ideology. First used by Kim Il Sung in 1966, the term captured the significance of national self-reliance. With a KWP led by people mostly with experience in Pyongyang and Manchuria, self-reliance had already become a theme. *Juche* represented a version of Korean nationalism that emphasised suspicion of foreign influence. The ideology accompanied the creation of a cult of personality around Kim Il Sung, who acquired grander titles and became the subject of more and more public displays of loyalty.

By the late 1960s, North Korea had undergone tremendous transformation since the writing of the Constitution in 1948. The concerns at the heart of the 1948 Constitution had been addressed or dissipated. Rectifying colonial injustice was a less pressing matter two decades on from the DPRK's founding. War had scarred society in multiple ways, and had convinced the leadership of the need for mass mobilisation and self-reliance. The leadership shifted from somewhat collective to mostly personal. The relationship with the Soviet Union changed. Finally, in 1972, the DPRK promulgated a constitutional revision.

[35] Balazs Szalontai, *Kim Il Sung in the Krushchev Era: Soviet DPRK-Relations and the Roots of North Korean Despotism, 1953–1964* (Stanford University Press, 2005) 241.

The 1972 Constitution can be understood in relation to constitutional revision the same year in South Korea. In late 1972, Park Chung Hee suspended the Constitution and later put out a new, 'Yusin' Constitution with restricted rights for citizens. The revised Constitution also freed Park from the pressures of direct presidential elections. In revising their Constitutions, leaders in both Seoul and Pyongyang were responding to the wider regional environment.[36] This was an environment characterised by Sino-American détente and US failings in the war in Vietnam.

B. The 1972 Constitution

The 'socialist constitution' of 1972 updates the Constitution for the significant changes in priorities and ideology that had occurred since 1948; it also reflects substantial shifts in the institutional structure. As an authority on North Korean politics notes, 'the drafting of a new constitution was long overdue,' as '[t]he ideological assumptions embodied in the old constitution as well as the political structure it had instituted had long been obsolete'.[37] The post-colonial emphasis on land reform faded and the tolerance for private property disappeared. Rights to private property and business were eliminated.

The 1972 Constitution has 149 articles, making it nearly 50 per cent longer than the 1948 version. The document comprising the 1972 Constitution has striking differences from the 1948 one. Besides being longer, a major difference is the extent of the text devoted to laying out rights, duties and principles. The first four chapters, in 72 articles or nearly half the Constitution, cover this subject. This stands in contrast to just 31 articles in three chapters in the 1948 Constitution. This quantitative point is a symptom of substantive development of the ideology.

'Independence' is the overriding theme of the articles on principles. The first five articles, save one, each refer to the word 'independence'. Article 4, which does not, contains the first reference to '*juche*'. The concept of *juche*, which literally means 'subject' but figuratively much more, was incorporated into ideology six years prior. The idea signifies an attempt to adapt Marxism-Leninism to local circumstances. The introduction of *juche*, along with the other opening articles, gives the 1972 Constitution a strong emphasis on independence. By independence is meant that the DPRK is independent of foreign influence, with

[36] Son Ho-ch'ŏl and Pan In-hyŏk, 'Nampukhan "chŏk tae chŏk ŭijon kwan'gye ron" e kwanhan pip'anjŏk yŏn'gu: 1972-yŏn namhan yusin hŏnbŏp kwa pukhan sahoejuŭi hŏnbŏp jejŏng ŭl chungsim ŭro' ['A critique of the "theory of enemy-versus-enemy relations" between South and North Korea: A study of 1972's Yusin constitution in South Korea and socialist constitution of North Korea'] (2012) 77 *Han'guk kwa kukje chŏngch'i* [Korea and international politics] 1.

[37] Chong-Sik Lee, 'The 1972 Constitution and Top Communist Leaders' in Dae-Sook Suh and Chae-Jin Lee (eds), *Political Leadership in Korea* (University of Washington Press, 1976) 192.

the implication that this includes independence from the Soviet Union. While other Communist constitutions included references to allegiance to Moscow, the DPRK's 1972 Constitution did not. This feature is among those that make it 'unusual' among eastern bloc constitutions.[38] So striking is the focus on independence that legal scholars have referred to the 1972 Constitution as a 'declaration of independence'.[39]

There are further ideological developments reflected in the 1972 Constitution. Article 12 introduces the 'Chongsan-ri spirit,' a slogan that refers to a battle in the anti-colonial struggle. The next article brings in Chollima, another symbol of the North Korean revolution. The tone of the first portion of the Constitution makes clear that ideological updating is a crucial task of this document. While independence is stressed, the issues related to post-colonialism fade. Land reform, for example, had been completed and did not need as much attention.

The state structure was also updated in the 1972 document. The 1972 Constitution introduced a presidency or chairmanship, more similar to the PRC than the USSR. The president is made head of government and head of state, whereas in the 1948 Constitution these roles were separate (with the former office being held by the premier). Chapter 6 outlines the presidency. In the 1972 Constitution, the capital is also finally moved from Seoul to Pyongyang.[40]

C. 1972 as Constitutional Founding?

The simplest argument for considering 1972 a moment of constitutional founding is the extent of change that occurred. This change was both substantive, in the arrangement of power and in official ideology, and formal. The supplanting of Marxism with *juche* thinking is one reason to think of the Constitution as more than a revision.[41] As one observer notes, in this Constitution, '*juche* supplanted Marxism'.[42] The stress on *juche* confirmed Kim Il Sung's power.[43] On the other hand, the simplest argument against this position is that a longer pattern of fundamental continuity from 1948 and beyond can be found.[44] While the Constitution was updated to address changing circumstances, the 1972 Constitution did not alter the vision and structures set out in the original Constitution. In essence, the DPRK was founded as a Soviet-style state and it remained one.

[38] China Kim and Timothy G Kearley, 'The 1972 Socialist Constitution of North Korea' (1976) 11 *Texas International Law Journal* 113.

[39] Christopher Hale, 'Multifunctional *Juche*: A Study of the Changing Dynamic between *Juche* and the State Constitution in North Korea' (2002) 42 *Korea Journal* 283, 294.

[40] Constitution of the Democratic People's Republic of Korea 1972, Art 149.

[41] Hale (n 39) 294–96.

[42] ibid 296.

[43] Ch'oe Ŭn-sŏk, 'Pukhan hŏnbŏp kaejŏng nugu-rŭl wihan kŏsin'ga?' [Who was North Korean constitutional revision for?] [2017] *T'ongil han'guk* [Unified Korea] 38–39.

[44] Kim (n 29); Yoon (n 30) 1292.

Both of these arguments are too simple. Neither takes proper account of the regular changes that have occurred in North Korea. A subtler perspective is needed in order to assess the 1972 Constitution.

The simplest continuity argument hinges on seeing the DPRK as more like the Soviet Union than, say, like China. This claim can be assessed by viewing the DPRK against these reference points. In China in the mid-1950s, voices for legal reforms grew louder. Mao responded with the Anti-Rightist Campaign in 1957, purging, amongst others, advocates of legal reforms. So-called 'rightists' were alleged to be going against the revolution. In steering away from legal reforms, the PRC departed from the Soviet path. Legal reform emerged as an issue in mid-1950s North Korea as well. Hazard argues that the DPRK did not follow the response seen in China.[45] Instead, the DPRK continued with a more Soviet-style constitution. The evidence for this claim is that the state structure laid out in the 1972 Constitution, with the exception of the provisions for a presidency, mimics the USSR.[46] In this view, the North Korean leadership took law more seriously than did the Chinese leadership.

There are grounds for casting doubt on claims of a Soviet path in North Korea. Those claims rest too narrowly on a formal reading of the parts of the Constitution related to state structure. In the later 1950s, Kim Il Sung opposed those who advocated raising the status of law. Kim saw moves towards legal reform as a challenge to the Party. Further, Kim resisted the de-Stalinisation that occurred in the Soviet-aligned world. Like Mao, Kim denounced legalism as an undesirable Western import.[47] A decade after the 1948 Constitution, legal principles had already undergone substantial transformation.

The shift in legal principles might lead to the conclusion that ideology or cults of personality superseded law. In China, where internal strife made the Constitution nearly irrelevant for long periods, the evidence for such a view is strong. In North Korea, ideology and law had a more complex relationship. The leadership made more frequent, minor adjustments to the Constitution, even before the 1972 Constitution. Moreover, a major purpose of the Constitution seems to have been to incorporate and codify ideological developments. These developments were among the key reasons why the 1948 Constitution did not endure and a new one was written.

So does the DPRK's 1972 Constitution more resemble a variation on the Soviet model or on the Chinese model? An accurate statement is that it departs in specific ways from both. Unlike the Soviet model, ideology remained important. Further, the content of ideology stressed separation from the USSR and independence. Unlike the Chinese model, ideology was codified in the Constitution. This development would occur only later in the PRC. Attempting to find only a

[45] John N Hazard, 'A Comparativist's View of the 1972 Constitution of the Democratic People's Republic of Korea' (1974) 7 *Studies in Comparative Communism* 74.

[46] ibid 79–80.

[47] Goedde (n 2) 1271.

PRC model or a Soviet model in the DPRK misses the differences from both. If the DPRK was not a continuously Soviet-style state, then one argument against viewing 1972 as a moment of constitutional founding is weakened.

Despite weaknesses in the Soviet continuity argument, the claim that a new constitutional founding occurred in 1972 remains overstated. The 1948 Constitution was promulgated after many fundamental parts of North Korea's socialist system had been created, and these endured. Much of the state had been formed prior, in revolution. During the years from 1946 to 1947, while the north was under a provisional government run by Soviets, most of the revolution was completed. This revolution brought a new order. The social and economic pillars of the DPRK were constructed before constitutional founding as well. Institutions of social control were also fully developed in 1946–47. Industry was nationalised. Armstrong concludes that 'Most of the political, economic, and social institutions of the new state were fully in place by the spring of 1947.'[48]

As in other Communist revolutions, class labels were created in order to distinguish groups and privilege those from 'good' backgrounds. In North Korea, as in China, this exercise meant establishing categories based on the class backgrounds of individuals. Those from peasant or worker backgrounds were given more opportunities. This system meant a reversal of old hierarchies. What the system had in common with Choson traditions was that hierarchy was taken very seriously, even though it was a reversed hierarchy. This hierarchy was also very rigid in comparison with those elsewhere in the socialist world. In this sense, Communism in North Korea took on local traditions.[49]

It is also necessary to consider what the Constitution's purpose is in the DPRK context. North Korea's Constitution is a way of recording and communicating current official ideology and basic governing arrangements. It is not, emphatically, a document that sets out to constrain government. If the Constitution is viewed with only a liberal democratic model in mind then the main features of the Constitution will be missed.[50] Instead, the DPRK is consistent in using the Constitution to give an update on the governing ideology and structure. As Goedde notes, 'the constitution must be studied as a changeable national charter that describes the state's political priorities, structural changes that consolidate leadership, citizens' rights in relation to duties, and markers in economic development'.[51] What it outlines is not, of course, comprehensive. The actual power wielded by Kim Il Sung vis-à-vis the SPA, for example, is vastly understated.

In the 1972 Constitution, this malleability of the Constitution was on full display. The revision updated the Constitution to reflect the significant changes

[48] Charles Armstrong, *The North Korean Revolution, 1945–50* (Cornell University Press, 2003) 216.
[49] ibid 71–72.
[50] Patricia Goedde, 'Beyond Sham: The North Korean Constitution' (2020) 44 *Asian Perspective* 1.
[51] ibid 6.

that had occurred. Further revisions, with a similar purpose, followed in later years. The 1972 Constitution confirmed a pattern in which the Constitution would be amended with some regularity to reflect ideological updates and shifts in state structure. The Constitution became a malleable document. None of this is to suggest that the Constitution reveals everything about power in North Korea, but it does indicate some consistency over time in how the Constitution is regarded. Contrast with South Korea's constitutional experience can sharpen our view of this role of the Constitution. Before making that comparison, further constitutional reforms deserve brief mention.

D. Post-1972 Revisions

Since the 1972 Constitution, there have been two especially significant moments of constitutional reform. These moments serve the same purpose as the 1972 revision – they enshrine changes that have been made. These moments are revisions with the transition to Kim Jong Il and then to Kim Jong Un.

Kim Il Sung died in 1994. The regime waited until after the traditional three-year mourning period was over to undertake constitutional reform. The 1998 Constitution set the story for legitimising Kim Jong Il's ascent to power, which had already been achieved. The next moment of reform came in a series of revisions, most recently in 2019, after Kim Jong Un came to power. These revisions eliminated the language of *juche* ideology, replacing it with 'Kim Ilsung-ism'. They also formalised Kim's control over the military, a crucial part of the consolidation of his grip on power. The intent here, it is apparent, was to help justify the succession of the third generation of Kims to power.

Under both Kim Jong Il and Kim Jong Un, constitutional reform followed the pattern of 1972. Revisions updated shifts in the governing structure and outlined the new leader's ideological framework. As Goedde notes, 'Constitutional changes sometimes occur after the fact, acknowledging, updating, and essentially legalizing undergoing developments.'[52]

Besides revisions to the Constitution, there have also been changes to the relative significance of the Constitution. North Koreans who have left the country report that another document, the Ten Principles of the Party's Single-Ideology System (*tang ŭi yuil sasang che'gye hwangnip ŭi 10-tae wŏnch'ik*), is far more important than the Constitution. Ordinary people are familiar with these principles, as they have received training in them, but they commonly know less about the Constitution. As a guide to DPRK ideology, the Ten Principles might be more relevant than the Constitution. The Ten Principles were initially proposed in 1967, the year after *juche* was first mentioned, but were not announced until 1974. The Ten Principles stress the Kim family's position at the heart of

[52] ibid 19.

the state, which reflects their creation alongside the 1967 purge.[53] In the original version, loyalty to Kim Il Sung featured in all 10 articles. The document has been revised from time to time, including with updates for the shifts from Kim Il Sung to Kim Jong Il to Kim Jong Un.

VII. CONSTITUTIONAL FOUNDING IN RELATION TO SOUTH KOREA

The theme of state building in relation to the ROK can be expanded further. Leaders on both sides of the Korean peninsula in 1948 had to keep in mind the thoughts and responses of their superpower allies. South Korean constitution drafters needed a document that signalled to Washington a commitment to building a democratic order. Actually building a democratic order, or even making the Americans believe they were building an American-style democracy, was unnecessary. For the Americans, security and keeping Communists out of power were the priorities in Seoul. But lip service had to be paid to the recognisable symbols of democracy. This consideration was crucial in producing the ROK Constitution. In Pyongyang, too, Soviet advisers needed to be respected. The temporary people's assembly drafted a document that contained the socialist commitments (not only for Moscow's consumption) while also responding to the very different priorities of an agricultural society just coming out of colonial rule.

North Korea's 1948 Constitution set a powerful precedent for what a constitution should be in the country. That Constitution and subsequent revisions were concerned first of all with setting the justification for rule. Later constitutional revisions continued that model, making adjustments in light of ideological updates.

Comparison with South Korea clarifies features of North Korea's constitutional order. South Korea continues – in name – to operate under its own 1948 Constitution, though this document has been revised on several occasions. Until the country's democratisation in 1987, the Constitution was rather a nuisance to leaders. When it got in their way, they used force or fraud to revise it (1952, 1954, 1969). Or they suspended the Constitution, declared martial law and eventually rolled out a revised constitution (1961–63, 1972, and 1980–81). These revisions had little to do with the legitimising formula of the regime. When North Korea's Constitution has been revised, it has not been mostly in order to grant more power to the leadership or to permit a change in direction. Rather, it has been to re-orientate the official ideology, to justify changes that have already transpired, and to set out a basis for new shifts in organisation and leadership. The contrast with South Korea on this count is strong.

[53] James F. Person, 'The 1967 purge of the Gapsan Faction and establishment of the monolithic ideology system' (nd) *North Korea International Documentation Project E-Dossier Series*, online at www.wilsoncenter.org/publication/the-1967-purge-the-gapsan-faction-and-establishment-the-monolithic-ideological-system.

Consider, for example, a comparison of the South and North Korean Constitutions that were promulgated a day apart in December 1972. In South Korea, President Park Chung Hee had declared martial law two months earlier and dissolved the legislature. Citing the need for a 'revitalization' of society, Park removed the authority of institutions that could limit or check his power. Under the revised Constitution, the President was no longer directly elected and opposition parties were immensely disadvantaged in winning legislative seats. The 1972 Constitution ushered in a period when Park could use his various security forces to rule through terror. This was a reform that personalised power and made dictatorship harsher. Further, it followed on the heels of an extremely controversial recent constitutional revision, in 1969, to allow Park to run again for President. In North Korea, on the other hand, the 1972 Constitution was a careful statement of changes that had occurred in the decades since the first Constitution. It was not an excuse for leaders to grab more power, but rather a reflection of how authority and ideology had shifted over time.

There are indications that the Constitution is taken seriously by the North Korean leadership. If it were merely a charade, why undertake a major re-writing in 1972? It could either be left as it was, and ignored, or be updated frequently with the whims of the leadership. Neither of the scenarios unfolded. Instead, revisions have come infrequently. The effort of 1972, in particular, indicates that the Constitution was reformulated with great care.

The key point here is that constitutional reforms in North Korea were not mainly instrumental revisions designed to enable the powerful to circumvent rules. Such revisions had been the speciality of Presidents Syngman Rhee and Park Chung Hee in the south. Those Presidents each undertook a constitutional amendment to extend their terms in power; each also turned to coercion to pass amendments to the Constitution. The situation in the north has been different, since the Constitution is not primarily a document orientated to the constraining of power. Kim Il Sung could update the Constitution to restate official ideology. These symbolic purposes were relatively more important. This pattern continued under Kim's successors. Revisions shortly after Kim Jong Il gained power and after Kim Jung Un gained power also reflected adjustments made in the wake of consolidating their authority.[54] These constitutional revisions updated the ideology as well as state structures. On that count, these revisions also stand in contrast to those in South Korea's constitutional history.

VIII. CONCLUSION

Although the DPRK's founding Constitution of 1948 delineated rights for citizens, the document and its successors have not mainly been concerned with restricting the state or occupants of high office. This trait stems from the

[54] Goedde (n 50).

Constitution's context. The North Korean Constitution was for a post-colonial society where the Government had gained power through a revolutionary and nationalist movement. Comparison and contrast with South Korea is instructive. On the conflict-ridden peninsula, legal process has been a secondary concern in claims to authority. Even though South Korea's Constitution put formal limits on power, these were repeatedly ignored or forcibly changed – until the country's democratisation. For the first four decades, though, governments on both sides of the peninsula made claims to authority that were based more on things other than legal process.

Colonialism and war had shredded these societies. In the south, a counter-revolutionary group came to power with claims of delivering security. That group referenced its American backing to underscore its security credentials. But security legitimised breaking rules. The decades after liberation were violent in South Korea. Whatever rules were in the Constitution were peripheral to the actual bases of power and authority. In the north, a revolutionary group took charge with credentials from fighting the colonial overlords – a source of legitimacy that the leaders from 1948 forward in South Korea could not claim. Anti-imperial revolutionary credentials were the key to legitimacy. The Constitution was a serious articulation of the legitimising formula; that purpose was more significant than a role in limiting authority.

9

The 1924 Constitution: Towards the Modernisation of Mongolia

AMARSANAA BATBOLD AND CHADRAABAL UNURBAYAR

INTRODUCTION

As a people, the Mongols trace their origins back to the time of the Hunnu (Xiongnu) Empire that lasted from the third century BCE to the late first century CE. Over the centuries, various Khaganates ruled the Mongols in what is roughly the area of present-day Mongolia. Today, Mongolia is a small and developing country. As of 2021, its population is just over 3 million, even though there are over 10 million ethnic Mongols around the world. Mongolia has achieved 100 per cent literacy of its population since the 1940s, and Cyrillic letters have been used as its national script in preference to the old Mongolian script. From 1924 till 1990, Mongolia was a socialist state and was an integral part of the Soviet socialist bloc. It thus comes as no surprise that socialist legal ideology has prevailed, especially since the 1940s, and legal scholars and professional lawyers consider Mongolia a member of the Continental legal family. As such, little remains of the impact and influence of its pre-1924 legal order.

Since 1924, Mongolia has had four different constitutions. The first was adopted in 1924, and this was followed by new constitutions in 1940, 1960 and 1992.[1] However, Mongolia had begun its modern constitutionalising process some time before 1924 through the adoption of several proto-constitutional documents. These documents addressed such important matters as limiting the powers of monarchy, rules relating to the Temporary Parliament, local government and decisions that declared the Mongolian state republican. The years between 1921 and 1924 were particularly crucial in this development, since real

[1] Besides these Constitutions, there is an opinion by some researchers that Mongolia had adopted a Constitution in 1949. See B Bayarsaikhan, *Tradition of Constitutionalism in Mongolia: Legal Analysis of 1949 Constitution of People's Republic of Mongolia* (Б.Баярсайхан, *Монгол Улсын Үндсэн Хуульт Ёсны Уламжлал: БНМАУ-Ын 1949 Оны Үндсэн Хуулийн Эрх Зүйн Шинжилгээ*) (2017).

progress was made in creating the necessary preconditions for the adoption of a modern constitution, all of which culminated in the Constitution of 1924.[2]

After suppressing Buddhism and its leaders in 1930s, and winning the 1939 Khalkhyn Gol Battle[3] between Mongolia (militarily supported by the Soviet Union) and Japan (which colonised part of China and established the puppet state of Manchukuo), Mongolia adopted a socialist-style Constitution in 1940. By this time, Mongolia was well and truly under the influence of the Soviet Union and its legal system, and it even adopted the system of single-party (Communist) rule. It leaned further and further towards the Soviet Russia's legal system and ideology, but maintained the private ownership of stock. However, in 1960, Mongolia further cemented the Communist Party's role and completely abolished the concept of private property and property rights under the Constitution. As the Cold War ended in the late 1980s and the socialist bloc collapsed, Mongolia became increasingly nationalistic, and restored private property rights by way of a constitutional amendment in 1990. By this time, Mongolians had decided to adopt a new constitution modelled on liberal-democratic lines – the 1992 Constitution of Mongolia.[4]

I. PRELUDE TO THE FIRST CONSTITUTION

At the start of the thirteenth century, the Mongols became a military force to be reckoned with, after Ghenghis (Chinggis) Khan united the various tribes and forged them into one of the most fearsome fighting machines in history. At its height (around 1294), the Mongol Empire – which included China – was the largest contiguous land empire in history. The death of Ogotai, Ghenghis' son, in 1241 led to a fracturing of the Empire, which by 1260 was made up of four distinct parts, including the Yuan Dynasty that ruled China from 1271 to 1368. It was at this time that the Mongol Emperors converted to Tibetan Buddhism. With the collapse of the Yuan Dynasty in 1368, the Mongols retreated to the Mongolian Plateau and established the Northern Yuan Dynasty, which lasted till 1635.

The Northern Yuan was divided into three parts: the Khaikha, Inner Mongolia and the Buryats. By the end of the seventeenth century, the territory that makes up present-day Mongolia came under the control of the Manchu-led Qing Dynasty of China and was administered as Outer Mongolia (on account of its distance

[2] B Chimid, *Respecting the Constitution* (Б.Чимид, *Үндсэн Хуулийг Дээдлэн Шүтэх Ёс*) (2006) 14–15.

[3] Uradyn E Bulag, 'The Nomonhan Incident and the Politics of Friendship on the Russia-Mongolia-China Border' (2009) 7 *The Asia-Pacific Journal: Japan Focus* 1 at https://apjjf.org/-Uradyn-E.-Bulag/3263/article.html, accessed 19 April 2021.

[4] J Amarsanaa and O Batsaikhan, *The Constitutions of Mongolia 1924, 1940, 1960, 1992* (Academy of Sciences of Mongolia, 2009). This collection of Mongolian Constitutions is published in old and new Mongolian scripts, as well as in English translation.

from the Chinese capital, Beijing). But there were many Mongols living outside this territory, including in what is now the Inner Mongolia Autonomous Region of China and part of the Russian Empire (whose population comprises mainly Buryat, Kalmyk and Tuva Mongols). Today, most Mongols live in Mongolia (3 million), the Siberian part of the Russian Federation (Buryat, Tuva, Kalmyk) and the Inner Mongolia Autonomous Region of the People's Republic of China. Mongolians also live in many parts of the world, such as Europe, the United States, and Australia, India and Afghanistan (Hazara Mongols).

In 1911, capitalising on the collapse of the Qing dynasty in China, Mongolia attempted to make itself 'more independent of China'.[5] Tsarist Russia took advantage of the situation to expand into Outer Mongolia, as well by negotiating an advantageous treaty in 1912, giving itself trading privileges in Mongolia[6] and promising to 'lend Mongolia its assistance in order to preserve her present autonomy and also her right to keep her national army, forbidding entry to Chinese armies and colonization of her lands by the Chinese'.[7] This was the start of Russian (and later Soviet) interventions and influence in Mongolia that would last till the late 1980s.[8] Between 1911 and 1920, Russia entered into a number of secret treaties with China in which it paid lip service to Chinese suzerainity over Mongolia in exchange for the Chinese acknowledging Mongolia's autonomy and control of domestic policy over its own territory.[9] At this time, as almost a third of Mongolia's male population were Buddhist monks, the Mongols established a theocratic khanate and installed the 8th Bogd Gegeen – the highest-ranked lama of Tibetan Buddhism in Mongolia – as the Bogd Khaan (or 'Holy Ruler'). He was to rule Mongolia till his death in 1924, afterwhich Mongolia proclaimed itself a republic[10] and adopted its first socialist-style Constitution.[11] In the course of the next seven decades, Mongolia was to enact three more constitutions. Those of 1940 and 1960 were socialist-orientated, while the 1992 Constitution was a 'revolutionary' democratic-type constitution.[12] Thus, for most of its twentieth-century history, Mongolia functioned as a socialist state.

At the point of its breakaway from China in 1911, the idea of constitution-making was new to Mongolia and, indeed, the rest of Asia, despite the singular example of Japan's Meiji Constitution of 1889. Even so, several attempts were

[5] William B Ballis, 'The Political Evolution of a Soviet Satellite: The Mongolian People's Republic' (1956) 9(2) *Western Political Quarterly* 293, 294.

[6] Bruce A Elleman, 'Secret Sino-Soviet Negotiations on Outer Mongolia, 1918–1925' (1993–1994) 66(4) *Pacific Affairs* 539, 540.

[7] Ballis (n 5) 294.

[8] See generally, Henry S Bradsher, 'The Sovietization of Mongolia' (1972) *Foreign Affairs* 545.

[9] Elleman (n 6) 541.

[10] M Sanjdorj (ed), *The First State Great Hural (8–28 Nov 1924)* [М Санждорж, *Бугд Найрамдах Монгол Ард Улсын Анхдугаар Их Хурал (1924 Оны XI Сарын 8–28)*] (Institute of History, Academy of Sciences, People's Republic of Mongolia, 1984) 6.

[11] Central Archive of Mongolia ТБА, Х-11, Д-1, ХН-2, Эх.

[12] Chimid (n 2) 12–33.

made to draft a constitution for the autonomous region of Monglia.[13] These efforts may be divided into three phases. First, there is ample evidence that the Government of the Bogd Khaan had drafted a constitution; second, Mongolia adopted several constitutional documents prior to the promulgation of its first Constitution; and, third, several different drafts were prepared, including those of the Tseveen Jamsarano,[14] Prime Minister D Bodoo,[15] and a draft of the working group headed by Prime Minister Tserendorj. All these formed the basis of the first Constitution.

There have been few scholarly attempts to study Mongolia's first attempt at drafting its Constitution just after the Revolution of 1911, although we know for sure that such an effort had indeed been made. During this time, the Bogd Khaan was declared the King of Mongols as well as its religious leader. Although the Bogd Khaan's Government was an absolute monarchy, there was, from 1914, also a functioning legislature – the Upper and Lower State Chambers (Улсын дээд, доод хурал). These Parliamentary Chambers discussed internal and external matters, and adopted statutes such as the *Codes issued by Edicts*.[16]

It seems that in 1912 the Government informed scholars[17] and the progressive democrats of the time that it intended to establish a parliamentary system and constitutional order similar to that found in the west.[18] Although the complete draft has not been uncovered and the principal drafter hitherto unknown, a Russian language source published certain texts of the constitutional draft

[13] Although the 1921 Constitution of Mongolia is considered as the first Constitution in Mongolia, constitutional documents mentioned here, or documents that established the State Upper and Lower Chambers of Parliament during the Bogd Khaan Autonomous Government, can be considered as the first Constitution (or constitutional documents) in Mongolia. It should be noted that these constitutional documents need to be further scrutinised in more depth. The Eight-Item Charter on the State Upper and Lower Chambers (*Улсын дээд, доод хурлын газрын найман зүйлийн дүрэм*'), which was promulgated by the Bogd Khaan on 23 March 1914, established the State Upper and Lower Chambers of the Parliament. See Preface to J Amarsanaa, B Bayarsaikhan and R Shajinbat, *Introduction to the International Constitutions /Groundwork of the First Constitution* [*Олон Улсын Үндсэн Хуулийн Оршил /Анхдугаар Үндсэн Хуулийн Судалгааны Эх Сурвалж/ (/)* (Хууль зүйн үндэсний хүрээлэн) (National Legal Institute of Mongolia, 2009).

[14] The manuscipt copy and its transliteration in cyrillic can be seen in Tseveen Jamsarano, *Draft of the First Constitution, 1924* [Анхдугаар Үндсэн Хуулийн Талаар Бичсэн Санал (1924)] in *The Law of the State* [Улсын эрх], tr S Idshinnorov (2014) 95–109 [hereinafter *Law of the State*]. The 2014 re-publication of the manuscript in old Mongolian script in *The Law of States* does not include the title 'Draft of the First Constitution (1924)' [hereinafter '*The Law of States*']. The manuscript is archived in the National Archive of Mongolia YTA CX-31, Д-1, XH-10.

[15] Manuscipt of D Bodoo's draft can be found in the National Archive of Mongolia YTA, X-11, Д-1, XH-1

[16] These compilation of Codes adopted during 1913–18 is published in *Codes Issued by the Edict* [*Зарлигаар Тогтоосон Монгол Улсын Хууль Зүйлийн Бичиг*] (1995).

[17] G Munkhtulga, *Quest for the Draft of the Constitution of Mongolia During Bogd Khan's Rule* [Богд Хаант Монгол Улсын Үндсэн Хуулийн Төслийг Эрэн Сурвалжлах Нь] (2018) 67 *National Legal Institute of Mongolia Law Review* [Хууль дээдлэх ёс] 15.

[18] Chimid (n 2) 15; 'Reconsidering History of Drafting the First Constitution in Mongolia', *Unuudur* (newspaper) [*Өнөөдөр сонин*] (23 November 2004); and Z Lonjid and N Lundendorj, *Development Tendencies of State and Legal Thought* [Монголын Анхны Үндсэн Хуулийг Боловсруулсан Түүхийг Сөхвөл] (2002) 226.

that related to Bogd Khaan's power. This monthly periodical, entitled *Far East* (*Дальній Востокъ* in old Russian transcript) published synopses of contemporaneous Asian pediodicals. In Issue 36, dated 1936, there is a brief report on 'A Talk about Autonomous Mongolia's Future Constitution'.[19] The report cited the German language daily newspaper *Der Ostasiatische Lloyd*, which was published in Shanghai, as the source of this information. According to Munkhtulga, this partial text of the draft Constitution bore a striking resemblance to Japan's Meiji Constitution of 1889,[20] at least in the extract published in *Far East*. Moreover, according to Soviet Union's well-known diplomat and scholar, Ivan M Maisky, who was very conversant with early Mongolian history, there was another failed attempt to draft a constitution based on the idea of establishing Great Mongolian State or Pan Mongolian State.[21] This failed as it lacked popular support.

The Chinese military invaded Mongolia in 1919 in a bid to regain control of the state, but they were successfully repelled in early 1921, first with the help of White Russians (part of the Russian Empire military who were expelled by the October Revolution of 1917) and then with the help of Red Russians (Soviet Russia). With that, the Bogd Khaan emerged as king and religious leader of the Mongols, while the People's Temporary Government was established with support from Soviet Russia. Between 1921 and 1923, Mongolia adopted several constitutional documents,[22] such as the 'Temporary Rules of Procedure of the Hural of the People's Government of Mongolia' of 1921–24 (12 September 1921); 'Rules of Provisional State Meeting' (20 September 1921); 'Oath Agreement' (1 November 1921); 'Regulations on Local Administration of Mongolia' (5 March 1921); 'Resolution of the People's Government on the Establishment of a Republican Government' (13 June 1924); and the 'Charter on the State Great Hural' (19 September 1924). Of these, the Oath Agreement of 1921 was of great importance because, for the first time, it declared and proposed a move towards a constitutional monarchy, and it contained provisions on the relationship between athe monarch and the People's Government. This document was drafted and enforced by the People's Government from 1 September 1921,[23] and it created the legal preconditions for the creation of a republican state. After the Bogd Khaan died in May 1924, the Presidium and Plenum of People's Party and the People's Government issued a number of decrees. One of these, issued in June that year, declared Mongolia a republic.[24] This was just a few months before Mongolia's first Constitution was adopted in November 1924.

[19] (1913) 36 *Far East* [(*Дальній Востокъ*) 5–6.

[20] Munkhtulga (n 17) 20.

[21] Ivan M Maisky, *Modern Mongolia (Autonomous Mongolia at the Beginning of the 20th Century* [*Орчин үеийн Монгол (Автономит Монгол XX зууны гараан дээр)*] (2005) 301.

[22] Ch Enkhbaatar, *Constitutional Law* [*Үндсэн Хуулийн Эрх Зүй*] (2007) 45–47.

[23] J Boldbaatar and D Lundeejantsan, *Historical Overview of Mongolia's State and Legal Tradition* [*Монгол Улсын Төр, Эрх Зүйн Түүхэн Уламжлал*] (Admon, 1997) 213–14.

[24] D Dash, *History from the Declaration of the People's Republic of Mongolia*, ed Sh Natsagdori [*БНМАУ-Ыг Тунхагласан Түүхээс*]) (1984) 67–69.

II. THE PROCESS OF CONSTITUTION-MAKING

The 1924 Constitution was the end-product of several constitutional drafting attempts and the incorporation and consideration of earlier constitutional documents, and of research into the constitutions of foreign countries. The attempts to draft a constitution and efforts to understand the constitutional systems of foreign states gained momentum from 1911. After the 1921 Revolution, renewed attempts were made to put together a constitution, and several drafts emerged. First, there was the constitutional draft principally written by Tseveen Jamsarano (1880–1942), a Buryat Mongolian born in the present-day Aginsky region of the Russian Federation. Jamsarano was a leading figure of Mongolian political life and one of founders of scientific education from 1911 till the end of 1920s. Educated at the prestigous St Petersburg University, Jamsarano taught as a professor at Irkutsk University, in the early days of Soviet Russia.

Second, there was another draft by Prime Minister Dogsomyn Bodoo (1895–1922), acting on his own initiative. We know very little about this draft, but since it was written before the Bogd Khan's death, it probably pertained to the expansion of the ruler's role in state affairs, especially since the Oath Agreement only accorded the constitutional monarch control over religious matters. It appears that both of these drafts were written by persons fluent in European languages, since their drafts were influenced by foreign constitutional ideology and examples. Both these early documents have been preserved in the National Archive of Mongolia.[25]

Two years after Bodoo was stripped of all public offices and executed in January 1922, Decree No 1 of the People's Government was issued on 5 February 1924 covering matters relating to constitution-making. As a result, a new working group to draft a constitution was formed, and Soviet Russian and/or Comintern experts arrived in Mongolia to assist it. However, there were several versions of the draft constitution (drafted with the help of the Russian and Comintern experts). and these were either revised or abridged versions of one another.[26] Subsequently, the 1924 Constitution was promulgated by the First State Great Hural based on one of these versions.

According to Boldbaatar and Lundeejantsan, the constitution-making process officially commenced with the decision of the Central Committee of the Mongolian People's Party and People's Government on 10 October 1921. However, the government body that oversaw the drafting was established on 19 May 1922, headed by Khatanbaatar Magsarjav (1877–1927), Minister of Justice

[25] S Idshinnorov, 'One Draft of the Constitution of Mongolia in the Course of History'[Түүхийн Нугачаан Дахь Монгол Улсын Үндсэн Хуулийн Нэгэн Төсөл] (2000) 4–5 *National University of Mongolia Law Review* 178; and Ch Unurbayar, *Penetration of Constitutionalism in Mongolia (1911–1921)* [*Монгол Улсад Үндсэн Хуульт Ёсны Үзэл Санаа Нэвтэрсэн Нь (1911–1924 Он)*ˆ] (Arildal, 2005).

[26] Regarding these versions of constitional drafts and comparison of each version, see Dash (n 19) 70–73.

of the People's Government. To facilitate the process, the People's Government issued a Decree at the 39th Cabinet Meeting on 1 September 1922, mandating the working group 'to draft a Constitution by abridging laws of limited state ruled by people such as England and in line with present-day government position'.[27] Since the Bogd Khaan was a religious leader, the expression 'limited state ruled by people' in the Decree meant that a constitutional monarchy with public participation was preferable. However, this attempt at drafting was halted and the official body responsible was dissolved on 29 December 1922, on the ground that the drafters had wrongfully neglected the significance of Soviet Russia and its constitution(s), and had relied too much on European models when looking at modern examples. This abrupt collapse of the drafting process resulted from conceptual differences between the Mongolian leaders, as well as from pressure from the Soviets and Comintern.[28]

The 1924 Constitution was adopted at the First State Great Hural (*Улсын анхдугаар их хурал*) comprising 77 representatives from the various local administrative units.[29] According to Balkhaajav, the First State Great Hural was a major focal point for the People's Party and People's Government, and they dispatched their representatives to local administrative units to explain the importance of the Hural and assist in and observe the election of representatives thereto. Moreover, the People's Government had adopted a specific Charter on the State Great Hural. The First State Great Hural thus commenced in Niislel huree (present-day Ulaan Baatar) on 8 November 1924.

Of the 77 representatives, 92.2 per cent or 71 were common persons, while 64 of them were members of the People's Party or its youth organisation.[30] Amongst those who participated in the First State Great Hural, 70 were literate in Mongolian,[31] while some were proficient in Russian, Khazakh, English, Tibetan and/or Esperanto languages. Their ages ranged from 21 to 58 years old.[32] To elect representatives of the First State Hural, elections had been held in September, and 90 reprepresentatives were elected by secret ballot from local assemblies and 77 of them participated.[33] The representatives came from different parts of the country, including some representatives from military units. According to Article 12 of the Charter on the State Great Hural, Cabinet ministers, Speakers of the local assemblies, governors of local administrative units, all high-ranking and other lamas were disqualified from becoming representatives of the State

[27] Boldbaatar and Lundeejantsan (n 23) 224.

[28] ibid 223–24.

[29] B Bayarsaikhan, *Legal Dictionary of State and Legal History of Mongolia* [Хууль Зүйн Тайлбар Толь (Монгол Улсын Төр, Эрх Зүйн Түүх)] (2003) 172.

[30] Ts Balkhaajav, *The First State Great Hural, The First Constitution of the People's Republic of Mongolia* [*Улсын анхдугаар их хурал БНМАУ-ын анхдугаар Үндсэн хууль*] (1956) 10–11. See also Sanjdorj (n 10) 7.

[31] Sanjdorj (n 10) 7.

[32] Archival number of the list on representatives of the First State Great Hural can be found at УТТА Ф-11, Т-5, хн-12, хуудас 1-17. See also Sanjdorj (n 10) 304–07.

[33] Balkhaajav (n 30) 7.

Great Hural. In the meantime, Article 16 of the Charter required all Cabinet members (including the Prime Minister and Deputy Prime Ministers), a member of Military Council, the Commander in Chief, all other Ministers, top ranking advisers and the Head of the Academy of Sciences to sit in during State Great Hural Sessions.[34]

According to some historical sources, the working group headed by then Prime Minister Balingiin Tserendorj (1868–1928), mandated to draft the 1924 Constitution, was established on 24 October 1924, and had only three weeks to complete its task.[35] Moreover, at a session of Parliament convened on 7 November 1924, it was resolved that the draft constitution should be presented on 25 November for deliberation. The draft was then discussed for two days and was approved by its 14th resolution on 26 November 1924 at 4:17pm.[36] During the parliamentary deliberation, more than 60 representatives expressed their views on every provision of the draft. It is documented that some of the provisions, such as the relationship between the State Upper and Lower Chambers of the Parliament, were amended based on the representatives' opinion.[37]

Thanks to the availability of earlier constitutional documents and drafts, and the excellent research done since 1911, the adoption and deliberation of the new Constitution proceeded relatively smoothly and swiftly, with few differences among representatives in Parliament.[38] One contrary view is that strong pressure from Soviet Russia and Comintern played a role in ensuring that it was drafted and approved within such a short time. It is thought that the previous drafts were either too conservative (as being in favour of a constitutional monarchy (Bodoo draft)) or too liberal (Jamsarano draft), which was the opposite of what the Soviets and Comintern wanted. As a result, the Mongolians were left with no choice but to rely on Soviet Constitution as a model.

III. QUESTIONS DEBATED DURING THE DRAFTING

The first and foremost issue debated in Mongolia during the drafting of the Constitution (1911–24) was the model of exemplary constitutions to be consulted. Intellectuals and statesmen discussed three primary options. The first group was keen to adopt a constitution similar to those of western European

[34] To see relevant articles of the Charter, ibid 312.

[35] On 24 October 1924, Government Decree #39 covering this matter was issued. For more on this, see *Comintern and Mongolia* [*Коминтерн Ба Монгол*] (Publishing House of Science & Technology and Information Co, 1997) 93; and Unurbayar (n 25) 80.

[36] Sanjdorj (n 10) 266, 291; see also S Jalan-Aajav, *Mainstream of the Legislative Activities of the Peoples' Revolutionary State, 1921–1940* [*Ардын Хувьсгалт Төрийн Хууль Тогтоох Үйл Ажиллагааны Үндсэн Чиглэл (1921–1940)* (1967) 76.

[37] Boldbaatar and Lundeejantsan (n 23) 226–27; and Sanjdorj (n 10) 10.

[38] Sanjdorj (n 10).

(bourgeois) countries, arguing that to modernise Mongolia and its society, western Europe and the United States of America were better examples, being modern industrialised countries. Two separate drafts were prepared following this trend of thought: the Jamsarano and Bodoo drafts.

A second group of intellectuals were more cautious and were anxious to incorporate the best elements of Mongolia's cultural traditions and practices while modernising Mongolia. They advocated designing a constitution in line with western ideals while considering Asian values. Japan's Meiji Constitution thus served as their primary model. In particular, a letter submitted to the State Great Hural by Ch Dandaa, a government official and scholar, stated that 'it is a complicated and crucial issue of our time, and it should not be taken lightly. A closer look reveals that the law of Riben (Japan) among other countries contains a complete summary of the detailed secrets of laws of those countries.' Nevertheless, it was not just an attempt to directly copy the Japanese system of law and government, because the lawmakers also studied the constitutional documents of developed democracies, such as the United Kingdom (UK) and other European countries, as well as laws that existed before the 1911 Revolution, in accordance with the orders of the Central Committee of the Party and the Government.[39]

The third group of statesmen advocated a socialist-type constitution similar that of Soviet Russia. As we shall see later, foreign experts were instrumental in the drafting of the 1924 Constitution of Mongolia. Between 1911 and 1923, there was strong interest in studying constitutional models of the west, especially those of the UK, the USA and France, as well as those of Japan. However, after the Russian Revolution of 1917 and the Mongolian People's Revolution of 1921, the shift toward a Soviet-type of constitution occured. In the end, the socialist-type of constitution modelled after the 1918 Soviet Constitution was drafted[40] with the help of Russian experts. In any case, these various efforts demonstrate the high degree of legal and constitutional consciousness that prevailed in Mongolia at that time.[41]

At the First State Great Hural in November 1924, the Head of the Drafting Committee gave a speech in which he stated that there were three types of constitutions around the world. The first was an absolute monarchy; the second a constitutional monarchy; and the third a bourgeois republic exemplified by the Republic of China. He then expressed a preference for a wholly different type of constitution, like that of the People's Republic (Soviet).[42] It should be observed that prior to the Bogd Khaan's death in 1924, Mongolia had never accepted

[39] Lonjid and Lundendorj (n 18).
[40] Bayarsaikhan (n 29) 176.
[41] Chimid (n 2) 39.
[42] Sanjdorj (n 10) 256.

a republican form of government. Indeed, the idea of a monarchy surfaced naturally, after the Revolutions of 1911 and 1921, which led to the Bogd Khaan emerging supreme. However, after the 1921 Revolution, the idea of a constitutional monarchy rose to prominence and was pushed unilaterally by the People's Temporary Government. This concept was later incorporated in the Oath Agreement.

But when the idea of a constitutional monarchy was being discussed, the republican form of government was pushed by those who initiated the 1921 Revolution as an alternative. They reasoned that the Government should rely on the people, and that there should be limits on those who rule and govern.[43] It was a new idea for Mongolia, because up until then, noblemen and high-ranking lamas were regarded as the natural and perpetual rulers of the land. With the death of the Bogd Khaan in May 1924, the idea of abolishing the monarchy and adopting a republican form of government came to the fore and was quickly incorporated in the 1924 Constitution. This signalled a move towards greater secularism among the Mongolians. As a result, state–religion relationships were more heavily scrutinised. And by the late 1920s and early 1930s, the Communist Government took an increasingly harsh position toward religion.

After the 1921 Revolution, equality became increasingly important, especially for the People's Party and People's Government. They had defeated the Chinese with the help of the Soviets, who had already rejected the old feudal ways of Imperial Russia.[44] Before the 1921 Revolution, Mongolia was a feudal state where nobles, high-ranking lamas, usurers and wealthy merchants who treated commoners as their servants. But as the Revolution succeeded with the help of the Russians, Mongolians took the 1918 Soviet Russia Constitution and the 1924 Soviet Union Constitution as examples of a democratic constitution.[45] In doing so, it became all the more important to abolish the social stratification within Mongolian society that oppressed the common folk. The concept of equality for all persons was thus woven into the 1924 Constitution.

The other critical matters were Mongolia's future economic path and the guaranteeing of social-economic rights. Before 1911, Mongolia's peasantry ran what was essentially a subsistence economy. It was outmoded and registered low productivity yields. The monetary regime was also primitive and poorly regulated. The Revolution thus provided Mongolians with an opportunity to overhaul the economy following a socialist, rather than capitalist, programme and agenda, while allowing private property. Although there was not much evidence that the wider public discussed the above-mentioned matters, it was clear that these questions were discussed or studied in great detail among the statesmen and intellectuals for number of years.

[43] Jalan-Aajav (n 36) 21–22.
[44] For more about this, see Balkhaajav (n 30).
[45] ibid 17.

IV. DRAFTING MONGOLIA'S FIRST CONSTITUTION: INTERNAL AND EXTERNAL FACTORS

A. Internal Factors

In the case of the first Constitution of Mongolia, internal factors were the driving force in making the 1924 Constitution. As discussed, the efforts to understand constitutional law seemed to start just after the 1911 Revolution in Mongolia. The will of all classes of Mongolian society to regain independence and establish a nation-state was the driving factor, and regardless of politicial or ideological differences, and social differences, this had prevailed.

i. Role of Intellectuals

Internally, local intellectuals like Tseveen Jamsarano and D Bodoo played a vital role in understanding and creating the first Constitution of Mongolia. For instance – the scholar Jamsarano, acting on Prime Minister T Namnansuren's instruction – conducted a comparative study of the constitutional laws in the developed Western and Eastern countries, and wrote a book entitled *The Law of States*.[46] In his book, Jamsarano stated that 'the supreme powers of the state are to rule, govern and defend itself, and deal with foreign countries'.[47] Another scholar, Ch Demchigdorj (also known as Dandaa), proposed ways to overcome the country's backwardness and to spur a national revival in his *Matters of New Government*,[48] written in 1915, and *The Main Rule of New Government*,[49] written in 1922.[50] At the beginning, most likely during the 1910s, Dandaa supported the idea of reforming the Government while preserving the monarchy. Later, around 1922, he supported the creation of a republican state.[51]

A manuscript, most likely written by Jamsarano, entitled *Introduction to the International Constitutions*, which comprises a legal history from the Magna Carta of England to the Constitution of Japan (1889), is still in the National Library of Mongolia.[52] We will discuss the contents of this paper in section V

[46] Since Tseveen Namnandorj was Prime Minister between 1912–19, this book might have been written before 1919. It was republished as *The Law of the State* (n 14). About the manuscripts, see (2003) 2–3 Эрх зүй сэтгүүл. [2003] *Шинэ толь сэтгүүл.*

[47] *The Law of State* (n 14) 51.

[48] There are four versions of this manuscript archived in the National Library of Mongolia according to B Batbayar, 'Research Overview on Ch Demchigdorj and his Publications' in *The Main Rule of New Government* [Удиртгал Ч.Дэмчигдорж Хийгээд Түүний Бүтээлийн Тухай Судалгааны Тойм, *Шинэ засгийн гол ёс*] (2015) 25.

[49] Ch Dandaa, *Main Rule of New Government* [Шинэ Засгийн Гол Ёсон]. This manuscript was later re-published as Ch Demchigdorj, *Main Rule of New Government* [*Шинэ засгийн гол ёс*] (Эрх зүйт ёс сан, 2015).

[50] Batbayar (n 48) 29.

[51] ibid 23.

[52] Manuscript Fund of the National Library of Mongolia with location number F2898-96. The author is unknown, and some researchers suggest that it may have been produced by Tseveen Jamsarano. This manuscript was later published as Amarsanaa et al (n 13).

of this chapter. At the same time, there are archival materials that prove that the constitutions of numerous countries were translated at the Institute of Scriptures and Manuscripts, a pillar organisation similar to that of the present-day Academy of Sciences of Mongolia.[53] Another famous book of that time was a treatise on public international law written by American diplomat and lawyer Henry Wheaton. It was translated into Mongolian from the Chinese translation of 1864,[54] and there were frequent references to this book by Mongolian negotiators at the tri-partite negotiation between Mongolia–Russia–China during 1915. And as international law deals with the relations between nations, it comes as little surprise that as a independent country, Mongolia was interested in the law of nations.

ii. Revolution

Another very important internal factor impacting the making of the Constitution was the succession of revolutions leading up to 1921. If no revolution had taken place in Mongolia, the constitution-making process may well not have gotten underway, at least in the way that it did. In 1911, Mongolia declared its independence from China. This was widely known as the National Liberation Revolution. In this movement, progressive statesmen, noblemen and Buddhist lamas of Mongols under the leadership of the Bogd (who, at the time was not a king but a religious leader) played a vital role in staging a comparatively peaceful revolution. From the beginning of the Revolution, Mongolia took a conscious step to re-build and reform its legal system.[55] In this, the State Upper Chamber and State Lower Chamber – consultative bodies to the Bogd Khaan – were very active in holding sessions. According to Professor Urangua, they convened 47 to 48 times a year.[56] One account tells us that the State Hural, comprising the State Upper and State Lower Chambers, received some 90 documents between 1914 and 1919.[57]

In 1921, with the help of Russian military, Mongolia repelled the Republic of China's invasion, and a new government under the Bogd Khaan was declared. However, within few months, with the support of Soviet Russia (the Red Russians), the Bodg Khaan Government was dissolved and a socialist People's

[53] *The Second Conference of the Mongolian People's Party* (Documents) (Ulaanbaatar,1974) 122–23.

[54] Munkhtulga (n 17) 17. This book was later re-published as Henry Wheaton, *Elements of International Law* [Б.Алтангэрэл], ed B Altangerel (Admon, 2006).

[55] B Sodovsuren, *Mongolian State and Law before the Revolution, 1911–1929* [*Хувьсгалын Өмнөх Монголын Төр Ба Хууль Цааз* (1989) 44–45. See also Khereid Jamsarano Urangua, *The Mongolian State at the Beginning of the Twentieth Century (1911–1919)* [*XX Зууны Эхэн Үеийн Монгол Улс (1911-1919)*] (NUM Institute of Historical Research, 2006) 93.

[56] Urangua (n 55) 90.

[57] *State Upper and Lower Houese of Mongolia, Compilation of Documents*, vol 2 [*Монгол Улсын Дээд, Доод Хурал. Баримт Бичгийн Эмхтгэл*] (2005) 10.

Government was established. As a result of these revolutions, Mongolia became one of the first Asian countries to secede from a former empire and establish itself as a sovereign state. With that break from China, Mongolia's early democrats worked assiduously to push the state towards self-government and to abolish serfdom. From 1921 to 1924, real progress was made to consolidate this achievement by creating all of the preconditions for the drafting of the main law of the state.[58]

iii. Socio-economic Conditions

Social-economic conditions in Mongolia before 1911 were poor, and there were compelling reasons to modernise the economy. The wealth gap among Mongolians was huge, and the entire state was economically dependent on and beholden to China, local usurers and the merchant class. Education was provided mostly at Buddhist temples or at home. Only those who were wealthy could afford home schooling, while the common folk could only send their children to the temples to be educated. There, children were expected to serve the temple, but were often also exploited. There were no secular educational institutions, and certainly none that exposed students to western scientific knowledge and developments. Primitive livestock husbandry constituted almost the whole economy, and most men became lamas, but religion proved too rigid and inflexible for the needs of the emergent Mongol society.[59]

iv. Political and Doctrinal Conflicts

In the lead-up to the drafting of the 1924 Constitution, there was much political and doctrinal contestation over the form the draft constitution would take. These differences even resulted in Prime Minister Dogsomyn Bodoo being overthrown, charged with treason and conspiracy to overthrow the Government, and executed in 1922. As a result of the difference of opinion between national democrats and Comintern supporters, the earlier western liberal-orientated commission was disbanded[60] and another commission, headed by Prime Minister Balingiin Tserendorj, was established.[61] The Commission then drafted a new Constitution of the People's Republic of Mongolia with the substantial participation of the Comintern, and submitted it to the State Great Hural for approval in record time.

[58] Chimid (n 2) 14–15.

[59] For social-economic conditions in Mongolia at beginning of 20th century, see Urangua (n 55).

[60] See further Ch Unurbayar, *An Introduction of Constitutional Ideas into Mongolia* (Ulaanbaatar, 2005).

[61] Z Lonjid, 'Reconsidering History of Drafting the First Constitution in Mongolia' *Unuudur* (23 November 2004) no 274.

B. External Factors

Although internal factors were a primary driving force behind the concept and content of the 1924 Constitution, its drafting was also greatly influenced by external factors. These factors may be discussed from two perspectives. The first concerns factors that encouraged Mongolians to think about the Constitution and other key legal rules. The second pertains to the factors that influenced the content of the 1924 Constitution.

The Revolutions in Russia in 1905 and 1917 represented a significant break from the past. The Revolution of 1917 saw the Bolsheviks overthrow the Imperial Government and the Romanov Dynasty that had ruled Russia since 1613. This development significantly affected Mongolia, which was not only geographically proximate but also socially and culturally tied to Russia through the Buryat Mongols who lived on Russian soil. At the same time, many Russian travellers, diplomats, scientists and merchants either lived in or transited through Mongolia. The Buryat Mongols, who were educated in Russia, were familiar with western ideas and ideology, and actively shared these ideas and other developments in Russia and elsewhere with their fellow Mongols.

At the same time, the constant internal unrest within China during the nineteenth and early twentieth centuries invariably affected Mongolia. Indeed, at the start of the twentieth century, China began looking for ways to reform its state structure and understand constitutional monarchy, and this development was keenly observed by Mongolian nationalists.[62] In many ways, these developments in Russia and China weakened these respective empires' influence on territories lying on the outskirts of their borders, such as Mongolia. The Qing Government's 'new policy of government'[63] in Mongolia led to increasing frustration amongst the Mongols.[64] But the collapse of the Qing Empire in 1911 presented Mongolia with the perfect opportunity to dissolve its connection with China[65] and declare its autonomy. From this point on, the process of constitution-making was seen as a means to transform Mongolian society, and as a signal to the rest of the world that Mongolia was modernising.

In drafting their Constitution, the Mongolians were keen to learn from foreign precedents. Indeed, there is an evidence that Mongolians studied foreign constitutional experiences and ideas in great depth from the beginning of 1911, as evidenced in archival manuscripts in old Mongolian script. Amongst these,

[62] For more on this, see Unurbayar (n 20) 31–34.

[63] At beginning of the 20th century, the Manchu Qing Dynasty implemented a new policy toward Mongolia known as '*шинэ засгийн бодлого*' in the Mongolian language or 新政 in Chinese, meaning literally 'new government'.

[64] On this situation, see Urangua (n 55).

[65] 'The Mongol-Manchu relationship was conceptualized as an alliance rather than conquest.' About this, see Uradyn E Bulag, 'Independence as Restoration: Chinese and Mongolian Declarations of Independence and the 1911 Revolutions' (2012) *10 The Asia-Pacific Journal: Japan Focus* 4 at https://apjjf.org/2012/10/52/Uradyn-E.-Bulag/3872/article.html, accessed 7 April 2021.

three documents stand out: (i) *Introduction to the International Constitutions*; (ii) *The Law of States*; and (iii) *The Main Rule of New Government*.

Introduction to the International Constitutions covered a number of foreign constitutions and constitutional documents, and contained a research article as a preface. In the part that discussed England, it touched on the relationship between the king and barons, tax, religion, etc between the reigns of Henry III and Edward I in the context of the Magna Carta (1215, 1225 and 1297). This manuscript also excerpted parts of the Norwegian Constitution and the whole of the American Constitution, including its subsequent amendments, as well as a narrative on the making and adoption of the Constitution. The text of the Meiji Constitution of Japan (1889) was translated into the Mongolian language and included in this manuscript. Most importantly, it contained an article explaining the importance of the US Constitution in the modern world, and the role of the French Revolution and the influence of Jean-Jacques Rousseau on constitutional monarchy. This manuscript further set out brief accounts of constitutional developments in the Netherlands (1814), Norway (1814), Bavaria (1818), Grossherzogtum Baden (1818), Wuerttumberg (1819), Portugal (second Constitution in 1822), Saxony (1831), Braunschweig (1832), Belgium (1830), Spain (1834, 1837 and 1845) and Greece (1844), in declaring independence or constitutional monarchies by adopting constitutions. It also gave the example of Poland's becoming part of Russia after the 1830 Revolution and how its Constitution was abolished. The manuscript provided a brief history of constitutional developments (adoption, amendment and abolishment of constitutions, transplantation experience) in England and western and eastern Europe in the late nineteenth century. The document highlighted the American Constitution, the constitutions of its constituent States and their relationship inter se, and the notion of constitutional review, as well as some unique characteristics of the English and Russian constitutional orders. The manuscript stated that the Hispanic countries of the Americas were very difficult to understand, and added that the Meiji Constitution of 1889 should be considered carefully, since adaptations were needed as its model was transplanted from western Europe. Professor Jugnee Amarsanaa and his colleagues have concluded that the constitutions in *Introduction to the International Constitutions* were translated from the slavic language,[66] while historian D Dash argues that these translations were not made for 'ordinary purposes' but in preparation for the drafting of the first constitution.[67]

These influences were significant, at least up till 1921, when increasing pressure from Russia and the Comintern dramatically changed the thinking of key Mongolian officials. As we saw earlier, Russia become increasingly interventionist in Mongolia from 1911. After 1911, Russian influence in Mongolian affairs increased steadily, save for the brief period around the 1917 Russian Revolution.

[66] See Preface to Amarsanaa et al (n 13) 3.

[67] *The First Great Hural of the Mongolian People's Republic* (Ulaanbaatar, 1974) 341–42.

The establishment of a Communist regime in Russia following the 1917 Revolution, and the subsequent formation of the Communist Mongolian People's Revolutionary Party in 1920, cemented the ties between the two states.[68] These ties were further boosted in 1919, when the Soviet army helped the Mongolians repel the Chinese forces that sought to re-establish control over Mongolia. This culiminated in the retreat of Chinese forces in 1921, after which the Soviet Government and the Provisional Government of Mongolia signed a treaty that provided for mutual recognition.[69] As Alan Sanders, a noted scholar of Mongolian studies, observed:

> Mongolia's ties with Soviet Russia were constantly strengthened, and in August 1924, at its Third Congress attended by 108 delegates representing 4,000 members, the Mongolian People's Party opted for the 'non-capitalist path of development' advocated by Lenin. The party was renamed the Mongolian People's Revolutionary Party (MPRP), the name evidently given to it by the Russian Communist (Bolshevik) Party.[70]

When the constitution-drafting process began in earnest in 1922, it was envisaged that a constitutional monarchy would be created, with the Oath Agreement of 1921 forming part of it. Tseveen Jamsarano joined the drafting commission in 1922, and his own early liberal draft was used as the basis for discussion. However, the drafting commission was dissolved, ostensibly because it was unable to complete its work, and the task was relegated to the legislative department of the Mongolian People's Government.[71] The Bogd Khaan's death in 1924 led to the jettisoning of plans to create a constitutional monarchy, and developments and power struggles between the Mongolian elites threatened and jeopardised Mongolia's independence. The Soviet Government took the opportunity to strengthen its influence in Mongolia and sent in more advisers, including Vasilevich Vsesviatskii (1884–1938), Comintern envoy Turar Ryskulov (1894–1938) and a third unnamed expert, with explicit instructions to help 'speed up the work' in drafting of the first constitution. According to Sablin, Badagarov and Sonomova, it was Vsesviatskii who drafted the Constitution, and translated into Mongolian by Elbeg-Dorjui Rinchino.[72] A new commission – chaired by Prime Minister Balingiin Tserendorj and comprising Jamsarano, Rinchino and Ryskulov – was established to review Vsesviatskii's draft. Ryskulov noted that the Constitutions of the USSR and the Far Eastern Republic[73] were the main sources of Vsesviatskii's draft.[74] While there were some disagreements

[68] Ballis (n 5).
[69] ibid, 302.
[70] Alan Sanders, 'Parliament in Mongolia' (1998) 4(4) *Legislative Studies* 131, 137.
[71] Ivan Sablin, Jargal Badagarov and Irina Sonomova, 'Khural Democracy: Imperial Transformations and the Making of the First Mongolian Constitution, 1911–1924' in Simon Wickhamsmith and Philip P Marzluf (eds), *Socialist and Post-Socialist Mongolia: Nation, Idenity and Culture* (Routledge, 2021) 14, 32.
[72] ibid.
[73] The Far Eastern Republic or the Far Eastern Soviet Republic was a nominally independent state in the easternmost part of Russia, which existed between 1920 and 1922.
[74] Sablin et al (n 71) 32.

as regards the draft, these were quickly ironed out, with the Russians dominating the proceedings. The Russian experts even participated in the deliberation process, by answering questions and providing explanations of the draft at the First State Great Hural.[75] According to Jamsarano, the ultimate choice of a constitutional model was inextricably tied to the degree of support Mongolia received from Russia.[76]

V. THE STRUCTURE AND NATURE OF THE 1924 CONSTITUTION

The 1924 Constitution was adopted with a preamble, six chapters and 50 Articles. This Constitution had a brief official interpretation.[77] The structure of the Constitution was as follows:

- Preamble
- Proclamation of the Freedoms of the Mongolian Common People (Articles 1–14)
- The Organs of the State Supreme Power (Articles 15–29)
- Local Administration (Articles 30–33)
- The Right to Elect and to be Elected (Articles 34–36)
- The State Income and Expenditure (Articles 37–46)
- The State Seal, Coat of Arms and Banner Flag (Articles 47–50).

Chapter Two, on the Organs of the State Supreme Power, dealt specifically with the State Great Hural (Articles 7–11); the State Small Hural (Articles 12–17); the Presidium of the State Small Hural (Articles 18–26); the Government (Articles 27–28); and the Economic Council (Article 29).

Article 4 of the Constitution vested the state supreme power in the State Great Hural and, during an interval of convocations, in the State Small Hural. During an interval of convocations of the latter, power vested between the Presidium of the State Small Hural and the Government. Representatives of the State Great Hural were elected for one year only. Thirty members would be elected to the State Small Hural, which was accountable to the State Great Hural and was in charge of adopting statutes, rules and resolutions once the Presidium submitted a draft (Articles 11 and 20). The Economic Council was in charge of business and economic policies under the Government (Article 29). The preamble declared the end of the constitutional monarchy and the adoption

[75] Part of the minutes of the meeting with Ryskulov's speech at the First State Great Hural about his involvement in the drafting process; see Sanjdorj (n 4) 258, 264 and 266.

[76] Urangua (n 55) 79.

[77] B Chimid, *Importance of New Research Aspects of the Constitution: The Concept of the Constitution* [Үндсэн Хуулийн Хөгжлийг Судлахад Шинэ Хандлага Чухал: *Үндсэн хуулийн үзэл баримтлал*) (2017) 123.

of republicanism, with the State Great Hural and Government exercising the supreme power of the state. Article 2 declared the state's goal of strengthening the foundation of the republican order and the eradication of the old oppressive regime. It further provided that all political affairs be vested in and exercised by the people.

Article 3 contained several elements of human rights. For instance, it declared the freedom of religion, freedom of assembly, right to criticise, freedom to form associations and cooperatives (right to entrepreneurship) and the right to free education. The right to elect and to be elected was considered particularly important, and this was addressed in a whole chapter of the Constitution. Under Article 34, all men and women (with some exceptions) had the right to elect and be elected to State Great and Small Hurals and local assemblies. However, certain persons were limited or prohibited from voting and being elected – those who exploited others, nobles, high-ranking and other lamas who live permanently in monastries, usurers, 'big merchants', and insane and convicted persons.

The Constitution also enshrined the principle of equality of all persons and abolished the titles and ranks of princes, dukes and lords, as well as the right of high-ranking and re-incarnated lamas to take part in political life. As noted earlier, Mongolia had been, up till the Revolution of 1921, a feudal country with a highly hierarchichal and stratified class system. The Constitution guaranteed all persons the equal enjoyment of rights and freedoms, irrespective of their origin, religion or gender. The most obvious evidence of the 1924 Constitution's being a socialist-type constitution is found in Articles 3 and 4. Article 3 declared that Mongolia would 'strive for socialism and communism'. And, as already noted, the old elites and bourgois classes were banned from political participation and leadership.

VI. SOME ESSENTIAL CONCEPTS IN MONGOLIAN CONSTITUTIONS

A. Acceptance of the Basic Concepts of Human Rights in the Constitutions

While the Mongolians had fought for independence and freedom on the basis of national liberation and human rights,[78] the concept of 'human rights' was rather alien to the Mongolian people. Although ideas about respect for human rights and fundamental freedoms, and guaranteeing them by law, came from the West, it was not long before they took enthusiastic root in Mongolia. One of the first things Mongolians accepted from Western legal thought and culture was a national democratic ideology based on people's rights and humanitarianism,

[78] Unurbayar (n 25) 42.

especially in response to the oppressive policies of the Qing Government. For instance, a daily newspaper at the time published the following:

> The following are important things in self-determination and the Rule of Law: first, gaining freedom of the people and the State must always act in the best interests of the people. If people should achieve their freedom by their efforts, it is called real freedom. The freedom gained with the help of other foreign oppressive rulers is a fake one.[79]

Progressive intellectuals had long studied how the idea of human rights became the basis of constitutions in Europe. This scholarship was reflected in the works of Tseveen Jamsarano and Ch Demchigdorj, and it is also considered important in the framing of the 1992 Constitution. In particular, Jamsarano noted in the preface of his *The Law of States* that

> [t]he original purpose of politics was not to enslave the masses and benefit a few, but to try to benefit the general public. Politics was created to free the people from all of the sufferings and to bring them up in peace.[80]

Jamsarano considered not only state systems of foreign countries, but also human rights as the foundation of any state. He emphasised that 'the rights and freedom of people are enshrined in the laws of many current powerful countries in the world'.[81] Jamsarano also acknowledged the universal constitutional principle that human rights should not be violated by either state or individuals, and noted that the Government had a duty to protect individual rights:

> Everyone has the right to develop his or her body, mind and language, and to create his or her benefit in his or her discretion, so the state administration or common persons should not oppress and violate another person's personal rights. That is why the government must protect human rights equally.[82]

B. Recognition of the Main Principles of Parliamentarism

Mongolia has been acquainted with the ideas and basic principles of parliamentarism since the early twentieth century, although it had similar organs like the *great huraldai* (assembly) in the distant past. One of the major political and legal reforms in after the 1911 Revolution was the establishment of State Upper and State Lower Chambers with consultative powers in 1914. This was similar to the Western-style parliamentary model and marked the beginning of the development of parliamentarism in Mongolia. In this regard, scholar Sh Natsagdorj

[79] *Mongolian Truth* [*Монголын үнэн*] 1920, no 1.
[80] Amarsanaa et al (n 13) 45.
[81] ibid 53.
[82] ibid 53–54.

concluded that it was similar to the parliamentary bodies of Western and Eastern countries, meaning Europe, America and Asia.[83]

Tseveen Jamsarano, Ch Demchigdorj, S Danzan and D Bodoo had studied the basic principles of parliamentarism as constitutional achievements in Europe. Jamsarano briefly described the reasons for the establishment and development of the first Parliament in the West as follows:

> [I]f we look at the situation of many small and large countries from ancient times to the present, the rulers of the state value their interests and prestige. When the people complained and struggled, and the political situation deteriorated, the authorities had to convene a meeting of representatives from each region to discuss the country's misery, happiness, benefits, incomes, and expenditures, to adopt law governing the State and establish a national assembly (Parliament). The country was strong under the auspices of the national assembly, and there are over sixty countries, whether large or small, which have national assemblies, in the world today.[84]

It was thus desirable for the people of Mongolia to establish a people's government in this manner and not return to the old feudalistic form of government.[85]

Jamsarano studied how to establish the State Upper and Lower Chambers of the Parliament and what challenges they would face, and critically compared the bicameral legislatures in other countries,[86] concluding that a small country need not have two chambers.[87] He analysed the methods of election for each chamber, its criteria and its process, and proposed how Mongolia should implement it, providing detailed analyses of the mandates, structures, legal frameworks and powers of parliaments, in particular in Western Europe. The national democrats sought to transplant European legal culture and thoughts in combination with their traditional values in Mongolia, as can be seen in the *Zarligaar togtooson Mongol ulsyn huuli züiliin bichig*. On this point, Professor S Narangerel concludes that this codified law contains both Mongolian legal traditions and foreign legal experience.[88] A letter requesting the establishment of the Upper and Lower Chambers by Bogd Khaan said:

> There are state assemblies in many powerful and wealthy nations. In those countries, delegates to the Upper Chamber discuss state political issues while those of the Lower Chamber discuss regional issues. Both chambers appoint a leader to unify public policy.[89]

As a platform for expressing the different views of the different political forces in Mongolia, the State Hural provided an opportunity for different ideologies

[83] Sh Natsagdorj, *The Main Path of Feudalism in Mongolia* [*Монголын Феодализмын Үндсэн Замнал*] (1978) 331.

[84] Amarsanaa et al (n 13) 45–46.

[85] *Mongolian Truth* (March 1920).

[86] Amarsanaa et al (n 13) 46.

[87] ibid.

[88] S Narangerel, *Legal System of Mongolia and the World* (2001) 101.

[89] *State Upper and Lower Houese of Mongolia, Compilation of Documents*, vol 1 [*Монгол Улсын Дээд, Доод Хурал. Баримт Бичгийн Эмхтгэл*] (2005) 24.

to compete with each other, thus creating the conditions for the development of pluralist democracy. Subsequently, in 1914, the Bogd Khaan issued 'the Eight-Item Charter on the State Upper and Lower Chambers'.

The State Upper Chamber was made up of unelected officials with the right to advise the Khaan, to protect the interests of ministers in some way, but it was otherwise similar to the parliaments of many states. Although the State Hural (Parliament) from 1914 to 1919 did not fully reflect the real nature of parliamentarism, its approach to the Western-style parliamentary model had a distinct advantage over antecedent bodies such as the *great huraldai* and *hoshuu chuulgan/banner* meetings. It was a good start to the development of parliamentary democracy, even though it did not endure. We see these ideas reflected in the 1921 Rule of the Temporary State Assembly, the preamble to which stated:

> The most popular international event in the world, whether large or small, is the national assembly. Now our Mongolia is a sovereign state like many other countries in the world, it is important to convene the same assembly, adopt laws and regulations that will benefit the people forever, and enlighten the general public and strengthen the ancient roots of our people's government. Let the government immediately announce and establish a real national assembly.[90]

While these parliamentary ideas and principles were primarily advanced and advocated by progressive statesmen and intellectuals, they gradually took root and eventually became embodied in the Constitution.

VII. THE IMPACT AND INFLUENCE OF THE 1924 CONSTITUTION

It is a widely-held view in Mongolia that the 1924 Constitution was especially significant in twentieth-century Mongolian history. According to Professor B Chimid, the significance of the 1924 Constitution may be summarised as follows:

> It provided Mongolia with the legal basis for its independence and its consequent acceptance by international community;
>
> It abolished feudalism and made all the persons equal citizens of the country;
>
> It abolished the theocratic monarchy, established a republic and created new state organs (Great and Small Hural, Government, Ministries);
>
> It unified the country through local government;
>
> It established the economic and fiscal foundations of the state; and
>
> It became the basis of a new legal system similar to continental civil law legal family with Soviet influence.[91]

[90] *Compilation of the Constitution and Relevant Acts of the People's Republic of Mongolia* [*БНМАУ-Ын Үндсэн Хууль, Түүнд Холбогдох Актын Эмхтгэл*] vol 1 (1972) 33–34.

[91] Chimid (n 77) 122; see also Jugnee Amarsanaa, 'Development of Constitutionalism in Mongolia' (2006) 3(1) *Asian Law Review* 97, 102–03.

To these can be added Professor Ch Enkhbaatar's point that the Constitution stressed the separation of state and religion.[92]

The influence of the first Constitution on its subsequent progeny may be elaborated in two parts: first, the concepts embodied in all the Constitutions; and, second, the concepts that persisted in subsequent socialist Constitutions, such as the republican form of government, the separation of state and religion, parliamentary democracy and human rights. In the twentieth century, Mongolia established a number of different parliamentary bodies under the different constitutions, and these were considered main components of these constitutions. Indirect democracy and public participation – all ideas drawn from the 1924 Constitution – were to become cornerstones of Mongolian society and pillars of subsequent Constitutions. However, it has been argued that during the socialist period, elements of democracy were distorted, especially the right to criticise the state and its ideology, and while both the 1940 and 1960 Constitutions declared and guaranteed all the human rights, they were never observed in practice. During this time, as religion was considered taboo, the separation of state and religion was not an issue at all.

A. Concepts in the 1924 Constitution to the 1940 and 1960 Constitutions

Of the Constitutions of 1924, 1940[93] and 1960,[94] the first was somewhat unique. The first Constitution is not strictly speaking a pure socialist-type constitution but a socialist-orientated one.[95] Professor Chimid argued that a key feature of the legal system during the socialist period was a progressive and ultimately distorted approach to modern European legal culture as modified and mediated through Russian and Soviet law.[96] Even so, some concepts or features of that first Constitution endured in its successors.[97] For example, both the 1940 and the 1960 Constitutions retained the provisions on social class, privileging the working classes[98] as the foundation of society while prohibiting private property and commerce. In this respect these Constitutions were detrimental in politically dividing the people through the partisan ideology of 'class destruction'. At the same time, the fact that Mongolia became a single-party state and the Mongolian People's Revolutionary Party was given primacy in the Constitution, especially the 1940 and the 1960 versions, meant that the policies, ideologies

[92] Enkhbaatar (n 22) 48.

[93] This Constitution was based on 1936 Constitution of the USSR and was promulgated on 30 June 1940.

[94] This Constitution was adopted by the People's Great Hural on 6 July 1960.

[95] Chimid (n 2) 14.

[96] B Chimid, 'Orienting Appropriate System is an Effective Foundation of Legal Reform' [Зохистой Тогтолцоог Баримжаалах Нь Эрх Зүйн Шинэтгэлийг Үр Нөлөөтэй Хийх Үндэс Болох Нь) in Chimid (n 77) 138.

[97] Amarsanaa (n 91) 105–06.

[98] Art 2.

and programmes of the Communist Party were the main sources of law.[99] However, these socialist features were abandoned by the time the 1990 amendment to the Constitution came to be drafted. Despite these distortions, the three Constitutions had a positive effect on the constitutional law and thinking of Mongolians, and laid the ground for the 1992 Constitution.

B. Adopting the Democratic Constitution in 1992

In the late 1980s, the ruling Mongolian People's Revolutionary Party set itself the task of revising the 1960 Constitution. However, this effort ended with the outbreak of the Democratic Revolution of 1990,[100] after which the process of developing a brand new constitution began. This process was spurred by the resurgence of national consciousness. By this time, it was clear to Mongolians that their country was lagging far behind the rest of the world in political and economic terms, largely as a consequence of Mongolia's totalitarian regime and theory of social and economic organisation or formation.[101] In the late 1980s, Mongolian democrats led a successful movement to overthrow the one-party regime and carry out political, economic and social reforms. As a result, the one-party regime was abolished, and democratic reform, in particular the legal basis for political transition, was introduced by the 'Law on Amendments to the Constitution of the Mongolian People's Republic (MPR)', adopted by the People's Great Hural in 1990. According to this law, the permanent legislative body would be the State Small Hural.

In 1992, the current Constitution was promulgated at the People's Great Hural. The new Constitution strengthens Mongolia's sovereignty, independence, and the democratic foundations of society and state institutions. It fortifies the legal status of human beings, the state structure, the distribution of state powers, and organisational and local governance. Although the current Constitution retains the unicameral parliamentary system, the State Great Hural, the notion of checks and balances and the separation of powers were not clearly embodied in the first Constitution and subsequent Constitutions except the current one. Unlike previous socialist or socialist-orientated constitutions, the 1992 Constitution does not define a strategic goal or programme, but it does solidly enshrine the rule of law.

VIII. IMPLICATIONS

Mongolia's 1924 Constitution was seen by progressive intellectuals and statesmen as a *sine qua non* for statehood. Historically, we have seen that leading progressive

[99] Lonjid and Lundendorj (n 18) 237.
[100] Chimid (77) 92–93.
[101] Chimid (n 2) 27–28.

intellectuals and statesmen of the time played a key role in formulating the draft of the first Constitution and advocating modernisation. Although political factors, especially foreign forces, were important in shaping the direction of the country and its consequential constitutional type, Mongolians were keen to adopt the highest standards of human rights in the country's Constitution. The realisation of these rights was, however, extremely challenging, due to the prevailing socialist ideology and authoritarian form of government.

Despite the fact that Mongolia was a socialist state for almost 70 years, we saw how the legal conscience of intellectuals, statesmen and other stakeholders surfaced time and again, especially in the making of the 1924 and 1992 Constitutions, as opportunities arose for the creation of an idealised Mongolian society embodying values like equality, human rights and the limitation of state power. One observable pattern in Mongolia is the fact that its constitutional framers had always learnt from comparative studies. During the socialist regime, Mongolia was strongly influenced by the Soviet Union, but by the time of the drafting of the 1992 Constitution, it could freely choose which constitutions it could aspire to.

Index

www.ingramcontent.com/pod-product-compliance
Ingram Content Group UK Ltd.
Pitfield, Milton Keynes, MK11 3LW, UK
UKHW020804290926
15470UKWH00003B/954

9 781509 940189